THE IRISH-AMERICANS

THE IRISH-AMERICANS

The Catholic Church and The Knights of Labor

HENRY J. BROWNE

ARNO PRESS

A New York Times Company

New York — 1976

Editorial Supervision: ANDREA HICKS

———◆———

Reprint Edition 1976 by Arno Press Inc.
Copyright © 1949, by The Catholic
  University of America Press, Inc.

Reprinted by permission of The Catholic
  University of America Press and
  Henry J. Browne

THE IRISH-AMERICANS
ISBN for complete set: 0-405-09317-9
See last pages of this volume for titles.

Manufactured in the United States of America

Publisher's Note: The map facing p. 34 has
been reproduced in black and white for this
edition.

———◆———

Library of Congress Cataloging in Publication Data

Browne, Henry Joseph, 1919-
  The Catholic Church and the Knights of Labor.

  (The Irish Americans)
  Reprint of the ed. published by Catholic Univer-
sity of America Press, Washington, which was
issued as v. 38 of Studies in American church
history.
  Originally presented as the author's thesis,
Catholic University of America, 1949.
  Bibliography: p.
  1. Church and labor--United States--History.
2. Knights of Labor--History. 3. Church and
labor--History. I. Title. II. Series.
III. Series: Catholic University of America.
Studies in American church history ; v. 38.
HD6338.2.U5B76 1976   261.8'5   76-6326
ISBN 0-405-09323-3

THE CATHOLIC CHURCH AND
THE KNIGHTS OF LABOR

THE ILLUSTRATED CATHOLIC AMERICAN.

A JOURNAL OF INFORMATION AND RECREATION FOR THE PEOPLE

VOL. XV.—No 11.}   NEW YORK, MARCH 12, 1887.   {PRICE TEN CENTS.

HIS EMINENCE CARDINAL GIBBONS, ARCHBISHOP OF BALTIMORE.

The Catholic Church and The Knights of Labor

BY

HENRY J. BROWNE
Archivist and Instructor in History
The Catholic University of America

FOREWORD
BY
JOHN P. MONAGHAN
Chaplain-Founder
Association of Catholic Trade Unionists

THE CATHOLIC UNIVERSITY OF AMERICA PRESS
WASHINGTON, D. C.
1949

Nihil Obstat:

JOHN TRACY ELLIS
Censor Deputatus

Imprimatur:

✠ FRANCIS CARDINAL SPELLMAN
Archbishop of New York

New York, January 28, 1949

Printed in the U. S. A. by
THE PAULIST PRESS
401 West 59th Street
New York 19, N. Y.

TO

MY FATHER AND MOTHER

TABLE OF CONTENTS

PAGE

PREFACE xiii

FOREWORD xvii

CHAPTER
I. PRECEDENTS 1

II. FORMATION AND REFORMATION 34

III. THE ATTENTION OF THE HIERARCHY 70

IV. QUEBEC AND BALTIMORE 105

V. CANADIAN CONFUSION 138

VI. TWO MEETINGS: OCTOBER, 1886 182

VII. AFFAIRS IN ROME 228

VIII. THE REACTION IN THE UNITED STATES 275

IX. AFTERMATH 313

APPENDICES
I. THE "SECRET WORK" 359

II. PROPOSED SPEECH OF BISHOP JOHN J. KEANE FOR THE
RICHMOND CONVENTION, OCTOBER, 1886 363

III. THE QUESTION OF THE "KNIGHTS OF LABOR," ROME,
FEBRUARY 20, 1887 365

ESSAY ON SOURCES 379

LIST OF ILLUSTRATIONS

PAGE

"His Eminence Cardinal Gibbons, Archbishop of Baltimore"....Frontispiece

A Popular Picture of Terence V. Powderly... 138

"The New Ally of the Knights of Labor".. 275

"A Business Alliance" 313

Map—Trouble-spots in Church-Labor Relations in Pennsylvania........ 34

Abbreviations Used in Footnotes

AAB—Archives of the Archdiocese of Boston.
AAC—Archives of the Archdiocese of Cincinnati.
AAM—Archives of the Archdiocese of Montreal.
AAQ—Archives de l'Archêveché de Québec.
AAT—Archives of the Archdiocese of Toronto.
ACUA—Archives of the Catholic University of America.
ADC—Archives of the Diocese of Cleveland.
ADPM—Archives of the Diocese of Portland, Maine.
ADR—Archives of the Diocese of Richmond.
AUND—Archives of the University of Notre Dame.
BCA—Baltimore Cathedral Archives.
NYAA—New York Archdiocesan Archives.
PP—Powderly Papers, Mullen Library of the Catholic University of America.
RDA—Rochester Diocesan Archives.

PREFACE

THE scandal of the nineteenth century, it was reportedly said by Pope Pius XI, was the loss of the workingman to the Church. The story told in this study is intimately linked up with that phenomenon in that it shows the interrelationship of the American labor movement with the Catholic Church during the period of the ascendancy of the Knights of Labor. The scope of this investigation is limited in general from 1879 to 1891. Never before or since have these two forces come into such sharp conflict, and the happy outcome of their differences explains in good measure how the Church in the United States was spared much of the scandalous loss of membership witnessed among the laboring classes of Europe. Catholic workers everywhere were affected by its outcome, for the case resulted in the approval by the Holy See of their membership in a non-religious or neutral trade union which showed no antipathy toward religion.

The history of the Knights of Labor has never been fully written, nor does this work presume to add anything new to it apart from the ecclesiastical chapter. This, however, could not be told without continued emphasis on the secular development of the Knights. For this background the writer has leaned on the accepted and standard histories of labor in the United States and Canada. Although the papers of the leader of the Knights of Labor, Terence V. Powderly, are here used extensively for the first time, no attempt is made to recast any of their story except insofar as it pertains to the interest of the historian of the Church. Material for this treatment had of necessity, therefore, to be sought in the diocesan archives of the two countries in question. The contents of these archives are discussed in the Essay on Sources at the end of the volume.

The question dealt with in this study is a many-sided one. Apart from being another phase in ecclesiastical history it should interest students of labor, who may profitably pause amid the pressures of present tasks to look at the past. Furthermore, it is part also of Canadian history, for the problem of the Knights of Labor was one of the most important points of common interest affecting in these years the development of the Catholic Church in Canada as well as in the United States. Likewise in the light of much new material Powderly's version of what he entitled in his autobiography, "Ecclesiastical Opposition," has to be re-examined. Up to the present the only accounts of the relations of the Church with the Knights of Labor written by Catholic historians have been in episcopal biographies, and these are far from definitive.

The present investigation was approached in the hope of pursuing the elusive goal of historical objectivity—the truth—which Pope Leo XIII in 1883 admonished Catholic historians to tell fearlessly. The result is meant neither to defend nor to edify, but in itself it does teach sound lessons to those of both the Church and labor who would learn from the experiences of their predecessors. The author has tried to remain conscious of the prejudice which at times asserts itself in every man. The success with which he has overcome the dangers to objectivity which might arise by reason of his religious, social, and other ties, the reader alone will judge.

In the preparation of this work many debts of gratitude were incurred. The names which follow represent usually whole groups of people who, by their interest, co-operation, and hospitality assisted in the collection of material. The writer wishes to thank first Miss Mary R. Powderly, of Washington, D. C., who gave him full freedom in the use of her uncle's papers. He extends his thanks to the Right Reverend Joseph M. Nelligan, former chancellor of the Archdioceses of Baltimore and Washington, the Very Reverends William J. Gauche, of Mount Saint Mary's Seminary of the West, Cincinnati, and Walter J. Leach, vice-chancellor of the Archdiocese of Boston; and also to the Reverends Jean-Marie Beauchemin, assistant archivist of the Archdiocese of Quebec, Alex. Carter of the chancery of the Archdiocese of Montreal, Clarence H. Coughlan, chancellor of the Diocese of Portland, Maine, M. Herbert Delaney, vice-chancellor of the Archdiocese of Toronto, William K. Dolan, former chancellor of the Diocese of Scranton, John Krol, vice-chancellor of the Diocese of Cleveland, Justin D. McClunn, vice-chancellor of the Diocese of Richmond, Bartholomew F. Fair of St. Charles Seminary, Overbrook, Thomas T. McAvoy, C.S.C., of the University of Notre Dame, Robert F. McNamara, of St. Bernard's Seminary, Rochester, William J. O'Shea, S.S., of St. Mary's Seminary, Roland Park, Honorius Provost, of the Seminary of Quebec, and Edward A. Ryan, S.J., of Woodstock College.

No less deserving of gratitude are those, noted elsewhere, who co-operated with the writer through less personal contacts in searching out records. Similarly, the help and courtesy of the staffs of the following libraries are gratefully acknowledged: the Mullen Library of the Catholic University of America, the Library of Congress, the Riggs Library of Georgetown University, the Widener Library of Harvard University, the New York Public and the New York Historical Society Libraries, the John Crerar Library of Chicago, the Wisconsin State Historical Society Library, the Scranton Public and Lackawanna Historical Society Libraries, the Provincial Library at Toronto, and the Laval University Library.

The critical reading of the original manuscript by Professor Richard J. Purcell of the Catholic University of America and the Reverend George G. Higgins of the National Catholic Welfare Conference was most helpful and very much appreciated. For work on the map gratitude is due to Sister Consuelo Maria Aherne, S.S.J. Above all, the writer is deeply grateful to the Reverend John Tracy Ellis, professor of American church history in the Catholic University of America, who as guide and friend directed the project from the time he first suggested it. In its original form the present work appeared as a doctoral dissertation.

In the writer's own archdiocese he wishes to thank first His Eminence Francis Cardinal Spellman for the opportunity of continuing his studies at the University. To the Reverend John P. Monaghan, an inspiring teacher of his years in Cathedral College, New York, he is most grateful for the words of introduction to this volume. He is likewise appreciative of the interest and help of the Right Reverend John M. A. Fearns, Rector of St. Joseph's Seminary, Dunwoodie, the Reverend Jeremiah J. Brennan, archivist of the Archdiocese of New York, and Mr. Thomas F. O'Connor.

To all those who have aided or encouraged him in any way the author is sincerely grateful. He hopes that seeing the story of the Church and the Knights—to which they so often had to listen— now published for a wider audience will in some small measure repay them for their assistance and encouragement.

HENRY J. BROWNE

The Catholic University of America
September 29, 1948

FOREWORD

THE subject matter of this book was once a burning issue that involved the Catholic Church in the United States so intensely that its social program today is still enlightened by it. The embers of the controversy are still hot and could be enflamed again by a myopic partisan of "the Church" or of "Organized Labor." Father Browne has composed from the issue of the Church and the Knights of Labor a true social history. He knows all the facts and has documented them thoroughly, but more importantly, he has insight to the pattern of these facts in the minds of the men involved and so permits us to see that between the Catholic Church and the Knights of Labor there was much more in common than ever was in controversy.

Each group was anxious and devoted to the needs of the ordinary man for social well being and job security. The activity of the Knights of Labor eyed right alone, could be rebellion, eyed left alone the restrictions of the Church would be repression. Too few of these involved in the controversy saw the end apart from the means. Each, and they were nearly all honest men, tended to identify the well-being of the workers with his own means of securing it. Fortunately, there were men, particularly Cardinal Gibbons, who, over the fences and offences, saw the common issue. They knew the last word on the matter was neither with the law nor with the prophets of social reform.

It has taken a long time for the science of history to evolve a social consciousness. For a long time it was assumed that history should be partisan or apologetic. This kind of history was not always wrong but it was seldom true enough and for this reason, it was unable to compass the future and as men increasingly sought to read the future out of the past they discarded it arbitrarily in favor of scientific history, meaning that the historian was expected to recognize facts as impersonally as a chemist might recognize the contents of a test tube. This dehumanized history in popular practice helped to uphold the authority of many modern despotic confusions, such as racism and communism.

Too many of the scientific historians were not scientific enough since they excluded from their light all the sciences whose laboratory is the mind of man.

To uncover the collective mind with which men did things, to know what men had in mind to do in any historical situation is a kind of knowledge which comes from the discipline of study but more valuably from the discipline of one's own experience. Thomas Aquinas says that "What pertains to moral science is known mostly through experience." Too many historians are illiterate in the humanities.

Father Browne is an intimate in the household of the Church. He knows the laws and he knows the spirit of Christ that lies beyond any human equation of it; besides he is most fortunate that he has been a wage-earner. He knows the frustration of the common laborer. Sweat and knotted muscles is a braille that too few authorities have read to their own human loss and the gain of communism. Father Browne might have defended factually the right or left viewpoint of the controversy. He could have set out safely the facts as one sets out a chemical prescription. He has achieved the more difficult task of recording the resolution of a passionate controversy within the framework of scientifically compiled data under the enlivening light of authentic experience.

Society is the community of human experience. Much of it is wordless. As in this case, no man can record a major event accurately who has not been a part of it, in his mind at least.

One has to know how the Church had suffered from secret societies in Europe to understand Canadian nervousness about the oaths and secret rituals of the Knights. One has to appreciate the contemporary rugged individualism of the rank and file, clergy and laity, to explain how so kindly a man as Archbishop Corrigan could be frequently arbitrary and humorless in human relations. One has to have hungered and thirsted after justice, in muscle as well as mind, before he can know how much a prophet Powderly was to a generation of men who had been exploited and belittled in the industrial expansion of America.

Probably more than half the membership of the Knights of Labor were Catholic. The most dynamic and important were the Irish who had kept the faith and lost all else. They would have followed the Church. To our great honor and historical prestige, no bishop's unhappy experience with labor or Masonry or his own clergy was permitted to become the norm of action. Against all passionate, personal experience there prevailed in the controversy between the Church and the Knights of Labor the discretion of Christ Who condemned only what was already damned, and Who turned away from no man no matter how erratically he was traveling His way.

Father Browne, to the glory of the Church, has set down here, scientifically and sympathetically, the story of a conflict within the body of the Church in America that resolved itself into a pattern of behavior toward organized labor, that is still, thank God, our Catholic commonplace tradition.

JOHN P. MONAGHAN
Chaplain-Founder
Association of Catholic Trade Unionists

CHAPTER I

PRECEDENTS

In order to understand the deep concern of the Catholic Church over the affiliation of some of its members with a particular labor organization during the 1880's it is necessary to trace, in so far as it is possible, the precedents of the problem. These include not only the official tenets guiding its action on the matter, but also the contacts which the Church had experienced with organized labor in the United States before that time. Long before the Knights of Labor became an object of scrutiny by ecclesiastical authority certain principles concerning anti- and non-religious organizations had been repeatedly formulated by churchmen. It was only the next to the last decade of the nineteenth century that witnessed the outstanding example of a concrete application and adaptation of these abstract principles to the American scene. Some knowledge, however, of the development of the labor movement and its prior relationship with the Catholic spiritual authority is required as background to this story.

The chronicle of the efforts of the workers of the United States to combine for their own welfare has been given manifold divisions.[1] With regard to these various phases of the uphill struggle of American labor, no real attempt has hitherto been made to point out the contribution of the Catholic Church and its members. This is especially true of the earlier years of the century and the principal reason in this case is that there was not much to claim.[2] Even con-

---

[1] John R. Commons and Associates, *History of Labor in the United States,* 4 vols. (New York, 1918). This standard work gives six divisions: Colonial and Federal Beginnings (to 1827); Citizenship (1827-1833); Trade Unionism (1833-1839); Humantarianism (1840-1860); Nationalism (1860-1877); Upheaval and Reorganization (since 1876). This work will hereafter be cited as Commons, *History.* It is quoted throughout with permission of the Macmillan Company, publisher.

[2] Patrick J. Healy wrote a popular and rather ineptly titled sketch, "Catholic Economic Thought," in *Catholic Builders of the Nation* (Boston, 1923), III, 92-107.

sidering this question under the division of the pre- and post-Civil War eras, instead of the more limited segments the theoretical truth at least should be evident with regard to both periods, namely, that:

> Though the essential purpose and end of the Church are neither social reform nor economic revolution, nevertheless the maintenance of fixed standards of social and distributive justice and the insistence on definite principles of conduct always placed the Church in the position of being a powerful agency for social betterment, and more and more equitable distribution of the goods and resources of nature.[3]

During the decades before the Civil War, the American labor movement was not only in constant ferment, but it began to take on a definite shape. Not until the late 1820's did the wage earners in different occupations become conscious of the interests which they had in common, and of the fact that such could be effectively pursued through an organization which would embrace these various trades.[4] This birth of organized American labor might be said to have taken place at Philadelphia in 1827, with the rise of the Mechanics' Union of Trade Associations. It was transformed into the Workingmen's Party in time for the election of 1829, and in a short while it spread throughout many of the larger cities. It did not augur well for the future that the party was accused of being anti-religious, and the unit in New York City included among its demands the abolition of tax exemption of church property.[5] By 1832 these politico-labor groups had ceased to function and the old trade societies, characterized by their benevolent features, were all that was left to sustain the aims of labor. They, in turn, were for the most part doomed by the financial panic of 1837. A new outlook developed, and in the twenty years between 1840 and 1860 the welfare of the working class was sought mainly through humanitarian movements. It was the heyday of such reformers as Fourier, Owen, and Evans, who rather sought to escape the rising industrial order than to face its problems.

[3] *Ibid.*, III, 93.
[4] Commons, *History*, I, 169. The account which follows is based on the same volume.
[5] *Ibid.*, I, 212, 274.

Only a slight Catholic reaction to the idealist approach of these years was reflected in the press. On the one hand, a leading Catholic paper enunciated editorially what only about a century later was to become a commonplace among Catholic social reformers. In concluding an editorial on "The Claims of Labor," it said:

> In remunerating others, we do not reflect, that the full labor of one of our species should at least yield the necessities of life. We, on the contrary, consider ourselves justified in estimating the toil and strength of our fellow-men in proportion to the demand for them and the supply in answer to that demand, and by no other or more elevated standard. This too, in a Christian community and where all are in theory at least, equal in the eyes of the law.[6]

On the other hand, Catholic churchmen were credited with joining in the general attack on Fourierism by opposing association for the reason that they considered co-operative workshops to be the "first step to Socialism." [7]

Despite these few examples it is not very strange that during these ante-bellum days the Catholic Church should, in general, have had little influence on or contact with the labor movement. One need but recall its position in the United States at that time. In one way the Catholic and the workingman were often akin in having to fight against the same evil, the abuse of political power by a privileged class. Yet Nativism, with more of an economic than a religious motive, flourished even among such workers' groups as the anti-alien Order of United Americans.[8] Besides the external opposition which came from this early flare-up of America's most persistent prejudice, there were internal circumstances and problems limiting the social activity of the Church. All of these may be summarized under the single heading of phenomenal expansion, for the best estimate of the Catholic population for 1840 is given as 663,000, and for 1860 as

---

[6] New York *Freeman's Journal,* March 15, 1845.

[7] Commons, *History,* I, 571, citing New York *Tribune,* September 3, 1850.

[8] Ray Allan Billington, *The Protestant Crusade, 1800-1860* (New York, 1938), p. 336.

3,103,000.[9]   The story of diocese after diocese shows the pattern of the same great need for priests, a growth of schools and teaching communities of religious, and the development of orphanages and other works of mercy.[10] At least one study, based on contemporary and representative Catholic papers, reveals that the Church, although carrying on its ordinary work in a hostile environment, did not fail to express, "her solicitude for the needy and unfortunate insofar as her restricted means permitted." [11]   Even without very specific evidence, however, it is not difficult to realize that during this period, "the Church was not in a position to intervene directly in the bitter economic struggle which was in progress, nor to make its influence felt as a guiding factor in the settlement of labor disputes." [12]

There were, nevertheless, even during the years before the Civil War some Catholic priests and laymen who had enough insight to sense the social implications of the teachings of the Church; this aroused in them at least indignation, if not a very positive action in behalf of the workingman. Matthew Carey, the Catholic publisher and philanthropist of Philadelphia, who arrived in the United States in 1784, is remembered in American labor history as the earliest to defend the working woman in his speeches and writings.[13]   Even an incident in the history of the Oregon missions involving the vicar general, Francis Norbert Blanchet, who in 1846 became archbishop of this second metropolitan see in the United States, indicated what should have been a common concern of most pastors, since also in the English-speaking areas their flocks were mostly of the working class. It is hard to go beyond a presumption in this regard because the parish priest generally remains inaccessible to the ecclesiastical historian and real parochial archives, apart from registers, have not

[9] Gerald Shaughnessy, *Has the Immigrant Kept the Faith?* (New York, 1925), p. 189.

[10] Cf. John Gilmary Shea, *History of the Catholic Church in the United States* (New York, 1890, 1892), III, IV, *passim*.

[11] Sister M. Gertrude McGray, "Evidences of Catholic Interest in Social Welfare in the United States, 1830-1850." Unpublished master's thesis, University of Notre Dame (1937), p. 72.

[12] Healy, *op. cit.*, III, 96.

[13] Commons, *History*, I, 354, 356. This is brought out in Carey's "Appeal to the Wealthy of the Land."

been kept. In his plea for permission to erect a new mission Blanchet reminded the Hudson's Bay Company of its obligations in regard to the spiritual as well as to the temporal welfare of its workers. However, it was made a matter of paternalism more than of rights.[14] Back in the crowded industrial section of New York City, the irrepressible layman, Thomas D'Arcy McGee, who considered ignorance second only to intemperance as a yoke on the necks of the Irish laborers, in 1849 attempted a short-lived night school. His name is linked also with the ill-fated attempts to alleviate the lot of the slum-dwelling Irish by western colonization. Unfortunately, it would now seem, McGee was not very kindly received by Archbishop John Hughes, and shortly he departed for Canada where he became a leader in the movement for national confederation.[15]

An observant Jesuit, Augustus J. Thébaud, while pastor of St. Joseph's Church in Troy, New York, from 1852 to 1860, showed a sympathetic awareness of the workingman's situation. These conditions remained in his memory:

> But apart from religion [the rich were mostly Presbyterians] what were the relations between employers and employees? They were strictly a matter of business, of wages and work. For every day's labor I will pay you so much, and this done we are quits. Should you fall sick, it is your affair, even in case you have given me satisfaction for years. Nay, more, should you be incapacitated in working for me, without any fault of yours or mine, I owe you nothing, and it is not to me you have to apply for relief, but to your personal friends—I am not one of them.
>
> Whenever any of my poor parishioners fell sick or met with an accident, if they had not previously been able to lay by something for a 'rainy day'—which was indeed seldom the case—they were forced to apply to their fellow workmen, who never failed to respond. And I did not hear that the rich factory owner ever headed the list of subscribers.[16]

14 Sister M. Laetitia Lyons, *Francis Norbert Blanchet and the Founding of the Oregon Missions, 1838-1848* (Washington, 1940), p. 53, quoting a memorandum of November 15, 1841.

15 Elizabeth Skelton, *Life of Thomas D'Arcy McGee* (Gardenvale, 1925), p. 180 ff. Sister M. Gilbert Kelly, *Catholic Immigrant Colonization Projects in the United States, 1815-1860* (New York, 1939), p. 263. John R. G. Hassard, *Life of the Most Reverend John Hughes* (New York, 1866), pp. 310-312.

16 Augustus J. Thébaud, S.J., *Forty Years in the United States of America (1839-1885)* (New York, 1904), p. 117.

Probably the staunchest, and certainly the loudest, Catholic defender of the laborer up to 1860 was the journalist and lecturer, Orestes Brownson. With his conversion to Catholicism in 1844, he testified that his interest in labor was simply baptized. "I abandoned, indeed, after a year's devotion to it, the Workingman's Party, but not the workingman's cause, and to that cause I have been faithful according to my light and ability." [17]   In 1857 he was able to say:

> I believed, and still believe, that the rights of labor are not sufficiently protected, and that the modern system of large industries, which requires for its prosecution heavy output of capital, or credit, makes the great mass of operatives virtually slaves— slaves in all except the name—as much as are the Negroes on one of our southern plantations.[18]

If, however, interest on the part of individual Catholics with regard to the labor problem was only scattered, group activity was almost non-existent. The Irish Emigrant Aid Society was established in New York (1841) after similar steps had been taken in Philadelphia and Savannah, to give temporary aid to newly-arrived Irishmen by directing them to likely places of employment and by counseling them against the moral dangers of their new country.[19]   Early German immigrants founded the nucleus of an organization which was to continue as an instrument of Catholic social education down to the present day. After preliminary steps in Rochester and Buffalo in 1854, this German Catholic Central-Verein was formally organized in Baltimore in April, 1855.[20]   This effort was probably one of the first contacts of the nascent American Catholic social movement with the more mature European programs of reform, for the first German Catholic Congress had met at Mainz on October 4, 1848, under the guidance of Bishop Wilhelm Emmanuel Von Ketteler,

[17] Henry Brownson (Ed.), *Brownson's Works* (20 vols., Detroit, 1884), V, 67.
[18] *Ibid.*, V, 63.
[19] Thomas F. Meehan, "Emigrant Aid Societies," *Catholic Encyclopedia*, V, 402-404. Cf. New York *Freeman's Journal*, 1841, *passim*.
[20] Alfred Steckel, "German Roman Catholic Society of the United States of North America," *Records* of the American Catholic Historical Society, VI (1895), 254-259.

whom Pope Leo XIII was to call his "great predecessor." Consequently, it was said of him, "He was the first to draw the attention of the Catholic world to the supreme importance of the social question and to the only means of solving it."[21]   An historian of the American Central-Verein claims that the desires and aims of Ketteler were carried out in the United States, since the component benevolent societies, from the outset, "made social action their characteristic feature and from year to year extended their field of action in this respect."[22]   The Central-Verein did much in the field of sickness and life insurance, immigrant aid and employment bureaus. It was not, however, until Leo XIII's letter to the universal Church in 1891 that the labor question entered into their education and propaganda efforts.[23]

However much Catholics singly or in groups might seek to uplift the workingman, there could be no meeting of the Church and organized labor until the hierarchy had seen fit to make some pertinent pronouncement. Before 1866 there was nothing definite said relating to labor unions except in so far as the American bishops had reflected the century-old concern of the Church about secret societies. This had begun with the constitution, *In eminenti,* of Pope Clement XII in 1738, which first condemned Freemasonry and prohibited Catholics from affiliating with it or aiding it in any way under penalty of an excommunication from which they could be released only by the Holy See.[24]   Such fulminations against anti-social societies, or those which threatened injury to Church or State, were repeated and elaborated up until the time of Pope Leo XIII. That pontiff issued five encyclicals which attacked the Freemasons and kindred societies, and finally these condemnations were codified in three canons of the Code of Canon Law of 1918.[25]

In the United States the hierarchy in their very first meeting in

[21] George Metlake (John J. Laux), *Christian Social Reform* (Philadelphia, 1912), p. 24.

[22] Joseph Matt, "The German Roman Catholic Central-Verein," *Offizielles Souvenir Goldenes Jubilaeum* (Cincinnati, 1905), p. 152.

[23] *Ibid.*

[24] Joseph Quigley, *Condemned Societies* (Washington, 1927), pp. 12-28.

[25] *Ibid.,* p. 22.   Canons 684, 2335, 2336.

1810 had expressed concern over the dangers of Freemasonry. This was in keeping even with the secular spirit of a later time which saw the unsuccessful rise of the Anti-Masonic Party of 1831. A quasi-Masonic fraternity which emphasized benevolence, namely, the Odd Fellows, had also begun to flourish in the United States after 1819.[26] These facts, plus a development in the field of labor, give meaning to the words of the pastoral of the Fourth Provincial Council of Baltimore in 1840. Up to the panic of 1837 which crushed their activities, trade unions had been growing rapidly. For example, in New York City between 1833 and 1837 thirty various groups had been organized and this activity had resulted in bitter strikes and street demonstrations.[27] It was only in the period from 1837 to 1852 that labor turned to various humanitarian approaches such as co-operatives and agrarianism.[28] Against this background the prelates gathered in Baltimore condemned the immorality of secret societies and continued:

> It is not our intention to confine the above remarks exclusively to any one Society. They extend to all that are accustomed to have secret proceedings, mysterious symbols, private tokens of recognition and oaths or other pledges of like solemnity, assuming to bind them to secrecy, especially not to divulge a communication to be subsequently made, upon whose nature they can pass no reasonable judgment when they undertake the obligation.
>
> Amongst these Societies we learn with deep regret that upon our public works where large masses of the laboring population are kept together, there exist associations of a most demoralizing and dangerous character.
>
> As far as we can discover, the pretext is their own protection, but the practice is monopoly, blasphemy, insubordination, drunkenness, idleness, riot, and the terror of the vicinity. This abundantly explains the rapid demoralization of a class that was originally virtuous, industrious, laborious, useful and peaceful.

[26] Fergus Macdonald, C.P., *The Catholic Church and the Secret Societies in the United States* (New York, 1946), pp. 5-7. This is a companion study to the present one in which the author deliberately left aside treatment of the subject matter of this volume.

[27] Commons, *History*, I, 464, 476. Selig Perlman, *A History of Trade Unionism in the United States* (New York, 1922), pp. 18-29.

[28] Harry A. Millis and Royal E. Montgomery, *Organized Labor* (New York, 1945), pp. 33-43.

When once the custom of forming secret Societies is established in any part of a community it rapidly pervades the entire, and demoralization is the necessary consequence. We earnestly conjure you, then, beloved brethren, to have no part in this pernicious practice, and to use your best efforts to guard others against the delusion that these associations are compatible with good order and religion.[29]

The bishops of the country, in their next scheduled meeting in 1843, repeated their usual warning and generic condemnation of secret societies. Just the previous year the Sons of Temperance, an expression of the reforming spirit that was abroad, had been organized and this was to be another secret fraternity which, although not anti-social in nature, was to fall under the surveillance of the leaders of the Church in the United States. The members of such an organization might have found comfort in the statement of the pastoral letter, "We would not judge unkindly of any body of men, or of any individuals, professing to have in view objects of philanthropy and mutual aid," but the bishops did protest against the rash use of the name of God and secrecy, "since all just objects may be openly avowed and pursued." At the basis of their admonition to the faithful that the Church would not tolerate any Catholic's remaining in a position, "so opposed to the positive laws of the Church, and so dangerous to the integrity of faith," was the apprehension:

that by assuming mere natural principles as their guide, they insensibly prepare themselves for discarding revealed religion, so that some find themselves divested of faith, before they are conscious of the tendency and influence of the society with which they have connected themselves.[30]

[29] Peter Guilday, *The National Pastorals of the American Hierarchy (1792-1919)* (Washington, 1923), pp. 141-142. The decrees passed on secret societies contain nothing on this specific point. Cf. *Concilia provincialia Baltimorensia* (Baltimore, 1851), p. 172. Similar action of the First Diocesan Synod of New York, in August, 1842, condemning membership in organizations, "which had wrought great evils among the laboring classes, leading to perjury and the sacrifice of human life" (Shea, *op. cit.*, II, 540), has been shown by Macdonald to have been meant as a warning to Irish benevolent societies. *Op. cit.*, pp. 14-19.

[30] Guilday, *National Pastorals*, pp. 153-154, and Macdonald, *op. cit.*, pp. 19-23.

The historian of this assembly of the hierarchy tells, on the other hand, of the most positive and salutary advice given to the faithful, which if it had been heeded certainly would have favored co-operation in economic enterprises for the common good.

> Catholics were encouraged to strengthen the social bonds which should unite them to their non-Catholic neighbor, and to practice strict integrity in the daily concerns of life, in the fulfillment of all engagements, in their peaceful demeanor, in obedience to the laws of the nation, in their respect for civic authorities, and in their unaffected exercise of charity as a barrier to the widespread animosity toward their Church.[31]

The year 1846 saw further action in the matter of illicit societies, a problem which was becoming complicated not only from the practical viewpoint of applying general principles, but also because the principles themselves were becoming more involved. The American bishops met in Baltimore in May but they said nothing about the question, either in the decrees of the council or in the pastoral letter issued at the close of their meeting, although a commission of theologians had presented some very keen observations to them. In August of the same year, there arrived an interpretation sent out by the Holy Office in Rome to the effect that the "Societates occultae" with which the Roman constitutions were concerned were to be understood as meaning all those which worked against the Church or the State in any way, regardless of whether an oath of secrecy was demanded as a condition of membership or not. Hence it was quite logical that Bishop Francis Patrick Kenrick of Philadelphia should on February 26, 1848, raise the question before the Holy Office of the status of the Odd Fellows and Sons of Temperance. These organizations purported to have no hostility to either civil or religious authority, and yet they held themselves to secrecy by an oath or solemn promise. When no reply to his inquiry came after three months, the bishop anxiously wrote again. However, he waited two years, to be exact until August 21, 1850, before he was told simply, "Comprehendi in Bullis Pontificiis." [32] Thereby these merely secret

---

[31] Peter Guilday, *A History of the Councils of Baltimore, 1791-1884* (New York, 1932), p. 141.

[32] Macdonald, *op. cit.*, pp. 23-26. The request and the reply are found in

and not anti-social groups were to be included under the papal condemnations despite the definition of four years before. A new dispute
arose among canonists as to whether such secret societies were to be
considered merely as condemned and to be avoided, or also as having been prohibited under penalty of censure.[33]

The growth of American trade unions on a national scale came
during the 1850's. It was in 1852, too, that the first national council
of the Church in the United States convened in Baltimore. At this
council six ecclesiastical provinces were represented.[34] Here the
hierarchy in plenary session resolved its doubts on Rome's responses
concerning secret societies by doing nothing. The acts of the council
say the question was discussed but the pastoral's exhortation merely
stressed how needless it was for Catholics to seek opportunity to
practice benevolence through agencies outside the Church, when
they had their own "holy associations." [35] The fact that they were
most likely doing just that is seen in a unique contact which the
Church and labor enjoyed just before the nation was split by the
Civil War. The meeting of the national organization of the Iron
Moulders' Union at Cincinnati in January, 1861, came to an end with
an "elegant repast" at the Catholic Institute of that city. The driving
spirit in this organization, William Sylvis, had succeeded in keeping
the trappings of a secret fraternity out of the national organization,
although some locals had used them.[36] Cincinnati's institute of higher
learning was hardly a representative Catholic agency, however, as
shown by Archbishop John B. Purcell's disowning it in 1864, and by
his stating that it had always lacked the support of "a large and influential portion of the Catholic community." [37]

Full and official Catholic attention was turned to the labor ques-

Appendix XXVIII, pp. 335-337 of *Acta et decreta concilii plenarii Baltimorensis
II* (Baltimore, 1868).

[33] Quigley, *op. cit.*, pp. 26-27.

[34] Oregon City had been established in 1846, St. Louis in 1847, and Cincinnati, New York, and New Orleans in 1850.

[35] Macdonald, *op. cit.*, p. 28; Guilday, *National Pastorals*, p. 186.

[36] Jonathan Grossman, *William Sylvis, Pioneer of American Labor* (New
York, 1945), pp. 30, 42.

[37] John H. Lamott, *History of the Archdiocese of Cincinnati, 1821-1921*
(Cincinnati, 1921), p. 284.

tion only in the more turbulent period of the emergence of modern industrial America. The two decades after the Civil War, roughly speaking, are considered the time of "nationalism" in the American labor movement. The country had been consolidated by a web of railroads, and with these connecting links arose competition between manufactured products of various localities. For this reason, especially, labor found it necessary to intensify the formation of national trade unions. The idea of labor leaders was to prevent the workers from suffering as a result of the competitive struggle, by keeping their demands at the same proportionate level in all sections of the country. These groups flourished from 1864 to the business panic of 1873.[38] Over and above these, there was the renewed attempt at national federation of all labor in the spirit of the National Trades' Union of the 1830's—in the National Labor Union (1866-1872). Thus labor now nationally organized and the Church, through its plenary or national councils, were destined to have an influence one on the other.[39] The twofold reason for this has been described as labor's secrecy and socialism.[40]

The pernicious character of these two developments within organized labor, especially in the eyes of the Church, cannot be gainsaid. The recommendation of uniting all workers on a secret basis was not a very general one until the Pittsburgh convention of 1876. This unification was to be "not antagonistic with the duty that they owe to their families, their country and their God." [41] The meeting in that city was another attempt at an over-all labor federation and was held under the dominance of the Knights of Labor, the most famous of all secret labor organizations which had been established in 1869. The Knights of St. Crispin, the shoemakers' secret trade union, had begun two years earlier. Similarly there were several other societies which could be called strictly workers' groups with economic aims— not mere fraternal societies which maintained secrecy. These were

---

38 Commons, *History,* II, 43.

39 The contact came near to being physical. In August, 1866, the National Labor Union met in Baltimore to form a nation-wide organization of many disparate worker groups, and in October of the same year the Catholic hierarchy assembled in council in the same city.

40 Healy, *op. cit.,* III, 101.

41 Commons, *History,* II, 239.

the short-lived Industrial Brotherhood (1873-1875) and the Sovereigns of Industry (1874-1878).[42] Unlike this note of secrecy, the additional menace of "socialism," at least in the 1870's, was less readily discernible, unless it be taken in a wide sense as designating many radical elements, some of which socialism had mothered. This, then, was the picture:

> Through the records of the American labor movement during the seventies stalk German refugees, English chartists, Italians of Garibaldi's red-shirt army, Irish Fenians, French Communards, Russian nihilists, Bismarck's exiles, and Marxian socialists bent on nothing less than a world revolution, philosophers of every school mingling with those hard-headed craftsmen who were indifferent to utopias and principally concerned with matters of fact—shorter hours and better wages.[43]

The radicalism of these years is generally conceded to have been even less successful in propagating itself than that of the 1840's. Nevertheless, the sprinkling of Irish Catholic names in these pages of American labor history makes one wonder if, perhaps, these early labor leaders, having no social program offered by their Church, did not wander away from its guidance completely.[44]

Despite the difficulties which arose from the occult and suspected nature of parts of the body of organized labor, the American hierarchy, convening for purposes of reconstruction in 1866 at the Second Plenary Council of Baltimore, made its first joint statement on the question.[45] The bishops spoke of secret societies, especially

[42] *Ibid.*, II, 196.

[43] Charles and Mary Beard, *The Rise of American Civilization* (New York, 1942), II, 215.

[44] Witness J. P. McDonnell, once a student for the priesthood in Ireland, who became secretary to Karl Marx and the International; cf. Samuel Gompers, *Seventy Years of Life and Labor* (New York, 1925), I, 103, and Commons, *History*, II, 222; also P. J. McGuire, Socialist leader in New York City, early active in the A. F. of L., and "Father of Labor Day," who had a parochial school education; cf. *Ibid.*, II, 231, and Francis J. Haas, "Three Economic Needs of the 1880's and of the 1940's," *American Ecclesiastical Review*, CXVII (December, 1947), 401.

[45] *Concilii plenarii Baltimorensis II acta et decreta* (Baltimore, 1868), pp. 260-265.

the Masonic ones, in order to reiterate the papal condemnation of them.[46] The reasons for their prohibition were given because difficulties and doubts had arisen about the inclusion of various kinds of "assemblages of workers" under the condemnation. Four were enumerated: the danger of corruption of the Catholic faith due to the close mutual association with men of such mixed religions, the narrow and impervious compact of secrecy about all their business, the oath binding to inviolable secrecy in defiance even of lawful authority, and finally the ill repute of such societies among good men.[47]

There followed in this twelfth title of the decrees the two unique contributions of this conciliar legislation on secret societies. The first was the exception made for labor unions and the second, a method of procedure to be followed in the future. If it was not an approbation, it was at least a declaration of tolerance to say:

> After carefully considering these things there appears to be no reason why the prohibition of the Church against the Masonic and other hidden sects should be extended to those associations of workmen which evidently have no other purpose than mutual help and protection in exercising their trade.

In the light of the times the prudent and precautionary provision which followed was a wise warning against the evils of secrecy and injustice:

> Care must be taken, however, that under this pretext nothing be admitted which favors the condemned sects; nor are the workmen who join these societies to be induced by the wicked and wily arts of evil men to oppose the laws of justice by withdrawing the labor which is due from them or in any way injuring the right of those to whom they are subject.

The fathers of the council protested strongly that this was not a toleration of any society in which a man would be bound by an oath

[46] Some new ones, the legality of which had yet to be adjudicated, were: the Knights of Pythias (1864), the Grand Army of the Republic (1866), the Patrons of Husbandry (1867), and the Ancient Order of United Workmen (1868).

[47] *Acta et decreta*, p. 262, from the apostolic constitution, *Providas*, of Benedict XIV (1751).

to blind and secret obedience: "For those groups are altogether illicit in which the members are so joined by a strict compact for mutual defense that from it there arises the danger of disturbance or bloodshed."[48] The good which might have been done by this clause was lessened by the fact that in the brief section on secret societies in the pastoral no mention was made of labor unions.

The second addition was not made so spontaneously. In preparation for their meeting the American bishops had been sent a communication on July 13, 1865, in which Alessandro Barnabò, the Cardinal Prefect of the Congregation of Propaganda, by order of the Holy Father, told them to promulgate the decree of the Congregation of the Inquisition of August 15, 1846, which, as has been seen, declared the "secret societies" of the papal constitutions to be those hostile to Church or State. Pope Pius IX further wished that in case of difficulty in applying this decree recourse should be had to the Holy See. Therefore, the council forbade any *nominatim* condemnation of a society by any one of any ecclesiastical rank whatever, unless he was certain it fell under the papal statutes as interpreted by the Holy Office. Beyond that:

> If, however, there shall be circumstances which seem to demand a further explanation of the teaching already given, to that end, "all the factors in the situation being clearly pointed out" we order that recourse shall be had to the Holy See, whose most wise judgment we shall follow with whole heart and soul.[49]

However, many of the American prelates were not whole-heartedly behind the method of appeal stipulated in this paragraph, and it was retained only on the insistence of the officials of Propaganda.[50] Although many practical difficulties arising out of this new legis-

---

[48] *Ibid.,* p. 263.

[49] It has the same reading in the "Editio Altera Mendis Expurgata" of 1877, p. 264.

[50] *Acta et decreta* (1868), p. 264, footnote, "According to the opinion of many of the Fathers the Decree under this number was to be omitted: but according to the wish of the S. C. it seems it should be retained." Reference was then made to pp. cxlii and cxliii, "Instructio S. C. de Prop. Fide Specialis, circa quaedam Concilii Decreta." Alessandro Card. Barnabò to Martin John Spalding, Rome, January 24, 1868.

lation had to be faced by the bishops, it certainly was a boon to suspected groups in that it prevented their hasty condemnation. In effect it tied the hands of the American hierarchy to a great extent since the societies with which they were concerned were not anti-social in Propaganda's sense, but simply secret. These latter, church-men could no longer condemn by name. Although they were forbidden to Catholics under pain of sin the bishops could not include them under those to which the penalty of excommunication, with its consequent denial of the sacraments and privileges of a member of the Church, was to be attached. Only with the next council of 1884 did the American episcopacy win back closer control over the matter.[51]

In the meanwhile both the conciliar decrees and the rising problems of labor made an increasing impression on the Church. An early and hostile reaction was expressed in a pastoral letter of Bishop James Roosevelt Bayley of Newark, who warned his flock against having anything to do with such labor associations. The bishop went out on his own when he undertook to condemn not only the evils, but the essence of the idea of combinations of workers.[52]

---

[51] Macdonald, *op. cit.*, pp. 66-69, discusses the shortcomings of the legislation, but he says nothing of the American reluctance to accept this provision.

[52] "It is true that those which have been formed in this country have not as yet, adopted the harsh rules, and sanguinary penalties, of the secret societies on the Continent, and the labour combinations in England, but the principle is bad and 'no bad tree can bring forth good fruit.' . . . Pastoral letter of February 2, 1868, quoted in Sister M. Hildegarde Yeager, C.S.C., *The Life of James Roosevelt Bayley, First Bishop of Newark and Eighth Archbishop of Baltimore, 1814-1877* (Washington, 1947), p. 309. The present writer is inclined to agree with Aaron I. Abell, "The Reception of Leo XIII's Labor Encyclical in America, 1891-1919," *Review of Politics*, VII (October, 1945), 468, as against the biographer of Bayley that the archbishop who later spoke of labor organizations as "miserable associations" whose "idea is communistic," was against unions as such since he thought they were all conspiracies against the social order. Yeager, *op. cit.*, pp. 388-389. (Bayley made these statements to a convention of Irish Catholic Benevolent Societies in Baltimore, October, 1871.) However, merely in the light of the provision of the council of 1866 the present writer would disagree with Abell's predicating this hostile state of mind of "most bishops and priests until shortly before Leo's encyclical appeared."

The section of the Baltimore legislation on labor unions was pointed out by the Propaganda in 1870 to Archbishop John J. Lynch of Toronto, as a good guide for his own vigilance against new secret societies. The appearance of such in his territory, especially the Société des Cordonniers, prompted the communication which he was told should also be sent on to his suffragan bishops.[53] Lynch apparently was more impressed by the part of the decree which exempted unions than by the warning against them. He was from the outset and remained to the end of his life the outstanding, but unpublicized, friend of labor unions in the hierarchies of both Canada and the United States.[54] Even the scanty and scattered remains of his correspondence show him twice in the same month not only considering them legal, but after investigation and according to principles, privately endorsing them. Lynch wrote to a priest in Windsor:

> . . . I did not give a formal approbation to the 'Moulders' Association' in as much as we do not approve of any save religious associations. But I told their local President, who called on me, that if they did not require an oath from the Catholics, or any acts against Society or the Church, or any act of injustice against their neighbor we would admit to the Sacraments Catholics belonging to them, if otherwise worthy. As far as I could learn their rules do not require any such acts, but is a society for self-protection, which appears to be necessary in these days of money monopolies.
>
> Nearly all the foundries in Toronto are worked under the rules of the 'Moulders' Union.' I was glad to see a way of securing for our people, many of whom work in those factories, the daily bread of both soul and body. . . .[55]

[53] AAT, Cardinal Barnabò to Lynch, Rome, November 16, 1870, copy. It was also sent to Quebec, *vide infra*, p. 31. Earlier that same year the Vatican Council had the matter of secret societies on its agenda but never reached it. Raymond J. Clancy, C.S.C., "American Prelates in the Vatican Council," *Historical Records and Studies*, XXVIII (1937), 31.

[54] Ordained in Ireland, he went to Texas as a Vincentian missionary in 1846. From 1848 to 1856 he was a seminary professor there, and then he founded the Seminary of Our Lady of the Angels at Niagara, New York. He was consecrated Bishop of Toronto in 1859, and became an archbishop in 1870.

[55] AAT, Lynch to J. F. Wagner, Toronto, April 30, 1873, copy. Also copy of letter of April 29, 1873, to Robert Pearson, representative of the locomotive engineers.

Probably more representative of the Catholic churchman's attitude toward labor in the 1870's was the sermon of the prelate destined to become known as the champion of the American worker. Yet, in this decade, unlike Bayley or Lynch, Bishop James Gibbons ignored the problem of association in preaching a sermon entitled, "Man Born to Work: or, Necessity and Dignity of Labor." The penciled outline between the paragraphs of his manuscript shows that he intended to bring home to his audience that labor was natural to man and while it was a penance and satisfaction for sin, it was also a means of avoiding it. He contrasted the idler and the industrious man and emphasized the dignity of labor. His practical advice to workmen, especially the young, was threefold: to avoid idleness, to take always an active and personal interest in the business of their employers, and to remain contented in the state and city where Providence had placed them.[56]

As timely as these sentiments were apparently judged to be by Gibbons, they stand out in sharp contrast to an expressed opinion of one of his predecessors in the See of Baltimore. Martin J. Spalding, it might be noted, did not preach it, but he wrote in private correspondence, the most understanding statement on labor conditions made up to that time by any bishop in the United States. Published shortly after his death in 1872, it read: "In our country capital is tyrant and labor is its slave. I have no desire to interfere with the poor in their efforts to protect themselves, unless it is proved that these societies are plotting against the state or the Church." [57]

These efforts at self-protection on the part of the laboring men came under the watchful eye of the hierarchy who, in turn, depended for their information on the priests of their dioceses with their more immediate contact with the workers. An interesting example, not only of solicitude but of prudent action was that of Bishop William McCloskey. The pastor of the cathedral in his Diocese of Louisville had inquired about a labor society to which some of his parishioners

[56] BCA, 72-G-5. Preached three times: Wilmington, North Carolina, 1871, Richmond, Virginia, Lent, 1876, and the cathedral in Baltimore, January 13, 1878.

[57] J. L. Spalding, *Life of the Most Rev. M. J. Spalding* (New York, 1873), p. 283. No name or date of letter are given.

belonged. The bishop conditioned his toleration, even of the oath, thus: ". . . if this object of these men was only to keep secret their proceedings at their meetings, which business was in all respects perfectly harmless, and with the assurance on their part that if anything objectionable were introduced, or any effort made to connect them with forbidden societies, they would immediately abandon the Society. . . ." The members had told the parish priest that Thomas Foley, a Baltimore priest, who had been elected Coadjutor Bishop of Chicago in 1869, had approved their organization. McCloskey's testimony continues:

> . . . supposing that he [Foley] had gained special wisdom from three Archbishops, I had Father Dunn write to him before I gave my answer. He said he had approved the union in the same sense I state and added that in doing so he had followed the practice of the Archbishops—that if we did otherwise 'we might as well close our churches.'

This final pragmatic note does not detract from Foley's having borne witness to the fact that the three Archbishops of Baltimore, under whom he had served from 1846 to 1869—the last two more closely as secretary and chancellor—had not objected to Catholic membership in labor organizations, even where bound to secrecy by an oath, so long as this was not just a cloak to cover dangerous tendencies.[58]

Although McCloskey unearthed this precedent, he felt conditions within the union had changed so that he was unable to follow the Baltimore example. Nevertheless, he showed both a friendly attitude and the ever-present tendency to push these practical problems of secret societies back to a higher authority when he wrote:

> I see now however that they have added conditions and among other things they refuse here to let even the party swearing to see the oath beforehand. Of course I have instructed my priests that that cannot be done, and I am studying up the question preparatory to giving, if I find it necessary, a public declaration. My reason for thinking that an oath might in the case first stated be taken, was that as things go nowadays, it seems difficult for the workmen to defend themselves. The conditions laid down

[58] These were Archbishops Samuel Eccleston (1834-1851), Francis P. Kenrick (1851-1863), and Martin J. Spalding (1864-1872).

in the Council of Baltimore are not always as clear as they might be but they go pretty far. I wish you would instruct me in the matter if you have any clearer laws than I can find. It is a difficult sand bar to clear and yet my own impression is that taking things as we find them, we must give these people all that in conscience we can yield, and they claim.[59]

Like hesitancy and doubt were naturally enough expressed also in the actions of the parish clergy, who normally would take their lead from their ecclesiastical superiors.[60] It is not surprising, therefore, to find in the same decade of the 1870's Catholic priests regarded as friends and again as foes of labor associations. John Fehrenbatch, president of the International Union of Machinists and Blacksmiths of North America, it was said by one who spoke for him, "has frequently spoken to priests about our organization and never yet found one who opposed it, when it is properly explained." The essence of the explanation seemed to have been to point out that nothing in the constitution or ritual interfered with a man's religious obligations.[61] In quite a different vein was the response of the president of the Miners' National Association, John Siney, an Irish-born Catholic, to the attacks of the operators and the hostile press.

> We have been called "agitators," we have been called "demagogues," because we have counseled the members of this organization to try and secure those objects. In some places even the clergy have placed their anathema upon the society and why. Is it wrong to teach men to seek a higher moral standard? If so, let them vacate the pulpits. . . .[62]

[59] AUND, Cincinnati Papers, William McCloskey to John B. Purcell, Louisville, March 17, 1873. William J. Dunn was pastor of the Cathedral of the Assumption and a member of the bishop's council.

[60] AAB, Records of the Diocesan Council, 1866-1906. Boston provided for this according to the minutes of a meeting of the bishop's council, May 20, 1872. On the question of secret societies it was agreed, *inter alia,* "that the priests should be warned never to condemn in the pulpit any new society, not expressly condemned by the Church—unless they first take the advice of the Bishop."

[61] PP, Edward McDevitt to Powderly, Cleveland, May 26, 1873.

[62] Charles Edward Killeen, O.Praem., "John Siney: the Pioneer of American Industrial Unionism and Industrial Government," Unpublished doctoral thesis,

For the sake of a complete picture, it must be remembered that the principal scene of Siney's activity was the Pennsylvania coalfields, which in the 1870's were filled with labor disturbances. This fact was not without influence, not only on the immediate attitude of the churchmen in that area, but also later when the tradition of the Molly Maguires proved to be very long-lived. Just as Siney and the Workingmen's Benevolent Association in their attempt to organize the northern coal fields had to face the charge of identification with the Mollies in 1868, so did Terence Powderly and the Knights of Labor have to face the same charge over ten years later.[63] The precise nature of this terroristic group has never been fully brought to light, but the latest student of the question, J. Walter Coleman, although failing to identify the Mollies, did survey what has been written on them and he concluded:

> The undisputed facts relative to the, Molly Maguires may be summed up briefly: A number of Irish Catholic coal miners, having common membership in an Irish patriotic organization, were accused of constituting a secret criminal society. Acting in an official capacity as members of this society which was designated the Molly Maguires by the community, they were said to have committed various acts of violence, including a number of murders, against officials of mining companies. Certain of the Mollies were arrested, membership in a common society was usually admitted readily, evidence was presented by a detective, and almost every man arrested was convicted. The Molly Maguires were then declared to have been broken up.[64]

Although some have termed them such, the Molly Maguires were never a labor union, but rather the result of the failure of trade unionism in the anthracite region of Pennsylvania.[65] Hence it is claimed that, "beginning with the early sixties, when the society first became known, until 1876, when it was finally stamped out, its criminal activity varied inversely in frequency and violence with the

University of Wisconsin (1942), p. 291, quoting *Miners National Record*, November, 1874.

[63] *Ibid.*, p. 133.

[64] J. Walter Coleman, *Labor Disturbances in Pennsylvania, 1850-1880* (Washington, 1936), p. 27.

[65] Macdonald, *op. cit.*, p. 51.

fortunes of the anthracite workers' union." [66]   As early as 1862 Bishop James F. Wood of Philadelphia tried to exercise influence over them and throughout this whole period, both by preaching and advice, his priests in the Diocese of Philadelphia continued their pacifying work.

The crime wave in the coal districts which aroused public authority to action began in 1874. Pinkerton detectives had been planted among the miners and they even took part in planning the murders, arson, and beatings which darkened the ensuing years. The Bishop of Philadelphia (archbishop after February, 1875), knew of this spy activity through Franklin B. Gowen, president of the Philadelphia and Reading Railroad. Gowen is usually considered chief villain in the piece, although he used his ecclesiastical contact as a sign of approbation. The blame for the Molly outrages was generally put on the Ancient Order of Hibernians, as was evident in the somewhat celebrated "Declaration of Seven Pastors" of October 10, 1874. Within two years Wood and several other Pennsylvania bishops condemned this Irish fraternal brotherhood, and about the same time the chief labor spy, James McParlan, turned informer. During the criminal trials in Pottsville Gowen claimed the warning revelation of the McParlan mission by Father Daniel O'Connor to his parishioners at Mahanoy Plane had given the prosecution the chance to use the agent, McParlan, as a witness. The detective had been promised originally that he would not have to act as one and even that his true character would never be revealed. But to clear the priest's name of "any intentional association" with the Mollies Gowen proposed to the archbishop the disclosure of his own role:

> To do this effectually however and to put at rest all suspicions as to his position and that of the Church I would like to have your permission to state publicly that you have been for some time cognizant of the means I had taken to break up the association of the Molly Maguires and that you had most earnestly desired to destroy or disperse their organization. [67]

[66] Commons, *History*, II, 181. In evidence there is cited the publication by the *Miners Journal* of March 30, 1867, of a list of fifty murders in Schuylkill County between 1863 and 1867 at a time when the union was weak.

[67] Molly Maguire Manuscripts of American Catholic Historical Society

This maneuver and similar court proceedings resulted eventually in the execution of seventeen convicted miners and by 1879 the Mollies came to an official demise. The A.O.H. quickly disclaimed any relationships with this workingman's group, although there is evidence that most of the Mollies were members of this benevolent society.[68] One writer has gone so far as to explain the confusion in the light of the archbishop's being influenced by Gowen. This he finds not too surprising in view of the fact that Wood was not only a convert from Protestantism, but of English ancestry.[69]

Though Coleman thought to emphasize the role of the Catholic clergy in these labor disturbances, he shows no evidence of having gotten anything out of the few priests who survived to his day. They preferred a silence which, while it may balk an historian, yet showed a love for the people whose confidants they had been and with whom they had both sympathized in their suffering and warned in their wrong doing. The subject, they believed, "reflected no credit on either the Irish miners who were involved or the men who ran them to earth."[70] The priests of the coal region, the author says, are unjustly maligned, either for not having taken part in the persecution or, on the contrary, for having condemned the group in any way.

of Philadelphia, Gowen to Wood, Philadelphia, May 14, 1876. Gowen remarked piously, "It seems to me that the Lord is on our side, for if it had not been for Father O'Connor we could never have had the success we are now meeting with in our efforts to crush the society." *Ibid.*, Pottsville, May 11, 1876. Cf. Coleman, *op. cit.*, pp. 109 and 75. The above evidence is the first corroboration of a constant tradition.

[68] Macdonald, *op. cit.*, pp. 53 and 61. The full text of the above mentioned statement of a group of pastors is on pp. 54-55.

[69] John O'Dea, *History of the Ancient Order of Hibernians* (Philadelphia, 1923), III, 1037. Cf. Marvin W. Schlegel, *Ruler of the Reading: The Life of Franklin B. Gowen, 1836-1889* (Harrisburg, 1947), p. 175, where O'Connor some years later is shown betraying his feelings to Gowen: "Archbishop Wood has been coupled with your name so often during the past two years that many believe ye are combined to run the P. & R. Co. and enslave the workingmen. . . ." March 15, 1880, quote from a letterbook of P. and R. Coal and Iron Company. Schlegel found no personal papers of Gowen.

[70] Coleman, *op. cit.*, p. 37.

Both of these criticisms are unjust, for despite the fact that the clergy recognized the injustice under which the laboring class was suffering, they adopted a fearless and uncompromising attitude toward improper methods of remedying the situation. They knew, furthermore, that when a secret society countenanced violent industrial coercion, it would attract evil men who would use it as a screen to commit crimes unrelated to social life.[71]

However inarticulate were the American Catholic priests on the labor problem, or however scanty the record of their opinion, the American episcopate did speak and leave behind them public pronouncements. Archbishop John B. Purcell of Cincinnati, whether he suffered from somewhat inaccurate reporting or not, expressed strong feelings on contemporary developments. At the commencement of St. Xavier College on June 26, 1872, the account of the Philadelphia *Catholic Herald* stated:

> . . . he was very severe on the strikers. He denounced the destructive and demoralizing influence of Internationalism, and said that if eight hours were acceded to now, four hours might be demanded to-morrow, as there would be no limit to such arrogance and dictation. No government could exist under such a system. The next cry would be for a division of property—every loafer and drunkard requiring a new subdivision every Saturday night. The remedy for these evils was liberal education.[72]

It was nearly always through the more formal medium of pastoral letters, however, that mention was made of workers' associations by members of the hierarchy. Generally such statements were included between a condemnation of secret societies and a recommendation of Catholic lay social organizations. Individual bishops throughout the 1870's often re-echoed and occasionally added something to the sentiments of the plenary council of 1866. In 1873 the hierarchy of the Province of New Orleans, assembled in council, approved associations, "which are honestly directed to objects of benevolence, or of mutual assistance and protection."[73] Two years

[71] *Ibid.*, p. 173.

[72] July 6, 1872. Cf. Commons, *History*, II, 151-152, on the successful strikes for the eight-hour day in the spring of 1872.

[73] "Pastoral Letter of the Archbishops and Bishops of New Orleans assem-

later the Bishop of Alton found in secret societies one of the great forces against religion in the United States. He instructed his priests:

> Wherefore, brethren, exhort those entrusted to your care to avoid all secret societies, and even to look with suspicion upon all societies which have not the approval of your ecclesiastical superiors—more particularly when such have a religious service of their own at funerals, as have v.g. the Grangers and such like associations, or open and close their meetings by a service which is not approved by the Catholic Church.[74]

The people of the Diocese of Portland, Maine, heard emphasized not the ritualistic or religious character of such societies but their secrecy. The bishop went so far as to say: "The ordinary subterfuge that the members are allowed to tell their confessor is only a subterfuge making more plain the character of the society." [75]

Other bishops' statements after the hectic days of labor strife in 1877 showed stronger allusions to labor organizations. Bishop Bernard J. McQuaid of Rochester, whose influence stretched beyond his own see because of his close friendship with the later Archbishop of New York, Michael A. Corrigan, laid down these rules for the faithful of his western New York diocese:

1. Avoid all societies, condemned by the Church by name.

2. Avoid all societies, whose principles are similar to those of the first class, as in any way inimical to religion, or legitimate government.

3. Avoid all societies, whose purpose is the doing of wrong or injustice to individuals or classes in the community.

4. Avoid all societies bound by oaths of secrecy against the rights of lawful authority, spiritual or temporal.

5. Avoid all societies whose rites and rituals are made up of

---

bled in Council" (1873), p. 5, *Pastoral Letters*, IV, Mullen Library, Catholic University of America.

[74] "Pastoral Instruction of the Bishop of Alton, to the Clergy, Secular and Regular, and to the Religious Communities, Etc. of his Diocese." Issued April 12, 1875. Treasure Room, Library of the University of Notre Dame. Peter Joseph Baltes was the bishop of this see from 1869 to 1886.

[75] ADPM. "Pastoral Letter of 1876 of James A. Healy."

forms, ceremonials and words partaking of religious character, or communionship of worship not according to the teachings and practice of the Catholic Church.[76]

Even with directives as definite as those just quoted the priests waited on the action of their bishops, just as the latter in turn often took their cue from Rome. The Congregation of the Propaganda, which had jurisdiction over the Church in the United States as still in a mission status, was keenly aware of the growing danger of secret societies in this country. The cardinal prefect, Giovanni Simeoni, for instance, launched an inquiry about the nature of the Order of the American Union. He had read about it in the New York *Herald,* and wanted more such samples to judge in the light of ecclesiastical condemnations! [77] The identification of this particular group stymied Archbishop Gibbons of Baltimore and Bishop Gilmour of Cleveland. The latter was unable to get a copy of its constitution, although he testified there were few Catholics in it, and he wisely suggested unity of action on such questions among the American bishops.[78] Such unanimity was to take a long time to develop; much more rapid was the manner in which the hierarchy agreed in taking up and promulgating two initial encyclicals of Pope Leo XIII's pontificate, *Inscrutabili* of April 21, 1878, and *Quod apostolici muneris* of December 28, 1878. The former lamented the evils of a society which had overthrown the "supreme truths" on which its foundation rested. Principally because it scorned the authority of the Church, it had given itself over to a lust for transitory pleasures, a fury of dissension and bad government. The second document attacked the "pest of Socialism," the adherents of which, "scattered all over the world, and bound together in a wicked confederacy," sought the ruin of society by undermining religion, the state, the family and private property. The Pope warned also against those among the revolution-

---

[76] "Pastoral Letter of the Right Reverend, the Bishop of Rochester" (1878), p. 15, *Pastoral Letters,* I, Catholic University of America.

[77] BCA, 73-V-10, Simeoni to Gibbons, Rome, August 22, 1878. The existence of seventy-eight fraternal orders before 1880, and the rise of 124 new ones in the following decade would show that there was plenty of work for all concerned. Cf. Macdonald, *op. cit.,* p. 100.

[78] BCA, 73-W-9, Gilmour to Gibbons, Cleveland, September 21, 1878.

aries who even distorted the Gospel to their ends. Before closing he advised the bishops of the world to encourage, "societies of artisans and workmen constituted under the guardianship of religion," since Socialism sought recruits especially among them.[79] The filial acceptance of his warnings, at least, among American Catholics was typified at the reception tendered to the first American cardinal, John McCloskey, in New York, his see city. He returned from Rome bearing besides "a double embrace and benediction for all American Catholics," the red hat and the text of the earlier of the two encyclical letters. McCloskey had no doubt of the application of the pope's words to the United States and the duty of American Catholics to resist "socialism and revolutionism." He said: "We have the elements of revolution and communism among us. It is threatening. Mischief is brewing on this side of the Atlantic, and it needs all our power to stop the iniquity that is sweeping all before it."[80]

Reflecting the influence of these papal statements and even more specifically speaking out on labor unions than had been usual, were some of the pastorals of 1879. The diocesan synod of Vincennes was the occasion for this advice: "We would especially warn you against the socialistic societies or Secret Labor Leagues of the day, such as the Ancient Order of Workingmen. . . ."[81] That Bishop Francis S. Chatard was strict in his attitude on suspected societies—even beyond the severity of the decrees of Baltimore—is shown by what he enunciated as a sure rule for his people's guidance, ". . . any society

[79] Cf. Joseph Husslein, S.J. (Ed.), *Social Wellsprings* (Milwaukee, 1940), I, 1-23, for a translation and edition of their texts.

[80] Scranton *Republican,* May 31, 1878. Cf. also George D. Wolff, "Socialistic Communism in the United States," *American Catholic Quarterly Review,* III, (July, 1878), 522-562, and M. F. S., "The Labor Question," *ibid.,* III (October, 1878), 721-746. Both of these articles saw the remedy in the Christian religion which should have influence alike on the poor, the wealthy, and the government. John Gilmary Shea feared the contamination of the poor by communistic organizations in "The Rapid Increase of the Dangerous Classes in the United States," *ibid.,* IV (April, 1879), 266.

[81] This group, however, was purely fraternal. Commons, *History,* II, 196. Also PP, Uriah S. Stevens to John F. Loftus, Philadelphia. July 29, 1879. "The A. O. of U. W. is a life insurance and Funeral Benefit institution I believe and does not include labor Reform and is not therefore a competitor against us."

that is oathbound, or not being bound by oath is nevertheless secret in its transactions, excluding from it directly or indirectly the supervision of the Church is a secret society condemned by the Church and any Catholic belonging to it is excommunicated." [82] Yet he admitted in print, "it is notorious that greed of wealth does not often allow capitalists to be generous or even just. Hence the poor hardworking man seeks support in combination and in his numbers." Chatard bemoaned, however, the intimidation practiced against workers who did not conform to the decisions of such unions. Furthermore, even if there were Catholic trade unions he did not see how they could co-operate with their fellow-workers of socialist leanings. He maintained workers should stifle their envy of capitalists by looking to heaven, but in the meanwhile, he held, "Ordinarily speaking, the daily support of the man himself and of his wife and children, might be the least remuneration a good workman should receive; what his wife could make should go to provide for the future." [83]

With less concern for the problems of labor Bishop Joseph Dwenger of Fort Wayne warned his people against secret and oathbound societies, pointing out that, although some otherwise good men belonged to them, they were basically anti-supernatural and, of course, anti-Catholic. He perceived a connection between the "secret and higher grades" and communism, and the bishop was led to remark further:

> Although the Catholic Church does not condemn mere labor associations, yet we are justly alarmed when we perceive the communistic tendency of so many of them. We warn our Catholics never to be a party to wrong. They may refuse to work except for a certain price, but they cannot by force prevent others from working; they cannot even countenance robbery and arson, much less be a party to it. . . . [84]

[82] "Pastoral Letter of the Bishop of Vincennes on the Occasion of the Diocesan Synod (Indianapolis, 1879)," p. 14. Treasure Room, UND.

[83] Francis S. Chatard, "Catholic Societies," *American Catholic Quarterly Review,* IV (April, 1879), 220.

[84] AUND, Fort Wayne Papers, "Pastoral of Bishop Dwenger, Septuagesima Sunday, 1879."

The Bishop of Cleveland, however, elaborated further on the labor question and, although agreeing on the workers' right to organize and to strike, he presented a view concerning wages that today is seen to be directly opposed to the later social teaching of the popes. Gilmour said first: "Men have also a right to band together to agree not to work for less than a given price and so long as men act freely and without constraint, there is no sin in labor banding together for self-protection." Before pointing out the evils of secret labor organizations, as well as of violence and coercion, the Cleveland pastoral read:

> Where Labor Unions sin, is when they attempt to force men to join these unions, or attempt to force men to work for the price fixed by these unions. If the Union has a right to fix the price at which its members will work, so have men, who do not belong to these unions, an equal right to fix the price at which they will work. All men have a right to sell their labor at whatever price they please, and no man, nor union has a right to force another to sell his labor at the price they may have agreed upon. Here is where Labor Unions fail and cannot be sustained. If men who join Labor Unions have a right to determine the price at which they will sell their labor, so equally men who do not join labor unions have a right to determine the price at which they will sell their labor.[85]

Bishop Thomas A. Becker of Wilmington, not only agreed with Chatard, Dwenger, and Gilmour in opposing the monopolistic character of some unions, but he may even have had an influence on their thought since a year before their pronouncements he had published his views in the Philadelphia periodical, the *American Catholic Quarterly Review*. He wrote:

[85] "Lenten Pastoral of Rt. Rev. Richard Gilmour, D.D., Bishop of Cleveland" (1879), p. 2. *Pastoral Letters*, II, Catholic University of America. Since there is no means of ready access to the pastorals issued in various dioceses over the years, it can hardly be claimed that the above is a complete coverage, but they would seem to be the principal occasions when episcopal opinions were expressed on labor. Further consideration of the broader aspects of the problem from papal and American documents may be found in Joseph L. Powers, C.S.C., "The Knights of Labor and the Church's Attitude on Secret Societies." Unpublished master's thesis, University of Notre Dame (1943).

Theoretically there is no wrong whatever in a simple combination of workmen for the purpose of preventing an undue lowering of the price of their labor, or for the purpose of gathering funds to support their fellow-workmen, should a *'strike'* become necessary. The wrong begins the moment such associations attempt by intimidation or actual violence to prevent other workmen from accepting what wages they please.

Becker went further to pass judgment on specific techniques of trade unionists, *"Rattening* is wholly wrong and unjustifiable; *Picketing* is just as fair and honorable as would be the insertion of an advertisement in the morning paper to that effect." He did not see any need for men to combine to secure economic reforms, since in the United States public opinion and law could work out the social problem. Yet he judged there was no harm in such combinations, nor in "merely beneficial societies." [86]

These opinions on organized labor expressed by some of the more articulate members of the American hierarchy, were indeed conservative and cautious, but events were to show that the most active opposition to the Knights of Labor was to come from the Church in Quebec. The Quebec situation, too, had its background in the question of secret societies as well as in the developing labor movement. Canadian unionism before 1850 was sporadic and local and suffered from the rebellion of 1837 in several attempts at organization. It was inclined to secrecy and made greater strides only in the 1850's when the chief troubles centered around the printers who struck in both Quebec City and Toronto. Of particular interest here is the fact that the Canadian hierarchy was holding its first provincial council in 1851 in the city of Quebec, and their hostility to the strikers was able to be overcome only by John J. Lynch, "present as a theologian," who thereby saved the printers from an edict of con-

---

[86] Thomas A. Becker, "Secret Societies in the United States," *American Catholic Quarterly Review*, III (April, 1878), 216-217. It is interesting that Becker had been with Thomas Foley a member of Archbishop Spalding's household in Baltimore until the fall of 1865. In December of that same year, there came to reside in the house as secretary to Spalding the young priest, James Gibbons, who was elevated to the bishopric, as Vicar Apostolic of North Carolina, at the same ceremony that made Becker Bishop of Wilmington, Delaware, in 1868.

demnation.[87] Further expansion of unionism in Canada took place in the 1860's and many craft unions crossed the line from United States. The post-Confederation industrial development helped along the cause from 1869 to 1873, and the first step to organize the various groups for the common interest of labor took place in March, 1871, at Toronto where a trades' assembly was set up after the pattern of American labor of forty years before. Only with the Trade Union Act of 1872 were Canadian trade unions given a legal blessing. National organization came with the Canadian Labor Union in September, 1873, at Toronto, but this, however, was affected so adversely by the depression of that year that it has been maintained that the Toronto typographical union was the only one intact by 1879.[88]

That very year saw the publication by Archbishop Elzear-Alexandre Taschereau of the *Discipline du diocèse de Québec* which showed an awareness of stirrings in the field of labor. The section on "Secret Societies" was based not only on the general papal constitutions, but also on their own Canadian conciliar action and such specific directives as the condemnation of Fenianism by the Congregation of the Inquisition of January 12, 1870, and the letter of Cardinal Barnabò of November 16, 1870. This latter document, which mentioned specifically the shoemakers, had been addressed to the administrator of the Archdiocese of Quebec, M. Careau, since Taschereau was promoted from his positions of seminary professor and vicar general only in 1871. This opposition in Quebec to the ritualistic Knights of St. Crispin had already proved effective, for their third annual meeting in Boston, April 19-30, 1870, reported failure in the capital of French Canada. Mention of opposition from the Church was not recorded, but the existence in their pledge of "sacred word and honor" of the exception allowing the revelation of secrets to a "religious confessor" indicated very definitely that it was present along with the

[87] Daniel J. O'Donoghue, "Labor Organization in Ontario," *Annual Report of the Bureau of Industries for the Province of Ontario, 1886* (Toronto, 1887), p. 245.

[88] The author is grateful for the background of secular events sketched in Douglas R. Kennedy, "The Knights of Labor in Canada." Unpublished master's thesis, University of Western Ontario (1945).

manufacturers' resentment of their aggressiveness.[89]   This attitude was far from being out of step with the times, for in current Canadian opinion, even among "the liberal statesmen and press," unions were regarded as "perversions." [90]   Within ten years, nevertheless, the powerful internationals in the United States had penetrated into Canada, and one of them found its way even into Taschereau's *Discipline.*

Specifically on labor, the *Discipline* spoke of a "certain society of workmen" which had been recently established in Quebec from the United States, and which was open to suspicion. Following the mind of the Second Plenary Council of Baltimore the Canadian archbishop pointed out that the prohibition of the Church did not extend to labor groups which simply sought self-protection. He continued, however, elaborating on his own:

> And all this was the judgment of many bishops in the United States whose opinion I sought. But since such associations ordinarily do not lack danger, either with regard to public peace or the faith and morals of individuals, we advise pastors and confessors to use exhortation and advice to turn them away from them as much as possible.

Such members were to be refused the sacraments only if they did not promise the following safeguards: ready withdrawal at the word of the Holy See or the bishop, avoidance of all injustice or violence, and the abstaining from any oath of complete and absolute obedience.[91]

This unidentified labor organization which brought on the Quebec ruling was not the Knights of Labor, for the latter entered the dominion only in 1881, but it did provide the setting in which the Knights were later to be judged. The Canadian pronouncement and

---

[89] Don D. Lescohier, *The Knights of St. Crispin, 1867-1874* (Madison, 1910), pp. 87, 77-78.

[90] R. H. Coats, "The Labor Movement in Canada," *Canada and Its Provinces* (Toronto, 1914), IX, 295.

[91] E. A. Taschereau, *Discipline du diocèse de Québec* (Quebec, 1879), pp. 216-217. A notation concerning the receipt of Barnabò's letter is in the margin of these pages in the archbishop's extant copy.

the American statements of ecclesiastical policy may serve to mark an end to the background of the Church and labor before the 1880's. By the year 1879, the Knights of Labor had taken on a national character. Terence V. Powderly was at their head, and it was already becoming evident that some of the points that worried the bishops about secret societies were directly applicable to the Noble and Holy Order of the Knights of Labor of America.

CHAPTER II

FORMATION AND REFORMATION

THE year 1879 witnessed not only an increased awareness of the growing importance of organized labor on the part of some Amercan bishops, but it marked as well the beginning of the national importance of the Knights of Labor. This period of the Knights' prominence can be said to date from 1879 to 1893, years which were coextensive with the leadership of Terence V. Powderly.[1] The full account of this organization would be almost a complete picture of its times, so widespread were its interests and activities. However, to appreciate the ecclesiastical aspects of its story it is necessary to know something of the origins of the Knights. Worthy of serious consideration, too, is the background with which Powderly approached his office.

The efforts of the National Labor Union and the Industrial Brotherhood to form a nation-wide structure had already failed when the first successful national labor society was born at Philadelphia in 1869. It began with the dissolution of the Garment Cutters' Union (1862-1869), when nine of the members decided to stay together in a new and secret group. Secrecy was not a new thing for such an association, for the Industrial Brotherhood had used a pledge as had

---

[1] Mary R. Beard, "Knights of Labor," *Encyclopedia of the Social Sciences* (New York, 1932), VIII, 581. No attempt will be made here to rewrite the development of the Order, but the treatment will follow the standard works of John R. Commons and associates, *The History of Labor in the United States* (New York, 1918), II, and Norman Ware, *The Labor Movement in the United States, 1860-1895* (New York, 1929). The latter's approach is more ideological, and attempts to show the Knights as a kind of half-way mark to industrial democracy. Ware had access only to the papers of John Hayes and he reflects his dislike of Powderly. There are also the contemporary works of George E. McNeil (Ed.), *The Labor Movement, the Problem of To-day* (New York, 1891), and Powderly's own, *Thirty Years of Labor* (Columbus, 1890), and *The Path I Trod* (New York, 1940). These last works will hereafter be cited as *Thirty Years* and *Path*.

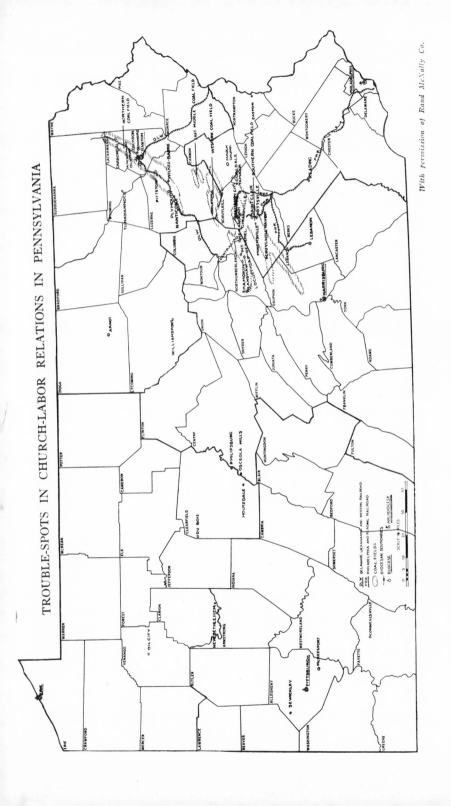

TROUBLE-SPOTS IN CHURCH-LABOR RELATIONS IN PENNSYLVANIA

With permission of Rand McNally Co.

many trade unions, but it was to become a detail of paramount importance in the Knights of Labor, due especially to the anti-labor attitude of capital during the depression of 1873-1879. It was maintained:

> The reason for the extreme secrecy was because it was claimed that open and public association had, after centuries of toil and struggle proved to be failures in one way or another. It was also claimed that when the association worked openly, so that its members might be known to the public, it exposed its members to the scrutiny, and in time, the wrath of their employers. It was deemed best to work in such a way to avoid comment and scrutiny.[2]

The practical means of enforcing secrecy were "the impenetrable veil of ritual, sign grip and password." In the case of the Knights of Labor, besides this very pragmatic reason and the natural human instinct for ceremonial, there was, moreover, the background of its founders which assured ritualistic detail for the order. An early sketch of their progress made this point clear:

> Mr. Stephens brought into the ritual of the new order many of the features of speculative Masonry, especially in the forms and ceremonies observed. The obligations were in the nature of oaths taken with all solemnity upon the Bible. The members were sworn to the strictest secrecy. The name even of the order was not to be divulged. . . .[3]

It was Uriah S. Stephens, former student for the Baptist ministry, a Mason, an Odd Fellow, and a member of the Knights of Pythias, who was elected first master workman of the Knights of Labor on January 6, 1870, and the retiring presiding officer, James L. Wright, was made venerable sage.[4] Stephens drafted an opening service and an initiation ritual which came into use in a manual

---

[2] Powderly, *Thirty Years,* p. 147.

[3] Carroll D. Wright, "An Historical Sketch of the Knights of Labor," *Quarterly Journal of Economics,* I (January, 1887), 142.

[4] Herbert Solow, "Uriah Smith Stephens," *Dictionary of American Biography* (New York, 1943), XVII, 581.

prepared in November, 1869.[5]   Another elaborate formula, called the founding ceremony, to be used when setting up new assemblies, is contained in an undated manual, also prepared by Stephens sometime in the early 1870's.   According to Powderly, in 1878 an exception was made in the oath in this ritual by the insertion of the words, "except to my Religious Confessor," and he insisted on adding, "at the Confessional."[6]   Years later one of the members of the first ritual committee, Robert McCauley, Irish-born and a Knight of Pythias, admitted that the ceremonial of the Knights of Labor "was taken verbatim et literatim from that of the Knights of Pythias."[7]   Although he mistakenly referred to them as seven in number, Powderly was probably right when he told a Catholic prelate that the founders "were for the most part members of the masonic order and the impress of their teachings in that order was stamped on the ritual and constitution of the K. of L."[8]   The ritual for the local assemblies was contained in a booklet entitled *Adelphon Kruptos,* meaning "Secret Brotherhood."   It came to be referred to as the A. K.   The "Secret Work," which was committed to memory, contained the official secret signs, grips, words, and symbols.   This was printed several times and sent out by the grand secretary for the sake of obtaining uniformity.   It was entitled "Secret Work and Instructions" and it was to be returned to that same official by registered mail within sixty days.[9]

With this extreme secrecy the Knights of Labor grew very slowly and it was only in July, 1872, that the "sojourners" who had been allowed into the garment cutters' group, Local Assembly No. 1,

[5] John R. Commons et al. (Ed.), *A Documentary History of American Industrial Society* (Cleveland, 1911), X, 19, note.   Information for the notes on these published documents was supplied by Powderly. *Ibid.,* X, 19.

[6] *Ibid.,* X, 25, note, and 28.   A cypher was used in it after 1878.

[7] New York *Sun,* June 8, 1889.

[8] Powderly to Archbishop Patrick J. Ryan, October 24, 1884, copy.   Since all the manuscript references but one in this chapter are from the Powderly Papers the symbol PP will be omitted herein, as well as the place of their origin, Scranton, when the letters were written by Powderly himself.

[9] Received by Powderly, April 1, 1882.   Ware, *op. cit.,* p. 41, inaccurately translates "Adelphon Kruptos" as "Secret Work," and in effect confuses these two distinct things. Cf. Appendix I, pp. 359-362.

also formed the second L. A. in Philadelphia. These early locals were not "mixed," i. e., composed of men of different occupations, but they were called trade assemblies. The swing away from the exclusive character of the trade unions to embrace all workers, and even those merely interested in the cause, showed an especially strong trend with the general assembly of 1878. In this were sown the seeds of ultimate dissolution of the Order. At all events, Philadelphia Catholics apparently were joining the Knights from the outset, for by the end of 1872, although there were only three assemblies in the city, the first information concerning the Knights of Labor had already reached the ears of the Catholic clergy. In this same year a committee, appointed by L. A. 1 and headed by William Fennimore, who had joined the local in January, 1870, called on Bishop James F. Wood. It was later said: "The result of the conference was an article in the *Catholic Standard* by the Archbishop [*sic*] in favor of the Order." [10] However, an examination of this paper revealed only an editorial endorsing the growing tendency of men to associate with one another, but pointing out the necessity of approval and guidance from the Church. In fact it postulated:

> The spirit of the world is always and everywhere the same, and societies organized upon a non-Catholic basis are likely to exert any but a good influence upon the Catholics who may join them. . . . The good sense, and still more the religious principles of the practical Catholics who belong to those associations, may, and often do, preserve them from the dangers to which we have adverted.[11]

Of course, the principles of the new Order as set down by Stephens in the secret ritual could have been made to sound quite harmless and even attractive to an ecclesiastic. Their organization was simply imitating capital in uniting to protect and advance the interest of labor where "open and public association" had failed. Intending "no conflict with legitimate enterprise, no antagonism to necessary

10 James A. Wright to Powderly, Philadelphia, August 1, 1888, giving the evidence of James L. Wright of the original founders' group.

11 *Catholic Standard*, April 6, 1872. Wood used the editorial columns of this paper for official announcements but they were always labeled as such. Cf. Essay on the Sources, p. 380, on lack of archival material.

capital," they offered as remedies, education, legislation, and mutual beneficence.[12]

By the end of 1873 these sentiments had been propagated sufficiently to have established in and around Philadelphia eighty assemblies, which on December 7 of that year formed the first district assembly out of delegates from all the locals in the area, whether mixed or trade in character.[13] Within a year another D. A. was established in Camden, New Jersey, but, "The first important expansion was westward through Reading to Pittsburgh and into the coal and iron districts, where the more rigid craft ideas of Philadelphia began to break down." [14] One of the leaders in this western part of the state was John N. Davis, editor of the *National Labor Tribune*. While the Knights were still known only as the "Five Stars," this Pittsburgh labor journalist gave them the highest recommendation for their success in Philadelphia and their broad inclusiveness. He concluded: "It is the best and most successful effort of labor to combine for its own defense. The obligation of secrecy gives it permanency and safety. The well-known Archbishop Wood of Philadelphia gives it his sanction." [15] Thus was continued the tradition of Wood's approval. Powderly, however, never used it when it would have seemed to his advantage to do so, namely, in his apologies to Archbishop Ryan and Cardinal Gibbons, although he expressed it in 1892 and it was later published.[16] The letter of James A. Wright, written in 1888 as Powderly was preparing his *Thirty Years of Labor*, told of a committee from Local 64 in Phil-

[12] Commons, *Documentary History*, X, 23-24.

[13] Here Commons, *History*, II, 199, remarks, "The ritual and other work of the Order were now put into written form, and the organization was complete." Powderly took credit for introducing a ritual for district assemblies after 1879. A copy of this "Archeon Work for District Assemblies" marked, "Received Feb. 14, 1883," shows the retention of symbolism but no oath or other religious features.

[14] Ware, *op. cit.*, p. 31.

[15] *National Labor Tribune*, March 13, 1875, quoted in Commons, *Documentary History*, X, 33. Philadelphia had been made a metropolitan see the previous month.

[16] Powderly to William Ayres, December 26, 1892, copy. Quoted in *Path*, p. 395.

adelphia which also called on the head of the see in 1875, "but they never held an interview with him, he was sick at the time." [17] Nevertheless, none of this information about Wood's friendliness was used by Powderly in his first publication.

It was in the same home city of the Order that Powderly claimed he was initiated into the Knights in 1874. But until 1876, when he was sought out by a member of L. A. 88 in Scranton, he "could learn nothing of the whereabouts of the order." [18] Nor does his diary reveal anything on this point until September 6, 1876, where it reads, ". . . joined a Labor organization. . . ." [19] Behind this statement, however, was earlier experience in societies of workers. This picturesque labor leader, who was to play the principal lay role in the relations between the Catholic Church and the Knights of Labor, was born in Carbondale, Pennsylvania, of Irish parentage in 1849. He was the eleventh of twelve children, and after spending six years at a public school at the age of thirteen he went to work on the railroad. In 1871 he joined the Machinists and Blacksmiths' Union and had trouble with blacklisting, and in 1874 he was also an organizer for the short-lived Industrial Brotherhood. His hitherto unexplored diaries show him to have been during these years of the 1870's very much of a "joiner." He was not only active but a leader in such non-labor groups as literary and debating clubs, and he was often associated with his Scranton parish groups, temperance meetings, and activities like the "Peter Cooper Club." Moreover, he sought to improve himself by serious reading, and even by drawing and playing the flutina. All this activity helped lessen the drudgery of work in a machine shop. He entered the married state in 1872 when he was wed to Hannah Dever. Powderly's daily chronicles show him to have been a faithful Catholic, for he carefully noted when he went to church and fulfilled his religious obligations. His receiving the sacraments only several times a year was representative for his day, since it was before the practice of frequent reception of Holy Communion had become common among

---

[17] James A. Wright to Powderly, Philadelphia, August 1, 1888.

[18] Powderly, *Thirty Years*, p. 196.

[19] His diaries give a very complete coverage of his daily life through the 1870's.

Catholics. In this regard, his diaries fail to corroborate two events narrated in his memoirs.[20] After joining the Machinists and Black-smiths' Union in 1871 Powderly relates he was turned away from the door of the Scranton cathedral since some one seeing the symbol of his union had reported him to Father Richard Hennessy as a Mason. Shortly afterwards this union symbol was also the cause of a public scene on the occasion of his attempting to go to confession to this priest. The diary of 1871 reports he was a union man by December of that year, but neither the entries for that year nor the daily accounts of 1872, although they tell the hour of every Sunday Mass he attended, even mention these two occurrences.[21]

The budding labor leader's entry for February 4, 1872, in some ways was kindly since he occasionally made a caustic comment on sermons. He went to the last Mass that Sunday and heard Bishop Wood who "denounced secret societies." [22] This would strengthen to some extent the truthfulness of his later admission that he entered the Knights of Labor with his Catholic eyes wide open to the teaching of the Church on such societies. He later told Archbishop Ryan of Philadelphia:

> I was admitted to it with a full knowledge of the oath and its bearings, I knew that Catholics could not join it, or if they did they could not remain members of it. That there existed a necessity for such an organization was apparent to every man who worked for wages, for at that time the Trade-Union was the only society that the workingman could look to for aid. When we reflect that the principal aim of the trade-union at that time was to lead its members into a strike, oft-times regardless of the consequences, you will see at a glance that a more conservative [   ] with which to carry on the business between

20 Powderly, *Path,* pp. 317-319.

21 Diary, 1876, April 30, Sunday. This item of some years later resembles the incident at the church door, "Went to nine o'clock Mass, and had the ill luck to meet Barney Reilly in the hall; he tried to put me out. I would not go. Called him everything I could think of." The next recorded confession was on May 9, and this to Father John W. Dunne with whom Powderly was always friendly.

22 Nowhere does he seem to give his opinion of this prelate, but one entry has a rather ominous ring, "gave Jimmy Ward my opinion of Bishop Wood of Philadelphia." Diary, 1876, June 8.

capital and labor was a necessity. To the trade-union no *laborer* could be admitted, simply because he was "only a laborer." The K. of L. recognized the rights of all men who toiled for a living to share in its benefits, no other labor society ever did it before. . . .[23]

This democratic vision of the Knights of Labor might have been clarified somewhat if the protest of a Brooklyn assembly in 1875 against extreme secrecy had proved successful. The discussion which followed brought on a national meeting at Philadelphia in July, 1876, but due to the predominance of the local group the question was quietly ignored.[24] Consequently, Powderly had to salve the slight stirrings of his Catholic conscience in another way. As M. W. of L. A. 222 in Scranton (founded in October, 1876) he entered into correspondence on the question of Catholic membership with Thomas King of D. A. 4 of Reading, which had been, established the previous January. King assured the anxious inquirer that the secrecy of the Knights of Labor was only a protective one; Catholics could always speak to their spiritual advisers about it, and even show the A. K. to the priest. In some places the clergy had already misunderstood the whole society. In Reading, on the contrary, Catholics "are encouraged by the Priests after having shown to them the A. K. and yet there are some hard working members who are Catholics who think it superstitious to tell the Catholics about confessing to the priests, although we know who we have to deal with sometimes. . . ." This last phrase may have referred to stern and domineering clergymen, but still he did not hesitate to advise a call on the Bishop of Scranton.[25] But Powderly had already called on his friend, Father Dunne about "the new Labor Society." The priest, he reported, "is in favor of it if the Church is." He returned to the rectory the following week to leave the A. K. for the bishop's perusal.[26] The entries for the following days show Powderly rather restlessly awaiting his visit to the prelate. It was after the turn

---

[23] Powderly to Archbishop Ryan, October 24, 1884, copy.

[24] Powderly, *Thirty Years,* pp. 225-233, gives the text of the proceedings.

[25] Thomas King to Powderly, Reading, December 21, 1876; also January 21, 1877.

[26] Diary, 1876, December 20 and 26.

of the year before he, hardly fortified by a report from Carbondale that Father John McGrath had been speaking against a secret labor society, made his call.[27]   Not very informative is his record of how after tea, "I went over to Bishop O'Hara's residence talked with him an hour and a half came home at half past nine o'clock read *Irish World* awhile then went to bed." [28]   There is no evidence to indicate it was anything but a friendly and pleasant discussion.   Powderly continued to attend the Knights of Labor meetings, to carry out his religious duties, and to maintain the friendship of Father Dunne, from whom he picked up the "Secret Brotherhood" the following week.[29]

The only available account of what took place between the bishop and the labor leader is in a letter of Powderly's written a few months later.   He told of receiving the advice of the secretary of his district assembly, and of how he followed it out:

> I took it [the A. K.] to the Bishop who examined it and told me he saw nothing in it that was wrong, and he thought the aggressive policy adopted by the Capitalists made it necessary for working men to join an organization for their own safety but he said the Church will not recognize secret societies. I told him this was not secret to the Catholic priest. He then said the thing he most objected to was the taking of a rash oath which he said the Church always forbids. I said I know it and I considered there was cause for this oath and that a great many Catholics (myself among the number) very often swore a very rash oath in an angry moment that was to all intents and purposes a grievous sin and then asked him if as a member I would leave the Society. His answer was: Do as you please. The Church does not approve of your Society but neither does it approve of a Building Association, for it doesn't ask of anyone to join it. You have taken a rash oath and that sin you cannot [sic] undo only by performing the penance imposed upon you by your confessor for as your Society is not secret to the priests why the sin falls on the rash oath you have taken and you cannot make that sin less by leaving the Society. I shall not say one word in denunciation of your Society unless I shall find that

---

27 Diary, 1877, January 2.
28 *Ibid.*, January 3.
29 *Ibid.*, January 12. The priest was expected to make a social call. *Ibid.*, April 14.

through it there are deeds of violence (such as the Molly Maguires commit) done. Then it becomes my duty to denounce such even though your Society were not secret.

This the Scranton leader thought should have been a pattern of action for Catholics. They should settle for ecclesiastical silence and the willingness to grant absolution in confession.[30] Brother O'Brien in Nanticoke took this correspondence to his pastor, Father "MacKingley," [Charles A. Mattingly] who reacted as might one who years later was to read Powderly's own version of his stormy relations with Bishop O'Hara. He called the letter nonsense. O'Brien felt he himself had a bad name with the priest since the last strike activity for which he had been blamed. Consequently he had declined from organizing any Catholics, although he claimed a precedent in Plymouth where the "principal Catholics" belonged and Father Patrick Toner had said "it was all right if the bishop said so." [31] O'Brien showed none of Powderly's fighting spirit with which he threatened to carry the battle against features objectionable to Catholics into the Pittsburgh national convention. This meeting of the National Labor League of North America, as the Knights had decided at Philadelphia to call themselves publicly, was scheduled to convene in July, 1877.[32]

Before that time, however, Powderly engaged in a preliminary skirmish in his own town by attacking religious bigotry within the local assemblies. At a meeting of L. A. 217 he "exploded a bombshell" by exposing the anti-Catholics.[33] Ironically enough two of them were Duncan Wright and George Starkey who seem to have been the very men who had brought Powderly into L. A. 88. John Lee, with whom he had joined, was the one perferring charges against

[30] Powderly to Jerry O'Brien, April 4, 1877, copy. The odd advice supposedly offered by O'Hara makes it all the more regrettable that the trip made to Scranton in April, 1946, by the present writer failed to uncover any of the records of Bishop O'Hara, but only the tradition that he was a strict disciplinarian. Cf. *Path,* pp. 317-328, for an account of Powderly's early difficulties in Scranton.

[31] O'Brien to Powderly, April 9, 1877; and March 18, 1877. *Sadlier's Catholic Directory* (New York, 1877), p. 360.

[32] Powderly to O'Brien, April 4, 1877, copy.

[33] Diary, 1877, April 23.

them.[34]   King of Reading thought they deserved expulsion if they
had violated the constitutional provision against political or religious discussion.   This would be the duty of D. A. 5 of Scranton
(established in February, 1877, and later called 16).[35]   Powderly
read his charges at the meeting of L. A. 222 and "came home after
resigning my Delegateship." [36]   This sacrifice of his place in the
district assembly and national gathering was intended to establish his purity of motive.   Whatever his reason, he did plead quite
sensibly, "Brothers, Protestant and Catholic, I call upon you as
you hope for eternal salvation hereafter to join hands in the amelioration of Labor for God knows we have enemies enough arrayed against
us in the ranks of Capital without our creating new ones among
ourselves." [37]   Apparently Powderly listened to the restraining advice of King, for he attended the D. A. meeting in Wilkes Barre,
although with disgust he noted that there he had seen "the most
disgraceful scenes I ever witnessed." [38]   The Scranton knight was
not, however, at the national conference in Pittsburgh on May 14,
1877, which superseded the one planned at Philadelphia the previous
year.   The western D. A. 3 had called this convention and hence
the Philadelphia faction was weak, although James L. Wright was
elected past master workman.   A resolution was adopted that it
would be his duty, "to instruct the new Initiate that are of the
Catholic Church, that their [sic] is nothing in this Order to prevent him from receiving the Sacrament, and if he considert [sic]
it his duty, to confess to his Father confessor, he may have the
power so to do." [39]

Here was the beginning on a larger scale of the attempt to placate
the authorities of the Catholic Church.   But the failure to put into
effect another resolution, namely, "That the name of the Order be
public," slowed up this effort.[40]   Powderly at this time was not in

34 Diary, 1876, October 10, 11.
35 Thomas King to Powderly, Reading, April 24, 1877.
36 Diary, 1877, April 26.
37 "To the Officers and Members of A. 222," April 26, 1877, copy.
38 Thomas King to Powderly, Reading, May 16, 1877.   Diary, 1877, July 11.
39 Powderly, *Thirty Years,* p. 235.
40 *Ibid.*

favor of publicity for the name, although in the West especially the
adoption of a public charter was considered actually necessary for
survival. Being a nameless society and the year being 1877 the
Knights readily acquired one name at least, that of the Molly
Maguires.[41] The great strikes which broke out in July in railroad centers such as Baltimore, Pittsburgh, and Scranton led to
scenes of violence which did much to confirm ecclesiastics like Bishop
John Tuigg in their hostility to the Order.[42] This Pittsburgh prelate's position on the Knights of Labor is not revealed in his diocesan
paper, but his disrespectful treatment by the mob when he appeared before them as part of a citizens' committee gave no evidence of friendship.[43] In general, as Norman J. Ware concludes,
"The courts began to see a riot in every strike, and a Molly Maguire
in every trade unionist." [44] As if such conditions were not enough
to bring about that result, the entrance of labor candidates into
municipal political campaigns gave further opportunity to their enemies to tar them with the Molly brush. In the election of February,
1878, which put Powderly into office as Mayor of Scranton, wherein
up to 1884 he had served three terms, one knight admitted they were
known locally by the name of Molly Maguires.[45] Although Powderly's political opponents were to concentrate on his "communistic
tendencies" as campaign ammunition, and also a little, in the opposite direction, on his Catholicism, the charge of "Molly" was more
suited to Pennsylvania and, therefore, longer lived.[46] For example,
an election day circular gave the testimony of citizens of his home
town that "he is neither a communist or a Molly Maguire." [47] Another aspect of this name-calling was the revival of the anti-labor ac-

[41] L. J. Brooks to Powderly, Mt. Washington, June 16, 1877.

[42] *Ibid.,* June 26, 1877.

[43] Pittsburgh *Catholic,* July 28, 1877. Most of the Protestant press of
Pittsburgh blamed the trouble on Catholic instigation, while the *Methodist
Recorder* agreed with the bishop's estimate that probably only about five per
cent of the mob were Catholics. *Catholic,* August 18, 1877.

[44] *Op. cit.,* p. 49.

[45] Peter Hill to Powderly, Tunkhannock, February 27, 1878.

[46] Powderly, *Path,* p. 76 and Mary J. Keenan to Powderly, Brooklyn,
March 4, 1878.

[47] Scrapbook, November, 1878-November, 1880, n. p., n. d.

tivities of Franklin B. Gowen, and his alleged use of priests and other clergy for his own ends, and this in Schuylkill County where the Molly terror was only then dying out. An organizer wrote to Powderly of the troublesome year just passed:

> . . . well the Catholic clergy told him [Gowen] that if he would not discharge men for keeping holydays, they would assure him that there would be no strike, the other clergy intimated similar things the result was that an order was issued that no man should be discharged for keeping holydays, and there was no strike.

He was hoping for the best after sending an instructed and well primed Catholic member to the priest with a copy of the ritual.[48] Even when the Knights first assembled in what amounted to a real national or general convention someone had to deny for the benefit of a newspaper reporter that they were Molly Maguires.[49]

This Reading General Assembly—even the location was neutral —succeeded in bringing the Philadelphia and Pittsburgh factions together harmoniously in January, 1878. Part of the business of forming a central body was to consider declaring the name public. Other items on the agenda were a central assistance fund, a bureau of statistics, and the problem of providing revenue for the organization.[50] Publicity was defeated by a vote of twenty-two to five, and neither Powderly nor any of the nineteen delegates from Pennsylvania voted in its favor. The preamble of the Industrial Brotherhood (1874) was adopted by the Knights and became not only an expression of the aims of the Order in the preamble of its own constitution, but it was also substituted in time for the religious fea-

---

[48] J. R. Thomas to Powderly, Mahanoy City, December 17, 1877.

[49] Scrapbook, November, 1873-January, 1878, The Reading *Daily Eagle,* January 4, 1878. This item entitled, "The Mysterious Meetings on Penn St.," shows how the reporter was given all kinds of misinformation, although some members tried to use secret grips and passwords on him. This exposé resulted in the expulsion of one delegate from the Knights of Labor. *Record of the Proceedings of the General Assembly,* pp. 24-25. Hereafter this series will be cited as simply, *Proceedings* with place and year of the session indicated.

[50] Powderly, *Thirty Years,* pp. 238-239.

tures of the part of the ritual called the "Founding Ceremony." [51]
Since the assembly went into secret session several times and their
minutes were not printed, there is only Powderly's word for it that
at Reading he began in earnest his campaign for an adaptation that
would have changed at least the ritual of the society to please the
Catholic Church.[52] He recalled:

> But while the oath stood as a barrier against the admission of
> the Catholic the order could make no progress. I at the first
> session of the general assembly ever held brought the matter
> before that body. I was the only Catholic on the floor so far
> as I know. I wish to say in passing that I was at that time
> acting under advice of a Catholic clergyman. The matter was
> not settled at that meeting. . . .[53]

Despite Powderly's clerical adviser, if the events of the years
1878 and 1879 are any criterion, the labor leader's hidden efforts
were about as much appreciated as they were known by Catholic
churchmen. Whatever their motives may have been, the outcry of
these ecclesiastics against the trappings of secrecy had the final result of aiding Powderly in building up a strong opinion within the
Order for stripping it of such. There was clerical action in Schuylkill County almost immediately after the Reading General Assembly.
Father Henry F. O'Reilly of Shenandoah, a man likewise well acquainted with Molly Maguire activities, was thought by the local
Knights to have learned their secrets. He had not yet spoken, and
the Scranton leader's aid was sought to win permission for Catholics
to join since the success of the Order in that section depended on

[51] Commons, *Documentary History*, X, 25. No date is given for the
change, but the stamp on Powderly's copy reads "July 12, 1882." The earlier
version calls for recitation of psalms and other scriptural texts, amens and
alleluias, organ music, and words in cypher.

[52] Cf. *Proceedings* (Reading, 1878), pp. 14 and 18, on going into secret
session.

[53] Powderly to Archbishop Ryan, October 24, 1884, copy. The identity of
the priest remains quite uncertain. Perhaps it was Father Dunne of the bishop's household, who had assured him a few months before that a Dr. Haggerty
was not opposing the organization. Diary, 1877, October 25. Since the convention was January 1 to 4, it could possibly have been the confessional advice of
Father Thomas F. Coffey, Diary, 1877, Dec. 27.

"an amicable solution at once." [54] A parish priest at Mahanoy was not as slow to speak. He reportedly denounced the Knights as a secret society, threatened with excommunication those who would not leave it, and classed it with the Mollies for wickedness. [55] The paper that carried this story some time later had an editorial based on the article in the *American Catholic Quarterly Review* on secret societies. The author had connected the Molly Maguires and the Ancient Order of Hibernians according to the popular view of those days. Applauding the article's candor, judgment, and liberality, this conservative Scranton paper agreed that the purposes of labor associations were better served without oath-bound secrecy. [56]

The Bishop of Scranton, William O'Hara, in a pastoral of February, 1878, had also commented on the evils of secret societies which held themselves aloof from the Church. He used these words as a springboard in his sermon in the Cathedral of St. Vincent de Paul one Sunday morning in May. The local paper, which was friendly to labor's cause, carried this story:

> The reverend gentleman's object in referring to and reading the above to the congregation was prompted by the reading of a letter from a prominent member of a secret organization known as the "Knights of Labor" in which the writer stated that that organization had the approbation and esteem of the bishop (Bishop O'Hara) and the priests of the diocese. It is entirely untrue, as neither he nor any of the clergy of this diocese had ever investigated that association, and consequently had given no approbation. [57]

The unfriendly Scranton *Republican* merely added that the letter containing the story of the bishop's supposed approval had come from the member of the society to whom it had been addressed.

---

[54] R. Rees to Powderly, Shenandoah, January 7, 1878.

[55] Scranton *Republican,* February 19, 1878.

[56] III (April, 1878), 192-219. "Secret Societies in the United States." Although the article was unsigned the table of contents for the whole volume shows it was written by Bishop Thomas A. Becker.

[57] *Daily Times,* May 20, 1878. This paper was sympathetic enough to attack the *Sunday Plain Dealer* for beginning an exposure of the Knights of Labor, January 20, 1879.

Bishop O'Hara administered to the writer, so the editorial said, "a sharp rebuke for his impertinence in having used his name without authority, and quoting him as being in favor of a society that had never done him the honor of submitting for his consideration its constitution and by-laws." This paper some days later had an item about Powderly's advising the meeting of the lodge "not to be alarmed at what the bishop said in church," and then leaving to enjoy a minstrel show, much to the annoyance of the workers when they found out about it.[58] The interesting thing is that Mayor Powderly's recollections picture himself being condemned from the altar as "a man who had hoodwinked the workingmen into electing him mayor," and being called among other things a fraud and an imposter. Forty years after the event he wrote out the exchange of words with the bishop which allegedly followed that sermon. Powderly blamed it all on a doctored letter which he had sent to a knight in West Virginia. In Powderly's own telling he quotes a report of a committee of the Scranton locals which had called on O'Hara and after "a patient hearing" had been reassured that, although he could not approve, he would not hamper their action unless he was able to find something objectionable in the "Five Stars." [59]

However much the Bishop of Scranton might have changed in his attitude toward the Knights since January, 1877, Powderly did not let it deter him from further action in the cause of accommodation of the labor society. There has been no evidence uncovered to date for the statement that he forced Stephens' hand into calling a special session of the general assembly at Philadelphia in June, 1878.[60] The special call of May 16, 1878, stated:

[58] May 25, 28, 1878.

[59] Powderly, *Path*, pp. 320-325. He claimed the account was written down ten days after the event, but the present writer could find no trace of it. The Diary for 1878 has a gap from February 10 to November 23. His additional recollection of the difficulty of explaining for the bishop's benefit how harmless the word, "international" really was (pp. 326-327) was not verified by the diary of that year.

[60] Ware, *op. cit.*, p. 76. Powderly, *Thirty Years,* p. 252, says merely he was written to and investigations were made.

> The business is to consider the expediency of making the name of the Order public for the purpose of defending it from the fierce assaults and defamation made upon it by Press, Clergy, and Corporate Capital, and to take such further action as shall effectually meet the GRAVE EMERGENCY.[61]

The fifteen delegates were blocked in their efforts since a two-thirds vote was required to carry such a constitutional change as to allow a local assembly or a district assembly to make the name of the Order public if requested by two-thirds of its membership. Powderly at that time made a compromise proposal to the effect that the district and local assemblies under the jurisdiction of the general assembly, "take into consideration and discuss the propriety" of making public the name of the society, of expunging all scriptural texts from the A. K., of modifying the initiation exercises in such a way as to remove the opposition from the Church, and finally of dispensing with the founding ceremonies for the district and local assemblies. In order to make the proposed change at the next general assembly, a two-thirds vote of the total membership was to be required and for that reason before December 1, 1878, an informal vote from each of the local assemblies was to be forwarded to the grand secretary.[62]

As the second regular session of the general assembly approached it would seem that Powderly was at peace with the churchmen, for he wrote, "I am not authorized to say anything regarding the views of our clergy upon it but I can say they never interfere with us here." [63] Stephens who, it might be suspected, would feel otherwise, was likewise at peace with the Catholic members, although their noise resulted in a compromise suggestion endangering his beloved ritual. He praised the "tens of thousands of Catholics in the Order" as being "among the best of our members," and this at a time when the total number in the Knights of Labor was 8,506! [64] Within a few months he was seeking to correct what he

[61] *Proceedings* (Philadelphia, Special Session, June, 1878), p. 40.

[62] *Ibid.*, pp. 44-45.

[63] Powderly to R. N. Martin, September 3, 1878, copy.

[64] U. S. Stephens to Harry Dubbs, December 2, 1878, copy. *Proceedings* (Chicago, September, 1879), pp. 116-117.

considered a unique phenomenon, an upcropping of anti-Catholicism in a local in Indiana.[65] He thought Catholics deserved sympathy since they "have a hard enough time with their church on account of their labor societies." [66] In 1879, however, Terence V. Powderly was to replace Stephens, and the former's ideas began to take precedence. This did not occur without ruffling the serenity of the society, although Powderly, too, sought to keep the Order flourishing by avoiding the disharmony of political and religious discussion at meetings.[67]

The vote of the locals on the four propositions of the Philadelphia session was too meager to tabulate, but it was reported by the grand secretary, Charles Litchman, that the majority of locals were against publicizing the name, although a majority of the votes were for it. On the other propositions both majorities were in the negative. He concluded:

> The *exposes* in the public press, the opposition of clergy, and other things, have made some of the brothers timid. I would recommend the passage of some law under which those sections desiring to work openly may do so, always strictly guarding those Locals and Districts which prefer to work secretly.[68]

Powderly framed a resolution giving local choice in this regard where two-thirds of the delegates in a district assembly, or of the members in a local assembly were willing. The way was also prepared for further action by the resolution of a Pittsburgh delegate which made an exception to the secrecy prohibition for "such members as hold private consultation with the clergy for the good of the Order." [69] This was as much as Powderly thought could have been done with but a few Catholics in the Order, but Stephens, nonetheless, attributed the change to the persecution inflicted by the corporations and the Church in certain districts of Pennsylvania where

[65] U. S. Stephens to Henry Gecker, February 6, 1879, copy. Also to Thomas Wybrant, February 6, 1879, copy.

[66] U. S. Stephens to J. R. Stephens, February 23, 1879, copy.

[67] Powderly to J. J. McLoughlin, February 11, 1879, copy.

[68] *Proceedings* (St. Louis, January, 1879), p. 63.

[69] *Ibid.*, pp. 75-76. Diary, 1879, January 6, ". . . had the satisfaction of putting my resolution through on making the name of the Order public."

the members, therefore, thought it better to make an "open bold fight."[70]

The Church to which these workers belonged shared with the railroad corporations the dubious honor of a publicity which pictured them working together in the Pennsylvania coal fields. The Scranton *Times* ironically described the problem: "The enlightened management of the P. and R. Railroad is again to the front with its disinterested effort to save Schuylkill county from the terrible effects of Labor unions. . . ."[71] Depending on the point of view of the paper, F. B. Gowen dreamed up or discovered a "McNulty Gang" of breaker burners who were part of the Knights of Labor.[72] His public letter admitted that, unlike the Mollies, most of the Knights were men of good will, but they were led astray by ruthless leaders who, of course, did not see eye to eye with him on labor negotiations. The *Republican* carried the item that "The Catholic Church at Pottsville and other towns have [sic] given notice that the Church will excommunicate all members of the new order."[73] The local Knights petitioned for a police investigation of the alleged destructive McNulty gang, while the *Times* attributed their very existence to "the distempered brain" of Gowen.[74] On March 2, however, Henry F. O'Reilly, pastor of the Church of the Annunciation at Shenandoah, read off the names of gang-men of that neighborhood, a list which had been supplied to him by the Pinkerton Detective Agency. The conservative press foresaw from this report the end of the Order in that region and it commended the "prompt and decisive action of the Catholic clergy."[75] Powderly, on the other hand, as an interested observer sought to check the facts, but without waiting to find them, he lamented:[76] "Br. Leary is getting some

[70] U. S. Stephens to R. B. Hanna, July 18, 1879, copy. Powderly to Archbishop Ryan, October 24, 1884, copy.

[71] February 17, 1879.

[72] *Republican*, February 15, 1879.

[73] February 17, 1879.

[74] February 25, 1879.

[75] *Republican*, March 4, 1879.

[76] Powderly to M. A. Leary, March 12, 1879, copy. The *Times* had doubts about early reports of Church co-operation (February 18) but then was silent except for a letter, the tenor of which was "Let the pulpit beware"

hard knocks from Father Riley [*sic*] but I guess he'll survive. When a priest calls in the aid of a detective he must have lost faith in his redeemer, and I prefer the religion of *Christ* to that of *Pinkerton*." [77]

Just as the affair of the McNulty gang gave the Church a bad press, so in the case of the Shenandoah picnic shortly thereafter the Mayor of Scranton, it would seem, was much more definitely victimized. In his posthumously published autobiography Powderly edited the documents pertaining to this matter and from them he launched into a tirade on the clergy and the doctrine of submissiveness which they preached to labor. [78] Although it was probably exaggerated by the labor leader in order to add to the picture of his martyrdom, the incident is interesting as an example of how in one instance the papal advice to form Catholic worker groups was followed and resulted in failure. The Knights in Shenandoah arranged for their first public demonstration on July 23, 1879. Before a large attendance of workers from all over Schuylkill County Powderly, in the midst of his speech, was asked to comment on the Catholic Workingmen's Society of Girardville. The Philadelphia *Times* of July 24 carried the story that he had defied the Church's power to break up the Knights of Labor by such means. His spontaneous reaction was expressed in his journal for July 24, ". . . came to Scranton at 7:15 went to the office and wrote a correction for the Phil. *Times*. . . ." In essence it said he "could see no necessity for any more labor societies; . . . this would act as a wedge between Catholic and Protestant workingmen and create dissension rather than unity." A few days later another privately written entry tells of seeing a poster for a local paper advertising him, "as defying the Church." He "got mad" and told the dealer he would stop the sale of the Sunday papers if "they didn't tell the truth." [79] The pastor of St. Joseph Church in Girardville, the Reverend Daniel O'Connor,

(March 14). These newspapers were the only evidence for the present writer, since neither diocesan, railroad, nor detective agency records supplied any. Cf. pp. 380, 384.

[77] Powderly to Charles Litchman, March 12, 1879, copy.
[78] *Path*, pp. 329-345.
[79] Diary, 1879, July, 26.

did not let the chance to defend his parochial society slip by. Still accepting the hostile version of the speech, he pointed out principally the pantheism in the ritualism of the Knights (which was undeniably present, but probably meaningless to most workers) and he tried to cajole Powderly into working toward the formation of Catholic associations of workingmen.[80] But this Powderly never did, and with the dissolution of the society in December of that very year he noted with obvious satisfaction, "Too good to live. R.I.P."[81] It is noteworthy that Powderly's position in the eyes of the Church did not suffer at all in Scranton, where he continued to hob-nob with Father Patrick Roche of St. Patrick's in Hyde Park, and to be an important member of the committee for the parish picnic—at which on this occasion he did not speak.[82]

A still more exalted honor was bestowed on the Scranton politician when he was elected "Grand Master Workman" at the Chicago meeting of the general assembly in September, 1879. Nothing was further accomplished there to do away with absolute secrecy, although Daniel O'Leary made an unsuccessful attempt "to have some alterations made in order to avoid the opposition of the Church," and David Fitzgerald brought up a resolution to have the name of the Order universally publicized which was defeated.[83] Yet the new head of the Knights of Labor very shortly gained enough experience to realize how urgent was the necessity of eliminating the oath, for although the opposition of the Church continued even where there was no apparent connection with business interests, still another example of such a supposed tie was reported. It concerned Bishop Francis S. Chatard of Vincennes who, it was charged, had been reached by the coal operators. This was the explanation of his hostility that the Knights used, although he was also known to have been a former rector of the American College in Rome, and

---

[80] Powderly, *Path*, pp. 335-337. O'Connor claimed the society in Girardville had been "heartily endorsed by Archbishop Wood." Letter to Gowen, March 15, 1880; Schlegel, *op. cit.*, p. 175.

[81] Scrapbook, November, 1878-November, 1880, marginal note, n. p.

[82] Diary, 1879, July 27 and August, *passim*.

[83] O'Leary to Powderly, Carbon, December 24, 1879. He had introduced a document on the Secret Work. *Proceedings* (Chicago, September, 1879), p. 95. Cf. also p. 119 on Fitzgerald.

supposedly, therefore, was a strict disciplinarian.[84] Litchman gave a similar report of the DuBois Pennsylvania mining area, where it was said, "the mine owners have resorted to the old, old trick of appealing to the Church to use its influence to destroy our Order." [85] Closer examination of this case in the Diocese of Erie indicated how inaccurate reports of ecclesiastical opposition could be. The report from that area itself was that even if all the clergy condemned the Knights, the only basic objection of Bishop Tobias Mullen would still concern simply the oath, for "he says he would be with us even with closed doors and also if the oath could be left out, and have a pledge of our Knightly Honor instead." [86] Within a week Powderly for the first time had taken up the phrase, "Knightly honor." Henceforth he was to continue to advocate this substitute until the oath was eliminated.[87]

Powderly's position against oath-bound secrecy was bolstered by Catholic pressure within the Knights of Labor. His correspondence reveals the simple obedience (founded in their faith) of the laboring men to their sometimes tyrannical pastors who had tremendous influence in public life, especially in the poor and rough mining towns. Their mere word or charges from the pulpit, not always spoken after close investigation and sometimes associated by the workers with the sentiments of employers or politicians, could often start a local on the way to its collapse.[88] The rank and file of the Knights of Labor never seemed to appreciate the Church's attitude on secret societies, perhaps because they appeared trivial beside the obvious and desperately needed benefits of organization. "The oath appears to be the only objection," was the optimistic re-

[84] D. O'Leary to Powderly, Carbon, December 24, 1879.

[85] Charles Litchman to Powderly, Marblehead, November 29, 1879.

[86] John Huron to Powderly, Du Bois, December 22, 1879.

[87] Powderly to M. A. Leary, December 27, 1879, copy. "I have no faith in the oath as a means of keeping men's mouths shut." After being reminded that honor could hardly be "knightly" before the initiation he dropped the adjective. E. A. Stevens to Powderly, Chicago, January 6, 1880.

[88] For example, a ninety per cent loss was attributed to this reason plus the inability to pay dues in a Shamokin assembly. Samuel Owen to Powderly, June 1, 1880. Also attesting similar influence, John Meehan to Powderly, Dickson City, September 27, 1880.

port, and the grand master workman began to feel that the substitution of a pledge of honor would stop the ecclesiastical trouble,
which by 1880 was sprouting up even outside the Pennsylvania coal
fields.[89] Yet he continued to interpret the ritual for interested
brothers, for in some places the nature of the Supreme Being of the
ceremonial came up for discussion. While deciding that it need not
be held that it was the "God of the Bible," at the same time he
became indignant at a Chicago knight, E. A. Stevens, of whom the
terms "atheist" and "socialist" were readily used, for suggesting a
circular to put an end to these "sectarian" discussions.[90] Stevens,
who averred "I'd see all the clergy in hell (always provided that
there is such a place) before I would change a word to suit them,"
was advised that only a fool would deny God, and, furthermore,
"There are questions of real interest to *labor* which should take up
our time and let these ninny hammers who wish to quarrel over
Scripture do so if they will." [91]

As the list of misunderstanding priests lengthened and Powderly's supposed influence with Church authorities widened, he
sought for the time being to keep himself out of the light of publicity.[92] One member of the Order at least expressed agreement
with his procedure of keeping the fire of the Church off himself lest
such a spectacle discourage other Catholics. This Pittsburgh correspondent spoke kindly of priests as human and liable to err, and he
gave it as his observation, "Of course they don't pander to the
wealthy and influential, like ministers of other denominations. . . .
The priests know there are thousands of Catholics who belong to
trade unions and they do not denounce them." Further he presaged,

[89] To a Doylestown, Ohio, knight he wrote, "Complaints are numerous of
the opposition from the Church." Powderly to Dominic Hammer, January 5,
1880, copy.

[90] Henry G. Taylor to Powderly, New York, September 25, 1880; Powderly
to Michael Mooney, January 24, 1880, copy; Richard Griffiths to Powderly,
Chicago, December 27, 1879; Powderly to E. A. Stevens, February 12, 1880,
copy.

[91] E. A. Stevens to Powderly, Chicago, January 6, 1880; Powderly to
Stevens, March 12, 1880, copy. For this latter answer he was applauded by
Griffiths, April 9, 1880.

[92] Powderly to C. C. Burnett, May 4, 1880, copy.

"Catholics will have to defend trade organizations." [93] Yet the main burden of letters complained of Church opposition, and the G. M. W. was moved to note on such a communication as he forwarded it to Litchman, "I get any quantity of such letters, I am getting sick of it." [94] To knights anticipating trouble in Schuylkill County and his own home town he insisted that the Order was "a bread and butter association," although he admitted a need for secrecy but not the oath-bound kind.[95]

Powderly also found support in his drive against absolute secrecy from another quarter than the Catholics. The German Socialists objected to their members belonging to such a completely occult group. As a consequence some socialistic locals and districts voted for a degree of publicity. This most likely confirmed Powderly in his belief that he had nothing to lose by continuing to hold his membership card in the Socialist Labor Party.[96] But despite Catholic and Socialist preference the next session of the general assembly in Pittsburgh did nothing about the G. M. W.'s favorite reform. The resolution in favor of publicity was reported on unfavorably by the committee on laws, and the delegates sustained its recommendation.[97] William Baird, who had initiated the attempt, came from Frostburg, Maryland, a detail that is of interest only in light of the fact that the organization in that area had brought the Order to the attention of Archbishop Gibbons of Baltimore. The local priest, Valentine F. Schmitt and Father James O'Brien of near-by Lonaconing, especially, had only quietly counselled Catholics against joining

[93] John Hirsch to Powderly, Pittsburgh, May 12, 1880.

[94] John Hart to Powderly, Cannelburgh, Maryland, April 19, 1880.

[95] Powderly to Christopher Byrnes, April 24, 1880, copy; to T. F. Mullaney, May 26, 1880, copy. In Carbondale the followers of the town's most famous son were reported to have been called, "dupes, heretics and what not," by Father John McGrath, the curate, T. F. Mullaney to Powderly, May 24, 1880.

[96] Philip VanPatten to Powderly, Detroit, May 20, 1880; J. T. Jones to Powderly, Collinsville, Illinois, July 9, 1880; VanPatten to Powderly, August 13, 1880.

[97] *Proceedings* (Pittsburgh, 1880), pp. 192 and 229. It was not mentioned in Powderly's opening address (pp. 169-176), but the secret session left no printed testimony. Therein he may have fulfilled his claim that "for two more sessions [1880 and 1881] I recommended that these ceremonies be abolished," to Archbishop Ryan, October 24, 1884, copy.

with the suspicion that the allowance made for Catholics to confess was "a catch in order to gain the good will of the clergy." Their moderate approach had been merely to advise those outside not to join and those already members to promise to leave if the Church should condemn it. The question was posed—to which no answer of Gibbons was found—"What shall we do in the future?" [98]

Although on the basis of Powderly's description of earlier conferences with ecclesiastics and from the action of the Frostburg delegates in 1880 one may suspect that the Church endorsed tactics of working from within in the cause of reform, it can hardly be sustained that the grand master workman led the fight for abolition of absolute secrecy and its protecting ritualistic oath primarily from religious motives. In fact, he professed that a man's religion or lack of it meant nothing to him, even if he took the oath with a very hazy or unorthodox notion of God, so long as his position on the labor question was satisfactory.[99] In the role of paternal adviser which he so often assumed, he stressed the need of men of integrity whose word could be trusted. Employing a scriptural reference, an ornament of style typical of him throughout his career, he said: "I don't think any oath no matter how strong can bind a man whom God created to play the part of *Judas*." [100]

More than any concern over the correct understanding of the quasi-religious features of the Knights, the objections brought to bear from predominantly Catholic sections loomed large among Powderly's worries. For example, the New Bethlehem District Assembly voted to ask the general assembly to do something to placate the Catholic Church, "as it is the whole and sole cause of weakening the order in this District and throughout the whole order." [101] Their spokesman's opinion was that this could be done, not by making changes in the A. K., but by sending delegations to the Catholic

98 BCA, 74-J-6, V. F. Schmitt to Archbishop Gibbons, February 19, 1879.

99 Powderly to Henry G. Taylor, October 7, 1880, copy.

100 Powderly to C. A. Lincoln, November 8, 1880, copy.

101 P. Ward to Powderly, n. d. (answered January 17, 1881); also May 10, 1881. A report from a traveling man was, "The greatest curse to our Order seems to me to be the priests. . . ." W. J. Hudson to Powderly, Willsboro, New York, May 13, 1881.

bishops, especially the most antagonistic, "such as Archbishop Wood of Philadelphia." [102] Powderly did not undertake this oft employed technique of a later day, but he contented himself with reporting that the matter was in the hands of the executive board. His dilemma was that by himself he was unable to change any law of the Order for the sake of reconciling a Catholic conscience and, of course, he could do even less about altering ecclesiastical law in order to relieve a troubled member of the organization, "when once he makes up his mind that it conflicts with the duty he owes his Church." [103] However, he indicated hope of a change on the side of the Knights, although Grand Secretary Litchman thought enough concessions had been made and that Church interference was inevitable.[104]

Powderly's hopes were dampened periodically by special clerical onslaughts on the Order in the form of "missions." These parochial services were of several weeks' duration and were conducted by special bands of preachers from religious orders, such as the Jesuits and Redemptorists. While they were being conducted in a parish, the local Catholic membership in the Knights of Labor usually dwindled. In the city of Philadelphia where many Knights were under the impression that the bishop had once blessed their society, some of the brothers were surprised at being refused absolution by the missionaries.[105] Powderly testified of Scranton: "We had a mission here in all the Catholic churches in the city and the *good* Christians are leaving us." [106] Although mission-preaching has not been studied such phenomenal results can be readily appreciated since, unlike the quiet retreat or even the parish exercises of more recent date, the mission of those days was the nearest thing to revivalism that the Catholic Church has experienced in the United

[102] Ward to Powderly, January 21, 1881; May 17, 1881.

[103] Powderly to Ward, May 12, 1881, copy.

[104] Powderly to Thomas J. Crump, June 28, 1881, copy. Litchman to Powderly, Marblehead, May 14, 1881.

[105] John J. Conway to Powderly, Philadelphia, May 2, 1881.

[106] Powderly to Litchman, June 15, 1881, copy. Also reports from DuBois, by John Huron, December 22, 1879 and James Walsh, Houtzdale, October 1, 1881. The latter said, "We have had a mission here and all that belong to the K. of L. and A. O. H. was told to stay away or give it up."

States.[107] As the Order became less secretive the mode of attack through missions fell off. Yet even later one pastor wanted a copy of the constitution and by-laws, "as I have a Jesuit mission now in progress," and also outside the State of Pennsylvania a little difficulty arose.[108] The sorrow of the grand master workman, he insisted, was increased not only by such ecclesiastical opposition, but also by the fact that he found, "that the best members make the best Catholics." [109] He pointed out how he was left alone to carry the fight to the general assembly by the annual desertion of fellow Catholics. Laying the blame and venturing a prophecy, he wrote, "If the priests would let us alone just two years, we could remove the oath easily." [110]

Although this revivifying operation was to take place within a few months, the dwindling fortunes of the Knights of Labor since mid-1880 made Powderly anxious about the future.[111] As the September meeting of the national body drew closer he urged consideration of the proposition that the hope of the Order lay in being opened to all by means of the elimination of the oath.[112] His characteristic expression of the problem was:

> I desire that all parts of the entire order be represented, that we may do one of two things, either adopt a plain simple honest straightforward plan of action for the future upon which the fullest light may be thrown when occasion demands it, or else disband and proclaim to the world that as an organization for the benefit of humanity we are a failure. I am tired of shilly shallying.[113]

The head of the Knights agreed heartily with the plan of the staff of the *Journal of United Labor* (founded in 1880 as the official or-

107 They were characterized by fire and brimstone and "stern, strong, rough words." Cf. John F. Byrne, C.SS.R., *The Redemptorist Centenaries, 1832-1932* (Philadelphia, 1932), pp. 277-279.
108 A. J. Gallagher to Powderly, Pottsville, February 7, 1882; John A. Johnson to Powderly, Providence, May 16, 1883.
109 Powderly to W. J. Hudson, June 20, 1881, copy.
110 Powderly to Peter J. Ward, May 12, 1881, copy.
111 Powderly to Griffiths, July 20, 1881, copy.
112 Powderly to Dominic Hammer, July 23, 1881, copy.
113 Powderly to Robert Nelson, August 17, 1881, copy.

gan of the society) to circularize the Order. Although appearing to be neutral and seeking only the opinion of all, the editors of the *Journal* favored publicity, a simpler ritual, and the word of honor as means of overcoming ecclesiastical hostility.[114]

Despite the prominence of the religious question, it would be out of all perspective to see the opposition of the Church to oath-bound secrecy as an isolated element in the affairs of the Knights. The *Proceedings* of the general assembly up to 1881 indicate the other problems which existed simultaneously with this one. Some of the difficulties which came to Powderly's desk had to be kept for the decision of the G. A., which the constitution referred to as having "full and final jurisdiction," and as being "the highest tribunal of the Order of the Knights of Labor." [115] The prevailing issues of the national gatherings of this body in 1878 and 1879 concerned strikes, politics, and co-operation.[116] In this same period the membership doubled, rising to over 20,000. An especially lively dispute occurred over the disposition of the so-called resistence fund which was collected by a tax on each local. Some recommended that it be used for the support of strikes, while others thought it might better be appropriated for educational, co-operative, or beneficent purposes. At every meeting of the delegates from various sections of the country, politics and the part the Order should play in them was discussed until finally it was left to the local assemblies to use their discretion in helping labor's friends at election time. The problem of the place of the trade union in the over-all organization of the Knights had to be faced, and finally it was, together with the mixed locals, made subject to the district assemblies. Among Powderly's chief tasks as demonstrated by his extensive correspondence was that of granting commissions to organizers who covered the country, but especially the industrial centers. Their work was often simplified by the Order's absorption of a weak national trade union, as in the case of the Knights of St. Crispin,

114 Gilbert Rockwood to Powderly, Marblehead, June 20, 1881; Powderly to Litchman, June 28, 1881, copy.

115 *Constitution of the General Assembly, District Assemblies and Local Assemblies of the Order of the Knights of Labor of America* (n. p., n. d.), p. 5.

116 Cf. Commons, *History,* II, 339 ff.

the shoemakers group. The gains, however, were often balanced by the losses sustained as a result of unsuccessful strikes.

Due, no doubt, partly to the difficulties of organizing, as well as to ecclesiastical ill-will, the chief interest and action of the regular session of the general assembly that met at Detroit in September, 1881, was in declaring, "the name of the order to be public property after January 1, 1882.[117] At the very outset in the address of the grand master workman on the afternoon of September 6, the lack of progress in the past year and the trials of the term just concluded were subjects of comment.[118] Powderly said:

> Many locals were already working under protest, the alternative of leaving the order staring them in the face. Night after night have I sat thinking and deliberating this matter over,—for gifted with what intelligence we may be, as unwilling to yield to its influence as we may be, yet we *must* admit that we want the men of all religions, and to get them we must make concession to the church, for its influence is too vast to be idly passed over.[119]

He described in a general way how he had undertaken to explain to churchmen the workings of the Order and the necessity of such strict secrecy. Several times he had written to clergymen, but this, he claimed, proved a failure because local knights were unable to answer satisfactorily further questions raised by their pastors. His eight personal calls, on the other hand, were highly effective.[120] Hence he was led to conclude that the best approach was the use of "a committee of intelligent members, thoroughly drilled in the

[117] Powderly, *Thirty Years*, p. 631. A later indication of the breakdown of complete secrecy, but the maintenance of another principle was the dispatch: "No objection to displaying grand seal unless it is on a beer stand." Powderly to D. A. Fenton, June 25, 1880, copy.

[118] Membership fell from 28,136 in 1880 to only 19,422 in 1881, Commons, *History*, II, pp. 343-344.

[119] *Proceedings* (Detroit, 1881), p. 271. Although he referred specifically to neither the Catholic Church nor priests, the context and the total absence of Protestant protests to that date among his personal papers indicate Powderly spoke exclusively of his own Church.

[120] No other record of these was found, but there are pages missing from the letterbooks of these years of the early 1880's.

methods, aims and objects of our Order," to call on fault-finding clerics. They would state the Knights' reasons, "for moving so secretly in our efforts to obtain living wages for a fair day's work." He professed his Catholicism and pointed out that the Church recognized "the right of men to combine for united protection," but it feared the danger of societies leading to "infamy and dishonor," and also the use of rash oaths.[121] Finally, the resolution to make the name public was passed. It was specified that it should be effective after January 1, 1882, and that the fact should be published in the national press.[122] However, Powderly did not make this proclamation, which may account in part for the repetitious character of clerical reactions to the organization as it spread into new sections of the United States. Henceforth, the name of the labor association would appear on its stationery, the designation of the name by the five stars was no longer necessary, and the words, "Noble and Holy," were to be omitted from the title.

The action on the oath was not revealed in the published proceedings, but Powderly boasted of it afterwards.[123] In relating the news of his re-election, he exulted, "Now comes the best part of it. The oath has been entirely done away with and a word of honor substituted. The new A. K. will go into effect January 1st, and I am glad of it." [124] It was February, however, before the new Grand Secretary, Robert D. Layton, instructed the Knights of Labor organizers: "The A. K. and F. and I. [Founding and Installation] Book has been revised, as follows: every portion in the least sectarian has been stricken out. The vow has been changed to a pledge of honor. All disguising or blindfolding in the initiation of candidates is abolished. . . ." [125] Powderly wrote to the father-founder, Uriah S. Stephens, who with his whole local assembly in Philadelphia was contemplating severance from the Knights of Labor,

[121] *Proceedings* (Detroit, 1881), pp. 271-272.

[122] *Ibid.*, pp. 290, 291, 302, 305, 306.

[123] Powderly, *Thirty Years,* p. 632. This session also opened the Knights of Labor to women on a basis of equality with men.

[124] Powderly to Peter J. Ward, October 9, 1881, copy.

[125] Received by Powderly, February 18, 1882.

because the Order had "drifted so far away from the primary land-marks." In reserved and diplomatic words he said:

> The changes made at Detroit were but few with the excep-tion of removing the oath from the initiation, and the shorten-ing of the initiatory exercises. And the popular sentiment was in favor of that step. Could we pick intelligent men only such a course would not be necessary but our Order must spread and must adapt itself to the times we live in.[126]

A short time later Powderly expressed the opinion that Stephens was unfair in being so highly displeased with the work done at De-troit, for just as he had stood by the organization although he op-posed the oath, so the Philadelphia leader should do the same after the change, "until it has had a thorough test." [127] Within less than a week the grand master workman came into possession of a letter of opposition circulated by his predecessor, and in forwarding it to Brother Richard Griffiths of Chicago, he let the rhetorical sparks fly:

> Bah, the old man is in his dotage. We'll get him a slice of the catacombs, one of the pyramids of Egypt, one of the Cyclops famous in mythology, the bones of Yepna Penoneah. Stir them all together with one of the oars that propelled Cleopatra's barge, toast over a slow fire to slower music, and when done, erect them on the ruins of the tower of Babel, while *Jim Wright* introduces to the new assembly a *spiritualistic medium.* If we could thus revel in the mysterious and marvelous, to say nothing of the *spiritualistic* and still more *ridiculistic* (if I may so speak), we would introduce a form of ceremony that would come up to the old man's conception of the proper thing. But the real question is *'Shall labor have all its rights?'* That and not the tomfoolery of the past is what we must consider, and while I respect Bro. S. if he insists on making a fool of himself he'll do it outside of this Order for I won't trifle with him much longer.[128]

[126] Stephens to Powderly, Philadelphia, October 22, 1881; Powderly to Stephens, October 25, 1881, copy.

[127] Powderly to Robert Layton, November 18, 1881, copy.

[128] November 24, 1881.

As a matter of fact, Powderly did not seem to care if the whole Philadelphia assembly took its threatened departure, since their attention was absorbed more by such things as symbols than anything else.[129] But there were objections from other quarters on the part of the "old school," especially from New York, where another split was feared.[130] Powderly was sustained against the Stephens-minded faction by Litchman who held that the old leader acted as if they were "all ministers and wanted to start a camp meeting." [131] Layton accused Stephens of wanting to thrust his religious views down the throats of every man whom he met at the outer veil of a meeting, and he concluded, "My advice to all, is get *God* in your heart, and it will never occur to you that His *name* is not in the A. K." [132] "Let them go," he also advised, and his assistant commented on the constitutional loopholes these locals offered, "New York and Brooklyn have made asses of themselves by the protests presented to the Bd." [133]

Yet some members felt differently, and Powderly had to write to a New York knight on the necessity of even the chief officer's obeying the law of the Order. He tried to point out from personal experience the uselessness of the oath, and the excess of the initiation

[129] This group did not leave the Knights, but it is only probable that Stephens was ever fully reconciled. Powderly told Archbishop Ryan that before his death he "became satisfied that a broader and more liberal plan should be adopted." October 24, 1884. However, the Knights of Labor alone among Stephen's fraternal orders were not invited to his funeral in the press. Ware, *op. cit.*, p. 94. The Pittsburgh office received word only on the morning of the funeral. Rockwood remarked, "It will seem strange perhaps, that no Grand Officers were present, but it is not our fault, as we did not get word in time" (to Powderly, February 16, 1882). Their informant was Frederick Turner, former member of the executive board from Philadelphia, but still Stephens' widow claimed both Powderly and Litchman had been invited but did not go, and only the latter had sent a word of sympathy. Scrapbook, April, 1882-January, 1884, *World* (n. p., n. d.).

[130] Theodore Cuno to Powderly, Brooklyn, October 24, 1881; James Connolly to Powderly, New York, November 14, 1881.

[131] October 28, 1881.

[132] Received December 6, 1881.

[133] December 20, 1881; Gilbert Rockwood to Powderly, Pittsburgh, January 7, 1881.

ceremonies. For nine years he had opposed them but without the thought of insubordination. He abided the "long formula of *words, words* that take all the time of the meeting," even though in the days of his unemployment, "all the ceremonies of the A. K. did not throw a single ray of light on my dreary pathway to show me *how* to get a situation and better my condition." [134] In this mood of resentment towards hymns and formulae, the grand master work-man refused the New York assembly permission to extend the use of the old form beyond the first of the year.[135] Even in September, 1882, at the general assembly session in the stronghold of the op-position he had to defend his Detroit action by pointing out that one consequence had been a considerable increase in membership from 19,422 to 42,517.[136]

The Catholics and other religious members, nevertheless, were not unanimous in their regard for the new ceremonial. For several years after the important decision their questions and doubts poured in on the grand master workman, and strangely enough some of Powderly's co-religionists were against the elimination of the oath. A representative of a group of assemblies in the New York area wrote in an attempt to explain their discontent at the change. He denied Powderly's charge about wasting time at the meetings, since

---

[134] Powderly to George K. Lloyd, November 24, 1881, copy. Partly quoted in Ware, *op. cit.*, p. 95. Powderly seems here to exaggerate his tramping "up and down this land looking for work and bread." According to *Path*, p. 27, the period was the winter of 1873-1874, when his Diaries reveal he had hard times but never went beyond Oil City, Pennsylvania, for work. Furthermore, the Diary for 1874 tells nothing of his first introduction to the Knights of Labor in that year, and even if it did take place he admitted later that full participa-tion came only in 1876.

[135] It is interesting to note in Powderly's autobiographical work which he had completed by 1921, his different appreciation of the ritual of the Order. His earlier sentiments were repeated in 1889, "The workmen of today are not the prosy fellows they were twenty years ago. Mystery and mummery have no place. . . ." New York *Sun*, January 8, 1889. After he had been a member of a Masonic lodge for twenty years he wrote his praise of the old secret cere-monial which concluded thus, "It inspired me in that far away time and abides with me now as a sublime truth coming through the years from Calvary." *Path*, p. 54.

[136] Powderly, *Thirty Years*, p. 561; Commons, *History*, II, 344.

their was only five minutes difference in the ritual, and all discussion was limited to one hour by the law of the Order, no matter how much time was saved. Powderly never answered this rebuttal.[137] This member professed to speak for the Catholics in saying:

> They consider that they had better be bound by an oath with the right to confess to there [sic] religious confessor than to be bound by a solemn promise with no rights of the confessional whatever unless they perjure themselfs [sic]. Objection is also raised to the taking of the name of God from the A. K. and other works wherever it appears as they regard it as brought about by the socialistic tendencies of the Western delegates who being in the majority consulted not the wishes or interest of the order in general but there [sic] own sweet will only.[138]

It was true enough the Socialists rejoiced at the changes made in the ritual, "so that our Germans can stomach it," but they were hardly responsible for it.[139] A few other assemblies outside of New York protested the withdrawal of God's name from the books, and the removal of the Bible from the "sanctuary." [140]

These comparatively few criticisms did not long bother the Scranton labor leader, for early in 1882 he was writing in an optimistic vein, "I am a Catholic and have striven for years to abolish the oath and now that it has disappeared and A. K. puts on a practical businesslike appearance I hear no complaint of the Church opposing us. It was while the old A. K. existed that the trouble arose." [141] In March the grand master workman handed down one of his "decisions" in making an exception for Catholics to reveal anything to their spiritual advisers under the new ritual, just as under the old one.[142] The Knights had nothing to conceal in the

---

[137] *Constitution for Local Assemblies,* article XI, upholds the correspondent.

[138] George K. Lloyd to Powderly, New York, November 27, 1881.

[139] Philip VanPatten to Powderly, Detroit, September 12, 1881.

[140] George P. Pierce to Powderly, Glassboro, New Jersey, February 28, 1882 ; Thomas Todd, Limestone, Illinois, March 4, 1882 ; W. S. Mullhuff, Coalton, Ohio, received March 20, 1882.

[141] Powderly to John S. B. Coggeshell, March 1, 1882, copy.

[142] Powderly to Thomas Todd, March 6, 1882, copy. These more official answers to queries usually involving the interpretation of a regulation of the

confessional for they were now as respectable as any trade-unionists.[143] They were not in a class with the societies condemned by the Church, Powderly claimed in writing to an Erie member:

> Different clergymen look with a different eye upon different societies except the Masons, Oddfellows, Knights of Pythias and kindred societies for no man *can* be a Catholic and belong to either one. That is a rule of the Church but a labor society is regarded in a different light. I have fought the oath from the start. It has been abolished and any Catholic may confess everything. He can even show the A. K. to his pastor if necessary. See page 272 of Detroit proceedings. I could not obtain a letter of approval from my bishop for the Church approves of none but strictly religious societies.[144]

It was beginning to dawn on Powderly that the oath was only one element exciting ecclesiastical disfavor. It was a persistent one, however, and for several years, especially in the new fields of the Knights' activities, he was insisting they had nothing to hide from priest or bishop.[145] Although he expressed surprise some years later to hear the charge of an oath raised again, nevertheless, in all his later negotiations with churchmen Powderly did not neglect to remind them of the elimination of the oath.[146] That this was far from meaning the end of secrecy is shown by the fact that as late as 1891 the provision of the A. K. was retained which forbade the revelation of any private work of the assemblies, and prohibited members from revealing "to any employer or other person the name or person of anyone a member of the Order without permission of the member." [147] Accordingly, part of Powderly's task

Order had extra weight and were later published together with approval of the general assembly.

[143] Powderly to Charles W. Mooney, April 14, 1883, copy; to [   ] Tecker, July 26, 1882, copy, "Our Order is now no more a secret organization than the Iron Moulders Union or any trade union."

[144] Powderly to Thomas Burman, July 25, 1882, copy.

[145] Powderly to John B. Hamelin, November 3, 1884, copy.

[146] Powderly to Thomas J. Lyons, April 9, 1885, copy.

[147] Quoted in Commons, *History*, II, 339. A further indication of how the Knights of Labor followed the pattern of most secret societies is shown in their use of regalia. Stephens advised on August 1, 1879, that anything but

in reconciling the Church to the Knights of Labor was to show that this secrecy was harmless to ecclesiastical and civil society. He saw early what was before him, for in lamenting his burden and making the perennial gesture of retiring from it, he wrote,

> I am afraid the Church will make trouble for us. Ever since I assumed control it has been uphill work. On one side capital fighting us, on the other hand the clergy have assailed me in many places without cause. Between the men who *love* God and the men who don't believe in God I have had a hard time of it.[148]

"neat tidy dress" would be against the A. K. (to R. B. Hanna). Powderly noted a growing sentiment for regalia to M. S. Finigan, June 8, 1881. The session of the G. A. in September (*Proceedings,* p. 314) decided on special badges to be worn at meetings, at funerals and public demonstrations. (Robert Layton, Special Instruction to Organizers, January, 1882.)

[148] Powderly to [   ] Tecker, July 26, 1882, copy.

CHAPTER III

THE ATTENTION OF THE HIERARCHY

THE turn of the year 1881 marked the removal of the religious coating from the Knights of Labor, but it did not, even temporarily, bring an end to ecclesiastical suspicion.[1] The oath had definitely been eliminated through Powderly's efforts but secrecy was still a major characteristic of the organization. With the publication of the name its secret character ceased to be as profound as a few years before when "Philadelphians noticed with trepidation that a few cabalistic chalkmarks in front of Independence Hall could bring several thousand men together."[2]

The revised *Adelphon Kruptos* and the *Founding and Installation Ceremonies* were ready for distribution shortly after the beginning of the new era of publicity.[3] Powderly's manual (the only one in his papers so dated) was stamped, "Answered July 12, 1882." It contained a ritual for setting up an assembly which was devoid of scriptural quotations and it employed in their stead the preamble of the constitution. The members of the new local were asked if they were willing to take "a pledge of honor that will not interfere with any duty you may owe to your country or creed, binding you to Secrecy, Obedience, and Mutual Assistance."[4] Some words, such as these last, which had formerly been in cypher were now spelled out. Likewise it dropped the exception made in the old form concerning the revealing "by word, act, art or implication, positive or negative, to any person or persons, whatsoever, excepting my Religious Con-

---

[1] Ware was happily ignorant of this when he wrote, "Thus the secrecy-religion problem was solved until, in 1885-88, when, with the tremendous growth of the Order, it was raised again by American priests and especially by a Canadian Archbishop. . . ." *op. cit.*, p. 97.

[2] Richard T. Ely, *The Labor Movement in America* (New York, 1886), p. 79.

[3] PP, Robert Layton, Official Notice, January 30, 1882.

[4] Revised Manual, "Founding Ceremony," p. 5.

fessor at the Confessional, the name or object of this order. . . ."[5]
The next section, the ceremony for installing officers, differed mainly
in the lack of a cypher and in the change of the expression, "solemnly
and sincerely swear (or affirm)" to "promise on my honor."[6] The
amended text of the A. K. indicated the discontinuance of the use
of the Bible as part of the furnishing of the "sanctuary," and, too,
as a source for readings. The expressions about "vows" were likewise no longer used. In place of swearing the candidate answered "I
do" to an affirmation beginning,

> You do truly promise, on your honor, that you will never
> reveal to any person or persons, whatsoever, any of the signs,
> mysteries, arts, privileges, or benefits of the Order, that may
> be now or hereafter given to, or conferred on you; any acts done,
> or objects intended, except in a legal and authorized manner, or
> by special permission of the Order granted to you.
> That you will not reveal to any employer or other person, the
> name or person of any one a member of the Order, when such
> information may render the member liable to be victimized or
> otherwise work to their injury. . . .[7]

With the only real change being the necessity of seeking the brother's
own permission to reveal his membership, this pledge continued in
use at least until 1891.[8]

Insofar as lessening secrecy was concerned the delegates to the
annual session of the general assembly in New York City in September, 1882, were of quite an opposite mind. They adopted a
resolution that the unintended and harmful openness of the Order
called for "a greater degree of secrecy" as necessary to achieve suc-

[5] Old Manual, "Founding Ceremony," pp. 6-7.

[6] "Installation Ceremony," Old Manual, p. 16; New Manual, p. 14.

[7] New Manual, "Initiation," p. 16. In the old form the candidate bound himself "under the penalty of the scorn and neglect due to perjury and vio-lated honor, as one unworthy of trust or assistance." *Adelphon Kruptos* (pencil marked, "1880"), p. 12.

[8] Commons, *History*, II, 339. It appeared in the publication of Ezra A. Cook, *Knights of Labor Illustrated. "Adelphon Kruptos." The Full, Illus-trated Ritual including the "Unwritten Work" and an Historical Sketch of the Order* (Chicago, 1886), p. 28.

cess.[9] Nevertheless, hardly anything more concrete seems to have been done after that date to conceal further the activities of the Knights of Labor, although at the next convention the grand secretary, Robert Layton of Philadelphia, expressed his personal preference for the absolute secrecy of previous years.[10] Powderly's position in 1883 was more of a compromise, for he said in his report that he favored "the adoption of everything which was formerly a safeguard, except the oath," and at the same time he sought to have the general assembly limit the activities of members in such things as "indiscriminate interviewing," which had injured the Order in some localities.[11] Nothing was done, however, and yet the Knights' activities remained sufficiently secret to bother the American hierarchy in the early years of the 1880's, and later their Canadian brothers. This was accentuated by the atmosphere of suspicion and uncertainty in which all societies functioned in those days, groups which, although composed at times in good part of Catholics, were outside the supervision of the Church.[12] Hence even before they ever met for joint action some bishops were venturing to take stands on the Knights of Labor because Catholic members were coming to them with their ritual and constitution in a puzzled and usually filial spirit seeking their advice.

It was not only with the elimination of the oath that the American bishops began to pay attention to the Knights of Labor, but the complaints of the earlier period, spasmodic in nature and confined mostly to Pennsylvania, became more constant and widespread, reaching even to Canada. Despite the approval that had allegedly been given by Bishop Wood of Philadelphia in 1872, an approval never fully authenticated, another committee made an unsuccessful at-

9 *Proceedings* (New York, 1882), pp. 307 and 351.

10 *Proceedings* (Cincinnati, 1883), p. 412. At this session the "grand" in the official titles became "general." *Ibid.,* p. 494.

11 *Ibid.,* p. 407.

12 An interesting example of the lack of episcopal harmony was the case of the Hibernians, who were finally exonerated of suspicion in 1886. This group was forbidden by Archbishop Wood to have a special Mass for its convention in Philadelphia in 1880, although in Cincinnati the previous year Archbishop Purcell had officiated at such a Mass. Scranton *Times,* May 11, 1880.

tempt to call on him in 1875.[13]   When Powderly took control in
1879 he hoped to put an end once and for all to the local troubles
with the Church by contacting the metropolitan whose province covered the entire State of Pennsylvania.   He thought the Knights
would be the subject of the bishops' deliberations in the First Provincial Council of Philadelphia in 1880, and he suspected, *"I may hear
from there also."* [14]   No record was discovered that he ever did, although the one pertinent document of ecclesiastical origin revealed
that such societies as the Ancient Order of Hibernians, the Emeralds,
and the Sons of St. Joseph were to be discussed as well as the Free
Masons and Odd Fellows.[15]   The decrees of the council likewise were
not specific on labor societies.   The bishops in Philadelphia merely
followed the Provincial Council of San Francisco of 1875 by asserting that in the case of associations that were doubtfully illicit, "absolution could be granted to a penitent only after he had seriously
promised to leave the society as soon as it should have been condemned." [16]   Yet even this conciliar authority would have been
by-passed by Litchman, who went Powderly one better in a suggestion which was to be heard again some years later: "How much
would it cost to send an ambassador to Rome to try to get a sanction at headquarters from the Pope for Catholics to join the Order?
How would it operate if a petition were drawn up setting forth the
objects of the Order and signed by as many present or former members (Catholics) and forwarded to headquarters?" [17]

[13] PP, James A. Wright to Powderly, Philadelphia, August 1, 1888.

[14] PP, Powderly to Litchman, Scranton, April 25, 1880, copy. Joseph
L. J. Kirlin, *Catholicity in Philadelphia* (Philadelphia, 1909), pp. 389-391,
gives the date of the council as Trinity Sunday, May 23, 1880, and besides that
only lists the officials.

[15] Archives of the Archdiocese of Philadelphia, "Quaestiones quaedam ad
Revmum Archiepiscopum Philadelphiensem ab episcopis provinciae transmissae
et de quibus in concilio agetur." The tenth of eleven titles was "De societatibus
secretis."

[16] *Decreta concilii provincialis Philadelphiensis I* (Philadelphia, n.d.), pp.
vii-viii. This was printed only after Propaganda's approval in 1886, and hence
there was added an appendix on this sixth decree, namely the legislation of
the Third Plenary Council of Baltimore, and the instruction of the Holy Office
of May 10, 1884, Appendix, pp. xii-xx.

[17] PP, Marblehead, April 29, 1880.

The position of Archbishop Wood is not clarified by the testimony that in his first call upon him James A. Wright was informed "that the Church was not against the Order," for in that same year of 1881 another brother concerned with the question of Church relations considered the Philadelphia prelate among "those who are hardest on us."[18]   One Philadelphia assembly at least continued to rest assured that a committee had won toleration from the archbishop.   Then the vicar general, Father Maurice A. Walsh, who, can be assumed, knew the ordinary's mind on such questions, held up a church funeral of a knight until "the letters K. of L. was stricken out of the funeral notice which was published in one of our daily newspapers."   The local asked point-blank about Wood and the alleged committee of some years past.   Powderly's answer was not discovered, but whatever it was it could not have been based on very solid grounds when seven years later he himself was asking James A. Wright the same question about Wood.[19]   In response this Philadelphia district master workman mentioned also his final effort to reach Wood, whom he did not see since the archbishop died that very week in June, 1883.[20]

Two of Archbishop Wood's suffragan bishops had been prompted to take positions on the Knights since the latter were very active in their jurisdictions.   Bishop Tuigg of Pittsburgh, even before his part in the trouble of 1877, was reported as strict on the question.[21] He was still considered such several years later when Powderly explained to several of the Pittsburgh Knights why he preferred no

18 PP, James A. Wright to Powderly, Philadelphia, August 1, 1888; Peter J. Ward, New Bethlehem, January 21, 1881.

19 PP, John J. Conway to Powderly, Philadelphia, May 2, 1881. Where the answer should be, since the letter is marked as answered, May 20, 1881, the pages are missing, Letter-book, 1880-1883, pp. 171-176.

20 August 1, 1888.

21 PP, L. J. Brooks to Powderly, Mt. Washington, June 28, 1877. Tuigg arrived in Pittsburgh only in 1876 and was having jurisdictional troubles. In a recent work on the Diocese of Pittsburgh one reads: "Perhaps what tipped the scale in favor of Bishop Tuigg was the news which reached Rome of his courageous behavior during the railroad strike in Pittsburgh at the beginning of July. This news created a sensation in Rome. . . ." John Canova, "Bishop Michael Domenec and Bishop John Tuigg," *Catholic Pittsburgh's One Hundred Years* (Chicago, 1943), p. 50. On lack of archival material, cf. p. 380.

publicity in the press, "published in the interest of Capital." He gave as an example his sad experience after the Shenandoah picnic in 1879, and he added that he knew Tuigg was severe, "and if the papers began to make a fuss, he would consider it his duty to say something about the order and if he did, the weak minded would leave the order." [22] In the See of Erie Bishop Mullen had come out positively against the oath as his reason for objecting to the society, but even after the oath was changed one of his parish priests, Father "Maher" [Martin Meagher] of Houtzdale, referred the committee of local members to the bishop for permission to belong. Although Powderly had endorsed such action the Knights themselves decided, "it is not worth while to bother the Bishop or the Priest about the order now for if they object to it now it is impossible to try to please them. . . ." [23]

Outside of the keystone state, besides Archbishop Gibbons, Bishop Chatard of Vincennes also had the Knights of Labor called to his attention in the days before the change of the ritual. Chatard's suspicion arose early and it was destined to be among the longest in duration. He was not content with a general statement of policy on secret societies in the early part of 1879, but toward the end of that year he specifically applied it to the Coopers' Union as an oath-bound society.[24] Several weeks later one of his diocesans who was a member of the Knights, relayed the news, "We have been condemned by name in this diocese," but he told the general master workman that he was going to make an effort to see the bishop.[25] Although Chatard never mellowed on the question of labor societies it would seem his main bone of contention at that time was the oath, for he found nothing worthy of formal condemnation in the *Constitution and By-Laws and Rules of Order of the Trade and Labor Assembly of Cincinnati and Vicinity* which he examined on August 11,

[22] PP, Powderly to C. C. Burnett; also John Hirsch, Scranton, May 14, 1880, copy.

[23] PP, James White to Powderly, Houtzdale, December 28, 1881; also November 28, December 13. *Sadlier's Catholic Directory* (New York, 1881), p. 275.

[24] AUND, Chatard Papers (microfilm), Chatard to the Reverend Ferd. Hondt, Indianapolis, November 1, 1879, copy.

[25] PP, Dan O'Leary to Powderly, Carbon, Indiana, December 24, 1879.

1881. He was prompted, however, to mark questioningly the clause favoring union management of producers' co-operatives.[26] In a less friendly spirit Bishop Chatard noted, on the evidence of an engineer acquaintance, that the Locomotive Brotherhood was Masonic in character and bound by oath to secrecy; hence Catholic non-union men had been at a premium since the railroad strikes, because "belonging to the Brotherhood was a reason for not getting a place." [27]

At the beginning of 1882 the attitude of some Catholic union members elsewhere certainly did not coincide with that of Chatard on the usefulness of labor organization. One of the results of these differences were such reports of clerical opposition as came from Pittsburgh, the industrial center of western Pennsylvania. Layton wrote on February 27, 1882:

> The Church just now is giving us a little trouble. This causes me some uneasiness at present although I think I can take the sting out of the bite next week when I go before the Bishop. Pray for me, for I have done considerable swearing over it and need assistance Divine or otherwise when the time comes for the interview.[28]

A few weeks later all was going well, probably as a result of the use of the familiar argument that modifications had been made in the Order to please the Church.[29] A worker in another city, however, "learned with regret of the recent opposition of certain of our clergy in Pittsburgh," and so set down his reflections for the general master workman. They included a very practical line of reasoning for priests and a little bit of venom. Man can get what he needs for the sustenance of himself and family, said this knight, only by a

26 AUND, Chatard Papers (microfilm).

27 *Ibid.* There is no name on the document but it is in Chatard's writing, most likely a copy of a letter sent. Greater detail on Chatard's position on the Knights was not found in his papers.

28 Wisconsin State Historical Society, John Samuel Correspondence. On the lack of archival material from the Diocese of Pittsburgh, cf. p. 380.

29 PP, Layton to Powderly, Pittsburgh, March 17, 1882. Powderly's interview to that effect was carried in the Pittsburgh *Leader,* May 7, 1882, Scrapbook, January, 1881-January, 1884.

united struggle against the master capitalists. His second argument was more pointed:

> Again the 5th commandment of the Church says 'Contribute to the support of your pastor:' in the eyes of the Church to bust one of her 6 commandments is as great a sacrilege as to break one of God's 10. Then how are we to choose between the two evils; obey the mandate of God and provide for ourselves, our families, and pastors and incur the wrath of the Church, or at least of a few of her teachers or, obey the mandates of mercenary clergy and allow our families and others dependent upon us to starve and thus incur the just wrath of a just God. In my opinion a man's own conscience must to a great extent be his guide in such matters (temporal) when our spiritual advisers differ so much. They certainly let us know quick enough if they don't get their share and to tell the truth I should like to see them with want staring them in the face and no other means left to relieve them but this very same one they oppose and I sincerely believe they with superior knowledge would make an obligation so strong and an organization so powerful that the combined efforts of nations could not overcome it; vide: *Jesuits.*

Nonetheless, this Detroit anti-clerical professed his continued loyalty to the Church, although he seriously anticipated trouble from the Bishop of Detroit.[30] As a matter of fact, almost at that very moment Bishop Casper H. Borgess, who never became an outstanding foe of the Knights of Labor, was lamenting the difficulty to a fellow bishop of determining the lawfulness of many labor associations. He proferred the opinion that they were, "at least to a certain extent, secret societies, and strongly tainted with the socialistic spirit." [31] In the bishop's see city the Order was coming more into the public eye, but at least one organizer felt it necessary to cease assuring people that the Church would soon sanction it.[32]

The publicity given by the press to the Knights of Labor was bound to arouse in separated parts of the Order some interest in

[30] PP, D. Barry to Powderly, Detroit, January 30, 1882.

[31] Archives of the Archdiocese of Detroit, C. H. Borgess to William H. McCloskey, Detroit, January 31, 1882, copy. This letter was copied for the writer through the kindness of John Tracy Ellis.

[32] PP, D. Barry to Powderly, Detroit, February 1, 1882.

the welfare of the whole group.   Thus a Catholic member in a healthy and growing assembly was led to inquire about some newspaper stories concerning adverse action by the Church.   He was silent on the clergy, but he professed his faith in the Church and in the Knights thus:

> Of course, newspaper accounts are liable to be in a great degree sensational but still we out west having no immediate access to the bottom facts are to some extent nervous when the welfare of our last venture and hope of bettering our miserable state is threatened by the hand of our cherishing mother the Church.   We can but think that either we or she are misinformed as to the practice of the order, and we hardly know what to think.   We cannot as Catholics refuse implicit obedience to the behests of the Church, but at what a cost would she exact that obedience if she commands us to resign our only hope of relief from the state of slavery to which the Vanderbilts, Goulds, Garretts, Perkins and other corporation magnates have reduced us owing to our hitherto isolated and consequently defenseless condition.[33]

Even though, notwithstanding its reformed status, the Order had already come into a renewed clerical disfavor Powderly serenely reassured the Iowa knight that he heard "no complaint from the Church." [34]   Quite the contrary was true during the years 1882 and 1883, for there was a scattered ecclesiastical opposition, and in several places it was reported as coming from the hierarchy rather than the ordinary parish priests.

One type of objection formerly made by the clergy seems to have died away by the middle of the first year of publicity for the Knights; that was the old charge of being Molly Maguires.   Formerly, any outrage or violence to property or members of management in certain Pennsylvania localities was feared as a new weapon in the hands of the enemies of the Order.   Public addresses by the officers of the society were used successfuly to dispel the notion that the Knights would ever resort to such tactics.[35]   About the time Pow-

[33] PP, Jno. S. B. Coggeshell to Powderly, Council Bluffs, Iowa, January 28, 1882. On the first two industrialists especially cf. Matthew Josephson, *The Robber Barons* (New York, 1934).

[34] PP, Scranton, March 1, 1882.

[35] PP, Powderly to Charles Litchman, Scranton, August 18, 1881, copy;

derly made a public disavowal of any connection with the old Mollies, he wrote the same thing substantially, but more vehemently, in answer to the charge of a Buffalo member:

> Our Order is not akin to the Molly McGuires, even though the G. M. W. is an *Irishman*. I am sick of that term being slung at us. There never existed such an association and as long as workingmen lend a willing ear to the slanders of capital just so long will capital be able to control us through our prejudices. . . . They can call me Molly McGuire, Communist, Socialist, Nihilist, and every epithet that the tongue of slander and malice can invent, but so long as the God who made me gives me life and strength just so long will I strive with what little ability I possess to win for laboring down trodden humanity all its rights and that without spilling one drop of blood.[36]

Thus ended for all practical purposes the identification of the Knights of Labor and the Molly Maguires, and in a later day when any charges of violence were leveled against the Order the finger of blame was commonly pointed, not so much at hot-headed Irishmen, as at foreign-born radicals of a different stripe.

But even before the days of the worst labor upheavals of the late nineteenth century, reports came to the general master workman of opposition on the part of the Catholic Bishops of Erie, Columbus, Cleveland, and Portland, Maine. He was told also of continued suspicion and ill-will, if not outright hostility, from priests, especially in Philadelphia and Chicago. In some cases one may be pardoned for questioning the complete accuracy of reports from the rank and file of the Knights of Labor. They could not be expected to be too reliable concerning the subtleties of the canon law on secret societies—a problem that worried even trained ecclesiastics—nor were they entirely immune to the exaggeration and distortion which arose out of rumor.

Bishop Tobias Mullen of Erie was the first member of the hier-

also John Lyttle to Powderly, Clarksburg, West Virginia, April 2, 1882, John Archbald, Arnot, Pennsylvania (answered May 25, 1882).

[36] Clipping without date among Scranton *Times* and *Republican* items of May 17, 1882, in Scrapbook, January, 1881-January, 1884; Powderly to William Hickey, Scranton, May 17, 1882, copy.

archy reported to have condemned the new form of the ritual in a pastoral to the clergy.[37]   Some months later he was represented as having seen only the old constitution, but still his lack of consent slowed up organization.[38]   An organizer in that territory saw hope for the Order only in the favorable proclamation from Archbishop Wood or, "else the clergy here dies and more liberal ones take their place." [39]   He was apparently a *persona non grata* there, for he suffered from pulpit denunciations by the pastor of Osceola, Father B. Lynch, and by "Father Maher" of Houtzdale. He even claimed the latter "stated at the Horse Races at Phillipsburgh I ought to be linched [*sic*]!" [40]   The society in another city of the same episcopal jurisdiction foresaw that without the bishop's consent, "it will be a fizzle here." [41]   Despite some internal opposition from those who "did not give a damn" for Bishop Mullen, a committee was set up to seek his consent for Catholics to join.[42]

In the spring of the same year, 1882, Archbishop Gibbons, on the contrary, was being approached not for any grant of toleration but with information that one of his priests was without doubt "not only a strong sympathizer, but an encourager of the Knights of Labor." [43]   This informing official of the Consolidated Coal Company, therefore, wanted another priest than Valentine Schmitt, the Frostburg pastor, to bring the blessings of religion to the foreign miners at Eckhart, Maryland. Any one of the German Redemptorists from Cumberland was considered more satisfactory than Schmitt

37 PP, Cornelius Cotter to Powderly, Osceola Mills, April 3, 1882. The pastor, Father B. Lynch, was reported as most agreeable, "We are all right . . . he says he was bound to read the Bishop's letter but he was not bound to act accordingly."

38 PP, Thomas N. Burman to Powderly, Erie, July 13, 1882.

39 PP, M. McPadden to Powderly, Osceola Mills, June 24, 1882.

40 Pittsburgh, July 20, 1882.

41 PP, James J. Dugan to Powderly, Oil City, July 24, 1882.

42 PP, Robert Simpson to Powderly, Oil City, September 20, 1882. Once again the story lacks ecclesiastical documentation. Cf. p. 380 on the Diocese of Erie.

43 BCA, 76-R-7, Charles F. Mayer to D. J. Foley (A Baltimore merchant, a close friend of Gibbons, and a brother of John S. who was a member of the archbishop's council, and of Thomas, late Coadjutor Bishop of Chicago), Cumberland, Maryland, June 6, 1882.

and the new pastor or someone else of the prelate's choice, was invited to ascertain to his own satisfaction, that, contrary to all the rumors spread by the Knights of Labor, the workers were treated exceptionally well. The mining executive maintained that his interest was more than personal since the Knights, if tolerated, would produce another Commune. Schmitt's answer to Gibbons on this charge was that he had been impartial, but he added, "It is true however that in my own mind I have a leaning toward the poor miners. For it is hard to see my people victimized and driven from their houses and homes." [44] The company had moved in aliens to take the place of striking miners and it had kept them in an enclosure "which in every respect looks like a military camp." The Catholic Irish had been ordered out of their company-owned homes and Schmitt, fearing violence, refused to co-operate with the company official by going into the encampment to offer Mass when they would not let the workers out. The Protestant ministers did likewise, but Gibbons' informant blamed Schmitt especially, and so the pastor recommended that the informer be stalled off.[45] The existing records do not disclose the archbishop's reaction, but the fact that the incumbent of the parish house at Frostburg was not changed might suggest a latent sympathy toward organized labor on the part of Gibbons.[46]

Disturbances of a different nature occurred over the Knights during the early part of 1882 in the Dioceses of Columbus and Cleveland. In both instances it did not take place until the suffragan bishops of their sees had returned from the Fourth Provincial Council of Cincinnati, which lasted from March 5 to 19. This gathering was convened by the coadjutor-administrator, Archbishop William Henry Elder, and Bishop William McCloskey of Louisville did the preliminary work on secret societies.[47] The completed decrees resulted in a statement that real labor unions were *per se* legitimate. The assembled bishops did, however, express the fear lest such associations commit injustices or be drawn to "condemned sects," especially since men of all kinds were mixed together in them,

---

[44] BCA, 76-R-9, Frostburg, June 8, 1882.
[45] BCA, 76-R-10, Schmitt to Gibbons, June 9, 1882.
[46] Schmitt was still pastor in 1885, *Sadlier's Catholic Directory,* 1885, p. 59.
[47] Lamott, *op. cit.,* pp. 218-220.

and the doctrines of socialism were making such headway among them. The council repeated Pope Leo XIII's admonition for the setting up of religious societies, particularly for young workers, but it immediately added, "Workers should not suspect that the Church in giving such advice is hindering them from demanding a just price for their work, and of using all lawful means of obtaining it." [48] A generous section of the pastoral letter was likewise devoted to labor unions. Since it was presented to the gathering by Bishop Gilmour for comments and emendation, it is not surprising that it should be almost word for word the same as his lenten pastoral of 1879 on the subject of the objectionable practices of labor organizations.[49] The letter of 1882, however, added some general advice in another vein:

> . . . capital must be liberal toward labor, and share justly and generously the joint profits which labor and capital have produced. . . . Capital has no more right to undue reward than labor, nor should capital be unduly protected at the expense of labor. . . . They are mutually dependent on each other, and should mutually labor for each other's interest.[50]

This message to the clergy and laity of the Province of Cincinnati was duly read in March, 1882, and within two months the Bishop of Columbus was reported to have condemned the Knights of Labor, not by proclamation but by refusing deceased knights Christian burial—one of the penalties for membership in a forbidden society.[51] Powderly's advice to Bishop John A. Watterson's subjects was long but quite resigned in tone. He began: "I regret exceedingly the stand your bishop has taken. Of course nothing that I can do will have any effect. . . ." Continuing in praise of their own labor organization, he added:

---

[48] *Acta et decreta quatuor conciliorum provincialium Cincinnatensium, 1855-1882* (Cincinnati, 1886), p. 234.

[49] *Ibid.*, pp. 246-247, 197. *Vide supra,* p. 29. In another place in condemning secret societies, Catholic membership in labor groups with non-Catholic religious features was deprecated, p. 252.

[50] *Ibid.,* p. 247.

[51] PP, Edward Brooke to Powderly, Zanesville, Ohio, May 23, 1882.

The Church always opposes secret societies but a great many divines hold different views of different societies. A Catholic *cannot* be a mason and remain a Catholic. Several other societies exist and every Catholic who knows his religion knows that he cannot become a member and receive the rites of his Church. I grant that he may receive these rites by deceiving his confessor but he cannot deceive Almighty God. But our society cannot be classed with these societies. It is simply and purely a labor society, a combination of trade union with the bad features of the trade union left out.

The oath was gone, Powderly pointed out, and now the obligation was like that of any union. "I wish to heaven," he interpolated, "that our members were as well instructed on the labor question as the Catholic clergy." The cause of the Bishop of Columbus' anxiety, he suggested, might have been loud-sounding radicals in the movement, but at any rate he could only conclude:

I cannot nor will not interfere between the Church and its members, only this far, you may show the priest or bishop everything in connection with the Order ritual included and then if they still command members of the Church to leave it, I have nothing to say.[52]

Another Ohio bishop, Richard Gilmour of Cleveland, who was to become more anxious about the problem of the Knights with the passing years, was said to have opposed the association as early as 1882. [53] The main action in his diocese was taken by the Reverend E. J. "Wattman" [Vettmann] of Canal Fulton, who began by calling some of his regalia-bedecked parishioners off the line of march in a Decoration Day parade and followed that up with pulpit denunciations. He based his action, not on any official pronouncement, but on "another priest's letter from the Bishop condemning it." [54] His threat of excommunication resulted in the loss

[52] Powderly to Brooke, Scranton, May 26, 1882, copy. Returned for postage and never forwarded. A search of the archives of the Diocese of Columbus proved fruitless, cf. p. 384.

[53] PP, John McBride to Powderly, Massillon, Ohio, June 29, 1882, "Bishop Gilmour of Cleveland, O. is against the Order. . . ."

[54] PP, Timothy T. O'Malley to Powderly, Alliance, Ohio, September 27, 1882; Salineville, October 23, 1882.

of great numbers and was considered an "ungentlemanly act." [55]
An interview with Father Vettmann by the local Knights resulted in
a promise of strong support from the pulpit if they could show him
one prelate's signature of endorsement.[56]

Without hoping for such positive approbation, Powderly and his
followers would have been content with mere passive toleration from
the members of the American episcopacy. Yet some bishops, such as
James A. Healy of Portland, went to the other extreme and seemed
destined to become a constant source of annoyance to the Knights
of Labor. This prelate, according to a report from Pittsburgh, began his campaign near the end of the year 1882 by threatening Catholic members with banishment from the Church. The leader of the
Knights wrote an explanation "at considerable length" to the master workman of the Maine assembly who was further advised by
one of the executive board to submit it for the bishop's perusal.
Powderly apparently did not intend it for posterity.[57]

The Mayor of Scranton by the early part of 1883 to all appearances was also ready to take up the offensive in person on two ecclesiastical fronts. These were Philadelphia and Chicago. He had certainly remained in good standing in his own diocese, if assisting
again in the management of the parish picnic can be interpreted in
the usual way, even though clerical opposition was occasionally felt
in other towns under the jurisdiction of Bishop O'Hara.[58] In quite
the same manner the Knights hardly ever had complete surcease
from the scrutiny of churchmen in the Archdiocese of Philadelphia.
Wood was said to have followed the example of O'Hara and con-

[55] PP, W. F. Sollau to Powderly, Canal Fulton, July 9, 1882.

[56] PP, O'Malley to Powderly, October 23, 1882. The knight had more
hope in the newly-ordained curate in his home parish at Salineville, who although he said, "if he was Bishop" he would not tolerate the Order, still seemed
to be open to conviction.

[57] PP, Jno. Campbell to Powderly, Pittsburgh, December 14, 21, 1882.
No copy of the letter referred to was found.

[58] PP, Powderly to Edward J. Clark, Scranton, July 26, 1882, copy; P. J.
Deegan to Powderly, Plymouth, April 3, 1882; O. S. Mloutz[?], Williamsport,
November 9, 1882, (They wanted to pacify the Irish and German priests, "both
men of liberal views," by a word from the bishop); John Whalen, Carbondale,
February 27, 1883.

demned the Order in a communication to his clergy and this, it was suspected, under the influence of Gowen.[59] Nonetheless, the clerical foray through the internal forum was on again in Schuylkill County where it was reported that the Catholic knights were given the alternative of giving up the Order or the Church. The suggestion that Powderly form a committee of three with Bishops O'Hara and Tuigg to call on the Archbishop of Philadelphia was answered by a mere promise to call on Wood about the matter.[60] On top of this came an urgent plea from Chicago, the first inkling that in that city the association was having trouble with the Church. The general treasurer wrote a strong appeal:

> For some time past I have received private reports from reliable sources that the clergy of the Catholic Church have been and are now tampering with quite a number of members of our Order, and so much so, that a very large proportion of our A's here, have become decimated in numbers, and it is strongly hinted that in a short time a manifesto will be issued against the order in this diocese; now considering this a very serious matter, it requires a master hand to deal with it, and knowing the experience that you have had in matters identical with this, I have considered it my duty to apprise you of it, and request you will come to Chicago as quickly as you conveniently can (as it is absolutely necessary you shall be here in person), and by your influence stop what may be a death blow to the Order, not only in Chicago, but in the States at large.[61]

The general master workman decided that both Philadelphia and Chicago needed him urgently, and practically at the same time.[62] Meanwhile he told Griffiths, "I have written to Church dignitaries, requesting a postponement of any harsh measure until I can see and explain in person, etc." [63] Powderly's plan of action was enclosed in a letter bemoaning his need of a secretary:

[59] PP, T. W. Griffith to Powderly, Coal Dale, June 15, August 14, 1882.

[60] PP, Patrick Moran to Powderly, Minersville, March 22, 1883; Powderly to Moran, Scranton, April 6, 1883, copy.

[61] PP, Richard Griffiths to Powderly, Chicago, April 11, 1883.

[62] PP, Powderly to Jno. Campbell, Scranton, April 13, 1883, copy; to Layton, April 13, 1883, copy.

[63] Scranton, April 13, 1883, copy. No copies of such letters were found. On the absence of evidence from ecclesiastical archives, cf. pp. 380, 384.

> I go to Philadelphia one week from tomorrow, ostensibly to attend Irish national convention, in reality to wait on Bishop Wood in relation to the Hechscherville men, he can remove the restriction there and may benefit us elsewhere. I must soon go to Chicago to arrange a similar matter. I think of applying for the position of Pope's Legate. I have had so much experience in ecclesiastical affairs.[64]

In the case of both Chicago and Philadelphia the lack of diocesan archival sources does a lamentable disservice here both to history and to the Church. These two very important centers of labor agitation—and in fact every diocese of the Pennsylvania province—have no documentary evidence to provide from the side of the churchmen either substantiation or refutation of the statements of the labor leaders. On the fulfillment of Powderly's proposal of the spring of 1883, however, not even his own extant records throw any light.

During these first years after the reformation of the Knights, "ecclesiastical affairs," moreover, were far from being the private preserve of Powderly. In local assemblies many a consultation was held with the parish priest and working agreements reached without benefit of the bishop. Sometimes the reports of knights on the clergy included also Protestant ministers. Such was the case in a letter from Rochester, New York, relating that the pulpit was neutral on the labor question though the clergy "were taking it up."[65] It was only the priests who were considered—and by "born Catholics" too— "sanctimonious religious fanatics" for their opposition.[66] There was still doubt in the minds of many Catholics about their right to belong and the influence of the priest's word within or outside the sacramental forum was recognized. When the clergy's reasons were given—even with the oath removed—they simply amounted in effect to, "Secret organization, no absolution."[67] On at least one occa-

---

[64] PP, Powderly to Gilbert Rockwood, Scranton, April 17, 1883. Archbishop Wood died on June 20, 1883, after about a year in which he was partially incapacitated. Kirlin, *op. cit.*, pp. 391-393. On Powderly's Irish connections see his *Path*, pp. 175-187. These activities helped him as much with Irish laborers as his temperance work did with many clergy.

[65] PP, Charles E. Robinson to Powderly, May 14, 1882.

[66] PP, Henry Fecker to Powderly, Lawrenceburg, Indiana, July 6, 1882.

[67] *Ibid.*, also M. J. Wynn, Centralia, Pennsylvania, September 30, 1882;

sion the priest concerned was accused of having political motives for his hardening change of heart.[68]

From the opposite side of the picture, however, the attitude of the Order toward the clergy underwent in general a more pleasant change. Powderly's reputation as a conciliator of clerics had grown to such an extent that one follower, on hearing of the refusal of his oft-proffered resignation, wrote, "Were the order to lose you now as its chief the R. C. clergy throughout the lenght [sic] and breath [sic] of the land would denounce it and its members in thundertones." [69] The official attitude of the Knights on clerical membership had also become more friendly. An admonition of an earlier date had ended, "Be very careful whom you take in. *Clergymen are not admissible.*" [70] Four years afterwards the general master workman's decision announced: "A clergyman of any denomination is eligible to membership provided he practice what he preaches, and provided he preaches in the interest of humanity instead of *Mammon.*" [71] This was in line with the general widening of the classes of people eligible to join the Order, the exception to which eventually narrowed down in practice merely to "rum dealers." It was hardly indicative, nevertheless, of any over-all policy of friendliness toward religious groups when a pamphlet entitled, "Knights of Labor," could speak of "your costly churches . . . where . . . even the Christ would be frowned upon unless hat in hand, he apologized and gave his name." [72] In fact it can only be surmised how far such a fraternal and ritualistic group as the Knights provided a substitute for active church attend-

R. C. Owens, Kansas City, April 20, 1883; John C. O'Brien, Volcano, West Virginia, May 22, 1883; John W. Latchford, Trenton, Missouri, May 27, 1883.

[68] PP, John Mulligan to Powderly, Lexington, Missouri, received March 23, 1883.

[69] PP, Patrick Coogan to Powderly, Heckscherville, February 16, 1882.

[70] PP, Powderly to Thomas H. Burns, Scranton, October 20, 1879, copy.

[71] This answer included also the technicalities of "blackballing." M. F. Cafferty to Powderly, Corsicana, Texas, May 9, 1883; Powderly to Cafferty, May 15, 1883, copy.

[72] The author was Ebenezer A. Hudson (Minneapolis, 1883). Many Catholic pastors would have smiled at the description of temples with upholstered pews and stained glass windows, "where fashion turns up its nose at mean attire."

ance, especially where ill-instructed Catholics were only mute spectators at an alien-language liturgy. Even Powderly was convinced that the best attendance at meetings was obtained on Sunday afternoons if the people were not "very religious."[73]

Yet no matter how loud were the cries of the Catholic knights, the chief difficulties of the early 1880's within the organization of the Knights of Labor were certainly not religious. As might have been expected, following what seemed to be the settlement of the basic objection concerning the oath and the consequent open character of the Order, a rapid and steady growth took place. After a drop in membership in 1881, 1882 showed 42,519 and the next year 51,914 on the list. These were centered, of course, in the industrial communities, for the organizers rarely entered into rural areas. The totals of the enrollment fluctuated greatly during these years, especially as a result of unsuccessful strikes. The telegraphers' strike in 1883 was not only the most important attempt to use this technique, but it also brought to the Knights much attention from the press and the public.[74] The influx of members included men of every school of political and economic thought, for the Order could hardly have been expected to examine the theories held by each candidate. Consequently, although the advocates of socialism never really dominated the Knights of Labor, they attempted to make inroads in it as well as in the trade unions.[75] Their influence is claimed in the constitutional provisions for the taxing of "all lands now held for speculative purposes" to the full value and for the government ownership through purchase of public utilities.[76] In addition, however much anarchism was theoretically opposed to socialism, it was equally true that to the public mind—which included the ecclesiastical— "their common opposition to the *status quo* was often of more importance than the divergence of their philosophies."[77]

[73] PP, Powderly to George W. Watthew, Scranton, October 9, 1883.

[74] Cf. Commons, *History,* II, 344-355; Ware, *op. cit.,* pp. 103-113; 117-134.

[75] Ely, *op. cit.,* p. 232. Joseph R. Buchanan, *The Story of a Labor Agitator* (New York, 1903), p. 135.

[76] Cf. Morris Hillquit, *History of Socialism in the United States* (New York, 1910), pp. 267-268.

[77] Ware, *op. cit.,* p. 304.

The three main groups of "radicals" which functioned and influenced the American labor movement during the 1880's do not seem to have been clearly distinguished by their Catholic contemporaries. Pope Leo XIII himself in his *Quod apostolici muneris* (also called *De socialistarum secta*) simply spoke of "that sect of men who under various and almost barbarous names, are called 'Socialists, Communists, or Nihilists.' "[78] It is small wonder that alongside the dangers that threatened from communism or anarchism, the local terrorism of the Molly Maguires, which has already been mentioned, faded into insignificance. As early as 1878 Allan Pinkerton for one was convinced the Knights were "an amalgamation of the Molly Maguires and the Commune."[79] How much he was influenced in his judgment by the desire to keep his detectives widely hired and how successful he was in coloring the mentality of management, is difficult to say. One industrialist did warn a Catholic prelate that the growth of the Knights of Labor by 1882 led him to expect in the United States "scenes not less terrible than those committed by the Commune in Paris."[80] The only foundation for such a fear could have been found in the program of the American anarchists. This "Black International" group, affiliated with the London headquarters of European anarchism which was set up only a few months before it in 1881, became the bogey of the American public, especially during the hectic events of 1886. The chief influence in this International Working People's Association was Johann Most, a German exile, who advocated "propaganda by deed," or what were to be acts of violence against not only capitalists but also officials of the State and the Church. Its most important center, however, was Chicago where one of the leaders, Albert R. Parsons, was also a member of the Knights of Labor.[81] From the trans-Mississippi section of the United States another leading knight, Joseph R. Buchanan, was also an important figure in a group—native American in character—which also declared allegiance to the London International. This was the International Workingmen's

---

[78] Husslein, *op. cit.*, I, 14. It was issued on December 28, 1878.

[79] *Strikers, Communists, Tramps and Detectives* (New York, 1900), p. 88.

[80] BCA, 76-R-7, Charles F. Meyer to Foley, June 6, 1882.

[81] Lucy E. Parsons, *Life of Albert R. Parsons* (Chicago, 1889), p. 15.

Association, established by Burnette G. Haskell of San Francisco in 1881, and called the "Red International" because of the color of its membership card and also because it favored socialism rather than anarchism. This latter fact was not always clear to the public, and Buchanan later explained that his mentioning of the use of force, especially in their journal, the Denver *Labor Enquirer,* was more in the way of a warning than a threat.[82]

The most inconspicuous and inocuous radical activity at this time was that of the Socialist Labor Party, which became amalgamated with the Red International in 1887. The former group had been founded in 1876, after the fall of the First International, out of the socialist factions of both the political and trade union stripe. Philip Van Patten, a native American, was the national secretary who registered Powderly as a party member, and Peter J. McGuire of New York, also a prominent knight, was active in the organization. After 1880 their influence fell off, and it was not until the important mayoralty campaign of 1886 in New York City that they took to politics again.[83]

In the ebb and flow of the labor movement the influence of these various radical groups was felt first within and later without the Knights of Labor. Stephens was not only opposed to their getting control since he considered them as "simply disturbers," but he said he detested even "the name of socialism." [84] Powderly's attitude was more pragmatic, for he claimed, "there are certain socialistic principles upon which we can all agree." [85] His opposition was not to their theories, which he considered sound, but rather to their injudicious advocates, "who drive good men off by shaking the *red flag* right in their face the first thing." [86] Powderly was particularly distracted by the antics of the socialist Theodore Cuno in New York,

[82] Buchanan, *op. cit.,* p. 129; Ely, *op. cit.,* pp. 240-251.

[83] Cf. Commons, *History,* II, 269-300, Chapter VI, "From Socialism to Anarchism and Syndicalism, 1876-1884."

[84] PP, Uriah S. Stephens to James S. Sullivan, n. p., August 19, 1879.

[85] "If socialism or communism means the restoration of man's natural rights I am a socialist and a communist, but I claim for myself the right to differ with my brother as to the means by which these reforms are to be brought about." Powderly to J. Mullane, Scranton, September 28, 1882, copy.

[86] PP, Powderly to Layton, Scranton, May 1, 1882, copy.

who was making unhappy statements to the press, attempting an authorized boycott, and issuing circulars abusive of the general officers.[87]

Indeed, the general master workman for a time feared socialist control in New York, but he was reassured on that point.[88] But besides the socialists in that city there were still what Ware called the fundamentalists, "the strict constructionists of Stephens' gospel of secrecy and ritual." [89] Powderly remained aware of their opposition, and he professed to know something of their intrigue, which remains unmentioned elsewhere:

> You have men in New York who would move heaven and earth to restore the old *Masonic* customs and make the order again oath bound. I *know* them. You have men in New York who have cooperated with men in Philadelphia to break up the order by going to a Catholic prelate of eminence and said, *'The oath is still in force the word of honor is but a blind to make cats-paws of the Catholic members and the G. M. W. is a party to this infamous transaction.'*

Yet in that very same letter he designated as "the curse of the K. of L.," as well as of the Land League, rather the fact that socialist speakers so often at public meetings "plainly hinted at the musket and gatling gun as the remedy for labor's ills." He hardly objected on principle, for he claimed he would resent such means being represented as those of the Knights—unless the Order should adopt them! [90] In a similar vein Powderly did not seem to mind agreeing with the pioneer organizer in Michigan who sent in a literary contribution to the Order's official paper and said: "Some fine-haired, thin-skinned cuss might kick, to use a graceful term, against

[87] Ware, *op. cit.*, p. 104, refers to this German newspaper man as "socialistic, somewhat scatter brained, and perhaps unscrupulous." This trouble filled much of the proceedings of the G. A. in 1882.

[88] PP, John Jay Joyce to Powderly, New York, May 21, 1882.

[89] Ware, *op. cit.*, p. 109, sees in the Cuno affair the solidification of these two sentiments, the socialist and Stephenite, which led to the intrigue so disruptive of the Order and helpful to the growth of the A. F. of L., namely, the Home Club which eventually removed Powderly from office. *Ibid.*, pp. 103-112.

[90] PP, Powderly to J. Mulhane, Scranton, September 28, 1882, copy.

communism or socialism being discussed in the *Journal of United Labor,* but I believe workingmen must be put right on these subjects, even though we do lose some damn fools." [91]

At least in time the general master workman came to realize that the expression of extremist views as to violent measures of social reform, "has caused not only clergymen but laboringmen to regard us with an eye of suspicion, and it will take somewhat of an effort to remove these impressions." [92]   He had tried previously to keep himself personally clear of such a failing by avoiding a public gathering of Knights in Philadelphia to agitate for Chinese exclusion legislation.   His *"confidential"* note read:

> I saw names at that meeting of prominent *Socialists,* and while I entertain socialistic ideas myself I like to see them practically set forth and had I gone down and appeared on the platform it would be telegraphed to the four corners of the earth that the K. of L. was a socialist society, and that would scare timid men away.[93]

By 1883 Powderly was privately and publicly disavowing any radical connections of the Order.   The now conservative leader claimed that only because of its strength was the Knights of Labor able to tolerate such members as P. J. McGuire and the other advocates of socialism which it sheltered.[94]   Further than this the chief of the Knights disclaimed before the world, "Mr. Most does not in any way represent the views and aspirations of the workingmen of the United States." [95]

This plea of conservatism was to be used by Powderly many times to win the benevolent forbearance of the American hierarchy.   By the end of 1883 some of the bishops had observed with no little concern the radical elements in the labor movement.   The Bishop of Detroit had observed the socialistic spirit of many labor groups

[91] PP, Joseph Labadie to Powderly, Detroit, May 30, 1882; Powderly to Labadie, Scranton, June 8, 1882, copy.

[92] PP, Powderly to Mulhane, September 28, 1882, copy.

[93] PP, Powderly to James McFeely, Scranton, June 6, 1882, copy.

[94] PP, Layton to Powderly, Pittsburgh, February 26, 1883.

[95] Scrapbook, March 1883—July 1885, Muscatine *Weekly News,* June 23, **1883.**

and he had characterized strikes as "limited revolution" called by arbitrary dictators. He did not miss the fact that "at several meetings in this city of late the Labor Associations openly advocated Socialism and imported German and English speakers of the darkest socialistic type to advocate the doctrine." [96]   Nor did the Fourth Provincial Council of New York fail to go a little beyond the usual condemnation of secret societies in its pastoral of September 30, 1883. Listed as groups to be considered dangerous, although not yet explicitly condemned, besides those with a religious ritual, were also:

> 1. Societies which prevent the lawful exercise of liberty, either on the part of employers or employees, especially if to further the end proposed recourse be had to violence. It is an injustice to prevent men by violent means from earning an honest livelihood.
> 2. Societies in which anti-religious, infidel doctrines are openly professed and advocated. No Catholic may remain united with men who assail Religion. [97]

Despite the fact that neither the Knights of Labor nor any specific radical excesses were mentioned by the New York bishops, it was quickly taken to heart by some of the Order, at least in Buffalo. [98]

[96] AADetroit, C. H. Borgess to William H. McCloskey, Detroit, January 31, 1882, copy.

[97] The letter was signed by John Cardinal McCloskey and his seven suffragans as well as Michael A. Corrigan, his coadjutor, and John J. Conroy, retired Bishop of Albany. The decrees were not published for three years and contained nothing so specific as the pastoral. *Acta et decreta concilii provincialis Neo-Eboracensis IV* (New York, 1886), pp. 9-12. Caput II, "De quibusdam obstaculis fidei." "Pastoral," pp. lxiii-iv.

[98] The only reference to radicalism was in speaking of papers "parading the title of Catholic," which preached "the worst kind of socialism and communism" p. lix. No names are given but it is interesting to cite from previous prohibitions. Gilmour condemned the *Irish World* and forbade its circulation in the Diocese of Cleveland (Lenten Pastoral of 1879, *Pastoral Letters,* II, CUA). Besides Ford's paper the Bishop of Alton, Peter J. Baltes, included McMaster's *Freeman's Journal,* and the Reverend David S. Phelan's *Western Watchman* of St. Louis as subversive of Catholic teaching and undermining episcopal authority. (Pastoral Instruction, January 23, 1879, Treasure Room, UND). Professor

One of them rushed to the bishop's house—only to find him out—in order "to prove to him by our A. K. that there is nothing communistic in our order." [99]   It would probably have done little immediate good if Bishop Stephen V. Ryan of Buffalo had been consulted, for he had just approved of a decree with his fellow bishops in New York which said that the scandalous differences in the judgments of ecclesiastics concerning secret societies were to be removed only by the proscriptions of the ordinaries. They were to confer on such a question and if it proved necessary to settle the difficulty, they were to have recourse to the Holy See.[100]

Whether it be explained by a mere failure of initiative, or by the lack of an ultra-montane and anti-liberal tradition among the American bishops, the fact remains that, while the Americans gave voice to such generalities, the question of the Knights of Labor was already being sent to Rome from Canada. It was rather the action of one man, Archbishop Elzear-Alexandre Taschereau of Quebec, the head of the hierarchy in Lower Canada, who could not have had nearly as much contact with the organization as his southern neighbors but who was more prompt to display suspicious fear.

The Knights of Labor had entered Canada in the fall of 1881 at a time characterized by expansion throughout the whole Dominion in the building of railroads, the influx of immigration, and increased industrialization. All this helped to bring on the revival of trade unionism which was marked by the establishment in July, 1881, of the Toronto Trades and Labour Council. While eschewing direct political action, it lobbied very actively for labor legislation. A new approach was represented by the first local assembly of the Knights of Labor in Hamilton, whence it spread to Toronto by August, 1882. By July of the following year the young society was supporting the Toronto council in the telegraph operators' strike, which failed in Canada just as it did in the United States.[101]

Ely's evaluation is significant, *"The Irish World and Industrial Liberator,* which is said to have an immense circulation, has been claimed as an exponent of socialism, but with how much truth I am unable to say." *Op. cit.,* p. 279.

[99] PP, John P. Bulman to Powderly, Buffalo, November 12, 1883.

[100] *Acta et decreta,* p. 12.

[101] Cf. O. D. Skelton, "General Economic History, 1867-1912," *Canada and*

The Order naturally grew more rapidly in Upper Canada, not only because of a more urban life there but also because it was a more hospitable environment for a secret quasi-fraternal organization than French Catholic Canada. For even in 1882 the Canadian Knights maintained temporarily absolute secrecy until they should have gathered sufficient strength to show themselves.[102]   By 1883 the Order had also entered Montreal but its growth would hardly indicate the same success there that it enjoyed throughout the Province of Ontario.[103]   Its origin in that commercial city of Lower Canada, however, is certainly worthy of note. William Keys later recounted how the first assembly was founded on January 12, 1883, and that with the blessing of Bishop Edouard Fabre. After contacting the Pittsburgh headquarters of the Knights he had thought it well to consult the churchman. His own account reads:

> Of course I would not have anything to do with the Order if Bishop Fabre disapproved of it. However I called on his Lordship and after explaining the object of my visit I handed him the constitution and secret work for examination stating that if he found anything objectionable that is to say that would conflict with our Holy Religion I would stop right there. His Lordship told me to call back in a week for an answer which I did, and he told me that he had not completed his examination. I called a week later when his Lordship handed me the constitution

its Provinces (Toronto, 1914), IX, 148-190; R. H. Coats, "The Labor Movement. in Canada," *Ibid.,* IX, 300-306; Harold Logan, *The History of Trade-Union Organization in Canada* (Chicago, 1928), pp. 43-80; Daniel J. O'Donoghue, "Labor Organization in Ontario," *Annual Report of the Bureau of Industries for the Province of Ontario, 1886* (Toronto, 1887), pp. 44-45.

[102] PP, James N. Brown to Powderly, Oshawa, Ontario, September 29, 1882.

[103] There were only three locals in Montreal by July, 1884, according to *Proceedings* (Hamilton, 1885), pp. 175-225, at least among those which submitted reports. Hamilton at the same time had a D. A. already functioning (*Ibid.,* p. 192), and there were no signs of any in Quebec. E.-Z. Massicotte, "Les chevaliers du travail," *Le bulletin des recherches historiques,* XL (August, 1934), 452-453, mistakenly gives 1882 as the date of the first assembly at Montreal, and arbitrarily claims the French Canadians were attracted by the ceremonies of the K. of L. since the Church barred them from "those fraternal organizations popular in the English speaking provinces."

and other documents stating that he did not see anything in the Organization that the Church could object to so, said he, go ahead and I hope your efforts will be crowned with success.[104]

In view of this auspicious beginning among French Canadians, it is not surprising that the first ecclesiastical flicker of doubt came instead from Hamilton, Ontario, the scene of the Order's first foundation across the border. Since that episcopal see was then vacant it was the Reverend M. J. Cleary of the cathedral staff, who wrote seeking the advice of Bishop Bernard J. McQuaid of Rochester. He wanted to know if he could legally give members of the growing labor group sacramental absolution and, if not, could he use McQuaid's name in his condemnation. The Canadian clergyman was being pressed into action by the brothers in the Emeralds, an Irish fraternal society of which he was chaplain. He concluded: "I have no reason to think that the constitutions of the 'Knights of Labor' *in force here* differ in any respect from the constitutions of the same order in the States." [105]

This same constitution had come into the hands of the Archbishop of Quebec who did not take the friendly, but independent, step of Montreal or the prudently cautious approach of Hamilton, but rather sought immediately a decision from Rome. What moved him to this action the extant and available documents have not revealed, except that his own letter to the Holy See showed that he was in the midst of investigating the progress of Masonry in his territory at the request of Rome. He referred to the problem of the Masonic-like labor societies, such as the telegraph operators and railroad workers, however, as "another very serious question the solution of which is most important and it seems ought to be defined by the Holy See." The basis for his action was given in recalling the distinction in favor of genuine labor unions made by the Second Plenary Council of Baltimore (1866) and also the mandate from the Congregation of the Propaganda (1865) on having recourse to Rome when there was difficulty in applying the decrees on

[104] PP, William Keys to Powderly, Montreal, January 25, 1887.

[105] RDA, M. J. Cleary to Bernard McQuaid, Hamilton, February 26, 1883. No answer was found, cf. p. 384.

secret societies. This was precisely what Taschereau was doing, although his consultation was rather brief to fulfill the requirements of the phrase, "all the factors in the situation having been clearly pointed out," ("et quidem adamussim omnibus expositis rerum adjunctis."). He simply handed the Roman officials the problem and made this wise suggestion:

> I transmit the enclosed constitutions of two associations, the 'Equitum laboris" (Knights of labor) and the 'Telegraphistarum' (Telegraphers), in order that a judgment may be more readily passed on the nature, purpose and means of these societies. The former might be examined more carefully since it seems to be more general in its extension to all kinds of labor.
>
> Since at the invitation of the Supreme Pontiff all the Archbishops of the United States of North America are soon to assemble in Rome to examine many questions which concern the discipline of the whole Union, I humbly ask that the question of these associations be examined by those Prelates who are better equipped to clear up the matter since such societies are more numerous in their provinces.
>
> The principles are most clear, but the practical application most intricate; and no better occasion can be found for putting an end to all doubts.[106]

No response came from the Propaganda for almost a year. Furthermore, there is no available evidence that the American archbishops while in Rome preparing a schema for the future council with the officials of the congregation were ever consulted on this specific problem. This series of Roman conferences from November 13 to December 10, 1883, nevertheless, did put the hierarchy of the United States on the stage of the Universal Church for the first time since the Vatican Council of 1870 and several of the American bishops were found quietly speaking up in defense of labor organizations.

[106] Taschereau to Cardinal Bilio, Quebec, October 5, 1883, in "Circulaire au clergé au sujet de deux sociétés secretes," contained in H. Têtu and C. O. Gagnon, *Mandements, lettres pastorales et circulaires des évêques de Québec* (Québec, 1890), II (Nouvelle série), 444-445. *La Vérité* (Québec), August 25, 1894, gives the only evidence that he received an "authentic copy of these constitutions and by-laws" printed by the Knights of Labor from a Catholic in the United States.

Since the interesting and involved story of the council of 1884, one of the most notable achievements of the Church in the United States, has never been definitively told, some of the procedure in Rome must be recounted here.[107]   The American prelates on arrival were presented with an outline of subjects which the officials of the Propaganda thought should be discussed in preparation for the scheduled national meeting.[108]   The second paragraph of the ninth chapter ("On Some Other Matters of Discipline") suggested merely that the decrees and instructions on secret societies should again be inculcated.   Doubtfully censured groups were to be considered among those prohibited if they demanded an oath of absolute secrecy or a promise of blind obedience.   The use of a ritualistic cult might make some of them subject to the penalty reserved for those falling into heresy or schism.   The bishops were advised to issue a decree on these matters in the council, "adding that in doubtful cases recourse should be made to the Sacred Congregation." [109]

This section of the preliminary plan was first discussed by the assembled prelates on November 24, 1883, in the presence of the Cardinal Prefect of the Propaganda, Giovanni Simeoni, and also Cardinals Giovanni B. Franzelin and Lodovico Jacobini, Bishop Luigi Sepiacci, "as consultor," and Domenico Jacobini, the secretary of the congregation.   Simeoni had twice told them they were to feel perfectly free to speak their minds on what was already prepared for discussion or on any other subject.[110]   Archbishop Gibbons was the first to comment on the paragraph on secret societies, and he indicated acceptance of it as it stood.   The Metropolitan of Oregon

[107] Peter Guilday, *A History of the Councils of Baltimore, 1791-1884* (New York, 1932), p. 224, says, "The inner history of these Roman meetings as well as that of the private congregations of the Council itself has not been written."

[108] "Capita praecipua quae Emi Cardinales S. C. de Propaganda Fide censuerunt a Rmis Archiepiscopis et Episcopis Foederatorum Statuum A. S. Romae Congregatis praeparanda esse pro futuro Concilio." (8 pages.)   Marked November 11, 1883, in "Documents, II and III Council of Baltimore," AAB.

[109] *Ibid.,* p. 5.

[110] *Relatio collationum quae Romae coram S. C. de P. F. Prafecto habuerunt archiepiscopi pluresque episcopi Statuum Foederatorum Americae* (Baltimore, n. d.), pp. 3, 4, November 13, 1883, the opening session, and his reassurance to Seghers, November 15, p. 7.

City, Charles J. Seghers, the Belgian-born "apostle of Alaska," spoke in detail of the difficulty of the bishops in applying the condemnation of secret associations. Not only were the members questioned deceitful, but the general norms such as were once more proposed for the council's consideration would again lead to varying and even opposite interpretations by the members of the hierarchy. Hence he pleaded for more specific rules which should be applied to individual societies. Concerning unions the report on Seghers follows:

> With regard to societies of workers, he added, it is scarcely possible to find any that can be considered licit. For most workers take an oath to stop work at the word of the chiefs of the association and also of keeping other workers from labor even through violence; moreover, in these associations there is always a prevailing number of heretics and so Catholics are forced to keep too great familiarity with heretics and therefore endanger their faith and piety; finally on account of the strength of heretics in these associations the Bishops can do nothing at all about directing them.[111]

Several of the attending prelates showed quick reaction to these sentiments. Francis Chatard of Vincennes hastened to second them and to add similar observations. But it was reported of James Gibbons and Patrick Feehan, "On the other hand, the Most Reverend Archbishops of Baltimore and Chicago said not all associations of workingmen had a bad and dangerous purpose. Many exist they said, which offer no reason for ecclesiastical condemnation or prohibition." [112] The Roman officials simply felt that the Holy See could not become more specific in its recommendations, but the individual bishops should be able to apply them after investigation of particular cases. They agreed that an oath, such as Seghers spoke of, was enough to condemn such groups as it was "de re injusta." The danger of contact with heretics, they observed, should be handled just as any case of those who are put in the occasion of sin, except where the danger to the faith of the Catholic came from the very nature of the association.

111 *Ibid.*, p. 22.
112 *Ibid.*

The question was again discussed in the session of November 29, and Bishop Chatard once more spoke on the difficulties of the problem. This time he concentrated on the Ancient Order of Hibernians ("Societatem Veterum Hibernorum!") and he aroused much disagreement among the other bishops, although Feehan, later their defender in the council itself, was absent on that particular day. The Propaganda prelates pointed out once more that the specific judgments on suspected societies had to be left to the bishops in council, or even arrived at "through a commission of prudent men," set up for that purpose.[113] In these observations they also added something which had not even been mentioned by an American prelate, namely, that the council should recommend the institution of societies of Catholic workingmen such as existed in Germany and France, "which although they propose a temporal and material end are subject to the clergy and directed by them."[114]

As the bishops returned to their American sees in the winter of 1883-1884 they carried away from Rome another outline, this time of the items considered at the Holy See and to be acted on at Baltimore. This showed that as a result of the discussions, and apparently just on the word of Propaganda, there was included the suggestion of the use of an investigating committee and the strong recommendation of religious labor associations on the European model. This final schema, at least in this regard, softened the expression to read, that the proposed societies "follow the counsel and direction of the clergy."[115] But recourse to the Holy See in case

[113] As Corrigan put it: "The Holy See declined entertaining question of fact, leaving to Ordinaries the duty of applying the principles of their guidance with instructions to recur to Rome in case of doubt." RDA, to McQuaid, New York, January 9, 1884.

[114] *Relatio*, p. 24. Their Eminences had little time for the opinion of Bishop Edward Fitzgerald of Little Rock, whom, perhaps, they remembered as one of the two negative votes on papal infallibility in 1870, to the effect that condemning secret societies did no good but laid the Church authority open to the "derision and contempt of the impious." *Ibid.*, p. 25.

[115] "Capita proposita et examinata in collationibus, quas coram non-nullis Emis Cardinalibus Sacrae Congregationis de Propaganda Fide ad praeparandum futurum Concilium plenarium habuerunt Rmi Archiepiscopi et Episcopi foederatorum Statuum Americae Septemtrionalis [*sic*] Romae congregati." (12 pages).

of their own inability to arrive at a decision, was the one item which remained uppermost in the mind of the American hierarchy, and in this respect Quebec had already anticipated them. They had not gone to Rome with a clear and undivided position on labor organizations, and so in that regard it would seem they were not able to be "united as one man" when they faced the congregation. This united front technique in most of the conferences had won the respect of official Rome, even to the extent of replacing Sepiacci with Gibbons as apostolic delegate to the coming council and of starting a rumor of red hats for both the Archbishop of Baltimore and Michael A. Corrigan, the Coadjutor Archbishop of New York.[116]

It was Taschereau, however, and not Corrigan, who was to receive the cardinalitial honor with Gibbons three years later, and it was he who several months after his first petition continued importunately to write Rome on the question of the Knights of Labor. With academic aloofness rather than hostility to the society he took the opportunity to mention the matter in returning the fifteen-page survey on Freemasonry in Canada which he had been requested to make by Luigi Cardinal Bilio. He repeated his suggestion that the American archbishops be consulted and expressed his anxiety for an answer. The two associations, about which he had inquired the previous October, were still classified as suspected societies, "which resemble Masonic ones, and about which it is not clearly evident that they machinate against the Church or the State, at least directly." He reported that such combinations had been labeled as "dangerous" many times in their councils and pastoral letters, but the Canadian bishops had not yet taken any step beyond exhortations to avoid or to quit them. In the case of those who could not leave such associations without great harm to themselves the archbishop had been accustomed to advise that no action be taken so long as they promised to follow the final decision of the Holy See and were meanwhile disposed to abstain from any acts of injustice. Thus Taschereau considered himself to be within the precedents prescribed by the Second Plenary Council of Baltimore, and he expressed further his

---

[116] AAT, J. J. Carbery to Archbishop Lynch, Cork, February 11, 1884.

perfect willingness to abide by any further instruction of the Congregation of Propaganda.[117]

The next word which came from the Holy See was from Pope Leo XIII himself. This was in the form of an encyclical letter on Freemasonry called *Humanum genus* of April 20, 1884. Since it was addressed to the bishops of the world it was general in character and like all such communications would not be considered as automatically binding with infallible authority. *Humanum genus* was particularly concerned with revolutionary European Masonry and could give no help toward the solution of the specific problem, which, although posed by the Canadian archbishop was of more vital interest to the bishops of the United States. Nevertheless it did call for "associations of guilds of workmen" under religious auspices.[118] An attempt to give this pronouncement teeth came in the form of an instruction of the Holy Roman and Universal Inquisition entitled, "De secta massonum" of May 10 of the same year.[119] At the command of the Holy Father it was sent to all ordinaries of dioceses. It outlined practical steps, such as the granting of faculties to approved confessors for one year to receive back adherents of condemned Masonic groups, advising a preaching and teaching campaign under the leadership of the hierarchy, and encouraging religious societies for youth and for parents, and for those giving themselves to prayers and pious works. Moreover, the instruction made a clarifying distinction between those Masonic and similar sects forbidden under penalty of excommunication *latae sententiae*, and "other prohibited sects which are to be avoided under pain of grievous sin." These latter were especially the ones which demanded an oath of absolute secrecy or of blind obedience to unknown leaders. Finally, there was a third classification of other groups which were to be re-

[117] AAQ, T. 202, "Rapport fait à Rome sur la Franc-maçonnerie au Canada," January 7, 1884. In general it played down the impression of "abnormal progress" of Masonry and proposed to counteract it by means of pastorals, the press, and the pulpit.

[118] John J. Wynne (Ed.), *The Great Encyclical Letters of Pope Leo XIII* (New York, 1903), p. 103.

[119] *Collectanea sacrae congregationis de propaganda fide* (Rome, 1907), II, 198-200.

garded as dangerous, on account of suspicious doctrine and untrustworthy leaders. Regarding the workers, among whom subversive forces were said to be always active, the bishops were offered the guilds as model associations which cared for the spiritual as well as the temporal welfare of their members. This reference to Catholic associations of workers must have sounded strange to American bishops, especially when it enjoined: "Nor are these same Bishops to fail to guard such societies, to prepare and approve laws for them, to win the favor of the wealthy, to keep them under their patronage, and to assist them in a practical way." They were advised, finally, that only by the united efforts of the archbishops and their suffragans could this work of saving society be accomplished. The congregation was desirous of receiving accounts as soon as possible of whatever action they might undertake, and thereafter it was to be made part of the regular diocesan reports to Rome.

Some of the hierarchy in promulgating these messages from Rome on Freemasonry elaborated a little of their own ideas on labor societies. Taschereau proclaimed such organizations to be dangerous and deceivers of the working class by their pretenses to mutual protection and charity. In addition he looked on them as responsible for much harm to public peace and order and the general welfare of the workingman.[120] Much less disturbed was the Archbishop of Toronto, John J. Lynch, who assured the Pope that the Irish Catholics who made up most of his flock were adverse to Masonry and had set up their own patriotic and benevolent societies to counteract any attraction which it might have. He praised Leo XIII's encyclical and detailed for the Pontiff the progress of his archdiocese.[121]

One of the closest American neighbors to the Canadian hierarchy, James A. Healy of Portland, Maine, made one of his pertinent public statements at this time. This bishop was distrustful of all secret societies, even though they professed only the highest purposes. On the labor scene he remarked: "Even the beardless boys in their unions

---

[120] Têtu-Gagnon, *op. cit.,* II, 434. "Mandement, 29 Juin, promulgant une encyclique du souverain pontife contre le franc-maçonnerie," quoting the pastoral of the IV Provincial Council of Quebec, 1868.

[121] AAT, copy or rough draft of letter to the Holy Father, only date, 1884.

must have not only signs and passwords, and grips known only to members, but ceremonies of initiation, oath, threats, which they do not publish even in their manuals." The Church approved, he continued, open and honorable "societies and guilds of mechanics," but "no union ought to succeed that is founded upon injustice and violence to outsiders; that pretends to take the bread from the mouth of all who are not union men; that ranks the imperfect tradesman or mechanic with and above the better workman simply because he is a union man." [122]

Healy in his border-line position in Maine also continued to be close to Taschereau in his outlook on the problem of the Knights of Labor. His pastoral, although somewhat specific, was an indication that the hierarchy in the United States by the middle of 1884 had yet to face the issue. In the previous few years some hesitant action had been taken by individuals among them, but as a body they were still only formulating general principles. Consequently their procedure was to be slower but, therefore, more lenient and more independent of Rome than was that of their Canadian counterpart.

[122] ADPM, Pastoral of July 10, 1884. Among the suffragans of the Metropolitan of New York only the Bishop of Buffalo made a pertinent remark, for he thought workers groups served "as feeders to Freemasonry." NYAA, S. Ryan to Corrigan, Buffalo, August 9, 1884.

CHAPTER IV

QUEBEC AND BALTIMORE

By the time the year 1884 had half elapsed the American labor scene had become more hectic than it had been for a long while. Serving to render the industrial expansion more acute for the toiler, the depression of 1883-1885, with its consequent wage reductions and unemployment drew many into the labor movement from among the less-skilled workers. As one historian has expressed it, "the idea of the solidarity of labour ceased to be merely verbal and took on flesh and life; general strikes, sympathetic strikes, nation-wide boycotts, and nation-wide political movements became the order of the day." [1] The Knights of Labor by 1884 had adopted the policy of supporting strikes when the executive board judged it wise, but though the organization was involved in many strikes during that year it was the guiding spirit of only a few. [2] These economic weapons were used in nearly every case to protest against wage cuts and to proclaim publicly the right to combine for self-protection. Generally speaking the strikes were failures, but this did not mean that the Knights were falling off, for their membership rolls by September, 1884, showed an increase of about 20,000 to bring them to a total of 71,326. [3] The Order, moreover, was not at this time as concerned with opposition from the Catholic Church as it was with more secular affairs. Ecclesiastics, on the other hand, while outwardly quieter than in the preceding years, were fashioning the canonical procedure by which the group would eventually be examined. This was demonstrated especially by the work of the

---

[1] Commons, *History*, II, 357. On the condition of the workers in general, Henry David, *The History of the Haymarket Affair* (New York, 1936), p. 13, says, "Implicit in the statistics of the distribution of national wealth and income is the fact that a considerable part of the American working class lived neither far from nor securely above the poverty line."

[2] Ware, *op. cit.*, p. 133.

[3] *Proceedings* (Philadelphia, 1884), p. 583.

Third Plenary Council of Baltimore in November, 1884, which followed closely on the first official action in Quebec.

Even before these steps were taken, however, there was still found on the local level a certain suspicion and fear on the part of Catholics toward membership in the Knights of Labor. The policy of Powderly was one of openness, and requests for advice from members puzzled by ecclesiastical relationships resulted in the formation of committees which, armed with letters from the master workman and copies of the constitution and the A. K., went calling on their pastors.[4] In Easton, Pennsylvania, for example, the pastor, the Reverend John R. Dillon, based his suspicion not on any particular knowledge of the Knights, but on the simple rule "that the Church was against all secret societies." After a pleasant interview he promised to refer the matter to higher authority in Philadelphia.[5] The parish priests of Schuylkill County were probably in Powderly's mind when he said he was not too anxious to see an attempt at reorganization in that trouble spot of Pennsylvania.[6] The pastors would have found legitimate reason to be upset if they had known that the old ritual was still in use in at least one town of the area in question.[7] From a more distant, but also very Catholic, center an apparently unanswered inquiry came to the G. M. W. from the prominent Catholic layman and publisher of the *Pilot,* Patrick Donahoe. After Powderly had made an address in Boston Donahoe told him that none of the city's three Catholic papers had taken note of it, and this silence led the Boston editor to ask him the Church's position on the association.[8] In pointing out that the New England Knights had met in an "infidel Hall" he put his finger on something that was quite common, probably as much because Masonic and fraternal brotherhoods controlled such

4 PP, George Wild to Powderly, Belleville, Illinois, November 27, 1883; G. H. Buck to Powderly, Humboldt, Kansas, June 16, 1884.

5 PP, James Hardcastle to Powderly, S. Easton, March 12, 1884; also March 2, 7.

6 PP, M. A. Leary to Powderly, Mahanoy Plane, April 21, 1884; Powderly to Leary, May 20, 1884, copy.

7 PP, Charles H. Carl to Powderly, Mahanoy City, August 4, 1884.

8 PP, May 10, 1884.

meeting places, as for any other reason. Yet, as far as the records show, the use of these halls was not so great an irritant to the Catholic clergy as might have been expected.

As a matter of fact, when the Order celebrated "the fifteenth and most successful year of Knighthood," in the city of its birth from September 1 to 10, 1884, there was no word of any difficulty with the Catholic Church. Several aspects of that gathering were, nevertheless, of some importance for the association's future relations with churchmen. In the first place, "the constitution underwent a radical change at this session," and the first alteration was affected in the preamble of principles of the Order, since the initial convention of the general assembly.[9] Thus once again the Knights were able to argue, as they had after the elimination of the oath in 1882, that they had sufficiently changed their character to warrant a new adjudication at the hands of the Church.[10] Of even greater interest, in the light of the source of the first clerical fulmination, was the fact that the general secretary was still complaining that he had been unable to get anyone to translate the ritual into French, although a German translation of it and of other items such as the constitution was already in existence.[11] Moreover, the official listing of local assemblies showed in the Canadian Province of Ontario eight such groups in Hamilton, nine in Toronto, three in London, and others scattered in over a dozen more towns, but only three existing in the Province of Quebec and those all in the city of Montreal.[12]

[9] *Proceedings* (Philadelphia, 1884), "Address of the General Master Workman," p. 569; Powderly, *Thirty Years,* pp. 636-637; text of changes, *Proceedings,* pp. 768-785.

[10] A circular, "Secret Work and Instructions," undated, but distributed by John W. Hayes, who was elected general secretary-treasurer in November, 1888, noted, "The general assembly at the Philadelphia session, decided to return to the old form of initiation, and the A. K. is changed accordingly. . . ." It would seem, however, that Hayes was referring to the order of procedure rather than content since in the 1886 publication of Ezra Cook the old quasi-religious trimmings were still missing.

[11] *Proceedings,* pp. 582, 795.

[12] *Proceedings* (1884) shows none in Lower Canada for the year ending July 1, 1884, pp. 797-843. But *Proceedings* (Hamilton, 1885) reveals the above condition as of that same date, pp. 175-225.

Nonetheless, it was to the clergy of the Archdiocese of Quebec that a circular went out under date of October 17, 1884, from the vicar general and administrator, Cyrille E. Legaré, who was acting in the name of the absent Archbishop Taschereau. Its brief introductory note merely expressed Legaré's belief that a knowledge of the two documents contained therein would be useful to the priests. They were the petition to Rome of their archbishop and the long delayed response from the Congregation of Propaganda which was dated simply September, 1884.[13] The latter document contained the formal condemnation passed by the Holy Office on the preceding August 27 after "accurate and mature examination." It read:

> After examining the principles, organization, and statutes of the Society of the Knights of labor, as they have been exposed, that society ought to be considered among those prohibited by the Holy See, according to the instruction of this Supreme Congregation of May 10, 1884 and according to its intention. Its intention is that it be commended to the Bishops to take steps with regard to those delated and similar Societies, and to use remedies according to the commands and counsel which are contained in the same Instruction.[14]

Quebec's private "Circulaire au clergé" served as a model for a similar announcement in the suffragan Diocese of Montreal on November 4, 1884, where Bishop Fabre thought he, too, should conform with the judgment expressed by the Holy See.[15] Although it contained a formal and *nominatim* condemnation of the Knights of Labor, *prout exponuntur* (passing over the question of the telegraph workers), the decision does not seem to have caused any immediate furor.

Actually Powderly at this time had just about finished a speaking tour of Ontario and it was the presence of the general master workman rather than any Roman directive that brought on a momentary flare-up of the religious issue. In this case it proved to be a blessing for the Order. Papers in London, Toronto, and Hamilton carried

---

13 Têtu-Gagnon, *Mandements,* II, 444-447. This response was printed in both the original Italian and French.

14 The original is found in AAQ, CMR, 28, Simeoni to Taschereau.

15 AAM, Consultation, Knights of Labor, August 17, 1886, Appendix I.

accounts of the labor leader's exposition of the aims and purposes of the Knights of Labor.[16] Although Powderly had disavowed communism and pointed out how men of all religions worked harmoniously together in the organization, the *Tribune* of Toronto took him to task for avoiding the issue of secrecy and the opposition of the Catholic Church toward the Order on that account. The *Tribune* was, in turn, answered by Dan O'Donoghue under the name of "Workingman." [17] This active Toronto laborite likewise undertook, at the request of the general master workman, to call on Archbishop Lynch armed with a copy of the filial apologia, dated October 24, which had been written by Powderly with special reference to Archbishop Ryan of Philadelphia. Echoing the Scranton leader's views, O'Donoghue felt sure of success, for although he had previously encountered unfriendly priests, he had remained undisturbed and "Catholic to the core." "My faith," he added, "never suffered, but rather the obverse, by trying to have the warmest sympathy for the ills and sufferings of my fellowman, and endeavouring to the utmost of my humble ability to lighten or mitigate them." [18]

O'Donoghue described himself as "jubilant" and "more than delighted" after his interview with "the far-seeing, enlightened and worldly-practical John Joseph Lynch, the venerated Archbishop of Toronto." He related how feeling very much at his ease, he had first explained his mission and agreement with Powderly's views, and had then assured Lynch that, "like you, I was ready to leave the organization if he so ordered." The archbishop's reaction was described thus:

> He heard me through with patience and attention. He then said: "I will put my answer to this gentleman (yourself) and yourself in a few words. I recognize the *right*—the *urgent*

[16] PP, Scrapbook, January, 1884-September, 1885, London *Advertiser,* October 10; Toronto *News,* October 14; *Evening Times* (Hamilton), October 14.

[17] PP, *Ibid., Tribune,* October 18, 25, 1884.

[18] PP, O'Donoghue to Powderly, Toronto, October 27, 1884. Cf. for an appreciation John G. O'Donoghue, "Daniel John O'Donoghue, Father of the Canadian Labor Movement," *Report, 1942-1943* of the Canadian Catholic Historical Association (Ottawa, 1943), pp. 87-96.

necessity—of organization on the part of labor as against greedy and unscrupulous capital. I never have, will not now, nor never will condemn the honest efforts of workingmen and women to protect themselves against the oftentimes outrageous exactions of selfish tyrants and monopolists. I am glad to learn of the conservative spirit evinced by this organization. Let it avoid violence, practice and preach temperance, and educate to a proper use of the ballot in their own interest, and I care but little for what its name may be, or the nonsense of its formularies. Don't come to me again on this subject, work away for the good of yourself and those of your class, and God bless you all." [19]

In the course of their talk, which lasted an hour and a half, the Archbishop of Toronto, to O'Donoghue's surprise, mentioned knowingly and with sympathy the recent unsuccessful strikes of the telegraphers—whose "treatment by the monopoly" he called "heinous"—carpenters, plasterers, and others. Strikes were justifiable, he asserted, when arbitration failed because of capital's refusal to be a party to it. He recalled also his activity years earlier in preventing the First Provincial Council of Quebec from denouncing the typographical union.[20] It is small wonder that the labor leader was led to describe Lynch as "one of those who believes that Catholicity if properly implanted in the first instance, will not suffer by education in the direction of the assertion of unquestionable right and justice." Seeming to put a final seal on his approval, the archbishop invited O'Donoghue to attend the celebration of the silver jubilee of his episcopal consecration. Over forty prelates were to be present, including Archbishop Ryan of Philadelphia as preacher, and O'Donoghue felt that he was to meet them all, and especially Ryan, since Lynch had told him, *"we* could talk the matter over at that time." [21]

It is not presently known whether such a conference ever took place, but it is at least certain that the two archbishops had a chance to discuss in person the Knights of Labor since a week after the events in Toronto, the Third Plenary Council of Baltimore opened on November 6, 1884, and toward the end of the council

[19] *Ibid.,* November 1, 1884.
[20] *Vide supra,* p. 30.
[21] PP, O'Donoghue to Powderly, November 1, 1884.

Lynch was present as a guest observer. Besides these two opportunities for enlightenment from the Archbishop of Toronto, Ryan was also directly briefed on the labor organization, by a communication from Powderly, and by direct contact with other officers. The contact grew out of the circumstance that about the time of the death of Archbishop Wood in June, 1883, the hostility of the pastor of Schuylkill Falls had been sufficient to cause concern to the district master workman, James A. Wright.[22] This parochial condemnation was apparently no passing whim, for it had to be faced again after the arrival of Patrick J. Ryan as Wood's successor in June, 1884.[23] This priest, William Walsh, not only "laid out" the general secretary, Frederick Turner, but he branded Powderly a Mason and in refusing to look at letters of explanation, he acted, in Turner's phrase, like "a perfect bulldog." Most illogically he said he was against the Knights or any union in his parish, although he did not care about other localities. The only benefit from the interview with Father Walsh arose from the fact that the officials of the Knights of Labor were sent to the archbishop who received them very pleasantly and said, "he had no objections to the K. L. but would not interfere with the parish priest as yet." [24]

Powderly took advantage of these circumstances to practice more of the ecclesiastical diplomacy in which he seemed to revel, and even to covet for himself, when the occasion of exercising it arose. He wrote to Turner telling of his letter to Ryan and the copy "to another Archbishop," and instructed him, "If Bishop Ryan sends

[22] PP, James A. Wright to Powderly, Philadelphia, August 1, 1888.

[23] Born in Ireland in 1831, coadjutor of Archbishop Kenrick of St. Louis, 1872-1884; died in 1911.

[24] William Walsh as late as 1883 was curate at St. Paul's Church, Philadelphia, where the Very Reverend Maurice A. Walsh, mentioned above as opposing the Knights, was pastor. PP, Powderly to Turner, September 25, 1884, copy; Turner to Powderly, Philadelphia, October 23, 1884. It would seem that at least James A. Wright was with the general secretary, since he speaks in the plural, and the D. M. W. later recalled, "I afterwards on death of Wood waited on Archbishop Ryan, the last visit was with Bro Turner. He also was in favor of the Order, and said, 'Any priest, or others who were disinterested and would oppose the K. of L. did not know its good mission.'" To Powderly, August 1, 1888.

for you tell him that you will leave the matter to me."[25] His explanation to the Philadelphia prelate first disabused him of the notion that he was a Freemason and laid the blame for the charge to the habit of many Irishmen of accusing any successful one from their ranks of being a member of a secret society. He further reassured him concerning his practical if not too devout Catholicism and he went on to detail his achievement in eliminating the elements in the make-up of the Knights that had been unacceptable to Catholics. On temperance he pointed out, with an allusion to local history, ". . . we are determined that the evils which sprung from the use of strong drink, sold to them by members of their own order, and which brought disgrace not only upon the laboring men of Schuylkill Co., Pa. but upon a *nation* as well will never with the help of God be visited upon the Knights of Labor." By quoting a letter written to an anxious member in Maine, the general master workman hoped to convince the archbishop that the Knights were not a secret society of the condemned sort, and that they were even hostile to socialists, communists, and anarchists. Powderly went so far as to claim, "They had a foothold in the order when I took charge of it but I instantly declared war on them and they *went out to stay*." If the final assertion here was of doubtful accuracy another sentence may have flowed from at least a momentary conviction. It read: "I wish to God that all of our members were as true to the cause of the poor and oppressed as the priest."[26]

The labor leader's approach was obviously to make himself and the "labor society pure and simple" as acceptable as possible to Archbishop Ryan before the convening of the council at Baltimore. His extreme good will was shown by his offer to bring Ryan at Philadelphia any other desired information, including copies of the constitution or the ritual. Furthermore, he said expressly: "We are willing to place everything before your Council and ask advice, promising that so far as we ourselves are concerned we will do everything in our power to remove objections." In depicting the alternative, Powderly foresaw the necessity of what has become a commonplace and authorized Catholic position concerning non-

[25] PP, Powderly to Turner, October 28, 1884, copy.
[26] Powderly to George N. McGregor, September 30, 1884, copy.

religious labor associations. He appealed also on the less noble grounds of preserving a supposed Catholic control, saying,

> If I am commanded to leave the order I am willing to do so but I hope and pray that no such order will go forth from the Baltimore council for if it does it will deprive the Catholic working man of the only remedy he now possesses, it will drive him from an order where he now has the controlling power and leave the order to those of other faiths. We must work with men of other religions and I know from bitter experience that what we are not able to take will never be given to us without the asking, and if we ask for living wages without having an organization at our back we will never receive them. Turn us out of this organization and it becomes a protestant association with a return to oathbound secrecy, and instead of a blessing to us it will prove a curse.[27]

The lack of any evidence of co-operative action—even an answer —on the part of Archbishop Ryan would indicate that a valuable opportunity to clarify the issue was lost.[28] The absence of documentation from ecclesiastical archives, of course, compels the historian to leave the reasons open to speculation.

Consequently the work of the American prelates in Baltimore, insofar as the records show, did not include any specific mention of the Knights of Labor. Labor organizations in general were considered, however, and, more important still, the machinery for judging suspected societies was set up. Since the meeting of the American bishops in Rome in the fall of 1883, it had been left to the metropolitans, together with their suffragans, to study further the "Capita proposita et examinata" and to concentrate especially on their assigned sections. The ninth chapter dealing in part with prohibited societies fell to the lot of Archbishop Corrigan, who formed a committee with three bishops of the Province of New York, John Loughlin

---

[27] PP, Powderly to Ryan, October 24, 1884, copy. He claimed therein that over half of 250,000 members were Roman Catholics, and nearly half of 150 convention delegates; but since the religion of the members was not asked his estimate was probably little more than a guess.

[28] BCA, 81-S-13, Powderly to the Reverend Francis Carew, August 31, 1886. He told his old pastor he never received an answer of any kind.

of Brooklyn, Francis McNeirny of Albany, and Winand M. Wigger of Newark. This committee drew up some suggestions. These were first submitted to the other suffragans and then forwarded to Baltimore where the final schema was prepared for the council.[29] The finished product of the deliberations of the various committees formed part of a forty-page booklet published and distributed by Archbishop Gibbons.[30] The bishops suggested that consideration be given to questionable societies under a four-fold classification, namely, those condemned by name, those constituting participation *in sacris* with heretics or schismatics, those with secrets not revealed even to the Church or an oath (or promise) of absolute obedience, and finally those which affected workmen. On these last they added a hitherto unmentioned note for conciliar discussion when they proposed, "that those associations be considered evil and forbidden which are unjustly prepared to prevent craftsmen or workers from exercising their industry or labor according to the laws of the country either in hiring the labor of others, or contracting for their own, and this especially if violence is added to injustice." [31]   These New York bishops agreed that in doubtful cases the members of the hierarchy should investigate before applying the principle and if uncertainty still remained, then as a last resort there should be recourse to the Holy See. Admitting that they could learn from the enemies of the Church, they advised also the speedy institution of "Associations and Societies of Catholic workingmen" on the European model suggested by the outline prepared in Rome for the council.

When the American hierarchy assembled in Baltimore they found in the *Schema decretorum* a section entitled, "De societatibus secretis." [32]   The discussion on this matter was held on December

[29] RDA, Committee Report, July 4, 1884.

[30] *Relationes eorumque disceptata fuerunt ab illmis ac revmis metropolitis cum suis suffraganeis in suis singulis provinciis super schema futuri concilii praesertim vero super capita cuique commissa* (Baltimore, 1884).

[31] *Ibid.*, p. 32.

[32] Pp. 72-77, the fourth chapter of the eighth title, "On Zeal for Souls." The deputation which previously worked on it was made up of Archbishop Francis X. Leray of New Orleans and Bishops Edward Fitzgerald of Little Rock, Martin Marty, O.S.B., Vicar Apostolic of Dakota, John J. Keane of Richmond, Dominic Manucy, Administrator of Mobile, Isidore Robot, O.S.B.,

1. As might have been anticipated Bishop Chatard of Vincennes showed a continued interest in this question. Due to the inquiry he had made previous to the opening of the council, the Propaganda had sent a reminder that the bishops were to take into consideration the instruction "De secta massonum" of May 10, 1884.[33] Chatard first suggested in council the condemnation of the Ancient Order of Hibernians, which resulted in a somewhat violent disagreement that was quieted only by Archbishop Feehan's defense of them.[34] The Indiana bishop, just as he had done before the Roman officials the previous year, was still seeking to decide on questions of fact, and Corrigan, for one, later pointed this out. The Coadjutor of New York, in dismissing Chatard's complaint about Gibbons' handling of the council, added, "It strikes me that if any opposition was manifested to Bishop Chatard in Baltimore during the Council, it was for a similar reason. We had not the *material time* to enter into such discussions; nor the means at hand of pursuing the investigation." [35]

Corrigan's observation was very true and the realization of it was shown by the suggestion of Bishop John L. Spalding of Peoria early in the debate on the Ancient Order of Hibernians that for the sake of uniformity a commission of five or more archbishops be set up, "who would prudently and accurately deliberate on these things and finally decide in the name of the Council." [36] This was a counter-proposal to the item of the schema which called for consultation and uniformity of action in doubtful cases only by the bishops within each separate province.[37] Alemany expressed his preference

Prefect Apostolic of Indian Territory. There were also eleven theologians and a notary, too, in the person of Charles P. Grannan. *Acta et decreta concilii plenarii Baltimorensis tertii* (Baltimore, 1884), p. ix. This private edition of the conciliar legislation contains also the minutes of the private congregations. The 1886 edition was the one edited for public use only after Rome's official approval had been given to the legislation.

[33] BCA, 78-Q-4, Simeoni to Gibbons, Rome, October 3, 1884; AAB, Simeoni to Williams, "De dispensationibus matrimonialibus et de societatibus secretis," October 2, 1884. Cf. Macdonald, *op. cit.,* p. 109.

[34] *Ibid.,* pp. 109-114.

[35] ADC, Corrigan to Gilmour, New York, September 4, 1885.

[36] *Acta et decreta* (1884), p. lxxvi.

[37] *Schema decretorum,* pp. 76-77.

for making all the archbishops members, and to this all the fathers of the council agreed. At the end of the heated remarks on the Hibernians, however, McQuaid arose to suggest a committee be designated to inquire into the nature and purpose of that society and to make a report to the council. The Metropolitans of Chicago, Philadelphia, San Francisco, and Baltimore were already nominated when Spalding reminded the assembly of what had already been said by himself and Alemany about the necessity of a "Permanent Commission of all the Archbishops who would inquire into societies about which a doubt had arisen and make a judgment on them." After that clarification once again the conciliar minutes merely record, "Quod omnes probarunt." [38]

According to the decrees, therefore, the process of judging particular societies was to begin with individual bishops. They were to examine personally, or through others, the workings of suspected organizations to see if they deserved condemnation from their very nature or whether it was rather from circumstances surrounding them. These groups would no longer be merely those militating against the Church or the State, but also those forbidden by reason of secrecy or blind obedience. Thus there was removed "the hampering restriction of the Second Plenary Council," which had excluded from condemnatory action practically all the secret orders in the United States.[39] The bishops, however, were restricted by the further clause calling for use of the committee of archbishops. It read:

> Moreover, in order to avoid having the confusion of discipline which results in great scandal to the faithful and detriment to ecclesiastical authority when the same society is condemned in one diocese and tolerated in another we do not wish any society to be condemned by name as falling within one of the indicated classes, before the Ordinary should have referred the matter to the Commission, which we have now set up to judge cases of this kind, and which will consist of all the archbishops of these provinces.[40]

[38] *Acta et decreta* (1884), p. lxxviii. J. S. Alemany, Abp. San Francisco, 1884.
[39] Macdonald, *op. cit.*, pp. 116-117.
[40] The pioneer historian of the Catholic Church in the United States, John Gilmary Shea, "The Coming Council of Baltimore," *American Catholic Quarterly Review,* IX (April, 1884), 350, had suggested a "permanent committee of bishops and theologians to investigate the facts about each association."

Even the heads of the twelve metropolitan sees were not to be a court of last appeal, for the final and key sentence of the decree read: "But if a society will not have seemed to all to be deserving of condemnation recourse shall be had to the Holy See in order to receive a sure judgment and preserve uniform discipline in our provinces." [41]

One item of the decrees of 1866 remained unchanged; that was the exception made for bona fide labor organizations, which was quoted word for word.[42] With regard to the recommendation for Catholic societies of workingmen on the European model the bishops found a rather watered-down version in the *Schema decretorum* under the heading "De societatibus honestis," which they accepted.[43] On Corrigan's suggestion the phrase, "nec semper peccandi [*sic*] libidine," was dropped. This had alluded to the bishops' belief that besides mutual benevolence and protection, or self improvement and recreation, there were often sinful causes that made "joining" such a popular American pastime. The prelates in council approved the setting up and promotion whenever possible under the patronage of the bishops, of "Societies of Catholic proletarians, workers and other citizens, which although they have a temporal and material purpose, nevertheless follow the counsel and direction of the clergy." [44] It may be noted that even the first draft of the decrees omitted the word, "proletariorum." [45]

Catholic societies of the type mentioned had been recommended by the Holy See as a more effective cure of the evils of secret so-

41 *Acta et decreta* (1884), p. 84. It was the same in the final edition of 1886, pp. 143-144.

42 *Acta et decreta* (1886), pp. 142-143.

43 *Ibid.* (1884), p. lxxviii. One of the public sermons given at the council was by Bishop John J. Keane on "Catholic Societies," *Memorial Volume. A History of the Third Plenary Council of Baltimore, November 9-December 7, 1884* (Baltimore, 1885), pp. 190-208. He warned, of course, against the secret societies which in effect substituted natural benevolence and religion for the Church, p. 206.

44 *Schema decretorum*, p. 77.

45 *Acta et decreta* (1884), p. 84. Denis O'Connell worked on this draft of the decrees of the council after its close in Gibbons' residence, and may, therefore, have been responsible for this verbal change. NYAA, O'Connell to Corrigan, Baltimore, December 13, 1884.

cieties than that of "penalties and fear"; but how widespread were the American attempts to carry out this recommendation, now re-echoed by the council, has never been thoroughly studied. One archival item revealed the existence of the Catholic Benevolent Legion, founded in 1881 "for the social, benevolent and intellectual improvement of Catholic men in a fraternal organization." [46] Another booklet, and this of only four pages, contains the "Constitution and By-Laws of the Catholic Workmen's Benevolent Union," organized in 1887. Its expressed object was "the union of Catholic workingmen under the banner of mutual benevolence, charity, temperance, social and material improvement," and its approval by Monsignor Thomas Preston, Vicar General of New York, was indicated. Of a similar nature were the Irish Catholic Benevolent Union with its headquarters in Philadelphia and the Catholic Knights of America which was incorporated in Kentucky in 1880.[47] That even such Catholic groups were susceptible to the spirit of the times was shown in 1881 when Bishop McQuaid, thinking they were aping secret societies, had required the Catholic Mutual Benevolence Association meeting in his see city to "abolish the ritual and all the emblems over the officers' chair." [48]

The pastoral letter of December 7, 1884, published by the American hierarchy at the close of the council in Baltimore, on the other hand, did give a special word of commendation to one social effort within the Church, namely, the Catholic Young Men's National Union. This was followed by a word of praise for "the various forms of Catholic beneficial societies and kindred associations of Catholic workingmen." The bishops continued: "It ought to be, and we trust is everywhere their aim to encourage habits of industry, thrift and sobriety; to guard the members against the dangerous attractions of condemned or suspicious organizations." [49] Much attention was given by the prelates in their message to the faithful to the evils of these latter societies. These words were not applied

[46] NYAA, Robert T. Rea, "An Address to Catholic Workingmen."
[47] This latter group paid upwards of $1,600,000 in benefits in seven years to families of deceased members. *Catholic Standard,* January 15, 1887.
[48] RDA, McQuaid Diary, January 31, 1881.
[49] Guilday, *National Pastorals,* p. 262.

directly to labor groups, but the exception made for genuine unions was not mentioned and only the admonition from the decrees of almost twenty years before about evil purposes being sometimes latent in workingmen's societies was read from the Catholic pulpits of the nation.[50] Yet the encouraging solution of the canonical procedure to be used with suspected societies at least made for a kindly caution which would prevent ill-considered condemnations. This regulation was translated into readily understandable terms for the laity thus:

> While therefore the Church, before prohibiting any society, will take every precaution to ascertain its true nature, we positively forbid any pastor, or other ecclesiastic, to pass sentence on any association or to impose ecclesiastical penalties or disabilities on its members without the previous explicit authorization of the rightful authorities.[51]

Such opinions of high ecclesiastics conceived in the cloister of council had little immediate practical value in influencing the hesitant, if not hostile, attitude of some Catholics toward the Knights of Labor which still lingered as a "stigma cast on it." [52] A letter of endorsement from a priest or just the word that Catholics were permitted to belong was eagerly sought.[53] A favorable report was made to Powderly that the Bishop of Fort Wayne before the council had allowed one of his priests to be lenient even after having examined the ritual.[54] Some months afterward, this same prelate, Joseph Dwenger, spoke very explicitly on the question of capital and labor. The neglect of Christian principles, he pointed out in his pastoral, had led capital to ignore the idea of justice in determining wages. Labor unions were wrong only when they coerced others to follow their opinion, and Dwenger seemed to frown on the closed shop when he wrote, "No labor union has a right to dictate that none

---

[50] *Ibid.*, p. 259.

[51] *Ibid.*, p. 260. Cf. Macdonald, *op. cit.*, p. 119.

[52] PP, John P. Bulman to Powderly, Buffalo, December 7, 1884.

[53] PP, P. W. McGowan to Powderly, Raleigh, September 24, 1884; George Lake, Meriden, Mississippi, October 5; John J. O'Connor, Easton, December 17, 1884.

[54] PP, W. H. Hanford to Powderly, South Bend, October 15, 1884.

but their members shall work in a certain place." He deplored the excesses caused by unprincipled men "leading the poor laborers into strikes, into riots, yea even bloodshed," and he warned Catholics if unions used illegitimate means they would have to give up their membership.[55]

Bishop Dwenger, in instructing his people, brought principles down to practical application as much because of the times as any other reason. He did not speak in a vacuum, for the year 1885 was one marked by great aggravation of what he referred to as, "the greatest question of the present age," that of capital and labor. The boycott came into widespread use when strikes generally failed, and the strikes in 1885 were far more spontaneous and unorganized than was true of earlier outbreaks. Especially was this true in so far as they affected the lowest brackets of workers, the unskilled and aliens. Railroad strikes were particularly frequent in 1885, and outstanding among these was that which began in March on the roads controlled by Gould in the Southwest. When Gould sat down to arbitrate with the executive board of the Knights of Labor it marked the high point in power of American labor organizations up to that time. This fact gave material for sensational columns to the newspapers which, in turn, added to the prominence of this new emancipator of the masses, and helped to spread the Order even more widely.[56]

As far as the Church was concerned, the year 1885 witnessed early reactions in Canada to Taschereau's Rome-inspired pronouncements. Across the border to the south there were widely scattered and totally variant positions taken by churchmen. The one case of exceptional and intense interest was that of the Bishop of Portland, Maine. On the whole the action emanating from Quebec led to an agitation of the matter, while that from Baltimore was as yet ineffective. The general secretary of the Knights, however, was convinced that the bishops' pastoral had not only succeeded in quieting Father Walsh of Schuylkill Falls, but that it had ended

---

[55] "Pastoral of Rt. Rev. Joseph Dwenger," Fort Wayne, Sexagesima Sunday, 1885. Treasure Room, UND.

[56] Cf. Commons, *History*, II, 364-371.

their troubles with the Church in the United States, leaving only "the battle with it in Canada." [57]

Turner accepted the latter as inevitable since Powderly had just forwarded to him a letter of William Keys and a committee in Montreal.[58] The news was that the French parish priest of St. James Church in that city had denounced the Order on the basis of the Quebec circular, and that he had threatened the Catholic brothers with excommunication unless they withdrew. Keys found things "pretty hot" since in organizing the local assemblies, the members of which he estimated were at least four-fifths Catholic, he had put to good use the story of his early and friendly interview with Fabre about the Order.[59] Once again, as at the time of its establishment in the city, a committee called on the Bishop of Montreal and again they had "a very pleasant interview." His advice was based on the presumption that since the decision came from Rome it would be promulgated in the United States as well as in Canada. Hence Fabre counseled the Knights that they should have Powderly see the Bishop of Scranton, not only to have him, in turn, contact Fabre, but to seek to bring the American hierarchy around to a favorable position which would be "a means for our bishops to write to Rome, showing the necessity of this organization in Canada as well as the United States." The bishop was described as surprised at Rome's order, and the Knights' committee was pictured as most willing to conform to any ecclesiastically inspired alterations within the framework of the Knights of Labor.[60] Whether from distaste for his own bishop or the desire to contact the ranking American prelate (or at least to appear to do so) Powderly, "sick of this crossfire business," resolved to go to New York "to see *Cardinal McCloskey* himself." [61]

The general master workman's answer and directives to the

[57] PP, Turner to Powderly, Philadelphia, January 15, 1885.

[58] PP, William Keys to Powderly Montreal, January 11, 1885.

[59] *Ibid.*, January 25, 1887.

[60] *Ibid.*, January 11, 1885.

[61] PP, Powderly to Turner, January 13, 1885, copy. No evidence has been found that he ever made such a trip. McCloskey was ill most of that year and died October 10, 1885. John Farley, *The Life of Cardinal McCloskey* (New York, 1918), p. 366.

Montreal Knights were not found, although his somewhat cryptic reaction was inserted into a letter about a projected trip through the South. He wrote,

> I am annoyed over that Keys letter from Montreal. I don't think any such order ever came from *Rome*. At any rate I must do some diplomatic work to be known only to you and I until I report in secret session. I know what I would like to do but that would not be the wise thing to do.[62]

Powderly's action, in the form of a letter to Montreal, did, nevertheless, please Fabre. In this second interview the bishop was also presented with "the contents of your envelope as instructed." Just what this was is not made clear, although it probably included the manuals of the Knights of Labor, for in returning some of the material Keys wrote, "We inclose your private sheet and a copy of your letter to Archbishop Ryan. We have left all the rest with the Bishop." [63] The committee "presented their case in as favorable a manner as possible" and, of course, fell back on Powderly's message of advice which the bishop perused and then exclaimed, "This man speaks as a true Catholic! Yes, he is a Catholic!" The report added, "In the opinion of the Committee, everything rested on the above exclamation." [64]

Bishop Fabre showed his friendly spirit by promising to hold off the section of his forthcoming lenten pastoral which was to have dealt with the Knights until they should first see Archbishop Taschereau.[65] More than that, he appointed a priest to accompany the Knights' delegation to Quebec for that purpose. The labor men consented to go in two weeks' time, and regretting the fact that Powderly could not make it for six or eight weeks, they chose William Keys and an unnamed French Canadian to represent them.[66]

---

[62] PP, Powderly to Turner, January 14, 1885, copy.

[63] PP, William Keys to Powderly, Montreal, January 19, 1885.

[64] PP, William Rawley (for the committee) to Powderly, Montreal, March 17, 1885.

[65] *Ibid.*

[66] PP, William Keys to Powderly, Montreal, January 19, 1885; January 25, 1887.

Fabre was to communicate with Archbishops Taschereau and Lynch, and he did in fact shortly tell the former of Powderly's letter with its spirit of submissiveness and willingness to reform the constitution as the prelates might wish. He explained his plan to have them send someone to Quebec with a clerical adviser to talk the matter over with the archbishop, since Fabre rightly thought that Taschereau was better informed on Rome's procedure than he was himself. The whole question, the Bishop of Montreal ventured to predict, would require the Knights of Labor to correspond with Rome and the bishops of the United States.[67] These negotiations with Quebec were undertaken by Fabre at a time when the Catholic unity of the province was strained over such issues as the half-breed rebellion led by Louis Riel in the Northwest, and a little later the division of the Diocese of Three Rivers. Even an American archbishop could write words to which the future would give an ironic touch, "Happy are we so long as we are united among ourselves, unlike the church of Lower Canada." [68]

The interview between Taschereau and the representatives of the Knights of Labor was recorded twice, although in neither case was the date on which it took place given. But it could have been held only subsequent to February 2, 1885, since that day was less than two weeks after January 19 when the Knights saw Fabre and arranged to go to Quebec, and, too, because under that date Taschereau issued another "Circulaire au clergé" explaining the one of the previous October. He applied to existing societies the three-fold division made in "De secta massonum." The Freemasons and others specified by the Holy See were forbidden under pain of excommunication *latae sententiae* reserved to the Pope. The second class, prohibited under pain of sin, were such as opposed legitimate authority, imposed inviolable secrecy, and maintained blind obedience to unknown leaders. In this category were the Knights of Labor, and Catholics persisting in membership in the Order were, therefore, to be denied the sacraments. The final group of societies

[67] AAM, Letters, VI, 11, Fabre to Taschereau, Montreal, January 21, 1885, copy. No indication was found that he communicated with Lynch.

[68] NYAA, Gibbons to Corrigan, Baltimore, February 17, 1885. Cf. Robert Rumilly, *Histoire de la province de Québec* (Montreal, 1943), V, 1-108.

were those which were "dubious and full of danger" because of their tenets and their management.   These included specifically such unions as the telegraphists, shipbuilders, and brewers.[69]

The three reasons advanced against the Knights in Taschereau's circular to his priests were precisely those which the Order's committee claimed to have answered to the archbishop's satisfaction "by presenting facts contained in our constitution."[70]   Keys' later and more detailed recollection was:

> . . . after the necessary formalities had been gone through we proceeded to business and discussed the constitution clause by clause for some hours.   Finally the Archbishop said that the constitution he had sent to Rome was not in any way like the one we had before us.   After I stated that the Order was the same in the United States as in Canada and that we had only one constitution his Grace said he must have been misled that the constitution was handed to him by a telegraph operator which I considered was done for the purpose of injuring the order because the Knights of Labor you will remember did not support them in their big strike which occurred about the time the Archbishop was given the Constitution.   However his grace told us that there would be no further trouble.   He would withdraw the mandement and let the matter rest where it was. . . .[71]

The earlier report made by Rawley on March 17, 1885, added that they would be permitted to announce in the press that the Knights of Labor were not condemned by the Catholic Church.[72]

The essence of the interview, to Taschereau's mind, was that he told the two delegates from Montreal that it was up to them to prove that they were not worthy of condemnation under the Roman decree against "a society of the same name established in the United States."   Accordingly, they were urged to send their

---

[69] Têtu-Gagnon, *Mandements,* II, 451-455. This last part, mentioning specific unions as suspect, was omitted from the apologetic article in *La Vérité,* August 25, 1894.

[70] PP, William Rawley to Powderly, Montreal, March 17, 1885.

[71] January 25, 1887. The only other hint of the source of this copy of the constitution was found in the article in *La Vérité* mentioned above, which described it only as "a Catholic in the United States."

[72] PP, Rawley to Powderly, March 17, 1885.

documents to Rome.[73] It would certainly seem, therefore, that Taschereau, at least by his inaction, temporarily tolerated the status quo, although no official statement was issued to that effect. O'Donoghue in Toronto had that impression since he accredited the "Papal bull" to the arbitrary use of power by the Archbishop of Quebec and the Bishop of Portland, Maine, who followed the former's example. Nothing had been said in Archbishop Lynch's see and that "great, good and truly liberal" prelate was "never forgotten at headquarters." Furthermore, he argued it could not have originated in Rome, since then Taschereau "could not, *as he subsequently did,* of his volition withdraw it and remove the ban." O'Donoghue offered Powderly an enclosed letter as proof of this statement but, unfortunately, it has not been found among the latter's papers.[74]

The fact remained that outside of Maine the action of the Archbishop of Quebec as well as that of the bishops of the United States assembled at Baltimore, had little practical effect during the year 1885 in bringing a settlement closer to realization. That spring Powderly pictured his ecclesiastical troubles in this fashion:

> We have such damn good Catholics in the order that they confess not only their sins but their virtues. If they want to get drunk, if they want to fight, to lie, to steal, to libel, to slander, to cheat, or act the rogue or scoundrel in any way they *act* and never consult the priest, but if they are asked to do something to improve the condition of their fellow men their conscience troubles them to the tune of 25c a month for dues, 20c Cannelburg assessment and G. A. tax. . . . Bishop Healy of Maine is going for us, the Bishop of Leavenworth, Kan. a priest in Chicago and another in Easton. I am distracted.[75]

Powderly accepted as part of the reason for the difficulties the unfriendly attitude of some labor papers toward religion. This had been called to his attention by a leading Kansas knight, John

---

[73] AAM, Taschereau to Fabre, December 25, 1885. Found only in Consultation, Knights of Labor, August 17, 1885, copy.

[74] PP, O'Donoghue to Powderly, Toronto, June 21, 1885.

[75] PP, Powderly to Turner, April 24, 1885, copy. Cannelburg was a co-operative coal mining venture of the Knights that failed.

T. Stewart who, however, denied being "aware of any of the Catholic Clergy having denounced our Order." [76]   He was prompted to make this observation because word had been sent to headquarters that the priests in that section of the country were hostile and that it might be well to consult the Bishop of Leavenworth.[77] The issue seems to have closed with Stewart's letter of April 16, promising to investigate and to meet with leading ecclesiastics if such were thought necessary. Yet Powderly a week later expressed his feeling that Bishop Louis Fink, O.S.B., was "going for us." [78]

There was more truth to the story of the opposition of the Pennsylvania priest than in the case of the Kansas clergy. The Reverend John R. Dillon of Easton had previously investigated the Knights through their official books, but now he took a new approach.[79] Although Powderly was urged by the local members to write to him, there is no indication the priest received an answer when, taking canonical procedure into his own hands, he told the labor leader:

> As you assert that you are a practical Catholic, and as you have been mayor of Scranton I will cheerfully, and from the altar commend your society, if you will send me a recommendation of the "K. of L." signed by Right Rev. Bishop O'Hara— otherwise I must await the action of the authorities.
> I am not the censor nor the approver in the case.[80]

An inquiry from Chicago, quite to the contrary, did not even mention a priest. It consisted in doubts about taking the new form of pledge which excluded the old exception granting liberty to a mem-

[76] PP, Stewart to Powderly, Scammonville, April 16, 1885.

[77] PP, Hugh Ferguson to Powderly, Ransomville, March 20, 1885; Powderly to Stewart, April 10, copy.

[78] More indicative still of the growing extent of the Knights of Labor was an earlier complaint that the bishop ruling in the Wyoming Territory (at that time it was James O'Connor, Vicar Apostolic of Nebraska, who became first Bishop of Omaha in October, 1885), had ordered their denunciation from the pulpit, and this under the influence of Union Pacific money. Nothing more was said of it according to the records and no answer was indicated to have been made. Frank Perry to Powderly, Evanston, January 1, 1885. Cf. Essay on Sources, p. 384.

[79] PP, James Hardcastle to Powderly, S. Easton, April 12, 1885.

[80] PP, John R. Dillon to Powderly, Easton, June 2, 1885.

ber to reveal the character of the Order in the confessional. Powderly quickly had the scrupulous brother in substantial agreement with his thesis that "the Church does allow the banding together of men for honorable protection." [81]

At this very same time when a few churchmen showed signs of a sympathetic approach to the ecclesiastical problem posed by the Order, Powderly failed to make capital out of their attitudes. From Fountain County, Indiana, came word that a priest there had not only been impressed with a letter of instruction from Powderly, but also after "our interview with the Bishop" everything was considered "satisfactory." [82] The pastor at Lonaconing, Maryland, likewise, was described as "friendly to the Labor movement" and permission was granted him to have the Archbishop of Baltimore look over the A. K. and constitution on his visit to the parish.[83] The subsequent report said that not just Archbishop Gibbons, but also "the most prominent priests in the state," had examined the ritual of local and district assemblies and a circular letter from Powderly and had raised no objections. The pastor at Lonaconing, the Reverend Peter C. Manning, therefore told them, "we may go on as we are going with the order, and they will not object to it." [84] The encouragement given to timorous Catholic members to stay in the Order was the way another Catholic pastor, the Reverend P. J. McManus of Grand Rapids, Michigan, showed his friendliness. An obituary in a labor paper noted his words and further quoted him as saying:

> There is no church in the country the members of which would receive so much benefit through the general betterment of the wage working classes as would the Catholic church—for the greater body of our members are poor.[85]

[81] PP, A. J. Corrigan to Powderly, Chicago, April 10, 1885; May 18.

[82] PP, Frank McCreanon to Powderly, Fountain County, Indiana, April 6, 1885. The bishop in this instance would be Joseph Dwenger of Fort Wayne.

[83] PP, Patrick Cowan to Powderly, Lonaconing, April 13, 1885.

[84] *Ibid.,* June 27, 1885.

[85] PP, Scrapbook, March 5-25, 1886, Grand Rapids, *Workman,* January 2, 1886, describing a call made by the priest to that paper's office the previous July.

The only really serious cause for complaint in Powderly's spring-time distraction of 1885 was in the statement, "Bishop Healy of Portland, Maine is going for us." Apart from this prelate's proximity to Quebec and his own personality it is hard to account for the extraordinary interest which he took in the case of the Knights of Labor. The activity he displayed made him easily the foremost episcopal opponent of the Order in the United States, although the non-industrial character of his diocese would not seem to have warranted such concern.[86] It all began on the picnic grounds during the meeting of the general assembly in Philadelphia when Powderly gave permission to show the A. K. to Father James Peterson of Rock-land, Maine. The priest later expressed no disapproval but he did inquire what the Pennsylvania bishops thought of the Knights in the light of the recent papal pronouncements on secret societies.[87] The Maine representative pressed Powderly for an answer as being vital to their welfare in that vicinity. He was told in reply that the general master workman did not know his bishop's mind on the matter, the Knights of Labor was not the type of society condemned by the Church, and it had no secrets in so far as the Catholic priest was concerned. If a pastor should persist in forbidding his flock to belong, the Scranton leader recommended compliance, saying, "Being a Catholic, I never advise one to oppose the wishes of his spiritual adviser." [88]

This letter of explanation to McGregor, who was a non-Catholic, was also suggested for the perusal of another brother in the same State of Maine who had successfully sought permission to show the A. K. and constitution—the old editions and the ones shortly to be off the press—to his pastor and to the bishop.[89] It was at this very time that Bishop Healy was demanding to see the ritual, since

[86] PP, Scrapbook, March, 1883—July, 1885, Portland *Daily Press,* May 16, 1885. This paper set the size at sixteen assemblies in Maine with about 3,500 members, but *Proceedings* (Hamilton, 1885), shows only about 1,900 members in nineteen locals in the state, pp. 202-203, 217, 219, 223.

[87] PP, George N. McGregor to Powderly, Rockland, September 18, 1884.

[88] *Ibid.,* September 27, 1884; Powderly to McGregor, September 30, 1884, copy in letter to Archbishop Ryan, October 24, 1884.

[89] PP, Turner to Powderly, Philadelphia, October 31, 1884; Powderly to John B. Hamelin, November 3, 1884, copy.

he maintained that the book contained the oath of secrecy and obedience which made the society forbidden to Catholics.[90] The bishop's curiosity continued through the period of the plenary council in Baltimore where, according to the chancellor of the Diocese of Portland, John M. Harrington, further confusion was created by a delegation claiming to represent the Knights of Labor and giving voice to such statements as that part of the secret work was known only to the leaders. Furthermore, as Father Harrington related, "after the Bishop got home he was so bothered by different delegations of the K. of L. calling on him that he telegraphed to Rome to know if the order was to be condemned and he received an answer it was." [91] The only other evidence for this move on Healy's part is his reply to the Prefect of Propaganda thanking him for his favor of February 6 in which he had answered two questions, one on a community of nuns in the diocese, and the other on secret societies. An instruction had been sent on the latter question, and the Bishop of Portland pointed out that though the American prelates had had "a divergence of opinion and conduct," he intended to endeavor "in the future as in the past to follow in all simplicity the instructions of the Holy See communicated through Your Eminence." [92] Any doubt or hesitancy on the part of Bishop Healy had probably been eliminated even before that time by Archbishop Taschereau's promulgation of his answer from Rome on February 2. "As we are neighbors," Healy later recalled, "I asked for a copy of the decision, which he was kind enough to send me in 1885. I then sent on several copies to some of our prelates, not thinking that in such a case we were to wait for our Metropolitans, when a decision had come from Rome." [93]

[90] ADPM, Healy to M. Dupont, Portland, October 30, 1884, copy.

[91] PP, Thomas Lyons to Powderly, Vinal Haven, April 20, 1885. Concerning the council, the only thing that was uncovered was Healy's relating how in conversation several of the prelates had maintained that some secret societies were not forbidden under pain of excommunication. Apparently forgetting the instruction of May 10, 1884, he inquired what Rome had to say on it. ADPM, Healy to August J. Schulte, December 17, 1884, copy.

[92] ADPM, Healy to Simeoni, Portland, August 23, 1885, copy.

[93] ADPM, Healy to Camillus Cardinal Mazzella (of the Holy Office), Portland, March 15, 1887. No mention was made therein of contacting Simeoni.

This Roman decision—whether an authentic version was supplied by Taschereau or Simeoni, or both—was promulgated in the Diocese of Portland by a pastoral of February 18, 1885. In both French and English the bishop announced, "By a recent Decree of Rome the Society of the 'Knights of Labor' is proscribed and condemned. You are to make known that no member of it can be admitted to the Sacraments." [94] This directive also barred people from the sacraments for selling strong liquor on Sundays. In fact, intemperance had shared with secret societies the recommendation that it be a special subject of instruction after the obligatory reading of the national pastoral of the Baltimore council. These remarks from the pulpit had an immediate effect on the Knights, who planned an interview with the bishop as soon as he returned from a trip he had taken for his health. [95] The chancellor of the diocese meanwhile explained in Vinal Haven that they must withdraw or suffer excommunication. Although he held that their local groups were unobjectionable, they were not made acquainted with all of the secret work and, furthermore, some assemblies still had the objectionable oath. [96] The bishop added to this evil feature of secrecy that of irresponsible leadership, and he upheld his position to a private inquirer by pointing to the Roman and Canadian actions. But apparently remembering the decrees of Baltimore, Healy promised to send the Order's books to the Archbishop of Boston and to write him about the problem. [97] There is no extant evidence that he ever did this, but at the same time Powderly's pen was ready with a reassuring denial of the prelate's charges. He stated:

No record of any request or answer of Taschereau was found. However, Letterbook, II, 414, contains a press copy of the decision of September, 1884, on the Knights of Labor. It has no date, but from internal evidence would be about February 15, and therefore, could hardly have been Simeoni's communication of February 6, but rather one from Quebec.

[94] ADPM, "Pastoral of Rt. Rev. James Augustine Healy," Portland, February 18, 1885.

[95] PP, Robert A. Williams to Powderly, Portland, March 4, 1885.

[96] PP, Thomas J. Lyons to Powderly, Vinal Haven, March 30, 1885.

[97] ADPM, Healy to Fred S. Carter, Portland, March 27, 1885. Neither the ecclesiastical archives of Boston or Portland disclosed anything beyond this.

I am glad you call my attention to this matter and am thankful that Father Harrington has spoken of it for it may be that some of these blood and thunder socialists or anarchists are making an attempt to capture us in Maine. If the priest would give you the facts on which he bases his objections I will go to Maine and assist in ferreting out the wrong doers in the order.[98]

Despite this purely arbitrary explanation of radicalism as the cause of its rise, the opposition to the Knights in Maine continued to be effective. While Father Harrington felt he had to fulfill a duty that was distasteful to him, many Knights delayed their withdrawal from the Order in the hope of a readjustment.[99] Their confidence in the general master workman was strengthened by his actual appearance in Maine about the middle of May.[100] As if in anticipation of his coming, Healy had sent a telegram to the Archbishop of Quebec for the books of the Order in Canada, and Taschereau had forwarded the request to Montreal, explaining that he had no copies of the constitution "of your Knights of Labor."[101] When he called on Healy, Powderly readily admitted the organization was the same on both sides of the border. Then the bishop, after hearing his account of the society, showed him "the writ of condemnation" and advised him "to see and consult his bishop and through him to learn from Rome which rules &c were to be modified, so as not to be in conflict with the laws of the Church." His story continued, "This Mr. Powderly promised to do. I have never heard that he did so."[102] Healy may have been skeptical of Powderly from the outset, for he asked Fabre if the Knights had promised him

[98] PP, Powderly to Thomas J. Lyons, April 9, 1885, copy.

[99] PP, Lyons to Powderly, April 20, 1885. There was some indication that French members were leaving, ADPM, Healy to M. Dupont, April 25, 1885. Healy was active against other societies also. He not only decided that the fraternal Order of United Workmen was forbidden by Church law, but also the Locomotive Brotherhood of Engineers. Healy to N. Charland, April 13, 1885, copy. He was gravely suspicious of the A. O. of H. and even more so of the G. A. R. *Ibid.;* cf. also NYAA, Healy to Corrigan, Portland, April 14, 1885; April 29.

[100] PP, Scrapbook, March 1883—July, 1885, carries clippings from May 16 on.

[101] AAM, Quebec, 1882-1903, Taschereau to Fabre, Quebec, May 12, 1885.

[102] ADPM, Healy to Mazzella, Portland, March 15, 1887, copy.

to change "quidquid Romae non arridet." [103] Neither to the Bishop of Montreal, nor to Corrigan, to whom he also wrote after the meeting, did he reveal his talk with the labor leader. He sent the Archbishop of New York "a document" on the Knights of Labor to help in passing judgment on the Grand Army of the Republic, but he merely remarked that they were "the same in Canada as here." [104]

Powderly's reactions to their interview were even less encouraging than the bishop's. In his memoirs he gave what purported to be the actual dialogue, which showed Healy's chief concern to have been Powderly's "speaking in my state without my permission." [105] From a point closer in time to the events the head of the Knights expressed himself as pleased with the meetings of the Order he had attended in Maine, but he concluded that the bishop was irreconcilably opposed and their meeting had been to no effect.[106] Powderly also explained that Bishop Healy had threatened to write to his own bishop, and so he attempted to see Bishop O'Hara of Scranton first.[107] A date was supposedly set for June 1, but a complaint from the committee which had called on Healy revealed that on the evidence of their bishop's correspondence with O'Hara, Powderly had after a month done nothing to find out from Rome through his own ordinary what was considered offensive in the make-up of the Knights of Labor. The Bishop of Portland asked the delegation to goad the general master workman to some action and promised to "hold a neutral position" in the meanwhile.[108] Powderly simply answered that he had called on the Bishop of Scranton and would make his "report and *recommendations*" at the next session of the general assembly and the ever-threatening "successor" could work it all out. Dramatizing his position, he wrote:

> God alone knows what I have gone through during the past year, it has been one of horrors for me. Anarchists fighting me

[103] AAM, E. U., 1868-1891, Healy to Fabre, Portland, May 25, 1885.

[104] NYAA, Healy to Corrigan, Portland, May 23, 1885.

[105] Powderly, *Path,* pp. 345-347.

[106] PP, Powderly to Turner, May 25, 1885, copy.

[107] *Ibid.,* May 31, 1885, copy.

[108] PP, George N. McGregor to Powderly, Rockland, July 5, 1885. No correspondence between Healy and O'Hara was discovered.

personally to get rid of my conservative policy, and the Church fighting me on the other hand I have been so puzzled at times to know which way to turn that animation almost suspends its operations.

Yet in the next line he said the episcopal opposition in Maine was unique, and he advised quiet continuation of the work of organizing:

> Do not move too openly for that may bring down censure where *neutrality* is all that we require. You must read between the lines of this letter it is a delicate question. Accept the *neutrality*. Go forward without believing every *rumor,* and leave the rest to *Providence.*[109]

McGregor's counter-suggestion which would not have left as much to Providence, namely, that through Bishop Healy the Knights in Maine should contact Rome, was simply marked by the head of the Order, "no answer required." [110] Powderly missed his chance here, for Healy's "neutrality" meant not the withdrawing of the condemnation but the lack of further hostile steps until the appeal could be made to the Holy See.[111] He also backed down on his promise by doing nothing at the meeting of the general assembly by way of making proposals, either to conciliate or to fight the Catholic clergy.[112] The bishop, despite his possession of "an authentic copy of the Roman decree," in time found the archbishops of the United States regarding it as intended only for Canada. He, therefore, notified his priests to admit to the sacraments those who promised to submit when a final decision arrived.[113]

Although things might at times grow quiet in Maine, such could hardly be said for the Schuylkill region (Schuylkill and North-cumberland Counties) of Pennsylvania, where clerical opposition continued against Catholic membership in the Knights of Labor.[114]

[109] PP, Powderly to McGregor, July 8, 1885, copy.

[110] PP, McGregor to Powderly, August 3, 1885.

[111] ADPM, Healy to Pierre Lamoureaux, Portland, August 27, 1885, copy.

[112] PP, Oliver Otis to Powderly, n. d., n. p., in Letter-file, October-December, 1885.

[113] ADPM, Healy to Mazzella, March 15, 1887, copy.

[114] PP, Robert Maggs to Powderly, Mahanoy City, June 23, 1885.

Powderly was never anxious for reorganization there, for not only was the Order suspected, but his own name was subject to slander on the score of his having maligned priests and bishops. He replied most generously seeking a chance to defend himself, "I know of no bishop against whom I could say anything, and I know of no priest against whom I would or did say anything except in conversation with themselves, and then only on matters of a temporal nature." [115] Yet it was common talk that the priests of the valley were suspicious of "something behind the Constitution" which was not apparent to the uninitiated. The denunciation by the Reverend John J. O'Reilly in Mount Carmel went so far as to declare if the Pope ever approved the Order he would "fling off the vestments." Unlike this pastor, the neighboring priests in Shamokin and Locust Gap, both likewise in the Diocese of Harrisburg, were reported as very slow to speak on the subject even in private.[116] Powderly admitted his helplessness, "I have no power to silence Father Reilly [sic] as you suggest. You must act for yourselves, if he would not heed the Pope he certainly will not heed me." He merely counseled the deliberate exclusion of drunkards and other disreputable characters in organizing locals lest the clergy be antagonized.[117]

Although most of these unfriendly Pennsylvania priests were of Irish origin, nevertheless it would seem that the Irish element among the American Catholic working class had, in general, endorsed the Knights of Labor. This is shown, for example, in the acceptance of Powderly by the popular *Irish World and Industrial Liberator* as "a man who has such sound views on all questions affecting the interests of wage-workers." [118] Besides this evidence the opening of the session of the general assembly in Hamilton on October 5,

[115] PP, Powderly to the Reverend Peter C. McEnroe, September 26, 1885, copy. He was pastor of St. Canicus Church, Mahanoy City.

[116] PP, James A. Donnelly to Powderly, Locust Gap, October 26, 1885.

[117] Powderly to Donnelly, October 28, 1885, copy; H. F. Reilly, October 28, 1885, copy. On the lack of archival material in Harrisburg, cf. p. 380. Letters from several other localities indicated that Catholic workers constituted a promising but somewhat hesitant field for organization. Dan Frazer Tomson, Hot Springs, November 4, 1885; S. H. Shea, Lexington, November 11, 1885.

[118] October 17, 1885.

1885, brought words of commendation from the Boston *Pilot* for what gave promise of being for the first time a general unity among all labor groups in the United States. In an even more concrete way this paper showed its sympathy for the cause by recommending to its readers its very down-to-earth, if not radical, labor correspondent who signed himself "Phineas." [119] In a few months the *Pilot* had high editorial praise not only for Powderly but also for the organization as "a potent influence in this land and a promise of hope for the wage-workers in the near future." [120]

Except for the Irish readiness to accept Powderly as a compatriot, however, the nationality of Catholics in the United States made little difference in their relation to the Knights of Labor. A report from the city of Albany showed the contrast between a pastor named Edward A. Terry, who recommended the Knights, and Monsignor John H. Cluever, pastor of the German church of Our Lady Help of Christians, who denounced them. In the case of the latter not only were the influential German bakers blamed for his action, but also Bishop Francis McNeirny! [121] A German Catholic paper in Columbus, Ohio, *Der Ohio Waisenfreund* was very doubtful about the relation of Catholics to the Order, and it feared that a deleterious effect would follow among the Knights who belonged to the Church.[122] Naturally not all the German members were Catholics, and it was the suspicion of great influence within the Order on the part of the "infidels" that later led an Irish traveling salesman to seek some action by the Church.[123]

The growth of German Catholics in the Knights of Labor was such, nonetheless, that it finally brought on some planned action in Milwaukee, the see city of the most important German prelate in the United States, Archbishop Michael Heiss. Because of the advice of the German priests many good candidates were lost, so a committee of English-speaking Knights consented to approach the archbishop.[124] Powderly gave them a hearty approval and, averring

[119] October 10, 1885
[120] January 2, 1886.
[121] PP, Robert D. Crone to Powderly, Albany, September 16, 1885.
[122] PP, Charles P. Carl to Powderly, Cleveland, September 27, 1885.
[123] NYAA, T. O'Brien to Corrigan, Newark, April 29, 1886.
[124] PP, Tim Cruice to Powderly, Milwaukee, December 29, 1885.

that Catholics often misquoted their priests, he said, "Yes, by all means consult the Bishop, speak unreservedly, conceal nothing." [125] They went to call on Heiss with the usual exhibits of the A. K., constitution, journal, and letters from Powderly to Robert Schilling. Their originally cool reception changed after a week when the archbishop had an opportunity to consult with his clergy, and Heiss was finally led to declare that he would not condemn them since they were about the same as trade unions; Catholics could, therefore, use their own judgment about joining so long as they lived up to their principles and did not use unjust means to gain their ends. Archbishop Heiss was quoted as saying, "I know workingmen are not used right in all respects and they have a right to unite and combine against the encroaching and hungry monopolists of the country but they must be law-abiding." This was an outstanding example of ecclesiastical good-will, but the prelate requested that his opinion be kept out of the papers.[126] Later that same year the First Provincial Council of Milwaukee advised the clergy to dissuade Catholics from joining labor unions, which were *in se* lawful but generally dangerous for them. Yet in the pastoral letter, which received more publicity than the legislative decrees, the council balanced the scales a bit by attacking the evils of capital.[127] It said:

> When capitalists follow the heathen rule, to buy labor on the cheapest market, God is not with them; and when laborers

125 Powderly to Cruice, January 5, 1886, copy.

126 Cruice to Powderly, January 18, 1886. The G. M. W. was pleased at their "judgment and patience." January 22, 1886. However, it was nothing like the active support given by the German Evangelical Protestant pastor in St. Charles, Missouri, who between April and September of 1886 produced a paper of over a thousand circulation, *Der Ritter der Arbeit,* the only Knights of Labor paper in German. He was master workman of a local, but at the request of his parishioners he used the name, Fritz E. Fleissighand, as editor instead of his proper name, Frederick E. Flickeissen. Wisconsin State Historical Society, John Samuels Correspondence, August 31, 1886. Powderly ignored him when he asked him to be godfather of a new-born son, October 7, 1886.

127 *Acta et decreta concilii provincialis Milwaukiensis primi* (Milwaukee, 1888), p. 50.

imagine that all men should have an equal share in the comforts and enjoyments of this earthly life, divine Providence has ruled otherwise.[128]

The pattern of action which was to be followed, therefore, was laid down by no particular national group in the United States. This can be seen in the very names of the ecclesiastics who held such varying opinions. It was rather the approach determined by the Third Plenary Council of Baltimore which gradually became a reality. Although Lynch and Fabre and Heiss had been tested and found friendly, and Taschereau and Healy at best suspicious if not unfriendly, the problem was no nearer solution until the immediate appeal to Rome on the part of Quebec was supplanted by the mediating action of the committee of the American archbishops set up in Baltimore.

[128] Cincinnati *Catholic Telegraph,* June 10, 1886.

CHAPTER V

CANADIAN CONFUSION

ORGANIZED American labor passed through such a hectic year in 1886 that it would not be too strong to characterize the social turmoil as domestic warfare. The upheaval was reaching its crest at a time when the Catholic hierarchy was slowly being brought to realize the necessity of reaching some form of Church-labor understanding. In effect, they continued to pursue the policy of "masterly inactivity," a term adopted by Archbishop Gibbons of Baltimore. Not until October of 1886 did the committee of archbishops appointed to deal with the question of the troublesome societies really begin to function. Meanwhile the Knights of Labor were losing ground with the ecclesiastical authorities in Canada, and the interplay of forces, both of the Church and of labor, across the border did not help the Order in the United States. Nonetheless, the Knights of Labor were winning increasing recognition in the Catholic press of the United States. This fact showed the effectiveness of Powderly's tactic of disassociating himself and the organization from the radical elements whose activities began to provide sensational copy for the newspapers generally.

Powderly as a politician had been subject to all kinds of name-calling. On the completion of his third term as Mayor of Scranton in April, 1884, at least one journal in that city commended him as an honest gentleman, "considering he is a Democrat, and had to associate with such company." [1] The ex-mayor shortly afterwards sought unsuccessfully the position of Commissioner of the Bureau of Labor Statistics and, although he considered himself an independent in politics, he felt it necessary to write Republican President Chester A. Arthur, "to disabuse your mind of the idea that I am a communist." [2] At the same time Powderly continued an

[1] Scrapbook, January, 1884—September, 1885, Scranton *Review,* April 12, 1884.

[2] PP, Powderly to Chester A. Arthur, November 11, 1884, copy. Even

T. V. POWDERLY.

academic interest in the growth of "socialism or communism" in Europe and its influence on workingmen, and asked an organizer in England to keep him informed of such trends abroad.[3]

Nonetheless, as the bogey of radicalism grew in the American mind, Powderly had to take steps to keep the Order clear of association with it. *The Journal of United Labor,* in which a few years previously he had not hesitated to print socialistic doctrine, had to be defended from the charge of socialism "(in the prevailing acceptation of the term)," even though it was "never read." [4] The pamphlet which had given this classification of the paper was to have been answered, but O'Donoghue had brought Powderly to agree on the wisdom of leaving the question out of the official organ. The Canadian knight was alone in introducing the religious motivation when he said that he did not "altogether relish being a member of an organization . . . where I would by my presence be presumed to be hostile to the teachings generally of the Catholic Church." [5] Powderly's scrapbooks, however, show that he publicly pleaded conservatism during 1885, a year filled with disturbing boycotts. He condemned the "torch of the incendiary, the dagger of the assassin, and the bomb of the dynamiter," as unworthy of a knight.[6] It need hardly be said that he was opposed to communism, revolution, and strikes, although agreeing with "some of the aims of the ad-

before losing out he felt it might be well if he did not get the position since he would then be free to "rake some of our Irishmen for slobering over Blaine and his extreme solicitation for the Irish and Catholic interests. Why will our people be so easily gulled?" Letter to Dr. Carroll Wright, June 20, 1884.

[3] PP, Powderly to A. G. Denny (Sunderland, England), November 18, 1884, copy.

[4] PP, Powderly to George Hess, December 31, 1884, copy; also to [ ] Sharpe, December 30, 1884. One of the earlier contributors had become an anarchist. Joe Labadie to Powderly, Detroit, March 25, 1886. The G.M.W. deplored "war-like friends . . . who preach violence." Powderly, to J. P. Goughy, December 30, 1884. Turner was told the *Journal* must not be "anything else than the organ of the Order." January 16, 1885.

[5] PP, O'Donoghue to Powderly, Toronto, December 8, 1884.

[6] Scrapbook, March, 1883—July, 1885, *Labor News Echo* (Flint, Michigan), April 10, 1885.

vanced socialists." [7]   The general master workman with some justice considered himself as "fighting the enemy at both ends," when he learned that men like Victor Drury of District Assembly 49 in New York, were behind an anarchist plot to displace him as head of the Order.[8]

At least some Catholic observers were aware of the growing turmoil in organized labor as the year 1886 approached. Phineas of the Boston *Pilot* analyzed the process that drove workers into socialist-dominated groups thus:

> Avaricious employers drive the workman to radical means; the press, through ignorance or maliciousness misrepresent his acts and motives, the 'best people' condemn him and of necessity the officers of the law seize him and drag him before a judge that corporate influence has lifted to the judiciary. Helpless and hopeless the workman turns to the kind-voiced gentlemanly Socialist.[9]

The Brooklyn *Catholic Examiner* gave hearty endorsement to the movement for an eight-hour day, but considering the boycott a "formidable weapon," it advised discrimination and discretion in its use.[10] For much of the lawlessness in the Pennsylvania coal region the *Catholic Standard* of Philadelphia was ready to lay the blame directly at the door of the operators who had imported, deluded, and cheated European aliens.[11] Even as Powderly was again insisting that the Knights of Labor was not "an anarchist school" or a "communistic order," Bishop Dwenger of Fort Wayne was once more instructing his Indiana flock against "infidel social-revolutionists" who were not "the true friends of the laboring man." [12] There was at least one public appearance of harmony on this matter when Powderly addressed a meeting in Providence,

[7] Scrapbook, January, 1884—September, 1885 *Evening Post* (Aurora, Illinois), July 15, 1885; *The Pioneer Press* (St. Paul), July 24, 1885.

[8] PP, Powderly to A. A. Carlton, July 7, 1885, copy.

[9] August 1, 1885.

[10] December 26, 1885.

[11] January 30, 1886.

[12] PP, Powderly to Calvin Ewiggi, January 25, 1886; AUND, Fort Wayne Papers, 1857-1915, "Pastoral of Joseph Dwenger," February 5, 1886.

Rhode Island, with the Reverend C. J. Burns of the Pro-Cathedral of SS. Peter and Paul, as well as the Reverend F. A. Hinckley of the Free Religious Society, on the same platform. He said in the course of the two-hour talk, "We often hear it said that our organization is an association of Socialists and Communists, but you can say to such charges from me that they are not true, and we have no use for men called by those names." [13] It was shortly after this Providence speech in February, but still before the full fury of the events of the ensuing months in the labor field tied him down to the business affairs of the Order, that Powderly answered in person the distress call of the Canadian Knights who sought his help in matters ecclesiastical.

Archbishop Taschereau had remained quiet for almost a year when a Montreal dispatch in the *Morning Chronicle* of Quebec came to his attention and led him to communicate with Bishop Fabre. The Knights of Labor were reported to be on the verge of entering the municipal politics of Montreal, and also to be seeking a wage increase on the Grand Trunk Railroad. Hence Taschereau inquired, "Are not these Knights of Labor before the Holy See protesting they have nothing in common with the society of the same name condemned by a letter of Cardinal Simeoni of September, 1884?" Fabre was advised to keep a close watch on them lest they deceive the Holy See.[14] Within a week Quebec was further shifting the burden of adjudication of the problem to Montreal, and for a very good reason. Taschereau's Christmas note read:

> Since they do not exist in my Diocese, I think that it is up to Your Excellency to see to it and to consult Rome. I have the general rule in hand; the question is to know if certain diocesans of Montreal are exempt from it or not. The recent conduct of these Knights inspires strong doubts concerning their orthodoxy.[15]

There could be no doubt, however, about the growing importance of the Knights of Labor in Canada. In 1883 the experiment of

[13] Scrapbook, September, 1885—March, 1886, Providence *Journal,* February 10, 1886.
[14] AAQ, 35-184, 5, Taschereau to Fabre, Quebec, December 18, 1885, copy.
[15] AAM, quoted in Consultation, Knights of Labor, August 17, 1885.

the short-lived Canadian Labor Union of 1873 had been successfully repeated when a federation of the unions of the whole Dominion was set up and became the Trades and Labour Congress of Canada. It was sponsored by the Toronto Trades and Labour Council, but at the first congress fifty-four of the sixty-nine groups represented were Knights of Labor.[16] Not only their absence from the listings of locals in the *Proceedings* of the general assembly, but also the fact that at the Canadian congress from 1886 to 1888 every union represented was in Ontario, show the truth of Taschereau's allegation that his archdiocese contained no Knights.[17] This connection of the Knights of Labor with the national congress of labor was unique to Canada as were their attempts at direct participation and representation in politics.[18] The labor candidate was usually also that of the Liberal Party, and although their successes at that time, even on a local scale were few they were apparently sufficient to arouse the suspicions of the Archbishop of Quebec, a fervent supporter of the Conservative Party headed by the shrewd Protestant politician, Sir John Macdonald.[19]

It was not, however, in Quebec itself but in the suffragan See of Ottawa (which with Montreal was to become a metropolitan see in June) that trouble first arose for the Knights in that year 1886.[20] Bishop Joseph T. Duhamel had condemned the Order "some time ago," but only in January was O'Donoghue called on. He had grown up as a boy with the bishop in Ottawa, and had even *"blackened both his eyes once,"* and so he felt rather confident of success with Duhamel.[21] Powderly himself was hardly depressed when he wished him well,

[16] Coats, *op. cit.*, p. 306.

[17] *Ibid.*, pp. 300-302; *Proceedings* (Hamilton, 1885), pp. 175-225.

[18] Kennedy, *op. cit.*, pp. 57-59. Politicians in Quebec considered it important to control their vote. Rumilly, *op. cit.*, V, 221.

[19] Cf. Joseph Pope, *Memoirs of Rt. Honourable Sir John Alexander Macdonald* (London, 1894), II, 250.

[20] P. Alexis, *Histoire de la province ecclésiastique d'Ottawa et de la colonisation dans la vallée de l'Ottawa* (Ottawa, 1897), II, 98. This volume makes no mention of labor troubles.

[21] PP, O'Donoghue to Powderly, Toronto, January 24, 1886.

In your interview with his grace of Ottawa may success attend you. Dominus Vobiscum, Dhig-eu-dhu-fdellie, Faugh a Sallagh. [*sic*] Walk on him lively. Ser Gut [*sic*] if I knew any more prayers in Latin, Irish or German you'd have them.[22]

The Canadian labor leader was so given to making long detailed reports after exploits of this kind that for lack of time he at first could only advise the general master workman that a report would follow and he mentioned that he might go to see the Archbishop of Quebec.[23] The mere mention of Taschereau was hint enough that the meeting of January 31 had not had too happy an outcome. Even in making the appointment on the previous day for the labor deputation, O'Donoghue had been told by the Ottawa prelate that he could do nothing until the Quebec circular was retracted. The labor leader's argument then that Taschereau had shown lack of hostility by his tolerating one assembly in Quebec and many more in Montreal meant nothing to the Bishop of Ottawa.[24] Duhamel and O'Donoghue parted to meet again the next afternoon after the former had been given a copy of the constitution. Yet even before that at the eight o'clock Mass the next morning the bishop preached on secret societies and, although he did not mention the Knights by name, O'Donoghue, who had Charles March with him in his old family pew, and some of his friends interpreted the sermon as directed at themselves. Undaunted, however, and accompanied by William McEvela, a trade-unionist bricklayer, and James Dufresne of the typographical union, both "intimately acquainted with the bishop," the two leaders called at the episcopal residence at two o'clock. Their spokesman recorded that Duhamel stood more on the Quebec circular and his dignity, than on his logic. O'Donoghue forced him to admit, "*so far as he could see* our principles were unobjectionable." Somewhat "nettled," the labor leader could only insist on his own sincerity and frankness and embarrass the bishop with the question of how membership in the Knights of Labor could be right in Toronto but wrong in

[22] PP, Powderly to O'Donoghue, January 27, 1886, copy.
[23] February 8, 1886.
[24] No other evidence of the existence of one in Quebec was seen. The listings in the *Proceedings* of 1886 and 1887 did not include the locals directly subject to the general assembly.

Ottawa. Without further detail O'Donoghue related, "my colleagues took an active part in the discussion throughout." He reached two practical conclusions as a result of his conference: not to advise Catholics in his jurisdiction to join the Order and with Duhamel's approval, to call on Taschereau if, while in Montreal around the end of February, he still thought it wise.[25]

But it was earlier than the end of February when Fabre, goaded by Quebec's warnings, and probably even more so by the fact that the Order's growth made the problem acute, called the Knights to a conference.[26] One report put the Montreal increase at over 20,000 in a few months,[27] and even if exaggerated the growth was sufficient to bestir the clergy again and to have the bishop call for George S. Warren "to settle the affair." While this knight had supplied the bishop with English and French constitutions, he still thought the head of the Order would have to go to Fabre in person.[28] Powderly was on the road and did not answer and so telegrams began to pour in urging his attendance at "a conference of clergymen" in Montreal.[29] The faithful Canadian lieutenant, O'Donoghue, hastened to Montreal to meet him, but it was scarcely in order to help his defense of the Knights of Labor, for Fabre had always proved himself friendly.[30] The prelate described his own feelings toward the Knights as being such that he considered their willingness to submit to all the demands of the bishops regarding their constitution as sufficient reason to give the assurance that "it was not necessary to disturb them." [31]

[25] PP, O'Donoghue to Powderly, Toronto, February 14, 1886.

[26] Keys' report does not give much help: "Everything went on quietly for another year when the storm raised again more violent than at any future period." To Powderly, Montreal, January 25, 1887.

[27] *John Swinton's Paper,* February 21, 1886.

[28] PP, G. S. Warren (an organizer) to Powderly, St. Johns, February 11, 1886. Marked by Powderly, "Answered in person, Feb. 18."

[29] PP, J. F. Redmond to Powderly, Montreal, February 13, 1886. The same day on hearing he was not at home, he said, "It is impossible for him to have anything on hand to equal this in importance." Redmond to Turner; also February 15 and 16.

[30] PP, O'Donoghue to Powderly, Toronto, February 16, 1886, telegram.

[31] AAM, Consultation, Knights of Labor, August 17, 1886.

For some undiscovered reason, unfortunately Bishop Fabre himself did not receive Powderly on February 18, 1886, but a group of his priests did. No details of the gathering were found beyond Fabre's brief description which read:

> Last winter, I did everything possible to bring the question of the Knights of Labor at Montreal under consideration. Their leader, Powderly, came here, and met with several priests, with whom I had brought him together. This gentleman left behind a favorable impression and one was left with the conviction that he was disposed to reject from the By-laws of the Society any propositions which should appear worthy of condemnation in the eyes of the Bishops or of the Holy See.[32]

Powderly in his own account was more explicit about the bishop's absence and the nature of the meeting:

> Last winter I called upon the Bishop of Montreal, at least I called at his residence for the purpose of talking with him on the subject of a change in the Constitution. I did not meet with the bishop but had an interview with four of the priests of the diocese who were there. The priests explained several objections to me and I determined to have them removed at the coming convention and so informed the clergymen who met me at Montreal.[33]

On February 21, shortly after this meeting, the blow which had been threatening in the neighboring Diocese of Ottawa for three weeks finally fell when Bishop Duhamel condemned the Knights.[34] The Montreal spokesman, William Keys, noted this fact as he told

[32] *Ibid.*

[33] BCA, 81-S-13, Powderly to the Reverend Francis Carew, August 31, 1886. However cf. *Path,* pp. 349-352, for Powderly's only account of a trip to Canada, in "the winter of 1886." His relation of how his conversation with Fabre consisted in a difference over the Knights' use of the word, "divorce" and how some of his remarks were carried back and antagonized Taschereau was not substantiated in other sources.

[34] AAQ, 35-234, 5, Taschereau to Duhamel, Quebec, February 25, 1886, copy. The archbishop merely noted that the papers had carried the story and he added, probably referring to Rome, "I have not yet received the document concerning this society."

Powderly that a priest from the bishop's residence had called—he suspected sent by Fabre himself—to tell him that pressure was being brought to bear by the local politicians, and that "the best way out of this difficulty is to go to Rome and lay the matter before the Pope." [35] Even before he had received this advice the general master workman had penned a most respectful letter to Bishop Fabre from Philadelphia. He told him a Canadian agent was to forward the bishop some more Knights of Labor literature although, "Both the constitution and manual are now in the hands of a special committee for revision, objectionable features will be removed and a term of five years will be given in which to test the work." Powderly promised to heed the instructions given by three priests he named as "Fathers Quinliven, Matengier and Leclers," and he said further that he had "already taken steps to comply with the advice of the former [sic] in placing our constitution, A. K. &c in hands of such gentlemen as he suggested." Taking the announcement in the previous day's news of the denunciation by the Bishop of Ottawa as a springboard, he maintained that such hostility of the Church gladdened the hearts of the anarchists and socialists, and he went so far as to claim that anything that hindered the Knights hastened revolution. On the other hand, he quickly disclaimed any responsibility for the news accounts in the New York press of his trip to the episcopal residence at Montreal.[36] These stories had represented the bishop as having been satisfied as to the legitimacy of the Knights of Labor after a personal interview

[35] PP, William Keys to Powderly, Montreal, February 24, 1886. The writer later repeated this, and then on the word of a Catholic doctor who was also a member of the local and who had it from a Redemptorist at St. Ann's Church, he claimed "J. J. Curran, M.P., was continually visiting the Bishop for the purpose of inducing him to condemn the Order." January 25, 1887.

[36] PP, Powderly to Fabre, Philadelphia, February 24, 1886, true-copy, not found in press-copy book or in the Montreal archives. Two of the priests mentioned were able to be identified as J. Quinliven of St. Patrick's and J. V. Leclerc, cure of St. Joseph's both in Montreal. The third was most likely A. Mallengier of St. Anne's in the same city. *Sadlier's Catholic Directory*, (New York, 1886), Part II, pp. 9-10.

with Powderly. At least one Catholic paper had cautioned Catholic workers against too ready an acceptance of that statement.[37]

Just the day before Powderly wrote his note of submission and warning to Montreal a dispatch from that city appeared in the New York papers telling of a condemnatory *mandement* ordered by Archbishop Taschereau to be read throughout the province on the following Sunday, February 28.[38] This report—completely false on the basis of archival evidence—circulated widely and was of importance because of the reactions it evoked. Powderly was interviewed in Philadelphia and was quoted as protesting his reluctance to speak on such a delicate subject, but then there followed a quite indelicate and odious comparison between conditions in the United States and Canada. Only in Canada was there a gulf between the priests and the people and the Canadian Church needed, furthermore, to be suspicious because of the many anarchists and those with volatile French temperaments.[39] The most radical of Catholic papers, the Brooklyn *Examiner,* attributed the reported action to some differences in the Canadian organization, for in the United States, it was only "a needed counterpoise against the aggression of the arrogant and soulless corporation" and the eliminator of "idle demagogues and socialists." [40] Of more weight than these disclaimers, since it came from an official Catholic source, was the publicized statement of the Vicar General of the Archdiocese of Chicago, P. J. Conway, who explained the alleged action of the Archbishop of Quebec as probably due to local abuses. At any rate, Conway continued, his jurisdiction did not extend across the frontier where such a pronouncement would affect 10,000 Catholics in Chicago alone. Conway concluded, "We see nothing reprehensible in labor organizations, but feel rather like encouraging them. So far as I

[37] Scrapbook, September, 1885—March, 1886, *Michigan Catholic* (Detroit), February 25, 1886.

[38] *John Swinton's Paper,* February 28, 1886. Swinton mistakenly had Powderly in conference with Taschereau.

[39] *Ibid.* The Montreal *Daily Witness* of February 26, 1886, did not let such charges pass, but pointed out the close ties of pastor and flock in Canada and the more blatant fact that Chicago was the "asylum of anarchism." Scrapbook, September, 1885—March, 1886.

[40] February 27, 1886.

know there is not the least clash between their principles and our Church's teachings." [41]

It was this public utterance that led Archbishop Taschereau to make a report to the Congregation of the Propaganda, requesting some action to remedy the scandal that was being caused by these varying interpretations put upon the Knights in different dioceses. This communication also indicated with certainty the source of the newspaper stories, which had presented the old decree as if it were being published for the first time in the churches. He wrote:

> Most recently agents of this society have tried to enroll Catholic members in such cities of this province as Ottawa, Marianopolis and Quebec. Thus the condemnation pronounced in September 1884 was promulgated again in the press, and since my name appeared both on the consultation and the response, the story was spread about by editors and telegraphists that I had pronounced this condemnation.[42]

Besides enclosing a copy of these two statements of the first judgment on the Knights, Taschereau also included the article on Vicar General Conway from a Chicago paper which had been anonymously furnished him by a Catholic of that city. This was briefed for Cardinal Simeoni in six Latin points. The request ended on this note:

> It can scarcely be supposed that the Archbishop of Chicago does not approve this statement. Up to now he has remained silent.
> It will be impossible for me and my suffragans to safeguard the decision of the Holy Office if this society *nominatim* condemned by the Holy Office is thus protected and praised in the United States of North America.[43]

[41] New York *World,* February 25, 1886. The *Freeman's Journal* carried this item, and was rebuked for it by a layman who stressed the evils of the boycott conducted by the Knights. AUND, McMaster Papers, A. M. Cooney to James McMaster, Arlington, Kentucky, March 6, 1886.

[42] AAQ, 35-238, Taschereau to Simeoni, Quebec, March 2, 1886, copy. This is not found in *La Vérité* article of August 24, 1894.

[43] *Ibid.* Although this last statement might seem strong some contemporaneous evidence is seen in Swinton's item about a bishop saying anonymously, "God speed the Order." March 14, 1886. On a lower level there was the approving word ("a movement in the right direction") of the Reverend T. W.

Obviously the Knights' side of the case was getting no representation in Rome. The suggestion of the Montreal priest that Powderly go to see the Holy Father was answered in a letter, forwarding more Knights of Labor literature to the Bishop of Montreal, "I do not think it will be necessary to go to Rome. There will be a special session of the G. A. called in a short time and it will deal with the question." [44] O'Donoghue, however, was persistent, for after giving the details of the Toronto streetcar strike he concluded:

> Meanwhile, I may tell you that I will write the Ex. Board my opinion that it is of vital importance that *you, if possible,* or some other fairly intelligent Catholic, be *sent to Rome* as soon as possible to interview the Pope himself, so as to settle the case. If such is done the accessions in Canada alone would much more than recoup the expense. I suggest this advisedly.[45]

Within ten days he had kept his word about contacting the board, and he jokingly told Powderly how good the trip would be for his health, although his wife might miss him. The suggestion had come, he said, from "some priests here in Canada who are favorable to our cause," and it had met with his hearty approval since under existing conditions he felt "chary as to *advising* Catholics either at Ottawa or in the Province of Quebec to join the Order." [46]

Their subsequent exchange of lengthy letters was characteristic of these two friendly but differing labor leaders. Complaining of his exhaustive travels, Powderly wrote:

> I pray to God with all the sincerity of my nature to relieve me of a burden that is paralyzing brain and body even though death be the agent. *I am tired of life.*
> Now a word which I hope I may never have to repeat, *I will not go to Rome.* It has been proposed to me before and I repeat

Graham of St. Joseph, Missouri, and of the Reverend Thomas Barry of Philadelphia ("commendable"). Scrapbook, March 5-25, 1886, *The Laborer* (Marinette, Wisconsin), March 11, 1886.

[44] PP. Powderly to William Keys, March 1, 1886, copy.

[45] PP, O'Donoghue to Powderly, Toronto, March 13, 1886.

[46] *Ibid.*, March 22, 1886.

it. I am an *American.* I have made every honorable proposition
to the clergy of this country to make changes in our laws, and
they either do not want to suggest any thing or else they do not
know enough and I am as positive that God gave me a soul to
save that I know more about the condition of the laboring people
and their wants than the Pope. I have done everything advised
everything in reason. Why am I not met in the spirit in which
I meet them.

Powderly expressed annoyance at the press reports that Fabre
had given the ritual and laws to two lawyers to revise them, and this
without consulting him. Yet a month before he had also placed
these in the hands of "such gentlemen" as had been suggested by
a Montreal priest.[47] He continued his letter in a furious vein:

God it makes my blood boil. Go to Rome! *Never.* I will
not leave *America.* And if the church wishes to array herself
on the side of Anarchy (in Montreal) let her do so. I will take
particular pains to place our side before the world in its proper
light. . . . Go to Rome indeed, and be spurned as Davitt was.
No Dan, I cannot bring *money* enough to make me acceptable
to his holiness. I am not a wealthy man, and the history of
the past proves that a poor man representing a *poor man's cause*
need not knock on the gates of Rome.
  I have an illustrious example before me in the action taken by
the Bishops of Ireland who, in matters relating to the political
and temporal affairs of the people of Ireland refuse to be guided
by Rome. The British government fears the advance of the
Knights of Labor in Canada and I am of the opinion that her
influence has reached the Bishop's palace at Montreal.[48]

[47] PP, Powderly to Fabre, Philadelphia, February 24, 1886, true-copy, not
in any letterbook.

[48] In February, 1886, Archbishop William J. Walsh of Dublin "on behalf
of a representative body of the Irish Catholic bishops," had written to William
E. Gladstone in favor of home rule and a settlement of the land question
which would begin with the suspension of evictions. The appointment of Walsh
in June, 1885, to succeed the politically unpopular Edward Cardinal McCabe
was made by Pope Leo XIII against English pressure, brought to bear in Rome
by the mission of the Catholic Lord George Errington. Cf. Patrick J. Walsh,
William J. Walsh, Archbishop of Dublin (Dublin, 1928), pp. 203-204, 131-178,
and also Shane Leslie, *Henry Edward Manning, His Life and Labours* (London,
1921), pp. 386-393. One of those who urged this action in favor of the milder

It was on a spiritual note that he launched into his peroration:

> Dan you must pardon me if I speak too plainly to you, but I am deeply stirred over this affair. Conscious of the justice of my cause I am willing to face hell itself in defence of it, so that if the die must be cast and the Church array herself on the side of wealth, usury, monopoly and oppression, I will array myself where I now stand, on the side of God's poor, along side of those for whom Christ died. I prefer to stand at the foot of the cross, aye, and be nailed to it, to joining hands with those who in this day and generation crucify over and over again the suffering patient image of the living God.[49]

Unabashed, O'Donoghue responded with a firmness softened by flattery and cajolery,

> I have recovered my breath, as you will allow before I close. After reading your letter I can always tell the humor in which you were in after getting home. So you are 'tired of life' are you. I am satisfied Mrs. Powderly is not to blame for this, and that is a satisfaction.

An ordinary man would certainly have long since been overcome by the work of the G. M. W. but Powderly was no ordinary man, O'Donoghue maintained. Avoiding the Irish parallel with a silence that seemed to give assent, he got to the heart of the argument:

disciple of the nationalist Archbishop Thomas W. Croke of Cashel was Michael Davitt of the National League. Although it was reported that he was well received there, Davitt's own account of "Rome and Ireland' contains not even a mention of the trip. (Walsh, *op. cit.*, pp. 140-141.) The Land League and its ladies' auxiliary had drawn "law and order" admonitions from Rome and the Irish bishops in 1881 and 1882; the Parnell Testimonial Fund of the spring of 1883 had benefited by a condemnation from the Congregation of Propaganda, and Peter's Pence had declined. Michael Davitt, *The Fall of Feudalism in Ireland* (London, 1904), pp. 397-408.

[49] PP, Powderly to O'Donoghue, March 23, 1886, copy. He was much more pithy with Turner, "Dan O'Donoghue wants me to go to Rome, D——— if I will, I will fight this battle out on American soil." Even more self-revealing was the following to John Hayes, "I have two fractured ribs and two boils to contend with, you can form an idea of the frame of mind in which I find myself." March 23, 24, 1886, copies.

Well, so you wont go to ——— but I am not to mention the name. But I reiterate that you will have to go *ultimately.* I am not talking to T. V. Powderly now as if he was an ordinary person; he is the head—aye, and the *brains,* apparently alone—of such an organization as the world never before heard of. Crude I grant it may be and is, but it is preeminetly Powderly's building nevertheless. You need not have told me that you are an *American;* but you have some Irish pluck in you also, as well as *perseverance.*

Illustrating his point from contemporary troubles, the Canadian held that just as the head of the Knights of Labor had gone from Vice-President H. M. Hoxie to the highest railroad authority, Gould himself, in an effort to settle the Southwest strike, so the same procedure should hold for the ecclesiastical sphere. Only by approaching Rome could he say he had "exhausted all honorable means." With a neat twist O'Donoghue continued, "It is just because *we know* that the Pope *does not know* as much as you know of our condition and wants that it is essential that you should see him. If he did there would be no occasion for your going." He advised, too, that a frank inquiry be made of Fabre. In view of Powderly's incriminations he remarked that since the Church had not yet definitely spoken on the Knights, "there is hardly cause to be too nasty." Asserting his own interest in the oppressed, O'Donoghue proceeded to have the last word which amounted to a dressing down of the general master workman:

My suggestion was with the object of helping that very class, and saving them the crucifixion as far as possible. My opinion has not changed. If *you will not practice* that calm untiring, and often unappreciated patience which you preach as essential to the success of our cause, why *preach* it to me and everybody else? While I love you the more for the pluck and spirit of the man, yet I question the wisdom of your view under all the circumstances.

He had already approached the executive board on the subject and he hoped Powderly's "whims" would not be honored, but if necessary he would bring it up in the general assembly. In conclusion he said:

I know you are sensitive, so am I. Yet how often do I 'swallow' myself in obedience to the will of those here in Toronto whose confidence I am proud to possess, when they hold that it must be done in the interest of my brothers of the Order.[50]

Not only did this Roman mission fail to materialize, but despite all the words of protestation and promise the constitutional amendments—along lines that remained unmentioned specifically at that time—were never made. If Powderly's "whims" opposing the trip were not the principal reasons for the trip abroad, the month of March brought the all-absorbing and distracting strike. On the complaint that the terms of the settlement they had won in the second Wabash strike of the fall of 1885 were not fulfilled, all the members of District Assembly 101, composed of workers on the Texas and Pacific and the Missouri Pacific, walked off the job under the leadership of Martin Irons between March 6 and 10.[51] The ensuing work stoppage, supported even financially by the executive board of the Knights of Labor, was marked by the issuance of injunctions and court actions, the obstructing of railroad traffic and battles with scabs, bloodshed, and killing. One of the worst outbursts occurred in East St. Louis where walkouts began on March 25 and before long, as a result of the halting of traffic for thirty days, the city of St. Louis "was for a time in almost as much distress as if besieged by a hostile army." [52]

In the midst of this turmoil there broke in the press of the country Powderly's "secret circular" of March 13, which ordered organizing to stop, decried strikes without efforts at conciliation and arbitration, and advised against the projected strike for the eight-hour day on May 1. It also brought to the Knights' attention the position of the Church in these words:

The Church has been watching our order for years. In our infancy we had but little power for good or for evil. Today we are the strongest as well as the weakest labor organization on earth. Strong in members and principles, strong in the justice of our demands if properly made, we are weak in the methods

[50] PP, O'Donoghue to Powderly, Toronto, March 29, 1886.
[51] Ruth A. Allen, *The Great Southwest Strike* (Austin, 1942), pp. 45-46.
[52] *Ibid.*, p. 87.

we use to set our claims before the world. Strikes are often the forerunners of lawless action. One blow brings another, and if a single act of ours encourages the anarchist element, we must meet the antagonism of the Church. I warn our members against hasty ill-considered action. The Church will not interfere with us so long as we maintain the law. If the law is wrong it is our duty to change it. I am ashamed to meet with clergymen and others to tell them that our order is composed of law-abiding, intelligent men, while the next dispatch brings news of some petty boycott or strike.[53]

The only reactions from men of religion, at least in the records preserved, came from Protestant ministers. Social Christianity had grown gradually in the post-Civil War years and by this time not only did pulpits carry its message, but in several cases Protestant clergymen held membership and even office in the Knights of Labor.[54] The pages of *John Swinton's Paper*, nevertheless, showed his disgust with most of them for their fear of offending wealthy pew-holders, but at the same time he revealed that he had not abandoned hope of getting them out of their pulpits to see the world about them. The burden of such comments from 1884 to 1886— none of which he directed at Catholics—was decidedly unfavorable, although he strove by conferences to bring ministers of religion to an awareness of the labor problem.[55] Powderly, on the contrary, in the spring of 1886 did not show them even the courtesy of an answer, although ministers congratulated him, wished him well,

[53] Quoted in *Freeman's Journal*, April 3, 1886, from New York *Sun* dispatch of St. Louis, March 26. *Proceedings* (Richmond, 1886), p. 39, has a reference to the circular as being in Appendix A, but such was not printed.

[54] It is hardly possible to say how many there were. Swinton cited several in his issue of March 7, 1886. Cf. also Joseph R. Buchanan, *The Story of a Labor Agitator* (New York, 1903), pp. 48, 239. Powderly at a much later date wrote across an envelope containing the typescript of his chapter "Ecclesiastical Opposition," (*Path,* pp. 317-382): "Had clericals informed themselves about the K. of L. by joining the Order as other ministers did Cardinal Gibbons would not have had the occasion to go to Rome."

[55] Cf. Charles Howard Hopkins, *The Rise of the Social Gospel in American Protestantism, 1865-1915* (New Haven, 1940), pp. 79-97 especially, and Aaron I. Abell, *The Urban Impact on American Protestantism, 1865-1900* (Cambridge, 1943), pp. 57-87.

preached on his words, sought his counsel and invited him to address their gatherings.[56] Perhaps the ready use of the stamp, "No answer required," on all this correspondence came from the fact that he was on his "sickbed." His illness had recently been the occasion for a labor paper to defend him against a professedly religious man, "the editor of the *Independent* of New York and his like, who sneeringly call him 'King Powderly.'"[57] The Protestant religious press on the whole, although it favored organization, was apprehensive about strikes and boycotts, and lack of regard for the individual worker's freedom in joining a union and following its decisions. For this reason it saw great hope in Powderly's temperance and conservatism for a victory over the "demons of rum and violence."[58]

No Catholic authority endorsed Powderly at this period, but the Catholic press did bestow upon him now for the first time a fairly generous blessing. Like their Protestant brethren they expressed strict disapprobation of violence and warned against union monopolies among workers. But they seem to have gone beyond the Protestants in their hostility to the abuses of big business and their advocacy of corrective legislation. An approvingly reprinted editorial of the St. Louis *Western Watchman* appeared in the *Catholic Telegraph* on "The Rights and Wrongs of Labor." It considered legislation necessary "to make the relations of capital and labor mutually compatible" as the courts were useless ("our judges show no disposition to political martyrdom") and arbitration was a "temporary truce a subterfuge rather than a solution." The Knights and all organized labor, the editorial advised, should bring their influence to bear on legislatures and forego taking the law into their own hands. The editorial writer complained of unions working more

---

[56] PP, C. C. McCabe to Powderly, New York, March 27, 1886; W. S. McKellar, Mattoon, Illinois, April 9, 1886; J. C. Delaney, Harrisburg, March 28, 1886; Lyman Abbott, New York, March 29, 1886; Joseph Anderson (American Congress of Churches), Waterbury, April 8, 1886.

[57] Scrapbook, March-June, 1886, *Granite Cutters' Journal*, April, 1886. Cf. Ware, *op. cit.*, p. 84, on his physical weakness and hatred of travel.

[58] Carl Warren Griffiths, "Some Protestant Attitudes on the Labor Question in 1886," *Church History*, XI (June, 1942), 138-148.

against non-union workers than against capital, and he said by way of explanation,

> The principle of monopoly is as dangerous in the case of labor as in that of capital, and should be resisted. But we must have patience with these Knights of Labor. They have been taught dangerous doctrine by demagogues and have received bad example from their employers.

Organized capital resorted to the law which did its bidding while labor could fall back only on coercion, which at best won but temporary success.[59] This same emphasis appeared in an editorial of the Pittsburgh *Catholic*. The Baltimore council had not legislated on the labor movement, this paper held, since it believed it legitimate, and "its aims commendable and its methods peaceful." Yet labor had to be careful because no organization "has the right—the moral right—to prevent non-union men from working, as has been done." [60] The Philadelphia Catholic paper, showing an awareness of conditions in the State of Pennsylvania, commented on the injustice of forcing unwilling workers to strike. Granting the unquestioned right to strike if the employer's terms were unsatisfactory, the editorial pointed out that although workingmen should be "united together by the common desire to place themselves in a position which will enable them to win a decent livelihood and resist unjust and oppressive exactions on the part of their employers," this should be done by moral suasion, not intimidation.[61]

Without expressing it, but probably influenced somewhat by the fact he was a Catholic, the Catholic journals heaped accolades on General Master Workman Powderly. None of them, however, spoke officially for the bishops of their respective cities. The *Catholic*

[59] Cincinnati, April 1, 1886. On April 15 it found two lessons in the strike which held the interest of the nation. These were the menace of "nefarious and fraudulent schemes of unprincipled financiers," and the general odium attached to an organization by "rowdy and revolutionary characters." Both showed the imperative need of "sound and adequate legislation."

[60] April 3, 1886; also *Catholic Telegraph*, April 22, 1886, and *Michigan Catholic*, April 29, which advised each man in a trade association to decide for himself, "whether the demand is reasonable or not."

[61] *Catholic Standard*, March 27, 1886.

Standard noted the wide approval of Powderly's circular and called him "a cool, clear thinker," who was conservative and had a regard for religion.[62] In a similar vein the *Catholic Columbian* remarked that the Knights of Labor "put the right man in the right place when they chose him for their leader." [63] The Boston *Pilot* not only answered the Chicago *Times,* which had called Powderly a "Czar" and a "Brazen Bandit," but rated his words as "wise," and editorialized on bloodshed in St. Louis as "First Blood for Jay Gould." [64] Accompanying the reminder that the Church was the great conservative force in society, and that "Capital is helpless without labor, and labor cannot satisfactorily exist without capital," there went the recommendation of editor James McMaster, that the workers stick with Powderly.[65] Within a few weeks the *Freeman's* had lost much of its trust in the ability of the head of the Order and even wondered editorially why a more American title such as "Brotherhood" was not used by the organization.[66] The *Catholic Review* lamented the enforced lack of the ailing Powderly's leadership in the strike which had given the capitalists a chance to play into the hands of more violent men such as Irons, whose alleged address, "to the Workingmen of the World," was incendiary, "even if backed by hard fact." [67] While the radical Denver *Labor Enquirer* protested even Powderly's mention of the Church in his circular, the almost equally bold but Irish and Catholic paper, the *Irish World,* carried a favorable account of his "life and works," and defended the Order in the Southwest to the extent of calling for a fight against Gould "all along the line." [68]

Although no high ecclesiastic gave expression to words of approval or of reproach on the occasion of this famous strike, the opportunity was used by one priest who was more closely in con-

[62] April 3, 1886.

[63] Scrapbook, April 3-16, 1886, Columbus, April 3, 1886.

[64] April 17, 1886.

[65] *Freeman's Journal,* April 10, 1886.

[66] April 24, 1886.'

[67] April 17, 1886, Allen, *op. cit.,* pp. 88-90.

[68] *Labor Enquirer,* April 17, 1886; *Irish World,* April 17, 1886, and also *Catholic Telegraph,* April 22.

tact with the Knights in the field than any other cleric. The
Reverend Cornelius O'Leary was one of 500 witnesses called to
testify before the congressional committee which sat from April 20
to May 14 to investigate the strike situation.[69] His testimony was
as bold and notable as were his deeds during the strike in St. Louis
for, although no standard history mentions O'Leary, Powderly bore
witness to his help at that time and again later in life. He told
the Archbishop of Baltimore, to whom he sent the priest with a
letter of introduction, that after calling citizens to his aid in St.
Louis, "no one rendered the cause of law and order more effectual
service at that time than Father O'Leary who proved himself indeed to be a true priest of the people." He sought a hearing from
Gibbons for him since he felt responsible for the troubles which
O'Leary had suffered from the time he co-operated with the Knights.
Powderly went so far as to say, "I thank Father O'Leary more than
any living man for the termination of the strike before violence
was resorted to."[70] He repeated this assertion in his memoirs
wherein he added the charge that the priest's trouble consisted in
losing his parish because of the complaints made by the railroad
interest to his superior, Archbishop Kenrick.[71] The historian of the
Archdiocese of St. Louis calls the priest, "energetic, but somewhat
erratic," but he adds nothing that would contradict Powderly, for he
relates that "During the railroad strike of 1886 his imprudence in
speech brought the threat of an early removal of the machine shop
from De Soto. This led to his transfer to Webster Groves in October, 1886."[72] When the story circulated that the Missouri Pacific
Railroad had offered to build a church in De Soto on O'Leary's

[69] In his testimony before this Curtin Committee—which filled nine pages—
the priest claimed he had counseled only peace, but he took the opportunity to
support the Knights very strongly, and to blame the railroad for the trouble.
U. S. Congress, *Investigation of Labor Troubles in Missouri, Arkansas, Kansas,
Texas, and Illinois.* House Report 4174, 49th Cong., 2d Sess., 1886, Part I,
pp. 468-477.

[70] BCA, 82-W-9, Powderly to Gibbons, June 30, 1887.

[71] *Path,* pp. 133 and 38.

[72] John Rothensteiner, *History of the Archdiocese of St. Louis* (St. Louis,
1928), II, 525-526. No archival evidence was available. Cf. Essay on Sources,
p. 384.

removal the general master workman sought to counteract the feared effect by proposing to undertake the project himself.[73]   O'Leary admitted that for the financial interest of the parish he thought it necessary to leave and he acknowledged there was a rumor to the effect that the company had proposed to pay off the debt on the church if he were changed.   More than that, he maintained the railroad had encouraged a petition for his removal and spread the story that the shops would be removed on his account.   The priest had not hesitated to defy publicly the employers, and in denying their charges he pictured himself only as a peacemaker in the recent strike.   His account read:

> *I was not at home when it was called nor for a week after.* . . . My only crime was to endeavor to bring about an arbitration by calling a mass meeting at the Court House in St. Louis and demanding a settlement.   I still, it is true, point out their fraud and the demoralizing influence of railroad corporations and publicly assert my adherence to the principles of the order.[74]

Not long after taking over his new mission at Webster Groves, Father O'Leary once more claimed his departure from that place was based on the arbitrary action of Archbishop Kenrick, who came under the influence of a prejudiced and influential layman.[75]   At any rate, O'Leary was out of the archdiocese from March, 1887, to January, 1888, and on his return he waited eight years till the resignation of Archbishop Kenrick before he was again entrusted with the care of a parish.[76]

Whatever opinions the members of the American hierarchy had on this labor struggle they were not made public.   The *Catholic Review,* however, in the midst of the agitation on Gould's Southwestern system, published a letter purporting to be directed to "a meeting looking towards the redress of certain wrongs of working men," from the secretary of Archbishop James Gibbons.   The Baltimore prelate assured them of the "cordial approval" of all the hier-

---

[73] PP, Powderly to O'Leary, September 27, 1886, copy.
[74] PP, O'Leary to Powderly, De Soto, October 25, 1886.
[75] PP, O'Leary to Powderly, Webster Groves, March 30, 1887.
[76] Rothensteiner, *op. cit.,* II, 526.

archy on "every movement consistent with justice and fairness of dealing toward employers" and he referred the group to the "regulations and counsels of the Plenary Council." [77]   It is more certain that several of the bishops were aware of the general problem committed to the archbishops at Baltimore. McQuaid of Rochester, thinking of the example of the Primrose League in England, was of the opinion that great caution should be used in condemning or approving societies among the laity.[78] With regard to the labor question, Chatard of Vincennes was inclined to favor the use of arbitration, and he remarked that Powderly also favored this solution, although he still "holds on to strikes, as his 100 ton Krupp gun. He wants both hands free to cope with the lion later." [79] Archbishop Corrigan was pictured as singularly free of such thoughts by Patrick Hickey's *Catholic Review*. In answer to a story in the Chicago *Tribune* that he was busily concerned with the Knights on orders from Rome, it quoted him as saying, "I have had no letter from Rome and no correspondence whatever with any human being in reference to the subject." [80]   The main concern of the Archbishop of New York at that time was the Ancient Order of Hibernians. In connection with this particular group Archbishop Ryan of Philadelphia repeated the distinction which he had offered previously at Rome and at Baltimore between Catholic societies with religious ends and societies of Catholics with secular purposes. With regard to the

[77] April 3, 1886.

[78] RDA, McQuaid to Corrigan, Rochester, March 25, 1886, copy. This secret English group of "younger, more democratic and more militant Conservatives" was established in 1883 under some Masonic and Orange lodge influence. Besides his supposedly favorite flower the league inherited from Disraeli his imperialism and this soon predominated over its aim of social reform. Janet Henderson Robb, *The Primrose League, 1883-1906* (New York, 1942), pp. 37-47. The opposition of some priests, and especially the Bishop of Nothingham, Edward Bagshawe, resulted in what Manning characterized as "scandal and ridicule and irritation," until the early part of 1886 when the cardinal sent Herbert Vaughan, Bishop of Salford, to relieve the mind of Rome. Leslie, *op. cit.*, pp. 446-447.

[79] Paulist Archives, Hecker Papers, Chatard to Lawrence Kehoe, editor of the *Catholic World*, Indianapolis, March 29, 1886.

[80] *Catholic Review*, March 27, 1886.

latter, Ryan suggested to Corrigan the policy of Archbishop Kenrick of St. Louis—whose coadjutor he had been from 1872 to 1884— namely, *"to let them alone,* unless anything really objectionable should develop itself and then condemn them if the obnoxious features were not removed." "The matter," he continued, "becomes of very grave importance in view of the great labor contra Capital movement in the country. The Knights of labor are in some places almost exclusively Catholic." [81] Ryan's interest was definitely aroused since he even expressed a desire to meet Powderly and talk things over with him, although there is no indication that the conversation was ever held.[82]

The hope of such a meeting was nowhere in the plans of Elzear-Alexandre Taschereau of Quebec. If anything this archbishop had grown stronger in his original position, nor had he remained oblivious of current events while awaiting a definitive answer from Rome. The numerous strikes of the Knights of Labor served to prove to Taschereau their danger, especially since they controlled "so many thousands of workers." [83] With this in mind on April 19, 1886, he issued his "Mandement sur certaines sociétés défendues," which was addressed to the diocesan and religious clergy and all the faithful of the Archdiocese of Quebec.[84] After recalling the effects of excommunication which cut one off from the Church, Taschereau exhorted those belonging to the Masons to take advantage of the papal jubilee year, in which all confessors were given the special faculties (without resorting to the bishop each time as was usual in such reserved cases) of absolving such penitents. He went quickly to affairs at hand and pointing to the upheavals in many cities of the United States, the Archbishop of Quebec blamed them all on the "strikes organized by one society whose branches extend everywhere and embrace workers of every kind." The real heart of the message read:

[81] NYAA, Ryan to Corrigan, Philadelphia, April 21, 1886. Cf. Zwierlein, *op. cit.,* II, 378-437 on the Ancient Order of Hibernians and its Irish background.

[82] PP, Martin Maloney to Powderly, Philadelphia, April 21, 1886.

[83] AAQ, 35-264, Taschereau to Duhamel, Quebec, April 10, 1886, copy.

[84] Têtu-Gagnon, *Mandements,* II, 554-557. *La Vérité's* version (August 25, 1894) leaves out the blame he put on the Knights of Labor.

Having learned that delegates of the Society of the *Knights of Labor* have endeavored to recruit members in some parts of this province, we believe it is our duty, dear brethren, to put you on your guard against it, and please remark we do not speak in our own name, but in the name of the Holy See whose advice we have sought.

The now familiar answer of 1884 was given, this time introduced as the product of a year's examination of the rules and constitution "with all possible care and prudence." The Canadian archbishop, referring to the many offers to conform to every ecclesiastical requirement, continued:

We do not ignore, dear brethren, that to elude this clear and precise condemnation it was believed that to change certain articles in the constitution would suffice. In connection with this we might remark two things:
1. That the judgment being based on *the principles, the organization and the statutes of the society,* everything would have to be altered from top to bottom in order to escape condemnation.
2. That the Holy See is the only judge competent to decide whether the changes effected are apt to render this society acceptable for the children of the Church. While waiting for this decision a Catholic must consider the society as forbidden.

The *mandement* went on to remind the subjects of the archdiocese that the Holy Office had exhorted the bishops to use against this and similar societies the "procedures and remedies" proposed in "De secta massonum," which in effect was "to regard as guilty of grave sin and unworthy of absolution those who persist in taking part in it." Taschereau further counseled them to stay close to their pastors, and he repeated the warning of the Fourth Provincial Council of Quebec (May 14, 1868) against societies which appealed to workers through a show of mutual protection and charity. He closed his instruction by ordering that after the public reading in the churches on the following Sunday all should join in reciting a *Pater* and an *Ave* for the conversion of those who were members of societies forbidden by the Church.

This Quebec publication, although in the main a repetition of the Roman response, was also somewhat of a clarification. At least

the *mandement* pointed out specifically that it was not the archbishop's own doing and that only Rome could decide whether any
alteration was sufficient to justify a change in its original judgment.
Hence, as if its import was striking home for the first time, it was
reported to have caused great excitement among the workers of
Montreal and of the whole neighboring Province of Ontario.[85] From
farther west in Canada, where it was even said to have "created a
regular panic among Catholic members," came the suggestion of
appeal to Rome on the precedent of the recent reversal in the
English case of the Primrose League.[86] Archbishop Lynch of Toronto, however, set the pattern which was closer to that in the
United States. He had relented a bit on his former position of
strict neutrality. As far as he was concerned, in Ontario only
further joining by Catholics would be forbidden until Rome came
to a decision on the second copy of the constitution of the Knights
of Labor, which, he maintained—though on what grounds he did
not say—was under consideration.[87] The prudence of his approach
in contrast to the hasty action in Quebec was praised by the *Irish
Canadian*.[88]

Meanwhile across the border to the south the Quebec pronouncement caused neither great excitement nor prompt action. In Chicago
Vicar General Conway again, "speaking for Archbishop Feehan,"
discounted Taschereau's condemnation as not applying to the
Knights as he knew them.[89] The New York reporters did not get
as good copy from St. Patrick's Cathedral, for Corrigan referred
them to Monsignor William Quinn, who said that as far as the
United States was concerned the bishops were still watching the
Knights and had not yet spoken on the matter.[90] This story was
spread through the Pennsylvania press, and Archbishop Corrigan's
secretary was asked how correct it was, "for many priests who cannot see their way to absolve the Knights are very anxious to know

[85] *Catholic Review*, May 8, 1886.
[86] PP, Richard Ryan to Powderly, Winnepeg, April 29, 1886.
[87] New York *World*, April 30, 1886
[88] Toronto, May 6, 1886.
[89] New York *World*, April 30, 1886.
[90] *Ibid*.

if the Holy See has condemned an order which is everywhere working such manifest injustice." [91]   This statement revealed the persistent mentality of some clergy of that region, but unfortunately for the picture of Corrigan's mind at this time, what this correspondent characterized as a "prompt and very satisfactory reply" was not found.[92]

An unexcited attitude was evidenced even by the usually volatile general master workman, Powderly himself. On the day he was marking the official end of the unsuccessful Southwest strike, he calmly noted the latest ecclesiastical eruption: "I see that the Archbishop of Quebec has launched his mandament [sic] against the order, well it may do some good and bring some of our hot heads to their senses." [93]

The attention of Archbishop Elder of Cincinnati was brought to the question by enterprising reporters and he, in turn, at least stimulated the thought of the Archbishop of Baltimore. Elder was interviewed by the Pittsburgh *Dispatch*, when its representatives were unable to see Bishop Richard Phelan of that city. They hunted out the Cincinnati prelate at the Passionist monastery in Pittsburgh. Wisely protesting his inability to form a decided opinion with his present knowledge of the subject, he pointed out that such Roman responses were usually able to be evaluated properly only in the light of the framing of the original question and the evidence that was sent with it. As to probable action in the United States, Elder simply referred them to the instructions of the council of Baltimore.[94] He sent Gibbons a more accurate copy of this interview as printed in his own diocesan paper, and he took the occasion to ask if any step was contemplated with regard to the Knights. The slow beginnings of joint action by the American archbishops was foreshadowed when he wrote:

It seems to me that the answer given to Msgr. Taschereau cannot be entirely ignored. I suggest in the first place that you

91 NYAA, D. J. McDermott to C. E. McDonnell, Philadelphia, May 13, 1886.
92 NYAA, D. J. McDermott to C. E. McDonnell, Philadelphia, May 14 [sic], 1886.
93 PP, Powderly to William O. McDonnell, May 3, 1886, copy.
94 *Catholic Telegraph,* May 6, 1886.

write to the Propaganda and ask that they await information from the United States, and that you proceed to send whatever information you have, and request the other Archbishops to do the same. Or perhaps—as the Council of Baltimore commits the matter of Secret Societies to the Archbishops, it might be well for us to consult together, and send a common statement, if we can agree on one. I confess I know very little about them. I will proceed at once to learn all that I can.[95]

The answer of the archbishop who was called on to take the lead revealed that he at least had a little more knowledge of the problem than his inquirer and had given it some thought. Gibbons replied:

With regard to the Knights of Labor it is not easy to determine what action if any should be taken. A masterly inactivity & a vigilant eye on their proceedings is perhaps the best thing to be done in the present junction. If the Holy See has disapproved of the society in Quebec, as has been represented—the decision was *juxta exposita.* My impression is that the metropolitans of the United States will be almost, if not unanimous in not condemning them. The society cannot be held responsible for the acts of individual members. There are however some features of this organization that ought to receive an official rebuke:

1. Their persecution of non-unionmen, forbidding employers to employ them &

2. The custom of boycotting.

At our university meeting to be held on the 12th, this question will come up, as well as the A. O. of Hibernians. I wish you could attend this meeting.[96]

It has occurred to me to propose to the Abps., that a formula of paternal exhortation (calling attention also to the irregularities which I have referred to) be drawn up, that the draft be submitted to each of the Abps., published in the name of all the metropolitans after they have approved of it.

[95] BCA, 80-U-3, Elder to Gibbons, Cincinnati, May 3, 1886.

[96] Elder was not a member of the committee and there is no record of a scussion of this question at that time. The university group on that day cided on Bishop John J. Keane of Richmond as first rector of the Catholic niversity of America and prepared to lay the whole project formally before e Holy See. John Tracy Ellis, *The Formative Years of the Catholic University America* (Washington, 1946), pp. 175-179.

But we should be careful not to be too hard on them, otherwise they would suspect us of siding with the moneyed corporations & employers.[97]

Gibbons' adherence to this last dictum was expressed in an
otherwise unsubstantiated newspaper story. It followed in general
the line of thought to which he had given private expression. The
Archbishop of Baltimore was reported as saying that Taschereau's
actions were likely based on local conditions, and although he admitted no thorough knowledge of the Order in the United States,
"yet from reading the newspapers and Mr. Powderly's public statement, I have inferred that the objects of the Knights are praiseworthy and in no way opposed to the views of the Church." He
added, "The Catholic prelates will to a man declare in favor of the
organization of labor." He distinguished the Church's position on
societies, her opposition when they were anti-social and blindly oath-
bound, and her lack of concern when "a man joins an organization
swearing to keep its workings, with the proviso that nothing therein
shall be contrary to the laws of the land, to his conscience and his
religious tenets." It was along these lines, the interview concluded
that the re-examination of the constitution in Rome would be
decided.[98]

The opinions of several other American bishops on the latest
condemnation of the Knights of Labor were publicized at this time
at least on a local scale. Both Bishops McQuaid and Phelan found
the Knights reprehensible only in their interference with the rights
of others. In the words of the latter, they agreed on the Canadian
situation, "The letter had no significance outside the jurisdiction
of its recipient."[99] Unlike Phelan, Bishop Caspar Borgess of
Detroit had not examined the constitution, so he confined himself

[97] AAC, Gibbons to Elder, Baltimore, May 6, 1886.

[98] *The Journal of United Labor,* May 10, 1886, reprinted it as a story obtained by a correspondent of the Philadelphia *Press.* The Washington *Republic*
carried it substantially on May 2, 1886, and added the consenting opinion of
Placide L. Chapelle, rector of St. Matthew's Church in the national capital.

[99] *Irish World,* May 8, 1886. This paper carried no editorial opinion of its
own, but its Boston counterpart, the *Republic,* simply spoke of the trouble in
Quebec as a local one. May 8, 1886.

o "general principles on the subject," which were mostly on the non-interference with "the liberty of a fellow laborer in selling his labor or such a price as he judges to be for his own interests, and the reasonable support of his family." [100] The Catholic paper in Borgess' diocese did not stop with listing the reported opinions of prominent prelates, but assisted by a "learned priest in another state," it gave its own opinion. It did not simply say Taschereau's words were to no purpose in the United States, but claimed he was wrong and would probably have to withdraw the condemnation which he had inflicted on a society that was not anti-social. The Michigan paper ignored the Roman origin of the decree, but protested that it had been applied without consulting the hierarchy of the country where the Order had its headquarters.[101]

It may have been for this reason, as much as for its coverage of episcopal sentiment on the question, that Taschereau shortly thereafter chose to delate the *Michigan Catholic* to Rome. His letter explained to Simeoni his renewal of the condemnation in April because the decree of September, 1884, "had been less solemnly promulgated in 1884." It was his contention that the latest public statement had raised a storm in the United States, "where there are innumerable Catholics affiliated with this prohibited society, with the knowledge and approbation of the clergy and even the episcopate." As evidence he presented five folios of clippings from the May 6 issue of the *Michigan Catholic*. He directed Simeoni to one folio where there were "two letters praising this paper from two bishops and hence one can conclude that these prelates more or less approve what is contained in this paper on the present question." In doing this the Quebec archbishop was making the most of letters of endorsement carried on the masthead from Bishops Caspar Borgess and Henry J. Richter which did not, however, make the paper an official organ of either diocese. He enclosed also a letter of congratulations which he had just received from a group of Catholics in New York in praise of what he now called his pastoral.

[100] *Michigan Catholic*, May 6, 1886
[101] *Ibid*. The editors of this Detroit journal were William H. Hughes and John Hyde and it carried the endorsement of the Bishops of Detroit and Grand Rapids.

It had found its way into the press of the continent and as a consequence he went on to say he usually received threatening and contumelious letters. Some of them tried to tell him that his condemnation stopped at the boundaries of his jurisdiction, forgetting that the case concerned the promulgation of a decree of the Holy Office. Stretching the facts a bit—at least in so far as the extant evidence shows—Taschereau concluded on the familiar theme:

> Many American bishops asked me in 1885 to send them a copy of the consultation made in Oct. 1883 and of the response given in Sept. 1884 by the Holy Office. This I willingly did and now I see them, just like the others keeping a deep silence concerning the condemnation by name of the Knights of Labor.
>
> As I have already said in my letter of March 2, 1886 it seems to be most urgent that the Holy See put an end to this scandal as soon as possible.[102]

While the "scandal" continued, it seemed to be less the concern of the general master workman than before, since he was taken up with other affairs of the greatest immediate importance to the Order. Although there were conflicting views on whether Taschereau's *mandement* constituted a "thunderbolt" or not, it was reported that Fabre refused to meet a Montreal committee for the revision of the constitution, and an Ottawa knight lamented the lack of progress because of clerical opposition.[103] Nonetheless, Powderly's real pressing trouble was in the United States. Shortly after the great strike of the spring of 1886 had subsided a friendly Catholic paper commented, "There is a misunderstanding as to the attitude of the Church towards the Knights of Labor, and now the Anarchists have stepped in to complicate matters." [104] It was referring to the Haymarket riot in Chicago on May 4, 1886, which with the Gould victory in the Southwest, is generally taken a

---

102 AAQ, 35-280, 1, Taschereau to Simeoni, Quebec, May 13, 1886, cop *La Vérité* later carried only the conclusion, August 25, 1894.

103 PP, George Gale to Powderly, Ottawa, June 7, 1886; and *John Sw ton's Paper,* May 23, 30, 1886.

104 Brooklyn *Examiner,* May 8, 1886.

marking the beginning of the decline of the Order.[105] In this famous case eight anarchists, including a former knight, Albert Parsons, were tried for the throwing of a bomb into a squad of police, and after a highly questionable trial three were hanged. Powderly was reflecting the general American opinion which was fostered by the press when he said, "This Chicago business is a shame and a disgrace to labor." [106] To face such unusual problems the general assembly was ready by the end of that month to meet in special session in Cleveland (May 25 to June 2). The delegates had to deal with questions of strikes, boycotts, and the increasing number of disputes with trade unions. Despite the promises, which went back to those made in Montreal the previous February, and despite as well the suggestion of John Swinton, neither the agenda nor the actual records reveal that any consideration was given to the problem of the Church and the Order.[107]

A sense of security on this problem could, of course, have easily lulled the head of the Knights if he had been guided solely by the Catholic press. These papers not only generally idolized him but spread broadcast all the favorable stories on the Order.[108] Powderly's leadership, already considered "conservative and intelligent," [109] and judged to be "almost irreparable" if ever lost,[110] was further enhanced by another circular against all forms of violence right down to intemperance.[111] Even in St. Louis it was conceded, "what the Knights in this part of the country most need is not Church discipline, but a little every day common sense." [112] It was universally held that the Quebec action would have no effect in

[105] Mary R. Beard, *op. cit.*, VIII, 582. This view is somewhat questioned in David, *op. cit.*, pp. 535-536.

[106] PP, Powderly to Turner, May 7, 1886, copy.

[107] *John Swinton's Paper*, May 9, 1886; *Proceedings* (Cleveland, 1886), pp. 1-78.

[108] The Gibbons interview, for example, was in the *Catholic Columbian*, May 15, 1886 (Scrapbook, March-June, 1886); *Central Catholic Advocate* of Louisville, May 20, and the *Catholic Review*, June 6, 1886.

[109] Brooklyn *Examiner*, May 15, 1886.

[110] *Catholic Knight*, May 15, 1886.

[111] *Catholic Standard*; *Republic*, May 15, 1886.

[112] *Western Watchman*, May 15, 1886.

the United States.[113]   McMaster politely reminded the Quebec weekly, *La Vérité,* that "Rome speaks to us through our own beloved shepherds" and he recalled the procedure for settlement laid down by the Baltimore council, namely, through the committee of arch-bishops.[114]   His paper also defended its stand against two Pennsyl-vania priests, although it became increasingly cynical about Powderly, who would be valuable, it said, if he put the principles of his religion to practice and did not get "puffed up with foolish pride." [115]   Another Catholic paper hit on what was closest to the future solution by suggesting that Archbishop Gibbons have Powderly consult with a committee of bishops.[116]

There were other definite signs of a *rapprochement* between Catholics and the Knights of Labor.   Several of the newspapers followed the doings of the Cleveland convention.   The *Catholic Mirror* of Baltimore pessimistically thought it marked the ruin of the Order, and expected the Home Club of New York would oust Powderly at the October gathering.   Hence it urged, "Let him act promptly now, and we do not doubt that, having smashed the old concern, as he is able to do, he can build upon its ruins a society of working men, strong, liberal, united and certain of ultimate victory." [117]   On the other hand, one journal praised its work highly, while another thought it looked into the future "altogether too far for the present stage of industrial conflict," and still a third dubbed Powderly the Parnell of the poor people of America.[118]   Perhaps even more significant was a petition asking him to visit the Shenandoah Valley.   Among the first to endorse the request for the visit was the Reverend Daniel O'Connor of Girardville, with whom Powderly had mixed in 1879 and who had been at last converted

113 E. g., *Connecticut Catholic,* May 16, 1886.

114 *Freeman's Journal,* May 15, 1886.

115 May 22, 1886.

116 Buffalo, *Catholic Union and Times,* quoted in *Connecticut Catholic,* May 16, 1886.

117 June 12, 1886. On this ring within D. A. 49 which opposed Powderly cf. Ware, *op. cit.,* pp. 111-112.

118 Brooklyn *Examiner,* June 5, 1866; *Pilot,* June 12; *Connecticut Catholic,* June 12.

to the cause.[119] Another Pennsylvania pastor sought to have him as an extra attraction at a picnic for the benefit of his church.[120] Such actions indicated his growing acceptability in Catholic circles. More oblique evidence of this same fact came in reports of some bigotry against him on the grounds that he ran the Order in the interest of the Church.[121]

While this general atmosphere of peace reigned in the United States, it was far from prevalent in French Canada. On the issuance of the pastoral letter (June 26, 1886) of the Seventh Provincial Council, Taschereau, this time with his ten suffragan bishops behind him, included under the condemnation of Freemasonry a special mention of the Knights of Labor. The latter was then called dangerous because of its cosmopolitan character. Its directors were in a foreign country, "which at a given moment could be in opposition to the interests of and even at war with the government to which these members owe allegiance." [122] This nationalistic tone struck a new note in the consideration of the problem, and may, of course, have been inspired by the international relations between Canada and the United States at that time. Only the previous month the long-lived fisheries dispute had aroused widespread interest when loud American protests had been raised against the seizure of a vessel.[123]

Besides this Quebec council the month of June, 1886, witnessed other notable events of ecclesiastical importance. Both Canada and the United States were honored when Taschereau and Gibbons were made cardinals of the Holy Roman Church.[124] The two new princes of the Church, who were later to take the lead on opposite sides of the labor question, amicably exchanged invitations to the ceremony of receiving the biretta from the papal ablegates in their

---

[119] PP, George S. Boyle to Powderly, Shenandoah, June 7, 24, 1886.

[120] PP, C. A. McDermott to Powderly, Connellsville, June 16, 1886.

[121] *Central Catholic Advocate,* June 17, 1886.

[122] Têtu-Gagnon, *Mandements,* II, 575. It is not included in *La Vérité.*

[123] Charles Callan Tansill, *Canadian-American Relations, 1875-1911* (New Haven, 1943), p. 27.

[124] In Taschereau's case among the forces working to get him the honor was Premier Macdonald who had contacted Cardinal Manning. Pope, *op. cit.,* II, 212-213; Rumilly, *op. cit.,* V, 144-145.

respective cathedrals.[125] Another innovation in the ecclesiastical picture in the Dominion of Canada which emanated from Rome was the setting up of Montreal and Ottawa as metropolitan sees. Henceforth these sees would be independent of Quebec, and around them would form separate ecclesiastical provinces made up of their own suffragan dioceses.[126]

All of this did not mean that the impact of the recent pastoral issued in the mother See of Quebec would be lessened. It was reported as causing "great excitement," [127] while from Montreal came word of stiffened resistance in the form of ignoring the denunciation.[128] A paper in that same city which was Catholic and very pro-labor, held that the council at Quebec had misunderstood the Knights of Labor. The Order did not work in secret, nor were the leaders unknown men. Furthermore, it argued against condemnation of the society on the authority of a favorable article in the Roman *Moniteur,* and it advocated an appeal to the Holy See. The carrying of this critical article marked the end of labor news in the *True Witness* for six months.[129] But with no fear of reprisal, a Chicago labor paper was inspired "with all due respect to the eminent prelates" to tell the Canadians in a similar vein that they were ignorant of the true Order.[130] Quite another approach was that of the Brooklyn *Examiner* which tried hard to be loyal to the Church and the Knights by discovering a secret society of anarchists in Ottawa which "may throw some light on the opposition of Cardinal Taschereau." [131] The Baltimore Catholic paper explained away the Canadian condemnation as applying to a copy of an old constitution of the Knights of Labor, and the writer in the *Mirror* went beyond that to say that on the whole the Knights "have been commended by learned prelates as a conservative element in the social

125 BCA, 81-E-8, Taschereau to Gibbons, Quebec, June 13, 1886.

126 Rumilly, *op. cit.,* V, 181-182.

127 *John Swinton's Paper,* June 27, 1886.

128 Chicago *Knights of Labor,* June 26, 1886.

129 Kennedy, *op. cit.,* pp. 97-99, quoting *True Witness and Catholic Chronicle,* June 23, 1886.

130 Chicago *Knights of Labor,* June 26, 1886.

131 June 24, 1886.

agitation." [132] In a contrary manner the *Michigan Catholic* did not harp on the decision itself, but commended the obedience of those in the Canadian province who were withdrawing from the prohibited society.[133] That the number of these Catholic members was not negligible was evident within a week after the pulpit denunciations, for a Montreal committee quickly sought Powderly's "wise counsel and advice." Rome seemed to come easily to the Canadian mind, for they wrote:

> It seems to be the almost unanimous impression among our Catholic members here that the action of the Council should be appealed from and sent to Rome for consideration and adjustment. What you advise will be obeyed, no doubt, but there is considerable excitement and comment here just now on the subject, and an immediate reply from you as to the best and wisest course to pursue will have an appeasing effect among the members of the Order here, and will be anxiously awaited and looked for.

They thought that Powderly or one of his choice should make the appeal in person, and they were ready to send a delegate to Philadelphia to confer with him.[134] The general master workman however, ignored this request as he did a later suggestion that he consult with the papal ablegate, Monsignor Richard O'Bryen, who was expected about July 17.[135]

At this very time, midway in the year 1886, when Powderly to all appearances was forsaking any attempt to influence Canadian churchmen, some few among the American bishops were studying the problem. Pennsylvania priests who had long acquaintance with the Knights had been supplying material on them not only to the Archbishop of Philadelphia, but also to Bishop Chatard of Vincennes.[136] Archbishop Corrigan, on the other hand, had called

---

[132] *Catholic Mirror*, June 19, 1886.

[133] June 24, 1886. The only uncovered formal notice of resignation from the Knights and submission to the authority of the Church was in AAM,—G., Octave Guerin, St. Jean, July 10, 1886.

[134] PP, Eugene O'Rourke to Powderly, Montreal, June 25, 1886.

[135] PP, Richard H. Leahey to Powderly, Quebec, July 9, 1886.

[136] AUND, Chatard Papers (microfilm), D. O'Connor to D. J. McDermott,

in a theologian consultant in the person of the Jesuit provincial, Robert Fulton. To him he submitted material pertaining to the Independent Odd Fellows, the Ancient Order of United Workmen, and the Knights of Labor. Fulton's analysis of the constitution of the Knights of Labor read:

> With regard to the last pamphlet I would add [he suspected none of them gave a complete picture of their organization] that some of the principles, political and social (for example, p. 62, man's inalienable inheritance and right to share, for use of the soil) are at least doubtful in theory and dangerous in practice, I say *doubtful,* because the wording is loose, and the meaning may seem worse than intended.
> If the question be, whether persons belonging to such societies should on account of anything contained in these pamphlets, be excluded from the Sacraments, I would answer *No.*[137]

As has been seen above, however, it was the bishops of the First Provincial Council of Milwaukee who had their work immediately recognized. Even the secular press, on the basis of the Wisconsin activity, publicized the Catholic hierarchy as more positive in discussing the labor question than the Protestant clergy.[138]

Despite this reputation for facing the issue boldly it could with as much truth be urged that the American bishops were also very cautious. Elder once again goaded the Archbishop of Baltimore by

Girardville, June 12, 1886. O'Connor explained he "sent most of the papers" to Ryan and apparently McDermott forwarded what little he could still supply to Chatard.

[137] NYAA, Robert Fulton, S.J., to Corrigan, St. Ignatius, New York, June 12, 1886. Corrigan forwarded this answer to a "Dear Monsignor," perhaps his vicar general, Thomas Preston, and marked it, "Please return at your convenience, for my own guidance." The copy of the constitution (approved 1885) found among the Corrigan Papers was penciled at the spot Fulton indicated and the corner of the page still turned down.

[138] *Catholic Standard,* June 19, 1886, quoted the New York *Sun,* which said Catholics could well be proud of the Milwaukee statement that when "capitalists follow the heathen rule of buying labor in the cheapest market God is not with them." Some of them even became a little smug about Protestant lack of sympathy with labor's cause, citing resolutions of the convention of German Lutheran Synod in Williamsburg, New York, and the Dutch Reformed Church in Grand Rapids. *Pilot,* August 14; *Catholic Knight,* July 3, 1886.

telling him that some of his suffragan bishops were expecting action from the archiepiscopal committee on secret societies. They were not all as sure as he was that according to the conciliar decree the process would have to begin with the recourse of individual bishops who would supply the facts in the case and the reason for condemnation.[139] Gibbons' understanding of the matter agreed with Elder's. "It would be impossible," he explained, "for archbishops to resolve themselves into an investigating committee, and pry into the affairs of other dioceses. I believe that more good will result from a vigilant, masterly inactivity than by any hasty legislation." [140] The bishops of the Province of Cincinnati were certainly not hasty when in settling many other questions, they agreed if no answer was given by Rome, "in view of the fact that so many illegal means are used by some unions, whilst others loudly protest that they do not countenance such, to ask the committee of Archbishops to investigate the case." [141] It is uncertain whether the reference of the Ohio prelates to Rome's new consultation on the Order was based on a current rumor or on some previous action of Cardinal Gibbons.[142] A letter from the rector of the American College to Gibbons said cryptically, "At one time the attention of Rome was monopolized by the noise made in Quebec; since the papers came that you sent on, all that is changed and papers and everything else is full of Baltimore." It is possible that this reference to papers had to do only with the excitement attendant on the announcement of the elevation of the new cardinals and not to the Knights. Further on in the same communication from Rome Chatard was said to be working for condemnation of the Ancient Order of Hibernians and O'Connell thought also of the Knights of Labor. He added:

> In fact I may say they are already almost condemned. There will be a delay however and probably more investigation. It is the work of the Holy Office. [Canon Donato] Sbarretti, our

[139] BCA, 81-N-6, Elder to Gibbons, Cincinnati, July 18, 1886.

[140] AAC, Gibbons to Elder, Baltimore, July 20, 1886.

[141] AAC, "Copy of Minutes of the Meeting of the Prelates of the Province of Cincinnati, held at the Archiepiscopal Residence, July 21, 1886."

[142] This story of re-examination was repeated about this time by Father O'Leary, St. Louis *Catholic World,* July 17, 1886.

minutante told me of it and I urged the gravity of the move and recommended caution. He said he wrote the Holy Office about that decree passed by the Council constituting a commission of all the Abps to examine these cases in their first instance. That's the only means of prudence.[143]

O'Connell, then only a year in Rome, did not show the acumen in these affairs that he later acquired, for, even as he wrote, Taschereau was broadcasting what he considered his vindication. It was a letter of July 12 from Cardinal Simeoni which simply repeated in identical terms the Holy Office's condemnation of 1884.[144] His fervent pleas to Rome had been answered and for the last time he held the center of the stage in relation to the problem of the Church and the Knights of Labor. Taschereau sent copies of the communication in a letter dated July 31, 1887, to the bishops of his province and also to the Archbishop of Montreal. He took care, moreover, to get it into the Canadian press.[145] He told again of his disinterested requests for a decision and he gave the re-affirmation of the old one which had been handed down by the Holy Office on June 27. He denied that any other recourse had been in progress:

> The absolute silence of the Holy Office on this pretended appeal on the decision which I have communicated to your grace, proves that this appeal has not been made to the Holy See and that they have invoked it as a means of protection against the decision of September 1884 in order to deceive Catholics.
>
> If this appeal had been lodged, it is impossible that the Holy Office would not have been made cognizant of it since this matter is under its exclusive jurisdiction. In that case the decision of

[143] BCA, 81-Q-3, O'Connell to Gibbons, Rome, August 1, 1886.

[144] AAQ, CMR, VII, 171, Simeoni to Taschereau, Rome, July 12, 1886. The inquisitors general had given this judgment two weeks before.

[145] AAQ, 35-313, 314, Taschereau to Simeoni, Quebec, August 18, 1886, copy. It was not published in the Quebec *Mandements,* but it is in *Mandements, lettres pastorales, circulaires et autres documents publiés dans le diocèse de Montréal depuis son érection* (Montreal, 1894), XI, 397-399. In the documents sent by Vicar General C. A. Marois to Corrigan, NYAA, November 23, 1891, it is marked, "Aux évêques de la province eccl. de Québec."

June 27, sent by His Eminence Cardinal Simeoni would be the response. The first sentence turns out to be confirmed in its form and terms.

Taschereau ended on a note that was later very much disputed, namely, that the case was now closed for everybody. Since in this last decision as in the former one the Holy Office recommended that the bishops take such steps against the Knights as had been pre-scribed for prohibited societies, he said: "I cannot see how anyone can now be doubtful about the rule to be followed by Catholics of the whole world, over which the jurisdiction of this sacred con-gregation extends."

In all the years of altercations and negotiations this was the high point for those Catholics who were hostile to the Order. But at this very time its leader, Terence V. Powderly, showed a min-imum of interest. He entered into correspondence with Canada but only to despair of doing anything with Taschereau. As "simply a layman" he was powerless and could not even understand the di-vergence between the Canadian and American hierarchies. He prom-ised to discuss it at the Richmond convention and he concluded ominously:

> I became convinced while I was in Montreal that nothing short of the total extinction of the order in the province of Quebec would satisfy the bishop. There are those who are uncharitable enough to say that it was all brought about by political influ-ence, if so then it seems to me that the duty of the members is plain. I leave it to themselves to take such action as they deem best.[146]

Edouard Fabre, however, now an archbishop and directly re-sponsible only to the Holy See, was aroused to take more specific action. There had already arisen differences on more distinctly Church affairs between the Archdioceses of Quebec and Montreal. Montreal had grown to be a larger and more important city than Quebec and its archbishop resented Quebec's efforts to keep it from having its own Catholic university. Likewise, on the incorporation

[146] PP, George Clarke to Powderly, Montreal, July 29, 1886; Powderly to Clarke, August 16, 1886, copy.

of the Jesuits and the legal settlement of their property holdings, while Fabre was favorable, Taschereau was opposed.[147]   The former was ready to take an independent position also on the Knights of Labor. With his chancellor, F. Harel, he prepared a brief for Cardinal Simeoni which included three appendices of past Quebec utterances.[148]   The last straw of annoyance for Fabre had been the Cardinal of Quebec's publication of Rome's response in the Montreal papers while, as he thought, it did not appear in those of Quebec.[149]   Paraphrasing in part Taschereau's letter of the previous December 25 to him, Fabre said of the action: "This is no doubt because *the Knights of Labor do not exist in his Diocese* (Quebec) or because it is up to the ordinary of Montreal, 'to see to it'; or also because Cardinal Taschereau has become the spiritual head of Lower Canada."   Fabre was perplexed, this document stated, by his inability to do anything against the action of his brother bishops in the Province of Quebec, even though they had condemned a society which he claimed was still non-existent among them.   He believed, too, a mistake had been made at the outset since Rome had not seen a genuine manual of the Order.   The Archbishop of Montreal found further support in the positions of several other archbishops whom he had learned had not condemned the Knights. He listed Toronto, Baltimore, Cincinnati, St. Louis, New Orleans, Oregon City, and Boston. Of New York he said Corrigan "eschewed answering." [150]   Resting his case on these facts, Fabre made a threefold request:

1. Would it not be apropos to question the Archbishops of the United States on this subject of the Knights of Labor?

[147] Rumilly, *op. cit.*, V, 87-88, 182, 242-249.

[148] AAM, Consultation, Knights of Labor, August 17, 1886.

[149] While Taschereau told Simeoni of promulgation only to his suffragans and generally "in ephemeridibus canadensibus necnon in parochiis civitatis" (August 18), *L'Événement*, March 8, 1887, testified it was sent to the press of Quebec City.

[150] There is archival evidence of direct correspondence only with Corrigan. His "évite de répondre," more likely alludes to Corrigan's taciturnity with the press. If it was to a former correspondence no trace or allusion to it was discovered. On the other hand, if Fabre knew the opinions of the four last named prelates from the newspapers he found more than the present writer.

2. Would it not be fitting that the Holy See reserve its judgment until it had received all the information and thus delay
publishing a general law on the subject?

3. Regarding Montreal, would it not be fitting that the Ordinary be able to declare publicly that *no one should disturb Catholic members of this society, provided that they are disposed to
to submit to the judgment of the Holy See.*

This "consultation" of Archbishop Fabre on the Knights of
Labor was never sent to Rome. The very day after drawing it up,
seeking the support of the Archbishop of New York, he had
written to Corrigan:

> The Knights of Labor are rare in Canada except in Mon-
> treal. Consequently I am the one most embarrassed. I would
> like to ask Rome what course of conduct I should follow. For
> this purpose I wish to be able to present to the Sac. Cong. of
> the Propaganda the two sides of the question. Would Your
> Grace have any objection to writing a letter which I could cite
> as authority to the Propaganda? [151]

With what would seem, on the basis of previous action, to have been
an unexpected precision Corrigan promptly replied:

> As for myself (and I do not remember speaking with other
> bishops on the subject), I consider the society as *undoubtedly
> forbidden,* and have answered all inquiries of the clergy in this
> sense.
> The newspapers have, I believe, stated that I entertained
> doubts on the subject; but this is a mere and mean trick, or stu-
> pidity, as I absolutely declined to see any reporter in this con-
> nection. Had I seen one, I would have said simply that the
> Knights of Labor are condemned everywhere; as the condemna-
> tion is based not on local circumstances, but on the ends and
> objects of the society, which are identical everywhere as far as
> ascertained.

Not answering directly the question posed by the Archbishop of
Montreal, but seeking to disabuse him of the idea that the position of the American hierarchy was contrary to that taken in Quebec, Corrigan continued:

---

151 NYAA, Fabre to Corrigan, Montreal, August 18, 1886.

Neither did H. E. Cardinal Gibbons speak as the papers reported; as your Grace will notice from the cuttings which I enclose.

Moreover, all that he said, *some months ago,* before the fact of the decision of the Holy See was so well known, was said in a private conversation, whilst traveling—which some *reporter* overheard accidentally, and published. I presume the Cardinal had forgotten at the moment that the question had been decided by the Holy See. There will probably be occasion to promulgate this condemnation in our Synod, which will be held this Fall.[152]

The clipping was from the Baltimore *Sun* and told of the American cardinal's reluctance to comment on the latest Canadian move. It discarded, as based merely on hearsay, the interview with Gibbons which that same paper had reprinted on August 12 from the Washington *Republic* of the previous May 2.[153] But the particulars of the origin of that newspaper story, which was so favorable to the Knights of Labor, seem to have been Corrigan's own contribution.

Thus it was that on August 24 the chancellor of Montreal noted on the back of the draft of a week before that after hearing from New York Fabre "revoked the project of writing to the Holy See." The next day a letter went out instead to Quebec, hinting that an American churchman had been found who approved the condemnation and would soon publicly follow it. Corrigan remained unnamed, but Fabre ventured to suggest that Gibbons had not used the language the papers attributed to him.[154] In one sense it was too late, for a French version of the earlier Baltimore news story (without the correction of August 18) was already on its way to Simeoni. In his acknowledgment of Propaganda's letter of July 12, Taschereau added this to other newspaper evidence of the continuing scandal, with no intention of condemning Gibbons nor even

[152] AAM, Corrigan to Fabre, New York, August 20, 1886. Despite this last sentence the bishops of the New York Province met in May and August and the minutes read: "Nothing decided on the Knights of Labor." RDA.

[153] Baltimore *Sun,* August 18, 1886, an item from Cape May, New Jersey. Yet the *Catholic Mirror* noted without rebuke that Gibbons, Heiss, Keane and others had told newspapermen that the Order in the United States had not been condemned. August 21, 1886.

[154] AAM, Lettres, VI, 228, Fabre to Taschereau, Montreal, August 25, 1886, copy.

of affirming the accuracy of the report. He joined the opinion of
the Archbishop of Halifax, Cornelius O'Brien, to his own in urging
the Holy See to make its decision known *"to all prelates of Canada
and of the United States, with the obligation of promulgating it
and of demanding its execution."* [155]

Yet before any universal decision was to come from Rome the
question was to pass first into the hands of the American archbishops.
There had been a stir of interest among them, and one of them had
very quietly halted Montreal's appeal for a reconsideration of the
case by the Holy See. Although Taschereau's eye was single and
a repetition of the Roman condemnation had arrived in mid-1886,
the ecclesiastical answer to the problem in Canada had been generally confused. The official "inactivity" in the United States, on
the other hand, where the problem was much more acute, had been
in the meanwhile only dubiously "masterly."

[155] AAQ, 35-313, 314, Taschereau to Simeoni, Quebec, August 18, 1886,
copy. The Montreal *Daily Witness,* August 16, 1886, was further evidence
since it pointed out the dilemma of Catholics in view of the Quebec condemnation and Baltimore's apparent blessing.

CHAPTER VI

TWO MEETINGS: OCTOBER, 1886

Rome's second condemnation of the Knights of Labor which was revealed by Cardinal Taschereau under date of July 31, 1886, received wide publicity. The publication of the news, at least in the Canadian press, was officially inspired, although it was likewise quickly seized upon by the American papers. In the United States, however, far from bringing Catholics around to the Quebec viewpoint, it only served to build up a strong sense of independence among their more articulate representatives. The Catholic journals which adverted to the problem took their guidance rather from the published and republished interviews, of a more favorable tone, which had been granted by American prelates. How much of their impatience with the French Canadian archbishop speaking from a British Dominion can be attributed to the fact that many of these editors were Irish, and to the general ill-feeling in the States toward Canada in 1886, is hard to say. Meanwhile, unnoticed amid the public clamor, preparations went forward for two important meetings that of the general assembly of the Knights of Labor in Richmond, Virginia, from October 4 to 20 and that of the committee of archbishops in Baltimore on October 28.

With the exception of *Le Propagateur Catholique,* the French language paper of New Orleans, none of the American Catholic press seems to have been served directly by the release of the Quebec letter of condemnation sent out by Taschereau's secretary under date of August 11. This paper, however, made no comment of its own. Similarly the German paper in Baltimore, *Katholische Volkszeitung,* of the same date had nothing to say, but in view of "all kinds of speculation," it did send a reporter to Bishop John Keane of Richmond, who expressed a very optimistic opinion about the Knights of Labor in the United States.[1] The Cincinnati *Wahrheits-Freund*

---

[1] August 28, 1886. The extant run of *Le Propagateur Catholique* which came closest to the years under consideration is in the custody of Roger Baudier

quoted the friendly views of Archbishops Gibbons and Heiss, but for itself was satisfied to point out that the Quebec action made it doubly desirable to clear up the matter in the United States.[2] Other journals were not so reticent. The *Michigan Catholic* hastily pointed out that the document "printed broadcast and made to appear as a precedent for the Universal Church" was no more binding across the border than "a mandate of the Governor General of Canada." Catholics in the United States, it said, would await action by their own leaders, and follow the Irish advice, "It is time enough to bid the devil good morning when you meet him." [3] The most prominent socio-political Catholic paper held up the friendly comments purportedly made by Gibbons the previous spring as encouragement to the Knights. These were to serve as evidence also of "the wisdom and prudence" of Powderly who in an interview printed on another page explained that he considered the boycott together with the strike only "a last resort," and this because employers still used it. Ford's *Irish World* in addition quoted Corrigan as saying he had received no word on the question, but "any message received by Cardinal Taschereau did not necessarily apply to the rest of the country." Added to this were the favorable statements of Bishop Keane of Richmond, Dr. Chapelle of Washington, and one of the vicars general of Toronto who spoke in Lynch's absence. Archbishop Ryan of Philadelphia was reported as declining to give an opinion until he had further information.[4] This caution was reflected in the Philadelphia *Catholic Standard* which, although consistently quite aware of labor problems, simply carried an editorial on lawful and unlawful oaths, "because of questions practically connected with them, which are of constant occurrence." [5] At the other extreme the Brooklyn *Examiner* showed its very sympathetic attitude by gleaning from the press the additional reactions of Monsignors Thomas S. Lee and Edward McColgan of Baltimore to the

of New Orleans. It contained only this one item of interest for which the author is grateful.

[2] August 18, 1886.
[3] August 19, 1886.
[4] August 21, 1886.
[5] August 21, 1886.

effect that the Knights in the United States were not included in any condemnation so far emanating from Rome.[6] The editor, Thomas Preston, nephew of the Vicar General of New York, and educated in philosophy and theology for several years at the University of Louvain, found such a state of affairs remarkable.[7] His editorial said that the clergy did not usually come forward to agitate for the temporal advancement of mankind till the victory was won. "It was so," he held, "in the old days of slavery and it is so in the present crusade against industrial slavery which has recently been inaugurated." This natural disinclination "to mingle with worldly affairs" for once had been overcome and two good effects might be expected from these friendly declarations of clerics:

> They will strengthen the order in the minds of many honest workingmen who have hitherto been forced lower and lower by the tendency of their employers to follow the pagan custom of buying in the cheapest market and selling in the dearest, who will gladly welcome any legitimate organization to prevent their degradation to the level of mere ununited machines.

Furthermore, more than any amount of preaching they would strengthen the Church for, "Let the Catholic toilers believe that the Church is actively in favor of their temporal as well as their spiritual welfare, and there will be less defection among her children and more earnest devotion." [8]

While John Swinton undertook to inform the labor world of the disagreement between the opinions of Gibbons and Taschereau, Catholic New England was also voicing an opinion.[9] Boston's *Republic* expressed its view by entitling an editorial, "Not Applicable Here," while its neighbor, the *Connecticut Catholic*, took up its position behind the interview of Cardinal Gibbons which seems to have become as widely dispersed as Taschereau's hostile statement.[10]

6 August 21, 1886.

7 AAC, Thomas Preston to Elder, New York, January 20, 1887. Besides editing this paper he was the Washington editor of the New York *Herald* nightly from 8 p. m. to 2 a. m.

8 August 21, 1886.

9 *John Swinton's Paper,* August 22, 1886.

10 Both August 21, 1886.

At the same time the more venerable and substantially Catholic paper, the Boston *Pilot*, merely reprinted the Gibbons' item on the fifth page without comment and in small print.[11] This was likely an indication of skepticism about its authenticity rather than of waning zeal for the cause of labor, for in a few weeks "Phineas" was lamenting the conservatism of the movement, and pointing out that without an aggressive attitude they would be "driven back to their former state of dumb obscurity." [12]

Whether a frontier influence be evoked or not, the fact remains that several Catholic papers in the West and South were more outspoken. One of them, the *Morning Star* of New Orleans, which carried also the approval of the bishops of five surrounding dioceses in the Southwest, was so bold as to merit quoting by the Brooklyn *Examiner*.[13] In an editorial which was completely out of character, for the usual run of them were on strictly religious subjects and even pious in tone, this southern paper characterized Taschereau's letter as showing, "a party spirit unworthy a Catholic bishop." It expressed annoyance at his efforts to make Rome's answer universal in scope.

> Every theologian knows how difficult it often is to decide whether a response of a Roman Congregation is general or particular. Cardinal Taschereau, in the light of his extreme modesty sees no difficulty at all. In a word, we have our own beloved Cardinal, Archbishops and Bishops who are the natural, or rather supernatural, channels by which are conveyed to us the will of Christ's Vicar on earth. Cardinal Taschereau has the grace to settle the petty squabbles of his illustrious subjects. We hope he will let us alone.[14]

This canonical approach was used also by the paper in Bishop Ireland's Diocese of St. Paul. It discussed more calmly, however, the notion of "juxta exposita," by which it explained the condemnation on special circumstances peculiar to Canada and it pointed out that the American hierarchy had been sent no such

---

[11] August 21, 1886.
[12] *Pilot,* September 4; cf. also October 2, 1886.
[13] September 11, 1886.
[14] September 4, 1886.

directive.[15] The *Western Watchman,* edited by the Reverend David S. Phelan, reminded Taschereau that the bishops of his neighboring country did not need the help of his chancery and it added: "Both civil and ecclesiastical Canada needs a little holding down at this moment." [16] Likewise in Leavenworth, John O'Flanaghan explained to a fellow editor what he considered the purely local nature of the condemnation.[17]

In Baltimore, Gibbons' own see city, the Catholic press carried no elucidation of his position. Yet it published Taschereau's letter and also the interview in an opposite strain of Dr. Chapelle.[18] It indicated, too, a continued trust in Powderly who was complimented, it maintained, in being held "worthy of the abuse of the convicted Chicago anarchist," Albert Parsons.[19] The leading Catholic paper in New York City likewise gave no space to Gibbons' supposed position on the Knights, but it was not quiet on the subject. Mc-Master, who had been impressed some months before by the proposals of Powderly's secret circular, had changed his mind on the general master workman. He pointed to the strikes, "disastrous to the interests of the laboring classes," as evidence of what he had feared might happen, namely, "that his fabric would tumble about his ears." He, therefore, pronounced:

> Mr. Powderly proves a *theorist,* a half-educated lecturer. . . . It is fully proved they heed him not. . . . We are sorry to use such harsh words about an organization of which we had hoped, no permanent, but a temporary good influence, towards securing for the laboring classes, *the right to live*—that Civil Society must give them, on terms other than they have now—or there will be a social upheaval that easy going people do not dream of.

The editorial continued, but without becoming specific, to claim that the position of the American hierarchy had been misrepresented. Finally, although with more verve than the others, he offered the

[15] *Northwestern Chronicle,* August 26, 1886.
[16] August 28, 1886.
[17] *Kansas Catholic,* September 30, 1886.
[18] *Catholic Mirror,* August 28; cf. also August 21, 1886.
[19] September 4, 1886.

familiar—but unfounded—position taken by Catholics in the United States:

> What is true is this. The Archbishop of Quebec, Canada, has, with approbation of his act by the Holy See, condemned an organization in Quebec calling itself, 'K. of L.' Which of the heterogeneous agglomerates, each claiming to be 'K. of L.,' has had its special 'constitution,' so exhibited and condemned, His Grace of Quebec has not specified. The incriminated document has not been given to the public. The *corpus delicti* is wanting. Which one of the bad boys that Mr. Powderly has undertaken to gather into his reform school has been in fault in Quebec, does not appear. That the whole school is badly reformed may be true, but the faithful in the United States are not to learn this from the Archbishop of Quebec, but from their own Bishops, each one of whom is under oath to hunt out, and expel all false sects from his Diocese.[20]

Besides the force of this ordinary pastoral obligation, secret societies in the United States had to contend with the special instrument of the Catholic hierarchy, namely, the committee of all the archbishops set up by the plenary council of 1884. Its individual members had not been inactive on the problem since its inception, but only in the fall of 1886, as the Catholic press so loudly discussed the Knights of Labor, were events quietly moving towards their first joint action. Of the dozens of fraternal societies in the United States, two especially had come to be the chief sources of concern to the bishops, the Ancient Order of Hibernians and the Grand Army of the Republic, the one predominantly Irish and the other peculiarly American.[21] The American canonical approach to the problem in 1885, when the committee of Bishops Moore, Dwenger, and later Gilmour, had been working in Rome for approval of the conciliar decrees, was highly commended by Bishop Luigi Sepiacci. Yet at that time the Roman prelate showed little comprehension of the situation in the United States, for he said, "Some bishops see Freemasons in everything, and some never see them anywhere." [22]

---

[20] *Freeman's Journal,* September 4, 1886.

[21] Fergus Macdonald, C.P., *The Catholic Church and the Secret Societies in the United States,* pp. 122-143.

[22] BCA, 79-I-13, O'Connell to Gibbons, Rome, April 12, 1885. On the prob-

But during the months of 1886 the society which aroused the greatest episcopal anxiety, and this especially on the part of Corrigan, was the non-Masonic Ancient Order of Hibernians. It was, however, the Archbishop of New York's negotiations with Propaganda over the more Masonic-like Grand Army of the Republic which proximately stimulated Rome to have the conciliar stipulation on suspected societies carried out. This mandate came at the end of August in the form of an acknowledgment of the receipt of a ritual of the Grand Army of the Republic and a request for its translation into French, Italian, or Latin. Simeoni then advised the Metropolitan of New York to tell Cardinal Gibbons that he wished the committee of all the archbishops convened in order to pass judgment on that society.[23]

It was several weeks before the Archbishop of Baltimore received this word which was to begin the canonical procedure at the top without waiting for the recourse of individual bishops. Nevertheless, his action in the meanwhile showed that he had not been merely waiting for Rome to take the first step in dealing with the leading organization of American workingmen. Gibbons this time did not even need the prodding of Elder. When the Archbishop of Cincinnati confessed he felt "a deep uneasiness" about the Canadian condemnation, even though no official word had reached the American hierarchy, the cardinal was able to reassure him. Elder maintained that not only was the condition a scandal to Catholics, but he had seen "no claim that there is any difference between the Constitution in Canada, and those in the United States." An additional reason for his worry was that "Bishops and priests are asking about it."[24] "I have not been idle on the subject," answered Gibbons, telling him how he had written to Rome to ask whether a copy of the constitution should be sent and also to Powderly's pastor requesting the latter to forward one to him. His further plans called for the presentation of their case in Rome by Bishops Keane and Ireland who were to make the trip in the interest of the new

lem of final approval of the decrees which came on September 10, 1885, cf. Frederick J. Zwierlein, *The Life and Letters of Bishop McQuaid,* II, 345-357.

[23] NYAA, Simeoni to Corrigan, Rome, August 28, 1886.

[24] BCA, 81-S-12, Elder to Gibbons, Cincinnati, August 31, 1886.

university following the committee meeting on October 27. Since the Metropolitans of Boston, Philadelphia, and New York as members of the university committee, were to be in Baltimore on that day, he thought it "an excellent opportunity for discussing the whole question." On the basis of inquiry already made on his own, however, Gibbons had reached a decision on the best policy to follow:

> A distinguished professor of Woodstock who is personally adverse to any condemnation of the Knights without better grounds than we have at present tells me that an eminent member of the Society informed him that he lived in Canada and the States, and that he knows the working and aims of the society in both countries. The sentiment of Woodstock and of a distinguished moral professor from Montreal who is here, is that the action of Quebec does not apply to us.
>
> In my judgment, our plain duty is to submit the matter to the Holy See and be guided by its supreme decision.[25]

Nonetheless, it was not beyond the cardinal's plans to contribute something to the formation of that decision. This he undertook to do on the very day, September 3, that he had answered Elder. In this he was doubtlessly influenced by the reception of a communication forwarded to him by the pastor of Carbondale, Pennsylvania, the Reverend Francis Carew.[26] Gibbons' second note to the Archbishop of Cincinnati told him how he had received not only a copy of the constitution of the Knights of Labor, but, what had not been

[25] AAC, Gibbons to Elder, Baltimore, September 3, 1886. From what followed it is highly probable that the Woodstock professor was Aloysius Sabetti, S.J. The only other "moral professor" whose opinion was found in the Gibbons Papers was Paulinus F. Dissez, S.S., of St. Mary's Seminary, Baltimore. His undated letter shows that he found in the constitution of the Knights of Labor expressions with regard to their end which savored of a "communistic or socialist spirit," such as regarding the right to "a share, for use of, the soil" (as Father Fulton had pointed out to Corrigan) and the workers' claim to full enjoyment of the wealth they create with no regard for the capitalist. As to the means they advocated, Dissez was suspicious of the "secret work" and hoped it did not mean an unwritten constitution. BCA, 86-Y-1, n.d., n.p.

[26] Gibbons' Diary, p. 209, reveals only the following: "I sent care of Dr. O'Connell a letter to Card. Simeoni deprecating a hasty condemnation of the Knights of Labor, & giving my reasons therefor. Today I recd a copy of the constitution of the order with a letter from its president, Mr. Powderly."

even sought or expected from Powderly, "a letter breathing a truly
Catholic spirit of obedience and respect for the voice of the Church,
and a willingness to amend the constitution if anything faulty is
found out."[27] The covering letter to Powderly's old pastor, even
more than the official document which it accompanied, was certainly
a most important one for the settlement of the Church's vexation
over the Knights, since Gibbons was to lean heavily on it.[28]

Cardinal Gibbons did not exaggerate in writing to Elder.
Powderly first reminded Carew that the constitution was under
revision, and he then recited his earlier efforts to placate the Church
through the priests in Montreal and by writing to Archbishop Ryan
in 1884.[29] He asked again:

> Will you, if it is not inconsistent with your duty, examine the
> constitution and give me your advice as to the parts of it that
> should be stricken out? The membership of the order at this
> time is nearly two thirds Catholic; and if it is condemned by
> the church it will simply make one more Protestant organization.

Referring to the Church's prohibition of membership in Masonic
societies, he went on:

> We do not complain of that but if we are deprived of having an
> organization wherein we can look after our own interests, side
> by side with our Protestant fellow workmen, it will in no way
> advance the cause of religion and will do a great deal of injury
> to the struggling Catholics who have to compete in the labor
> market with those who have the entry to the society where the
> 'boss' can meet with and give out to them the best situations.

Powderly reasserted for the priest's benefit that all the secrets
of the Order were open to the Church. Then he protested:

[27] AAC, Gibbons to Elder, Baltimore, September 3, 1886.

[28] It is found only in BCA, 81-S-13, and a handwritten copy made by
Gibbons in 81-S-13/1. The Powderly Papers reveal that pages 201 to 223 between letters dated August 31, 1886, were neatly removed from the letterbook
containing July-September, 1886. According to the undisturbed index (p. 3)
these pages were addressed to Father Carew. Inside the front cover a notation
reads, "Last page examined, July 27, 1918."

[29] *Vide supra*, pp. 145-146, and pp. 112-113.

I do not know what else to do. I am willing to do everything that lays [*sic*] in my power to have the order meet with favor in the eyes of the Church. I know that in this age of scandal the newspapers are enough to give a coloring of wrong to every movement having the welfare of the poor at heart, but the newspapers must not be depended on to speak for the K. of L.

Furthermore, he argued, only the "anarchist, infidel element" would rejoice in a denunciation by the Church, "since it would deprive the Order of the conservative strength which it now has in the Catholic members," and they, as well as Catholic workmen, would suppose "that the Church opposed the elevation of labor through the medium of organization."

The words which applied to Powderly's own person were most respectful in tone. Denying that he had ever had anything to do with forbidden societies, he professed:

I have not paraded my religion as a reason why I should be entitled to any particular credit or favor, yet six months have never rolled over my head in which I did not perform my duty as a Catholic in approaching the sacraments. I ask your indulgence while speaking of this but I deem it necessary since that matter has been discussed and you, who know me better than any other priest in the country, may have heard the rumor also.

As further evidence of his good will the G. M. W. hoped on the day after writing to Carew to put all the material connected with the Order into the hands of the Archbishop of Philadelphia for inspection. This was his hope and promise:

If I can only learn upon what point in particular the objection rests I will have it stricken from the constitution. I will treat as strictly confidential anything that either priest or bishop may confide in me. It need never be made known who pointed out any of the objections if such is necessary. All that I can do will be done.

Powderly concluded by reassuring the Carbondale pastor that if possible any advice he gave would be acted upon. There was no deception about the purpose with which Father Carew approached him through a certain J. J. O'Boyle, for Powderly said, "I am satisfied to place this matter in your hands for presentation to His Eminence Cardinal Gibbons." [30]

If ever Gibbons was quick to desert a policy of inactivity it was on this occasion. On September 3, he received Powderly's apologia, and the cardinal's personal defense of the Knights of Labor drawn up in Latin at Baltimore carries that same date.[31] Although by his signature he took full responsibility for this communication to Simeoni, it is difficult to ascertain how much of it was his own thought. A rough Latin draft in the Jesuit archives of Woodstock College in Father Sabetti's hand does not indicate the dividing line of collaboration, and the note on the containing envelope, "Letter written for Cardinal Gibbons to Cardinal Prefect of Propaganda," is not the Jesuit's.[32] The body of the letter presented a favorable picture of the Knights of Labor and the reasons against condemnation, and only in the postscript was there a promise to send on a copy of the constitution and a declaration of willingness to abide by whatever response was made. The result of Taschereau's promulgation of the decree on the Knights, Gibbons told Propaganda, was to disturb greatly not only the faithful but the clergy and bishops of the United States, for they feared its repetition or extension to their own country. Hence, he frankly stated, the organization "as it is constituted in the United States cannot and ought not to be condemned, unless we wish to expose the Catholic Church to many dangerous losses." The purpose of the Knights of Labor was not evil, and it had no connection either with condemned societies, nor, on the public testimony of their highest leader, with those "nefarious socialists" who had made such trouble in Chicago.[33]

[30] In the light of this document Powderly's later objections to statements based on it and made by Gibbons to the Holy See are ridiculous to say the least. He inferred he never sent the cardinal a copy of the constitution and even more blatantly did he deny ever making "the statement concerning my religious status," or promising to change objectionable features of the Order. This letter carries only his own distinctive signature and so his professed explanation of Thomas O'Reilly's using the rubber stamp in his name is untenable. *Path,* pp. 392-394.

[31] BCA, 81-U-2, Gibbons to Simeoni, Baltimore, September 3, 1886, copy C.

[32] Archives of Woodstock College, II, A-7b3.

[33] Gibbons' loose use of such terms was not uncommon among some members of the ecclesiastical and labor hierarchies.

It was their sole purpose, "that with united strength and within the law they might mutually protect themselves against the tyranny with which many very rich corporations, and especially those controlling the railroads, inhumanly oppress the poor workers." The means used by the labor organization were not essentially bad, for by secrecy they did not "intend to hide from legitimate authority, but only to protect themselves from those most powerful adversaries against whom they battle legally by means of this association." Moreover, the Knights, the cardinal brought out, had made frequent offers to change whatever the Church might indicate needed revision and the few evil men among them were not such simply because they were members.

Gibbons claimed finally that a great hindrance to the growth of religion would result from a condemnation. He said, in a tone which he was later to change, "for since our Government does nothing to protect the workers, these who are in great part Catholics, with a certain natural and pious instinct turn to the Church for sympathy and counsel." If instead, he continued, they should find penalties and condemnation, they would turn to those "who babble about the Church favoring the strong oppressors and leaving the oppressed to their fate." He added to this—on what evidence he did not say—"the metropolitans of all this region, as far as I know, are not against this society and are entirely of the opinion it should not be condemned." The existence of their committee according to paragraph 255 of the decrees of the Third Plenary Council was pointed out but, as Simeoni was told, none of the bishops had yet made the recourse which it called for in the matter of dubious societies.

Gibbons' plans at that time obviously did not call for convening all the archbishops, but only for having the matter of the Knights discussed when the university committee met on October 27, and thereafter forwarding the problem to Rome in the hands of Keane and Ireland. Elder, too, had been invited to this meeting, but he was prevented by his preoccupation with plans to pay off the debt left by his predecessor and to hold a synod. So he thanked the cardinal for his "wise action in regard to the Knights of Labor," and excused himself. In his interest in the problem, however, Archbishop Elder had also contacted Bishop Gilmour of Cleveland,[34] "expecting him to see your Eminence about an evil existing in many societies, which are not bad in themselves." He described it thus:

> They drag into them men of the loosest notions about the duties of men to God and to their neighbors. But these men do most of the talking, and they are most active in directing the proceedings, and the Catholics who are there, are not commonly instructed well enough to detect the evil.[35]

Despite growing hierarchical concern in the United States the Roman activities which Denis O'Connell witnessed and took some part in were of more immediate consequence. In early September O'Connell began his report to Gibbons, "The course of proceedings against the Knights in the U. S. has been stayed and I am sure the matter will be dealt with now with great caution." Letters from Baltimore of an undisclosed nature had already impressed Camillo Cardinal Mazzella, S.J., and led him to consult with Raffaele Cardinal Monaco, sub-prefect of the Holy Office, who "had promised some modifications in proceedings." After O'Connell's talk with Mazzella he had visited Simeoni, who had already received "a bundle of papers on the matter." Simeoni, however, was hampered by the fact that the material was all in English, and the Holy Office was scheduled to adjourn for vacation in eight days. The Italian cardinal's instructions for Baltimore were to send translations of the old and new constitutions of the Knights of Labor with the differences noted. One already supplied by Archbishop Feehan of Chicago had been remitted by the Congregation of the Holy Office since it was in English.[36] O'Connell himself had hopes that the procedure of the Baltimore council might be upheld and thus make the work of translation unnecessary. (He apparently did not know that some of the books of the Knights existed in French). He found

---

[34] ADC, Elder to Gilmour, Cincinnati, August 16, 1886. He also included a clipping which he approved to the effect that labor had an equal if not "an overruling right in determining wages, hours, safety, etc.," but any dictation as to hiring was "tyranny and oppression."

[35] BCA, 81-U-4, Elder to Gibbons, Cincinnati, September 7, 1886.

[36] Feehan requested and received a French copy from the chancellor of Montreal shortly afterwards, probably for Rome's use. AAM, Circulaires, P. J. Agnew to F. Harel, Chicago, September 17, 1886.

some encouragement in Simeoni's remark that "it might be safest to follow it and have the trial made in the first instance in the U. S. as is done when there is only one man's interests involved." Moreover, the Prefect of Propaganda was observed to have "said apologetically that the condemnation given Cardinal Taschereau was made before the council was held." Mazzella agreed at least that getting the bishops' opinions was a good idea, and Sbarretti, their *minutante,* went to work to include Gibbons' views in a letter to the Holy Office. Still apparently unaware of Corrigan's activity, the rector of the American College could only report to Gibbons that an archbishop "has written about the 'Grand Army of the Republic.' " [37] At the same time O'Connell told the Archbishop of New York in a few words of the new Roman policy of caution on the question of the Knights, for although calling himself the servant of all the American bishops, he was, in fact, more an agent for Gibbons than the others.[38]

Yet it was the word conveyed from Rome by way of Corrigan, rather than any disclosure of Rome's views by O'Connell, that put Gibbons in a position to achieve joint action by his fellow metropolitans. The Propaganda mandate of August 28, which was entrusted to Corrigan to be forwarded to Baltimore, was sent from New York on September 13. It called for putting the committee of archbishops to work on the case of the Grand Army of the Republic. The pertinent passage copied by Corrigan, in which he corrected Simeoni's mistake, read as follows:

> Before the Congregation of the Holy Office takes such a question under examination it is necessary to apply the arrangements contained in Art. 225 (255?) [*sic*] of the III Plenary Council. Hence the Commission composed of all the Archbishops of the United States will have to assemble to judge the nature of the aforesaid society. I pray you to communicate that to his Eminence Cardinal Gibbons who will then consider convening the Commission in order to render their judgment on the question.[39]

[37] BCA, 81-U-7, O'Connell to Gibbons, Rome, September 8, 1886; 81-V-3, September 17, 1886, reassuring him of Sbaretti's activity.

[38] NYAA, O'Connell to Corrigan, Rome, September 9, 1886.

[39] BCA, 81-U-10, Corrigan to Gibbons, New York, September 13, 1886.

Gibbons merely formalized the previous plans (which he had discussed with Elder on September 3) for a meeting in conjunction with that of the university committee. He set the date for the following day, Thursday, October 28. His thanks to Corrigan included a draft of his summons to all the archbishops with the request, "if you have any change or addition to suggest, I will thankfully receive it." [40] Whatever the undisclosed New York suggestions might have been—if any were made—the Baltimore letter of convocation included somewhat more than Simeoni had called for. It spoke of the Roman cardinal's wish

> that in accordance with No. 255 of III Plenary Council I would invite all the Archbishops of the country to a conference at which we should consider the condition of those societies whose good standing may have been brought in question, and that I should report to the Holy See the result of our deliberations.

Accordingly, Gibbons set the time for convening as the morning of October 28, and in his letters to Ryan, Williams, and Corrigan he inserted an indication that it was "the day following the meeting of the University Board." Those who might be detained at home were provided for by the concluding words:

> Should Your Grace be unavoidably absent, may I ask you to forward me any views you may have to offer regarding the Grand Army of the Republic, the Knights of Labor, or any other Society existing in your Ecclesiastical Province. [41]

Meanwhile in Rome O'Connell held back from submitting Gibbons' personal defense of the Knights of Labor. He did this knowing that Rome had convened all the archbishops, but only, so O'Connell thought, to decide on the Grand Army of the Republic. Even on the basis of the smaller and more informal gathering set for October 27, where the Knights were to be discussed, O'Connell explained:

---

[40] NYAA, Gibbons to Corrigan, Baltimore, September 14, 1886.

[41] BCA, 81-V-5, Baltimore, September 17, 1886, "Copy mailed Sept. 18 to each Archbishop of U. S."

There could be no need of it before Nov. 11 and I thought it more prudent to hold it over to see what turn things might take in the meantime. Then it appears that all the Bishops are not of accord in their views of the society, and that some letters of a different character have been written to the Prop.

Hence he wondered about Gibbons' statement on the total agreement of the metropolitans. His suspicion that the view in New York was "not very favorable" was based on McMaster's turning against the Order [42] and the attitude of Ella Edes who "has nothing to say in their favor and states that you are entirely on their side." [43] The delay in presenting Gibbons' document would, therefore, avoid the mistake of his misrepresenting "the real state of the case" and possibly save the good name of the Cardinal of Baltimore in Rome. A further bit of news that might well have made Gibbons wonder about Rome's opinion of himself was that Domenico Jacobini, Secretary of Propaganda and Consultor of the Congregation of the Inquisition, felt that the Holy Office would recommend the execution of the Baltimore conciliar decree on suspect societies "in the case of the Knights as it has done in the case of the Grand Army." [44] Yet the American cardinal on his own initiative had already done this very thing in his circular letter of September 17 to the archbishops of the United States.

[42] *Vide supra,* p. 186.

[43] Miss Edes played a part in practically all the major American ecclesiastical questions of the late century, either as an agent for Corrigan or a reporter for papers such as the New York *Herald* and the *Catholic News.* From those that remain, especially in the Rochester Diocesan Archives, one would conclude that her almost indecipherable letters were circulated between Corrigan and McQuaid, and sometimes Gilmour, and most of them were destroyed. An entry in the Diary of Archbishop Robert Seton for June 20, 1905 (New York Historical Society) shows not only her length of days in Rome, but her position. ". . . an American convert who lives in the *via della Mercede.* Is very well known in America. Was long a correspondent of some newspaper. A great friend of Card. Barnabo. [Prefect of Propaganda from 1856 to 1874.] Says he was her confessor. Grew blind as he grew old and she used to go up to Propaganda every evening and talk to him and tell him the news. I don't think she could ever have been good looking. New England family a great partisan of Corrigan. Detests Gibbons, Keane, Ireland and that side."

[44] BCA, 81-W-1, O'Connell to Gibbons, Rome, September 25, 1886.

Any efforts of Archbishop Corrigan to stop this consultation on the Knights of Labor have not left their traces in the available records. His persistence in the advice of the previous August to Fabre of Montreal was reflected somewhat in his sending to Taschereau points agreed on by his New York suffragans, "which ought to be discussed by the Archbishops of the United States at Baltimore this October." None of these was listed by either archbishop, but the Knights of Labor must have been in Taschereau's mind when he expressed great interest in the final decision on some of the questions.[45] Corrigan, at any rate, certainly did prepare most conscientiously for the coming meeting by requesting copies of rituals and constitutions for examination from his episcopal confidant, Bernard McQuaid, at whose Hemlock Lake summer home he had been vacationing shortly before.[46] Gibbons in the meanwhile informed the Cardinal Prefect of Propaganda of the step he had taken. He showed no sign of shrinking from what Rome might well have judged overstepping his bounds, in part possibly because O'Connell's last letter of September 25 had not arrived. At this time the cardinal made no mention of the Grand Army of the Republic, but he specified that the meeting was called to find out the opinion of the archbishops "on the Ancient Order of Hibernians, and the Knights of Labor, and other societies flourishing among us, concerning whose good standing in the eyes of the Church certain doubts have perhaps arisen." He not only promised Simeoni to inform him of their opinions, but he also pointed out his own independent diligence, "Before I received the above mentioned letter of Your Eminence I intended to obtain the advice of many of the archbishops in regard to suspected societies." [47]

As archiepiscopal circles stirred with preparations for the meeting in Baltimore, the affiliated labor groups throughout the United

[45] NYAA, Taschereau to Corrigan, Quebec, September 18, 1886.

[46] RDA, Corrigan to McQuaid, New York, September 25, 1886.

[47] BCA, 81-W-2, Gibbons to Simeoni, Baltimore, September 25, 1886, copy. Moreover, Gibbons followed up O'Connell's advice of his letter of September 8 by seeking a copy of the *"old* constitution," when he thanked Father Carew of Carbondale. BCA, Letterbook, Gibbons to Carew, Baltimore, September 27, 1886, copy.

States got ready for a much greater convention, that of the general assembly of the Knights of Labor in Richmond. From the outset this gathering, too, had its ecclesiastical implications. One of the delegates, although he realized McMaster was now unfriendly, asked the influential Catholic editor in New York what he thought of a plan whereby the difficulties between the Knights and the Church could be solved. It called for qualified and authorized agents of the Order to visit every bishop and to lay before them, "the constitution, secret work, written and unwritten laws of the Order, and explain the same." [48] Others among the Knights thought the removal of the secret features of the Order might help to mitigate the ill effects of the Canadian condemnation. Swinton alleged in a first page editorial that the proposals to this effect, made simultaneously by several organs of individual unions, had led to a "far-fetched inference in certain quarters that the proposition has been made in concert, so as to prepare the way for some action upon the subject next month." [49] One attempt had actually been made to improve Church-Order relations and this received an answer from the general master workman. His questioner admitted the fairness of the Catholic press and of the interviews given by clergymen, but he warned, "still there is an element working to produce a different state of affairs." The proposal, which he made in the name of the Catholic members of two locals, was to have the objects and aims of the Knights positively blessed by the Church.[50] Powderly answered in no uncertain terms:

> The request to have the aims and principles of the K. of L. approved by the Catholic Church will not be made by me. I am a Catholic and know that our church never approves of any, but a strictly religious society.
> We are tolerated and is not that sufficient? Had not your members better wait until there is cause for alarm? Why do they go to Canada to seek trouble when they are not molested by the Church at home?

[48] AUND, James A. McMaster Papers, John T. Cummings to McMaster, Wilbur, New York, September 15, 1886.

[49] *John Swinton's Paper,* September 12, 1886.

[50] PP, Oscar N. Marihugh to Powderly, Middleport, Ohio, September 11, 1886.

The Catholic Church has always denounced intemperance and vice of all kinds. Do our Catholic members always act strictly up to the advice given from the altar in these matters and do they shrink in alarm from the contemplation of a denunciation from the altar, of their bad deeds, as they now shrink from what is not even threatened by the Church, simply because some members in Canada have not behaved themselves. Have patience.[51]

Fortunately, the Canadian difficulties, whether arising from lay or clerical behavior, did not become prominent enough during the fall of 1886 to hinder the progress toward peace being made in the United States. While an anonymous correspondent denied publicly so much as a single desertion in the whole Provine of Quebec, at the same time a local in the chief commercial center of the province did confess that it was in a "critical condition" as a result of Taschereau's *mandement*.[52] The news from Toronto, on the other hand, was as encouraging as ever. Charles March and Dan O'Donoghue had taken on Monsignor Richard O'Bryen, the papal ablegate, in a two and a half hour visit in which O'Donoghue dubbed as liars those who had "outrageously misrepresented" Powderly and his mission to Montreal in the previous February. He spared the G. M. W. the details of "how and on what subjects we knocked him out," but mentioned how this gentlemanly diplomat while later being feted by Senator Frank Smith, "our bitter enemy," heard O'Donoghue referred to by a young priest, as "no Catholic anyway." [53] The ill repute in which some other Catholics held these two labor leaders, O'Donoghue and March,[54] did not influence Archbishop Lynch, of whom the former

[51] PP, Powderly to Marihugh, September 18, 1886, copy.

[52] *John Swinton's Paper*, September 12, 1886; PP, Arthur Herbert to Powderly, Montreal, September 13, 1886.

[53] PP, O'Donoghue to Powderly, Toronto, September 26, 1886.

[54] These men and their whole organization had been roundly denounced, with the assistance of many press clippings, for having "the germ of socialism" in an appeal for Lynch to join with Taschereau against "that vile Order." It closed with the reminder, "Your Grace will earn the gratitude and esteem of all the classes of respectable citizens on the continent and you will find it no loss to you . . . in any manner." AAT, Mary T. Smith to Lynch, Toronto, July 5, 1886.

aid warmly again, "God bless his liberal and radical heart." Quite
o the contrary, Lynch called them for a talk in the middle of
September and not only did he say he entertained no objection to
he Knights but he could not see where others had grounds for ob-
ection. He suggested a clarification in the preamble by defining
he capitalist's profits as at eight per cent and the rest to go to the
producer. Intending the interview for their private satisfaction
and requesting his name be used only in general terms, the Arch-
pishop of Toronto gave them his usual blessing and invited them
pack. Lynch felt, moreover, that the bishops of Ontario and the
United States were fundamentally agreed and he advised:

> Keep on at your good work without ostentation and untiringly;
> don't be afraid; the Church will mind its own business; I am
> able to attend to it in Ontario without going to Rome on this
> matter; don't be talking about what the Church should or should
> not do. I will attend to that; I am with heart and soul in the
> work which you are at. God bless you.[55]

The neighboring Province of Quebec exhibited neither the same
friendliness toward the Order nor the same harmony within the
Church. But these differences were shown only in the quiet exchange of notes. The report in a Detroit paper that a constitution
revised by the clergy in Montreal "under the direction of Archbishop
Fabre" was in the hands of two delegates who were taking it to
Richmond for approval, led Taschereau to write to Fabre who was
now his brother metropolitan and to send the extract.[56] It was
accompanied by a gentle rebuke:

> I believe I ought to call to Your Grace's attention that since
> the Holy See has been made aware of the matter and has given
> its judgment on it, it has exclusively also the duty of judging
> what modifications can make the society acceptable to the
> Church. I do not conceal the fact that this is a formidable
> problem which is daily disputed and takes on new proportions.

To Taschereau things seemed ominous, for now he had some Knights
in one of his own parishes. They were seasonal workers in the States

---

[55] PP, O'Donoghue to Powderly, Toronto, October 3, 1886.
[56] This enclosure was from the Detroit *Evening News*, October 7, 1886.

and had found it necessary to join the Order to get work. Never theless, they had had no difficulty with their American pastor i being admitted to the sacraments without resigning their member ship. This state of affairs had been reported to Simeoni by the Quebec cardinal but he had received no answer.[57] But Fabre was quick to respond, even if brief in doing so. He ignored the question of the supposed revision of the constitution of the Knights of Labor remarking simply that the Knights were "very numerous" i Montreal and adding that his priests had conscientiously pro mulgated throughout the Archdiocese of Montreal Quebec's *mande ment* on the occasion of the jubilee.[58]

Likewise, among the hierarchy of the United States the sign of a lack of uniformity of opinion began to appear, but this, too was in private. Although he had publicly denied that either himsel or any of his brother bishops had already denounced the Knights Bishop Gilmour's judgment was evoked by Elder in these words "The answer to Quebec on the Knights of Labor is intended to be general, and will be so if you in your meeting at Baltimore do not prevent." [59] Both Dwenger and Chatard also sent hostile answers to their metropolitan's request for opinions. The former was for a strong condemnation of the "unlawful means made us of in strikes," and likewise, "the socialistic and anarchistic principle often advocated in their lodges." [60] The Bishop of Vincennes, an old foe of the Knights of Labor who had already carried the figh to Rome, was strong against the Ancient Order of Hibernians and explicit in his objections to the Knights of Labor. He found evidence for the Order's socialism in the Chicago press and for anarchism

---

[57] AAM, Archêvequé de Québec, Taschereau to Fabre, Quebec, October 12 1886. This letter to the Propaganda was not found. On such migrant worker as these subjects of Taschereau during these years, cf. Marcus L. Hansen and John B. Brebner, *The Mingling of the Canadian and American Peoples* (New Haven, 1940), pp. 121-218.

[58] AAM, Lettres, VI, 250, Fabre to Taschereau, Montreal, October 13 1886, copy.

[59] *John Swinton's Paper,* September 17, 1886; AAC, Elder to Gilmour Cincinnati, October 1, 1886, copy; Gilmour to Elder, Cleveland, October 5 1886.

[60] AAC, Joseph Dwenger to Elder, Fort Wayne, October 2, 1886.

Powderly's opposition to the "wage system," while no one could
ny, so Chatard said, that the society countenanced strikes, boy-
tts, and persecutions of non-union men and scabs. Chatard dis-
sted any answers that such secret societies might make to bishops
t as yet he merely suggested that "the only prudent
urse to pursue, in practising indulgence, is to say not a word to
prove, and do no act to countenance them." Catholic members,
thought, should not be denied the sacraments but be won away
arguments such as those calculated to show them that they were
king themselves "servants of men." [61] While not as explicit as
rt Wayne and Vincennes, in his previous sentiments Archbishop
rrigan was at least aligned with Gilmour in his position. Cor-
an's stand, however, was not yet known to the other archbishops,
d meanwhile he proceeded with what appeared to be an objective
dy of the facts. As the time for the meeting drew near the Arch-
hop of New York had collected, "perhaps a dozen" constitutions
secret societies, only to find out that he had no time to read
m.[62] His secretary revealed that inquiry had been made of
me, but no satisfactory answer had been received. McDonnell felt
re would have been a more widespread promulgation of Rome's
ree against the Knights of Labor if Archbishop Lynch had not
erted that their revised constitution was under consideration by
man authorities. Of the New York scene he reported, "several
our priests, who were favorably disposed towards them and who
ored to put an end to strikes in this vicinity, later on expressed
ir hopes that the Knights would be condemned." In connection
h the coming gathering of the archbishops he merely remarked
t it was "not unlikely" the K. of L. would be discussed.[63]
The most effective preliminary work for the Baltimore con-
ence was done by Bishop John J. Keane of Richmond who acted
an ecclesiastical liaison officer with Powderly while the general
embly was meeting in his city from October 4 to 20. The Knights'
mbership of over 700,000 were represented there by 658 delegates,

[61] AAC, Francis Chatard to Elder, Indianapolis, October 12, 1886.

[62] BCA, 82-B-12, Corrigan to Gibbons, Troy, October 15, 1886.

[63] ADR, Charles McDonnell to O'Connell, New York, October 14, 1886.

a number "so large as to be almost unmanageable." [64]   Most
prominent in the order of business were the discussions of the
difficulties between the Knights of Labor and the trade unions.   In
such a gathering of inexperienced parliamentarians District Assembly
49 of New York, the most active of the anti-trade unionist factions,
took the lead and even succeeded in having members of the Cigar
Makers International Union barred from the Order.[65]   Such matters
as these were not, of course, the concern of the Catholic journals
which contented themselves with merely a comment on the convention, wishing the assembly well and giving Powderly special
applause.[66]   Two of the more Irish publications thought it in-
opportune to have raised the color issue in the southern city by
having a colored delegate from New York introduce the general
master workman and by attempting to resist the local custom of
segregation.[67]   The same editorial in the *Pilot,* nevertheless, readily
accepted Powderly's charge that the railroads had agitated strikes
and the Boston paper found him erring, "if at all, upon the side
of conservatism."   The *Irish World,* using Gibbons' words again
found the Knights perfectly in harmony with the Catholic Church
"which has always shown sympathy with every legitimate movement that aims at elevating mankind." [68]   Indeed, some were already
seeing more than "sympathy" in this case, for they considered the
Knights of Labor "too Catholic." [69]   Foreshadowing future outbursts
those disposed to be critical of the Church were convinced it was
making a "shrewd and subtle change of policy." [70]

There was no need of readaptation in the case of Bishop Keane

[64] Powderly, *Thirty Years,* p. 641.

[65] Commons, *History,* II, 409. For the background of this trouble with the
rising Federation of Organized Trades and Labor Unions, which in December
1886, became the A. F. of L., cf. *Ibid.,* pp. 396 ff., and the report of the minority leader among the Knights, Buchanan, *op. cit.,* pp. 313-316.

[66] Brooklyn *Examiner,* October 2; *Connecticut Catholic,* October 9; *Colorado
Catholic,* October 16; St. Louis *Catholic World,* October 16, 1886; Washington
Church News, October 20; New York *Catholic Herald,* October 16, 1886.

[67] *Republic,* October 16; *Pilot,* October 16, 1886.

[68] October 9, 1886.

[69] *John Swinton's Paper,* October 3, 1886.

[70] *Catholic Standard,* October 16, 1886.

a close collaborator of Gibbons, who used to good purpose the opportunity offered by this largest and most publicized gathering of labor held in the United States up to that time. Powderly attended services in St. Peter's Cathedral in Richmond on October 3 and noted on the back of a calling card, "Was at the Cathedral for three solid hours, had a high mass, incense so strong my head aches yet." [71] Yet after Mass he addressed the St. Vincent de Paul Society of the parish and compared its work of helping the poor with his own.[72] It is not clear whether the initiative came from the bishop or the labor leader, but on the evening of October 7 the two men conferred during what Powderly told the ubiquitous reporters was a purely social call. No mention, he insisted, was made of the Knights or of the colored question so much highlighted in the press just at the moment.[73] Keane's report to Gibbons revealed otherwise:

> It seems the newspapermen were anxious to make capital out of Powderly's visit to me, which they managed to learn of. But they have received no information from him or me. While there seems to be a rather general fear of some elements in their makeup, the impression, I think, is quite as general that we had better let such things correct themselves, as, in matters of mere pecuniary balance of interests, and in such a country as ours, is sure to take place.[74]

Apart from Powderly's contacts with Keane nothing positive came out of the Richmond session of the general assembly by way of aiding better relations with the Catholic Church. During its fourteen days over 400 documents were submitted, which were many more than could be considered. With regard to the constitution, only the first part referring to the general assembly was revised

[71] PP, Attached to letter of John M. Higgins to Powderly, Richmond, October 5, 1886, arranging to have him address the Catholic Beneficial Society that evening. A similar jotting addressed to Emma Fickenscher, his secretary, told of his forensic accomplishments, "I had that vast audience of the intellect of the order in tears. My God it was sublime. I tingle yet when I think of it. The *convention is mine*." n.d.

[72] Baltimore *Sun,* October 4, 1886.

[73] *Ibid.,* October 9, 1886.

[74] BCA, 82-B-9, Keane to Gibbons, Richmond, October 12, 1886.

and the rest was put into the hands of a committee.[75]   Hence the question of what was the most up-to-date edition of it continued to be of concern to the Catholic prelates even though their criticisms of the constitution had yet to become specific.   An extraordinary action of the Richmond convention was the commissioning of Thomas B. Barry to conduct negotiations in the Chicago walkout of 50,000 meat packers.   The following month this Chicago disturbance did come to have a bearing on relations with the Church, for the walkout met a demoralizing end with a sudden order from Powderly to give in to the forces of management.   This capitulation was attributed publicly by Barry to the influence of a letter of the Reverend P. M. Flannigan to the head of the Order.[76]

During the actual time of the convention, however, Keane was the only ecclesiastic in close touch with Powderly.   The Bishop of Richmond meanwhile not only continued his regular episcopal duties, but as he told Gibbons, he was preparing to leave for Rome on October 30 with Bishop Ireland to plead the cause of a Catholic university for the United States.[77]   His impression of Powderly could have been nothing but good since the leader of the Knights attended church every Sunday, and not only did this get into the paper but an interview was also publicized in which he explained that he had never had any active connection with the socialists and that any similarity between their principles and those of the Order was slight.[78]   No wonder, then, that the bishop and labor leader—this time allegedly accompanied by Thomas O'Reilly—had another cordial discussion immediately after the last adjournment and before Powderly left Richmond.   It would seem reasonable from this that the genesis of Powderly's part in the Baltimore conference might

[75] Powderly, *Thirty Years*, p. 644; *Proceedings* (Richmond, 1886), pp. 230-237.

[76] Commons, *History*, II, 418-419. For Powderly's defense of his action as taken on his own initiative, cf. *Path*, pp. 140-162. Ware, *op. cit.*, pp. 153-154, is inclined to discount the priest's influence.

[77] He had confirmation in Staunton (Richmond *Dispatch*, October 12) and the dedication of the chapel of the Little Sisters of the Poor (Richmond *State*, October 15). At the close of the convention these sisters received such things as the tables and muslin used by the Knights. *Church News*, October 31, 1886.

[78] Baltimore *Sun*, October 15; Richmond *State*, October 18, 1886.

have taken place in Richmond the week before. The only evidence
for that supposition, however, is found in two sources which will
hereafter be shown to have been doctored. Moreover, they are con-
tradictory in nature. The general master workman later professed
before the Order that he had "received a courteous invitation from
his Eminence the Cardinal to come to Baltimore, as his presence
there was urgently required for the purpose of offering testimony
on matters concerning the Order, and upon which his Eminence desired particular information." [79]   Ecclesiastical archives have revealed not even a mention of such an invitation, although Gilmour
and Riordan, speaking of the Ancient Order of Hibernians, suggested the same procedure of consulting the leaders at the meeting
of the archbishops.[80] On the other hand, Powderly's own initiative
was more emphasized in his unpublished, but also highly questionable, account of the Richmond preparations. The trip to Baltimore
was "advice given us by Bishop Keene [*sic*]." He had been assured "an audience" and, in fact, he believed that he was "expected
to present myself on that occasion and explain certain principles
and views of the Order." It was hardly an archiepiscopal summons
or even an invitation when—supposedly assuring O'Reilly—he said,
'Bishop Keene [*sic*] has instructed me as to the steps to take to
gain an audience and I have his word for it that you will be admitted and I want to have you with me on that occasion." [81]

Quite beyond counseling any procedure Keane, according to a
trustworthy record, had expressed some positive views which Powderly urged him to put in writing. To a certain extent the bishop
complied by sending him five sheets of a unique pencil-written
document. With it went this explanation:

You expressed this morning the wish that the view I was
urging should be embodied in a letter that you could use with

[79] PP, "The Order and the Church, Report by T. O'R." Certain sections
were crossed out apparently before Powderly presented it as his own at the
Minneapolis convention in October, 1887, and certainly before it was printed in
the *Proceedings* (Minneapolis, 1887), pp. 1644-1648.

[80] ADC, Gilmour to Gibbons, Cleveland, October 16, 1886, copy; NYAA,
Gibbons to Corrigan, Baltimore, October 18, 1886.

[81] PP. Powderly to Thomas O'Reilly, dated "October 25, 1886."

your associates. On the evening of our first interview, while riding to Richmond in the cars, I scribbled what would be the substance of an address to the Convention, should circumstances so form as to lead to my making one. Perhaps it may serve just as well for the purpose you contemplate—and as I am too pressed for time to revise or rewrite it, I send it to you in its present rough form—and you may make of it such use as you deem best and most provident and serviceable for good.[82]

In this religious and patriotic *fervorino*, which never saw the light of day, Keane heartily endorsed the cause of the Knights of Labor and warned them only to be ever respectful of justice and the law.[83]

It can be reliably established, then, only that Powderly alone had two meetings in Richmond with Keane, and it can but be surmised that they discussed there Powderly's trip to Baltimore. This is the case because the evidence of his correspondence with O'Reilly under date of October 25, 1886, is called into serious question. This influences not only the story of his arrangements with Keane, but more important still that of his appearance at the cardinal's residence in Baltimore since this same letter describes Powderly's preparations for his encounter with the hierarchy. Yet the message was written and falsely dated by Powderly after receiving instructions on August 15, 1887, from O'Reilly. These read: "The letter calling me to Philadelphia to accompany you to Baltimore to see the Cardinal should be dated Nov. [crossed out] October 25th, 1886." After the further request to date another order to proceed to Canada to see Taschereau as March 25, 1887, O'Reilly admonished, "Don't put these letters in your copying book. You understand!" Powderly, however, did make press-copies of both the desired letters, but in the back of a letterbook which covered the period from January to March, 1886.[84] A note of October 26, saying he was to be off on the next day to Baltimore "to attend the meeting of the Archbishops" was sent out by Powderly without mentioning O'Reilly or anyone else, and the copy was made in the proper letterbook for September-December, 1886.[85]

82 PP, Keane to Powderly, Richmond, October 21, 1886.
83 The full text is given in Appendix II, pp. 363-364.
84 Pages 316 ff. and 322 ff.
85 PP, Powderly to Gilbert Rockwod, Scranton, October 26, 1886, copy.

This letter dated October 25, 1886, may have expressed some truth as to Powderly's motivation, although it was written after the event, but it cannot be accepted as reliable evidence. Although it disagrees with O'Reilly's report, "The Order and the Church," on whether the group went to Baltimore by summons or through Powderly's initiative, it supports the assertion of the latter document that it was a committee that went. This report was published and became the official version of the Church negotiations after it was presented at the Minneapolis session of the general assembly in 1887.[86] In turn it was used by Powderly in his autobiography.[87] According to both the earlier documents, then, Powderly arranged to have O'Reilly and John Hayes accompany him. The long pre-dated letter was actually written in August, 1887, at a time when Powderly's Church connections were a target for his enemies. It was possibly a safeguard, therefore, against the charge of selling out to Rome on his own. Later there was to come up, too, the question of supplying O'Reilly with money to carry on ecclesiastical negotiations and in this Powderly had to defend himself. Both of the letters suggested by O'Reilly, concerning Baltimore and Quebec, would have given the appearance of work well done and worth their price.[88] Yet there is no evidence that Powderly ever had to make use of these letters before the Order.

Besides a possible explanation of why it should have been written almost a year afterwards, the other evidence which really dates from October 25, 1886, the supposed date of the letter of Powderly to O'Reilly, should be of help in establishing its authenticity. The letter itself expressed Powderly's belief in his duty to see the cardinal and archbishops and to put them straight, just as he would the leading churchmen of any denomination. However, he wanted a committee, not only as witnesses, but likewise to avail himself of O'Reilly's ecclesiastical etiquette (since he was an ex-seminarian), John Hayes' membership on the executive board, and also a John Howes as representative of the non-Catholic members. The only letter of acceptance found was that of O'Reilly, dated October 26, from New York.

[86] *Proceedings* (Minneapolis, 1887), pp. 1644 ff.
[87] *Path,* pp. 347-348, 392.
[88] *Vide infra,* pp. 289-291 and 299-300.

In it he spoke as if he already knew the cardinal, and that, "It will afford me much pleasure to present you to his Eminence," but a year later he was seeking a "letter of introduction" to the same prelate from Powderly.[89] Furthermore, the Baltimore *Sun,* which ferreted out the best of ecclesiastical news, made no mention of any companion of Powderly's on his trip to the cardinal's residence on October 28.[90] The whereabouts of Hayes on that day could not be established from his papers, but he was scheduled to meet Powderly on Wednesday evening, October 27.[91] This might have been a chance for the general master workman to get some last minute advice from another highly-placed Catholic in the Order.

The evidence which puts the negotiations with Gibbons and the other archbishops in the hands of a group of three Knights, instead of Powderly alone, is weak on other and lesser counts. When Gibbons did protest against their condemnation in Rome, O'Reilly congratulated Powderly, saying merely that the cardinal had "faithfully kept the promise made to you in Baltimore." [92] More than that, when Powderly first came under severe attack for his overtures to the Church, in Denver in May, 1887, he made no mention of the others who later were said to have been with him, but he remarked only, "When I held my interview with Cardinal Gibbons and other dignitaries of my church, I never betrayed any secret." [93] The minutes kept by the secretary of the meeting of the archbishops mentioned only Powderly, as did Gibbons' own recollections and his biography.[94] Due especially to the faulty character of the only

89 PP, The letters dated October 25 and 26, 1886, were not found in the regular chronological file of correspondence. O'Reilly to Powderly, n.p., received August 29, 1887.

90 October 29, 1887.

91 Hayes Papers, Powderly to Hayes, Scranton, October 25, 1886.

92 PP, O'Reilly to Powderly, Macon, Georgia, March 7, 1887.

93 *John Swinton's Paper,* May 22, 1887.

94 *A Retrospect of Fifty Years* (Baltimore, 1916), I, 189; Allen S. Will, *Life of Cardinal Gibbons* (New York, 1922), I, 327. It must be admitted that a difficulty arises from the sentence in Gibbons' memorial on the Knights of Labor later submitted in Rome, which reads, "After their convention, held last year in Richmond, he and several of the principal members, devout Catholics, made similar declarations [Powderly's letter of filial obedience sent to Father

evidence to the contrary, which purports to be contemporaneous, it is at least highly probable that Powderly was alone rather than with two other knights when he called at Cardinal Gibbons' North Charles Street house on the morning of October 28, 1886.

If there is doubt about the labor leaders, at least the ecclesiastical personnel present at the Baltimore meeting is definitely established. The secular papers, such as the New York *Herald,* announced the conference and told of the number of archbishops moving on Baltimore. They instanced Kenrick and Corrigan as likely to be hostile to the Knights because of local circumstances in their jurisdictions.[95] The issuance of a pastoral letter, which the *Herald* spoke of as a possibility, had received hierarchical support from only one bishop, John J. Kain of Wheeling. As a means of showing the conservative power of the Church, Kain pointed out, "the propriety of some official utterance warning our Catholic people against the unjust practices now so commonly resorted to by labor associations, whenever their members go on a strike." [96] Three out of the twelve archbishops of the United States were unable to be present and sent their excuses as well as their opinions to Gibbons. Archbishop Patrick W. Riordan of San Francisco, after promising if possible to attend, begged off for reasons of health, but he supplemented what he had told Gibbons orally by a "long communication." [97]

This letter of Riordan was not available, but his opinion was found at the end of a Latin version of the proceedings.[98] The Pacific

Carew, August 31, had just been alluded to without naming it] concerning the action of that convention. . . ." *Retrospect,* I, 193. It could also refer to such actions as that of the D. M. W. in Baltimore, J. J. McCartney, who put the case before his pastor, Monsignor Edward McColgan, the Vicar General of the Archdiocese of Baltimore who, in turn, was said to have forwarded it to Gibbons. Baltimore *Sun,* October 30, 1886. The possibility still remains that there were three in the delegation, but that Powderly did all the talking, and later on they wanted a document to prove their secret move and so the letter of October 25 was concocted.

[95] New York *Herald,* October 28, 1886.
[96] BCA, 82-D-2, Kain to Gibbons, Wheeling, October 27, 1886.
[97] NYAA, Gibbons to Corrigan, Baltimore, October 18, 1886. *Catholic Review,* October 16, reported Riordan had suffered injuries to his arm in a fall. On the lack of archival evidence from San Francisco cf. p. 384.
[98] BCA, 82-D-8. This was based on the English "Notes of proceedings of

Coast prelate was against disturbing any society unless there was an urgent necessity. Specifically he held:

> With regard to the Knights of Labor, some of them who are astute in politics are using it for their own end, for the majority are honest men who apart from this association know no other means of attaining their rights. If the deeds or words of some of the Knights of Labor ought to be reproved, the whole society ought not therefore be condemned. This association is already unmanageable on account of its size and will perish.[99]

The difficulties involved in leaving their sees kept two other archbishops away. William H. Gross of Oregon City had only two months before been in the East and besides he could not depend on the often impassable rural roads of his mission territory. So he reluctantly declined the invitation to his native Baltimore and simply gave his concurrence with Gibbons' views as stated in the press. He did add this observation of his own:

> I fear however that this question of capital and labor will cause trouble in the future. The preachers and politicians will run amuck with it as they did on the slavery question—and are now doing on the less dangerous question of Temperance. But I believe that it is our duty to speak out now in terms most unmistakable on this great subject.[100]

From Milwaukee came a copy of its provincial council's decrees which were not yet approved by Rome, plus some remarks of Archbishop Heiss. The German prelate explained his absence as due

meeting of Abps. Oct. 28, 1886 at Balt. to consider status of certain societies, made by Rev. M. F. Foley, Secy of meeting." The latter was found in an unindexed envelope among the Gibbons Papers. It contained also a rough pencil copy with many abbreviations, apparently jottings made on the spot which were later transcribed into this copy.

[99] The Knights of Labor had reached California by 1878. The press there held them in ill repute but among their fosterers was Burnette G. Haskell of the radical Denver *Labor Enquirer*. Ira B. Cross, *A History of the Labor Movement in California* (Berkeley, 1935), pp. 152-153. By July, 1886, that state had thirty-six locals affiliated and over 2,000 members listed. *Proceedings* (Richmond, 1886), pp. 326-328.

[100] BCA, 82-B-6, Gross to Gibbons, Corvallis, Oregon, October 9, 1886.

to the press of duties and the bother of rheumatism, and he undertook to warn the conference against being too harsh. He recommended "careful investigation" of the societies under consideration by three committees of bishops and priests in different sections of the country. Of the constitution of the Knights he had examined, he testified, "I could not find anything that would justify me to put them under the Societies absolutely forbidden by the Church." [101]

The meeting of the nine other metropolitans was held the same day that the Statue of Liberty was being unveiled in New York harbor, and Cardinal Gibbons had to excuse himself from that civic celebration in order to preside at Baltimore.[102]   The give and take of their discussion was duly noted by Father Foley, the secretary of the meeting. He did not state, however, and hence it is difficult to establish, just what part was played in it by Powderly—the only layman mentioned. O'Reilly's account, while it is "official," may not be, therefore, completely lacking in truth. Speaking, of course, in terms of three delegates,[103] he definitely indicated that only Gibbons received them:

> Upon our arrival at the Archiepiscopal residence, we were graciously welcomed and his Eminence expressed his keen appreciation of the obedience and readiness with which the invitation had been responded to. No one who has enjoyed the rare privilege of a personal interview with this able prelate can fail to have been impressed with the grace of his conversation, the kindliness of his manner, and to have gained an insight into the nobility of his life which makes him honored of all men, and beloved of Protestant and Catholic alike.[104]

[101] BCA, 82-C-5, Heiss to Gibbons, Milwaukee, October 19, 1886. There was as yet no coolness between the two archbishops over the German question, for Gibbons had shortly before given a letter of commendation to the Milwaukee priest, P. M. Abbelen, who used it at Propaganda in presenting his petition which so aroused non-German Catholics in the United States. Cf. John J. Meng, "Cahenslyism: the Second Chapter, 1891-1910," *Catholic Historical Review,* XXXII (October, 1946), 305.

[102] *Colorado Catholic,* November 20, 1886.

[103] The Protestant representative proposed by the letter of "October 25, 1886" is nowhere mentioned the second time.

[104] PP, "The Order and the Church. Report by T. O'R." These words were omitted in the published version, possibly as too strong for non-Catholic ears. *Proceedings* (Minneapolis, 1887), p. 1644.

The rest of the committee's report has them addressing themselves only to Gibbons and receiving an answer from him. They asked him to judge the Order by its good deeds and not by the "violent element" of which they sought to purge it. The cardinal's response was given "during the interview which was of long duration," and it noted the conservative leadership and declared the Catholic prelates would favor labor.[105] Gibbons was recorded as defending the Church's right to be vigilant of secret groups. He was quoted, furthermore, as showing the Church's friendship for the workers but her opposition to socialism and anarchism against which he warned the Knights. The cardinal concluded (as O'Reilly was to inform the Order) by promising the leaders of the Knights of Labor "to explain the purpose of the organization at the Vatican, and requested permission to pledge the Order to the maintenance of a lawful and orderly behavior." [106]

The difficulty arising from this account lies not only in a prejudiced version prepared by a man most likely not present at the time, but also in the fact that the recollection of both the cardinal and the labor leader agree on having the interview take place in the presence of the other archbishops. The Gibbons' memoirs have, "Mr. Pouderly [*sic*] telling the nature of the Order's secrecy to the Archbishops." [107] Powderly was acquainted with this work when he wrote his own life story and he mentioned the presence on that occasion of "a number of priests, bishops and archbishops," but he disagreed completely on the nature of the discussion. He maintained the cardinal's interest was not in their secrecy or ritual but in their "economic aims and methods of carrying them forward." [108] Although the Baltimore *Sun* erred the day after the interview in reporting that Powderly and a committee appointed at Richmond would soon call on the cardinal, it may have been more correct in later saying that the general master workman laid before him the

105 Deleted in the *Proceedings* was "We affirm that we are, and ever shall be, the enemy of plutocracy and of corporations of men with no soul," p. 1645.

106 *Ibid.*

107 *Retrospect*, I, 189; Will, *op. cit.*, I, 327. Will's assertion that there were several previous interviews is unfounded. II, 326.

108 *Path*, pp. 392, 348.

constitution and by-laws, and also in explaining that "the utterances of Mr. Powderly were carefuly noted and presented to the Archbishops." [109] This together with Powderly's version of the content of their talk would seem to be supported by the roughly composed minutes of the committee secretary giving, "First views of Archbishops-Knights of Labor." Foley began, "An opening statement was made by the Cardinal. He said that there were about 500,000 Catholic K. of L. in U. S. Their head, Mr. Powderly declares K. of L. against boycotting and against refusing to allow non-union men to work." Immediately after this the opinions of the individual archbishops are given and Powderly's name is absent, as no doubt was his person, when the meeting got under way.

The notes of Foley give the impression that the conference of archbishops was circled twice in search of their thoughts on the subject. Archbishop Francis X. Leray of New Orleans began with the erroneous statement that the constitution sent by Taschereau had been in Rome "more than a year," before action was taken.[110] Boston's Archbishop John J. Williams wondered if Ryan's suspicion that in places where the Order was weak the members could swear they did not belong to it, was a generally recognized principle of the Knights.[111] Apparently looking for such in the A. K., he read from the ritual of initiation some phrases, such as, "labor is the only creator of values and capital." Such a search for evidence was wasted on Archbishop Peter R. Kenrick, who gave no sign of being open to conviction on the matter. His see city of St. Louis had been the scene of great labor violence, and more than that, some months later he was said to have come under the influence of Gould's man, Hoxie. This information was advanced by Father O'Leary, ad-

[109] Baltimore *Sun,* October 29, 30, 1886.

[110] No opinion of his was found of a previous date except in PP, Scrapbook, September, 1885-March, 1886. Among the clippings here of March, 1886, was an unidentified and undated one which represented Leray as having no objection to the Order since it had no oath or blind obedience. New Orleans had 3,567 Knights in twenty-three locals. *Proceedings* (Richmond, 1886), pp. 326-328.

[111] Despite the apparent lack of commotion in the Archdiocese of Boston the Knights listed as of July, 1886, 402 locals in Boston, and fifty-seven in Lynn with a total of 92,775 members in that area. *Ibid.*

mittedly no admirer of his superior, on the word of the Reverend J. J. Hennessey, pastor of St. John's Church in St. Louis. His story was that "his Grace held a two hours' conference with Mr. Hoxie from whom he learned the correct position of the Order and straightway went to Baltimore to meet his brother bishops and archbishops and to discuss with them on the morality of the K. of L." [112] Since no further indication of what went into the formation of the prelate's opinion was available, one can only examine his viewpoint. He was opposed even to any episcopal communication with the Knights, for they were not only formidable, detrimental to society and untrustworthy, but they could change their constitution at will. Saying he "would be sorry if Rome should depart from its stand" the Archbishop of St. Louis expressed decided opposition and pointed for support to the experience of the previous winter and to their "refusal to allow others to work." Condemnation by the hierarchy, which should be on the basis of the organization's secrecy and anti-social character, would mean a loss for the Church but it would "gain in the estimation of intelligent men." To the presiding cardinal's request for a suggestion Kenrick replied that they should support Taschereau. Gibbons then countered by observing that the Holy See's reply had been *juxta opposita* and so the assembled committee should make its own statement. Kenrick simply insisted the society was an *imperium in imperio* and was made worse by the fact that there were "some well-meaning dupes among its members." Archbishop Elder of Cincinnati saw nothing wrong in the association's power as such. He asked if the same objection could not be raised against other organizations, such as capitalists or the liquor industry, which he considered to be "all powerful" in England and in the State of Ohio.[113] Williams was willing to agree with Kenrick on the dangers to the community and, of course, to agree with Rome, but from what he knew, and

[112] PP, O'Leary to Powderly, Webster Groves, Missouri, March 30, 1887. The Archives of the Archdiocese of St. Louis revealed nothing, nor did the records of the Missouri Pacific Railroad. Cf. p. 384.

[113] The liquor question agitated Ohio in the early 1880's. The Republican policy of taxing the liquor traffic, as opposed to the Democrats' advocacy of a licensing system, won out in 1886. Eugene H. Rosebloom and Francis P. Weisenburger, *A History of Ohio* (New York, 1934), pp. 349-352, 360.

that was confessedly only what he had read in the papers, he could see no "fixed point for condemnation." He favored an independent course of action and this approach was quickly taken up by Elder who suggested referring the case to Rome. Archbishop John Baptist Salpointe of Santa Fe who was French-born and had been a missionary in the troublesome Southwest since 1859, then also agreed to send it to Rome.[114] Possibly there was some influence exercised over Salpointe in traveling from St. Louis with Kenrick, for he added that from their effects he thought the Knights of Labor worthy of condemnation.[115] The Metropolitan of New York, whose city had also been beset by much publicized labor commotion,[116] and who had not been slow to express an unfavorable opinion on the Knights the previous August, merely suggested sending all their documents, public and private, to Rome. True, he had been advised in the meantime by as able a canonist as Richard L. Burtsell of his own archdiocese, to be lenient. The archbishop had asked his opinion on a woman's life insurance society, but Burtsell took the opportunity to extend his remarks to "societies established for the aid of the poor" and specified, "I have in mind also the Knights of Labor." Praying that the archbishops would be slow to take any action against them, the Roman-trained canon lawyer pointed out that Canada was no norm and that the threat of denial of absolution would not deter men. His advice to Corrigan had concluded:

> As much tolerance, as it is at all justifiable, should be used with them: even a tolerance of material for the sake of avoiding formal sin is advisable. The Church to-day is expected to protect, as far as possible the poor against the selfishness of and their legalized oppression by wealthy corporations.[117]

The idea of having recourse to Rome was taken up favorably by Leray, by Ryan, who wondered if their own condemnatory edict

---

[114] His province included New Mexico, Arizona, Utah, and Colorado, but not Texas which had been the center of labor strife. Denver was within the territory, but directly ruled by Vicar Apostolic Joseph Macheboeuf.

[115] Baltimore *Sun*, October 26, 1886.

[116] Especially in a street railway strike and the Henry George campaign.

[117] NYAA, Burtsell to Corrigan, New York, September 30, 1886.

would be heeded, and by Feehan of Chicago, who wanted the arch-bishops to take a position of "no approval, no condemnation," and thus let Rome take the responsibility. Ryan suggested that in all fairness to the Knights of Labor any constitution sent to Rome should have the latest changes noted, although no one seemed able to answer Leray's query as to whether or not the report that amend-ments had been made in Montreal was true.[118] The cardinal, with a diplomatic gesture toward the senior who had ruled as archbishop in St. Louis since 1847, agreed there was danger in such a formidable organization, but by transmitting the documents they would be obeying the Holy See. Kenrick, quite unmoved, declared "the assembly was called to express an opinion and ought to express it."

There is no hint in the minutes that a recess was held wherein a little private debating might have taken place. The archbishops, according to Foley's notes, were then called on for their "final views" on the Knights. Kenrick still opposed it as a dangerous organization; Elder said he would tolerate it "if all the objectionable features were eliminated," while Williams put himself down as simply against condemnation. Salpointe went on record for their condemnation, "as opposed to rights of others." Then Corrigan became more articulate, calling the Knights of Labor "an unhealthy organization," and "un-sound in ethics," but opposing positive condemnation, "as the poison has not yet sufficiently developed." If they really had a secret oath, however, the Archbishop of New York said, he would favor the sanction. His opinion was almost verbatim that contained in the "Report of J. J. Murphy, S.J. upon the Constitution, By-laws etc. of the *Ancient Order of Hibernians* and the *Knights of Labor*." [119] The Jesuit's judgment had been that the Knights were a "decidedly *unhealthy* organization for Catholics" because of their indifferentism and propagation of "theories which are ethically unsound." He went beyond the society's books to elaborate on its evils:

[118] E.g., *Freeman's Journal,* October 16, 1886.

[119] NYAA, n.d., n.p. The scribblings on the outside of these two folded pages seem to indicate Corrigan had it with him at the meeting.   John J. Murphy, S.J., was the president of the College of St. Francis Xavier in New York City.

Whilst in words deploring, it yet aims at a tyranny over the employer, and makes the same powerful by a no less baneful tyranny over the employee. It strikes at the rights of the capitalist by moral violence, and leads laborers and trades to coalesce for purposes of coercion, even though many of the laborers and trades may have no just grievance against the individual employer who happens to meet with the displeasure of the Society.

Murphy did not overlook the Order's resemblance to Masonic groups, although this was not raised by the Baltimore meeting at all. The very nuance of his advice against immediately condemning them was certainly to be that of Corrigan to whom the Jesuit had written, "it seems wiser to give them ample room to show forth the effects of the poison which seems to be in their system."

The hostility of the Archbishop of New York seems to have aroused the remaining prelates to a greater defense of the labor association. Ryan first said "as capitalists unite to protect themselves, working men have the same right, if their methods are not objectionable," and then he gave his usual vote for neutrality toward "societies of Catholics" which were not "Catholic societies," so long as the bad features were removed. Slowness in asking for a condemnation was favored by Leray, not only because labor had rights but also because of the evil consequences for the Church. In a more positive manner, the Archbishop of Chicago, whose city was the scene of many of labor's radical explosions, stated that the Knights were not a "menace to society" and that he was "most decidedly against the condemnation." The calm concluding remarks of Cardinal Gibbons were summarized thus:

> Labor has rights as well as capital. We should not condemn labor and let capital go free—would regard condemnation of K. of L. as disastrous to the Church—We should send documents to Rome and if objectionable features are eliminated K. of L. should be tolerated, should not be condemned—We have controlling influence over them: if they are condemned, a secret organization will follow in their wake and over that we will have no control.

That same day the committee held briefer discussions on the Grand Army of the Republic and the Ancient Order of Hibernians.

The archbishops decided not to disturb the former and they left the latter's position undetermined.[120] Thus the committee of archbishops as set up by the Third Plenary Council had done its work, but only in the case of the Knights of Labor had they determined that there was a lack of unanimous agreement and, therefore, the problem had to go to Rome.

Beginning with the report made after their adjournment and attributed to Bishop Spalding of Peoria, that most of the prelates had been hostile to the Knights, the press carried all kinds of stories on the significance of the latest ecclesiastical move.[121] Among the Catholic papers only the Brooklyn *Examiner* attempted to make editorial capital of it. Preston had it "on competent authority" that all that was awaited was the approval of Rome on the archbishops' decision that the Knights of Labor were legitimate. The *Republic* admitted they could only deduce that friendly relations still existed from Powderly's continued leadership, from the oft-quoted episcopal statements, and the Church's tradition as a "friend of labor." [123] In St. Louis the *Catholic World* was silent, while the *Western Watchman* said the deliberations should be a "caveat" to the Knights.[124] The *Freeman's Journal* branded press revelations on the subject as "purely imaginary," [125] and the *Morning Star* saw in the meeting merely the gathering of facts in Rome's slow process of passing a judgment.[126]

A correct version of the Baltimore affair was spread by the Archbishop of Cincinnati, and this, fortunately, reached even into Canada. Elder informed Gilmour by letter and told Bishop Camillus Maes of Covington about it personally.[127] The latter, referring to it as "a question whereon there is a regrettable disunion of action," probably betrayed his own feelings by referring to the Knights as, "les Chevaliers du Travail (d'industrie!)"—or sharpers. Maes did,

[120] Macdonald, *op. cit.*, pp. 147-148.
[121] *John Swinton's Paper*, November 7, 1886.
[122] November 6, 1886.
[123] November 6, 1886.
[124] November 6, 1886.
[125] November 6, 1886.
[126] November 6, 1886.
[127] ADC, Elder to Gilmour, Cincinnati, November 6, 1886.

however, on Elder's authority dismiss as inexact the press reports that the archbishops had pronounced in favor of them.[128] In Montreal Fabre seems, meanwhile, to have been keeping a discreet silence, although stories of opposition and even condemnation from the pulpit still emanated from that quarter.[129] The upshot of the constitutional revision which Fabre had not denied in writing to Taschereau and which delegates were supposed to have brought to Richmond remains only vaguely determined. Some explanation may lie behind O'Donoghue's observation that the Montreal Knights were fools for not taking Powderly's advice. This example of their "want of tact and discretion," which the Toronto leader did not further elucidate, demonstrated for him why they had such ecclesiastical troubles in the Province of Quebec.[130]

The general importance of the Canadian hierarchy in the whole problem of the Knights of Labor was definitely on the wane by the time Gibbons sent to Simeoni the report on the conference of the American archbishops. The Baltimore cardinal informed the Prefect of Propaganda that they had set forth their opinions on the Knights "about whom so much has recently been said," and he explained that their constitution had been given to the Bishop of Richmond, who was then on his way to Rome, and who would give Cardinal Simeoni an Italian translation. Foley's minutes were marked, "From these notes was condensed the official report sent to Cardinal Simeoni," and the report, of course, in the form of a Latin document was but a summary of the final opinions of the nine prelates and of those submitted by mail. No mention was made at all of Powderly.[131]

Almost on the same day there took place the departure of Monsignor Germano Straniero. This papal ablegate who had brought the biretta of his new dignity to Gibbons from Rome, had since

[128] AAM, Maes to Fabre, Covington, November 18, 1886.

[129] PP, William Lyght to Powderly, Montreal, November 28, 1886.

[130] PP, O'Donoghue to Powderly, Toronto, November 7, 1886. He was inclined to believe newspaper stories that Powderly was a "weekly communicant." The only account of this type seen was a later one by a Scranton priest in the *Irish World* of November 27, 1886, and reprinted in *John Swinton's Paper*, January 9, 1887.

[131] BCA, 82-E-12, Gibbons to Simeoni, Baltimore, November 12, 1886, copy.

traveled through the United States and Canada collecting material for a book, as well as gathering unto his person the ill-will of many of the native ordinaries. This was true to such an extent that O'Connell stated, "It is my impression that Monsignor Straniero's *carriera* ends with his mission to America." [132] Nevertheless, his gangplank interview included his notion on the Knights of Labor that "membership of the order is compatible with good Catholicism." Beyond this he claimed few American bishops were really hostile.[133] This story made the rounds of the press and months later it brought on Father O'Leary's acknowledgement that he had talked with him in St. Louis and given him material on the Knights.[134]

While the judgment on the Knights of Labor was being transferred to the officials in Rome, the forces of opposition in the United States were centering more about Archbishop Michael Corrigan who had already shown his unfriendliness.[135] This development was due, not so much to that prelate's legalistic conservatism, but rather to the obscuring of the issue of the Knights by the all-important problem in the Archdiocese of New York at that time, the case of Dr. Edward McGlynn.[136] The interlacing of these episodes was illustrated by the fact that shortly after his successful interview in the archiepiscopal residence in Baltimore Terence Powderly spoke on

132 BCA, 82-C-10, O'Connell to Gibbons, Rome, October 22, 1886.

133 Brooklyn *Examiner*; *Connecticut Catholic,* November 20, 1886.

134 PP, O'Leary to Powderly, St. Louis, April 4, 1887.

135 A letter to Cardinal Simeoni, November 4, 1886, the contents of which remains unknown, touched on the "labor movement." NYAA, Memoranda for Secretary, No. 1, Letters of 1880 to 1887.

136 There is no definitive study of this subject. For the pro-Corrigan side with emphasis on the part of McQuaid, cf. Zwierlein, *McQuaid,* III, 1-83; supplemented by the same author's *Letters of Archbishop Corrigan to Bishop McQuaid and Allied Documents* (Rochester, 1946), pp. 90-126; 134-139. The opposite bias is found in Stephen Bell, *Rebel, Priest and Prophet* (New York, 1937), and Henry George, Jr., *The Life of Henry George* (New York, 1900), pp. 459-503. The last two writers had no access to ecclesiastical archives. There are also Peter A. Speek, *The Single Tax and the Labor Movement* (Madison, 1915) and the sketch by McGlynn's friend Sylvester L. Malone in the volume he published, *Dr. Edward McGlynn* (New York, 1918) and one by John A. Ryan, *DAB,* XII, 53-54. Gibbons' role is brought out in Will, *op. cit.,* I, 361-378.

election eve in New York City in behalf of Henry George's mayoralty campaign. He made the speech to counteract a rumor that he opposed the choice of George.[137] The following day he drove around in an open barouche with the candidate, and Edward McGlynn, pastor of St. Stephen's Church. This was the climax of a local political fight which had widespread interest because it involved putting the social theories of George to the test of a popular vote for the first time. It had seen McGlynn's temporary suspension from his priestly functions for refusing to obey his superior and to desist from aiding George. Corrigan had based his action on Rome's procedure of three years previous when the doctor had promised public silence on the land question which the Irish agitated in the United States as well as in Ireland. On the other hand, the Tammany machine exploited a letter from Vicar General Preston which spoke of the logical conclusion of George's principles as being, "the ruin of the workingmen he professes to befriend." [138]

It was after the election of the Democrat, Abram S. Hewitt, in the middle of November, 1886, that Corrigan issued a pastoral letter. This was to lead to a further confusion of legitimate labor activity with the strife surrounding McGlynn's advocacy of what came to be called the single tax—or the appropriation by the state of the unearned increment in the value of land which society itself brings about. The archbishop's pronouncement to the faithful of New York dealt with matters of education, devotion, and discipline, but especially did it warn them against "certain unsound principles and theories which assail the rights of property," which, without naming names, he pointed out, "are loudly proclaimed in our day and are espoused by many who would not wilfully advocate what is wrong." [139] Regarding labor, he wrote briefly:

[137] *An Account of the George-Hewitt Campaign in the New York Municipal Election of 1886.* Prepared by Louis F. Post and Fred C. Leubuscher (New York, 1887), pp. 118-120. (A rare booklet in the Library of the Henry George School, New York City.)

[138] Zwierlein, *McQuaid*, III, 7.

[139] *Ibid.* The full text of the "Pastoral Letter addressed by the Archbishop of New York to the Faithful of His Charge on occasion of the Celebration of the Fifth Diocesan Synod, November 17th & 18th, 1886," is found in *Pastoral Letters*, II, Catholic University of America.

True indeed, in many painful instances, the rights of the toiler are trampled on, and fruits of his labor snatched from his grasp. True this is done too frequently with the concurrence, or at least the connivance of law. This is the evil that needs redress, but such redress can never be brought about by denying a fundamental right or by perpetuating a radical wrong.[140]

He concluded firmly entrenched behind a long defense of private property quoted from Leo XIII's *Quod apostolici muneris.*

The published reactions of McGlynn to what was considered by all an assault on George's teaching resulted in his further suspension from his priestly ministry until the end of that year. Others in Catholic circles however, were quite enthusiastic about the Corrigan pastoral. Cardinal Gibbons not only said Corrigan's remarks on land and property were well timed and would go far "to counteract the evil effect of loose utterances on that vital subject," but he also told him a few days later that his clergy and the Baltimore *Sun* had been favorably impressed.[141] A prominent Catholic layman of Philadelphia and an early member of the committee for the university, Bernard N. Farren, thanked Corrigan for sending him a copy of the pastoral and he remarked how pleased he was at the blow in favor of "the great conservative element." His attitude was, "I am glad you passed over the labor question with silence. It is so difficult to know just what is required, that time and patience alone can cure it."[142] Not quite as explicit was the Knights' perennial foe, Bishop Chatard, who wrote that the pastoral had been "most op-

---

140 *Ibid.,* p. 10.

141 NYAA, Gibbons to Corrigan, Wilmington, November 20, 1886; Baltimore, November 24, 1886. Still more enthusiastic was Corrigan's secretary who reported, "Henry George and his followers seem to reel under the blow the pastoral deals them." ADR, McDonnell to O'Connell, New York, November 24, 1886.

142 NYAA, Farren to Corrigan, Philadelphia, November 22, 1886. This is a clear instance of some relationship of the business mind and that of a church man. Similar, however, were J. S. Dennis, Chicago, November 27, 1886, and James Fenwick, New York, December 13, 1886. The latter was seeking the building contract for the new university and praised the letter "which ought to settle the unquiet feeling of the workmen, who, as a general thing are misled by demagogues."

portune and will do more for the Church in America, than the liberal Priests can do harm." [143]

The candid opinion of Archbishop Riordan of San Francisco was very much to the contrary. He thought Corrigan's pronouncement on property untimely, and liable to contribute to the loss of the Irish and the workers to the Church. Admitting also a "very deep and tender affection for Dr. McGlynn," who was possibly, "imprudent and obstinate," Riordan went on to say,

> I would wish that this constant interference with societies and labor unions should cease, and if some of the Bishops have leisure time for pastorals let them attack, if they must attack somebody, the gigantic corporations and monopolies of the land and say a kind and tender word for the great army of the labouring classes, that in our large cities are being reduced to the condition of slaves.[144]

The Catholic press meanwhile commented widely and favorably on the letter of the Archbishop of New York. The latest addition to the ranks, the New York *Catholic News*, when only a few weeks old sought not only to defend the archbishop but to disassociate the land and the labor movements. It reminded the *Leader*, a George publication, that "the support of the Catholic workingmen will not be won by sneers at the pastoral." [145] Again it insisted against two Protestant ministers that the Church's "benediction has been ever bestowed on labor unions and this spirit towards them has been evinced even by the present Sovereign Pontiff." [146] Its editorial answer to the charge that Catholics would have to leave labor unions founded on George platforms was that there were no such associa-

---

[143] NYAA, Chatard to Corrigan, Indianapolis, November 23, 1886. Of societies for "mutual advancement," he said at this time, "As long as they do not take up false principles of action hurtful to society, there is no harm in belonging to them." UND, Treasure Room, "Pastoral Letter of Rt. Rev. Francis Silas Chatard, D.D., Bishop of Vincennes, December 18" (Indianapolis, 1886), p. 5.

[144] ADR, O'Connell Papers, Riordan to "Rt. Rev. and dear Bishop" [Keane], San Francisco, January 22, 1887.

[145] December 1, 1886.

[146] December 8, 1886.

tions either among the Knights of Labor or the trade unions.[147]
At the same time the Brooklyn *Examiner* had no difficulty supporting both Corrigan and George. It recommended the archbishop's
defense of private property, but it held that the land doctrine the
followers of George advocated did not maintain otherwise.[148] Preston
pointed out the verbal resemblance of Corrigan's words about a
man's right to what he produces to those of the declaration of principle of the Knights, and he added, "This almost identical language,
let us hope, is only a sign of the harmony of the Church with the
cause of labor." [149]   The news of the following week was hardly
calculated to make for such a peace, for McGlynn was summoned
to Rome by a cablegram that arrived December 4. He subsequently
refused to go and at the turn of the year lost his parish and six
months later was excommunicated.   The *Examiner* carried the
opinions of Bishops McQuaid and Stephen Ryan of Buffalo, that the
first call to Rome was purely disciplinary, and the paper went on
to quote Bishop Ryan favorably on the righteous ways of the
Knights of Labor.[150]

The Knights of Labor, as seen in its official journal, did keep
quiet on the new aspects of religion in the labor movement. The
Journal only commented on the New York election as "Triumph
in Defeat," and lamented over press and pulpit attacks on their
plea for leniency towards the now condemned Chicago anarchists.[151]
The radical wing, although ignorant of his physical proportions, did
flay Corrigan as one of the "fat rascals" who opposed the new war

147 December 15, 1886.

148 November 27, December 18, 1886. Editor Preston would have been
pleased if he had known the opinion expressed privately to Manning by Archbishop Walsh of Dublin in a letter of January 7, 1887, concerning Corrigan:
"The mistake made by the Archbishop in his Pastoral was in ascribing to George
the doctrine denying the right of property, as if George held that no ownership
(in anything) could exist. I do not think it possible that anyone who had read
Progress and Poverty could have made such a mistake, or as regards the reasoning of the case, could have failed to see the irrelevancy of the arguments on
which His Grace relies." Walsh, *op. cit.*, p. 230.

149 December 4, 1886.

150 December 18, 1886.

151 *Journal of United Labor,* November 25, 1886.

on industrial slavery.[152] Likewise from Chicago came "vaporings regarding the Church and the Order." [153] Among the Catholic papers only the St. Louis *Catholic World* took upon itself to explain Powderly's part in George's campaign in a favorable light.[154] It was also glad, nonetheless, that Powderly had since professed to be out of politics.

Yet politics had already done much to confuse the picture of the relations of the Church and organized labor. In the New York mayoralty campaign the distinction between the labor party, the land movement, and the Knights of Labor had become very hazy. Moreover, the cause of a rebellious priest whose teaching was suspect had been linked with them. All this did little to produce the clarification of issues that was necessary for the solution of the problem. As the case of the Knights of Labor went to Rome, the eyes of workers and churchmen alike turned from Richmond and Baltimore to the Holy See. In 1887 they were to witness one very sensational news story emanate from the Vatican and this was to be followed by probably the most extensive publicity ever given to a Catholic question in the United States.

[152] Denver *Labor Enquirer*, December 4, 1886.
[153] PP, O'Reilly to Powderly, New York, December 27, 1886.
[154] December 25, 1886.

CHAPTER VII

AFFAIRS IN ROME

A variety of problems of the American hierarchy converged on the Holy See for adjudication in 1887. At home, besides the routine of pastoral administration, the heads of dioceses faced the bewildering ramifications of the immigration and assimilation of the foreign-born, made more acute by the fact that southern and southeastern Europeans began to increase among the incoming Catholics.[1] In Rome, questions which had arisen out of that American milieu awaited answers. The Knights of Labor case was only one among them. A neat summary of these problems was made by Bishop Keane, who along with John Ireland, arrived in Rome early in November, 1886, and found himself hard at work as late as the spring of 1887.[2] Of the "several matters" under consideration Keane considered as "most important," what later was called Cahenslyism, or the movement among some German Catholics in the United States against what they viewed as a non-representative Hibernian hierarchy.[3] On this question the non-German bishops readily united, and not only was the statement of the case made in the Abbelen memorial countered by Keane and Ireland, but it likewise met refutation in Corrigan's report to Simeoni, a report which received the backing of all the eastern archbishops at a meeting in Philadelphia on December 16, 1886. The McGlynn-George issue, however, did not find the same unity among this "American" group. It was at this time that McGlynn refused to answer the summons

---

[1] Some abortive efforts were made by the Knights of Labor to reach these peoples as was shown by the proposal to translate their books into Italian, Bohemian, and Polish. *Proceedings* (Minneapolis, 1887), p. 1756. From the side of the Church this is largely an unexplored problem. Cf. Henry J. Browne, "The 'Italian Problem' in the Catholic Church of the United States, 1880-1900," *Historical Records and Studies*, XXXV (1946), 46-72.

[2] ACUA, "Chronicles of the Catholic University of America from 1885."

[3] Cf. John J. Meng, "Cahenslyism: the First Stage, 1883-1891," *Catholic Historical Review*, XXXI (January, 1946), 389-413.

to Rome, and the advice given to him—at the request of the Holy
See—by Gibbons and his friends resulted in ruffled relations between
the Archbishops of New York and Baltimore. In addition, Gibbons'
successful plea against the condemnation of George's works on
February 27, 1887, was not unanimously endorsed.[4] Among these
thorny questions, and the one that had been the original reason
for the presence of Keane and Ireland in Rome, was that of winning
approval for the university, which was achieved on April 10.[5]

On the Knights of Labor the two American episcopal ambassadors
took action quickly after their arrival in the Eternal City. Within
two weeks they learned that Gibbons had sent the résumé of the
Baltimore conference directly to the Propaganda; consequently,
Keane proceeded to hand in the copy of the constitution and its
translation. O'Connell learned the exacting routine of the congregation when he was told that his French translation of "extracts from
another of their books" was incomplete without "also the *original
and complete* document from which the translation is made." [6] He
referred to it as the "rules of the Knights of Labor" which Gibbons
had sent. Simeoni sent him to Sbarretti, the *minutante,* to examine
the documents from Baltimore, but the original text was still demanded.[7] The Propaganda also knew about the Richmond convention, and so they awaited the revised constitution and "the
declaration of principles, the formulation of which was entrusted
to their Executive Committee and which Mr. Powderly promised to
send to your Eminence." This hitherto unmentioned item, Keane
warned the Cardinal of Baltimore, must also be translated for the
congregation's perusal. The Bishop of Richmond sent him at the
same time a clipping of an article on the "Social Question in the
United States," from the *Moniteur de Rome* of December 4. Through
Keane and Ireland's influence it had been published as an editorial
and served as a complement to one of the week previous. It defended
the Irish in the United States, and especially Powderly, for their

[4] Will, *op. cit.,* I, 362-367.

[5] Cf. John Tracy Ellis, *The Formative Years of the Catholic University of
America* (Washington, 1946), pp. 198-253.

[6] BCA, 82-G-4, Keane to Gibbons, Rome, December 4, 1886.

[7] BCA, 82-G-9, O'Connell to Gibbons, Rome, December 10, 1886.

conservatism, and it used the instance—later proved disreputable—
of the Haymarket trials as a reassurance that American civil
authority would always preserve public peace.[8]

On December 10, the same day O'Connell sought original material on the Knights of Labor from Gibbons, he wrote to assure
the Archbishop of New York that the German question was then
occupying most of the time of the Americans at the Roman curia.
He took it for granted that a discredited McGlynn would soon be
on his way to Rome as called on December 4. On the basis of this
belief he explained the postponement of any action on Henry
George.[9] New York's star was at the moment rising in Rome at the
expense of Baltimore's, and this was indicated with friendly frankness
by Keane to Gibbons. The same prelate's industry was also revealed
by the fact of his having submitted in less than a day three Latin
documents to Propaganda. They were reports based on a letter of
December 17 from Gibbons, and concerned the German trouble,
the coadjutorship of New Orleans, and the Knights of Labor, but
what they contained remains unknown.[10]

In the United States the beginning of 1887 saw new stirrings
within the labor movement, but the Church was not the agitator.
Among the Catholic laity Powderly's name had developed a drawing power and he even found himself sought after to lecture for
Church causes.[11] The Catholic priests in general became increasingly
friendly and helpful to the Knights through the year 1887.[12] Father

[8] BCA, 82-G-4, Keane to Gibbons, December 4, 1886, with enclosure.

[9] NYAA, O'Connell to Corrigan, Rome, December 10, 1886.

[10] BCA, 82-J-4, Keane to Gibbons, Rome, December 29, 1886. Eduardo
Soderini, *The Pontificate of Leo XIII* (London, 1934), I, 169, speaks of Gibbons
sending documents about this time accompanied by a letter, "in which he declared the condemnation would be a real calamity."

[11] PP, Gerald P. Coghlan to Powderly, Reading, January 27, 1887; Cornelius Cotter to Powderly, Osceola Mills, March 16; even his picture had a
value as a prize at a church fair, William R. Gleis to Powderly, Salina, Kansas,
December 31, 1887.

[12] PP, W. J. Cronin to Powderly, Corning, New York, March 22, 1887;
Reverend Peter Colgan settled a strike: Thomas Clarke to Powderly, Pitts-
burgh, July 8, 1887; Reverend M. J. McBride, Administrator of the Diocese of
Harrisburg, gave friendly advice: George S. Boyle to Powderly, Shenandoah,

Carew of Carbondale, for one, continued to act as a liaison man between bishops and the labor leader whom he had known so well.[13] Yet the labor scene as a whole was shaken by religious strife, some of which was re-echoed in the press. In the first printing of his new enterprise, the *Standard,* Henry George in justifying McGlynn said, "American workingmen might as well make up their minds that in the fight for the enfranchisement of labor they' must meet the opposition of the Catholic hierarchy."[14] This course was criticized to Powderly with a reminder that "quite a number" of the clergy who were their "staunch friends" would not feel complimented.[15] Neither did the Brooklyn *Examiner* go along with this tactic but, on the contrary, advised McGlynn to go to Rome.[16] Preston had already pointed out that the New York priest was not essential to the labor movement and that, on the other hand, Cardinal Taschereau was really aiding the infidel anarchists whom Powderly opposed, since they hoped for ecclesiastical prohibition.[17]

Some extremists within the Order, nevertheless, were more direct in trying to discredit the Catholic Church. One Polish assembly had the commission of such a radical in the person of a certain Anton Parysso withdrawn. Although he professed to be a follower of George and not an anarchist, the opposition he had instigated among the clergy had to be smoothed over by another knight who had two priest

June 21 and response of July 5, 1887; Reverend John Wolanski became a charter member of a new Polish assembly.

[13] PP, J. Powderly to T. V. Powderly, n.p., received January 1, 1887. The prelate in this case remained unnamed. Father Carew died that year and was eulogized by the bishop as "one of the diocese's oldest and most valued priests." *Catholic Record,* September 24, 1887.

[14] Quoted in St. Louis *Catholic World,* January 15, 1887. Under the new management of the conservative Conde B. Pallen this paper called George's article an anti-Catholic tirade. Unfortunately, the earliest issues of the *Standard* in the holdings of the New York Public Library are so badly deteriorated that they cannot be read.

[15] PP, P. J. Gilligan to Powderly, Cedar Rapids, Iowa, January 12, 1887.

[16] January 15, 1887.

[17] January 1, 1887. In answering a protest from Archbishop Elder, Preston revealed about his uncle, the vicar general, and the land question, "when I argued with him he had to admit that from my point of view I was right." AAC, January 20, 1887.

brothers.[18] While Powderly boldly professed in a speech at Newark that he need make no apology for his religion, farther west opposition to him was being based on his Catholicism.[19] The story of his alleged subservience to Father P. M. Flannigan in the Chicago packinghouse strike continued.[20] In addition, Barry, a fallen-away Catholic, persisted in giving interviews to the public press of an unfriendly nature, but at least one "liberal" Catholic made some response.[21] Furthermore, O'Donoghue and Keys undertook to clarify Barry's publicized criticisms of Catholicism in Canada.[22] Keys at this time not only vigorously denied current reports of failure in Montreal, but he praised the clergy of the province.[23]

The religious press in the United States showed some evidence of a devisive war, or what Swinton referred to as a "religious firebrand," in the camp of labor.[24] The *Catholic Telegraph* of Cincinnati answered the charges of the *Christian Standard* that the new democratic movements, such as the Knights of Labor, were incompatible with a "despotic" church.[25] The Catholic paper in St. Paul branded as foolish the accusations made in "certain quarters" that the Church was "the enemy of the working man and the friend of the monopolies." [26] As if in answer to the same argument, the *Catholic Standard* emphasized that the opposite was "emphatically true" in the United States.[27] The Denver *Labor Enquirer*, very

---

[18] PP, Parysso to Powderly, Detroit, February 13, 1887; M. Kruszka to Powderly, Milwaukee, February 2; Powderly to Frank Lux, March 11, copy.

[19] *Northwest Chronicle,* January 20, 1887.

[20] *Labor Enquirer,* January 15, 1887; January 29, "The report that Mr. Powderly had been summoned to Rome . . . appears to have been immature."

[21] PP, Richard Griffiths to Powderly, Chicago, January 25, 1887. He told of the work of a certain McAuliff.

[22] PP, O'Donoghue to Powderly, Toronto, January 12, 1887; Keys, Montreal, January 19, 1887.

[23] *John Swinton's Paper,* January 23, 1887. This may have been brought on by the friendliness of one of the priests in the bishop's residence who even advised that the general master workman visit there to bolster the Order. PP, Keys to Powderly, Montreal, January 10, 1887.

[24] *John Swinton's Paper,* January-February, *passim.*

[25] January 6, 1887.

[26] *Northwest Chronicle,* January 20, 1887.

[27] February 5, 1887; similarly *Catholic World,* February 9, 1887.

much to the contrary, explained the religious controversy in the labor field as simply an indication that reform necessarily antagonized "the Church" since that institution was "part of the machinery of oppression." [28]   Before long the Catholic papers announced that an authoritative Catholic statement on current problems was forthcoming from Cardinal Gibbons.[29] But the Baltimore prelate had already undertaken a more vigorous and direct course of action.

A cablegram from Rome had advised the cardinal to expect an early call to the Holy See where "important matters" would be referred to him. He had immediately informed Corrigan. His further regard for the Archbishop of New York was shown by his desire to consult him on a subject he felt would very likely come up in Rome, namely, the advisability of a papal nuncio in the United States. This was an innovation that Gibbons had always opposed. He also asked Corrigan's judgment on a canonical problem relating to the naming of a coadjutor for New Orleans, and he mentioned his refusal of an invitation to a banquet in New York since, as he said, "I would not enjoy the feast or honor without you." [30] Corrigan, likewise, was far from showing any displeasure with Gibbons when he expressed the opinion that the latter's two associates in Rome, the Bishops of Richmond and St. Paul, seemed to be "earnest in their work." [31] Yet unknowingly they were sowing seeds of disharmony between Baltimore and New York, for at that very time one Roman correspondent reported that the two American bishops were busy supplying Propaganda with details on the Knights of Labor.[32]

Likewise from Rome at this time came two somewhat more authoritative communications. One was Gibbons' call from the Secretary of State to receive the cardinal's red hat, and the other Pope Leo's own summons to the already recalcitrant and displaced

[28] January 22, 1887.

[29] *Catholic Telegraph,* February 10; *Church News,* February 13, 1887.

[30] NYAA, Gibbons to Corrigan, Baltimore, January 7, 1887.

[31] RDA, Corrigan to McQuaid, New York, January [ ], 1887. He had even wished O'Connell, "God speed to your labors." ADR, Corrigan to O'Connell, New York, December 20, 1886.

[32] Brooklyn *Examiner,* January 8, 1887.

New York pastor, Edward McGlynn.[33] The latter read, "The Pontiff commands the alumnus to come to Rome immediately." McGlynn, however, did not go and as Gibbons prepared to sail from New York he sent Corrigan his sympathy and thanked his secretary, Charles McDonnell, for sending the only copies of George's *Standard* that he had seen up to that time. Moreover, he planned to spend the "lion's share" of his time with the Archbishop of New York on Thursday, January 27, although he had already accepted Mr. John Keiley's invitation to be his house guest.[34] Taschereau, who was to sail on the same boat, was Corrigan's guest and he shared the place of honor with Gibbons at a dinner tendered them at the archbishop's residence. Out of it came a report from the vicar general's nephew that the problems of pressing interest "were incidentally discussed," and Taschereau announced his perennial opposition to the Knights while Gibbons said nothing.[35] The day before sailing Archbishops Ryan and Williams were also at Corrigan's house where a meeting was held, concerning the American College in Rome.[36] That evening in Keiley's Brooklyn home the cardinals, Corrigan, and several other "clerical gentlemen" were feted and the press reported Taschereau as saying he would join Gibbons in favor of a statement of the Holy See on George's doctrine which all the prelates opposed, but on the Knights of Labor he replied, "I shall do what I can to have it denounced." [37]

Besides the two cardinals with diametrically opposed views who left for Europe on January 29, there were two other interesting departures from New York City that same week. Archbishop Corrigan and his secretary set out to visit the missions of the Bahama Islands which at that time were under the ecclesiastical jurisdiction of his see.[38] A steamer for Ireland carried home the

---

[33] ADC, Elder to Gilmour, Cincinnati, January 20, 1887. The archbishop had been invited to confer with Gibbons before he sailed. AAC, Corrigan to Elder, New York, January 20, 1887. Zwierlein, *op. cit.*, III, 22.

[34] NYAA, Gibbons to Corrigan, Baltimore, January 20, 1887.

[35] Brooklyn *Examiner*, February 5, 1887.

[36] *Catholic News*, February 2, 1887.

[37] New York *Daily Tribune*, January 29, 1887, in Corrigan Scrapbook, p. 41.

[38] Brooklyn *Examiner*, February 5, 1887.

Irish agitator, Michael Davitt, who in a farewell rally in Madison Square Garden on the evening of January 21 had attacked Cardinal Simeoni as opposed to Father McGlynn for his Irish activities. This, moreover, was said to be because of the influence of the British agent in Rome. Although the charge was later retracted, the night it was made Terence V. Powderly, introduced by editor Patrick Ford and "blushing like a girl," gave the Davitt statement his public and full endorsement.[39] This appearance of the general master workman in Corrigan's archdiocese, as was true the previous November, was certainly not calculated to make for Church-labor harmony. The circumstances surrounding Powderly's presence in New York further obscured the central issue of the right and necessity of labor organization with local and Irish politics and the land question. But Powderly can hardly be blamed in one sense, for he was a reformer rather than a down-to-earth trade unionist, and all these questions were intimately related in his mind.

The practical mind of the Cardinal of Baltimore, however, remained clear and fixed in its purpose as he made for the center of Christendom, while at home the eloquent conciliator of the American hierarchy, Archbishop Ryan, eulogized him as being like the monk of old descending into the arena to bring peace between the gladiators of capital and labor.[40] Whether their differing opinions were sufficient to mar in any way the companionship of the two traveling prelates, the existing records have not revealed. At least they agreed in the first end and object of their journey, the reception of the red hat. Together Gibbons and Taschereau received a cordial reception in Paris and continued on to Rome where they arrived on February 13. Each had his first private audience with Leo XIII on the following Wednesday, February 16.[41] As far as the Knights of Labor was concerned, Gibbons did not enter upon an unprepared terrain. The ground work had been laid by Keane and Ireland in the form of a "respectful protest" entered

[39] *Ibid.*, January 29, 1887. Davitt's retraction was printed in the *Tablet*, May 7, 1887.

[40] *Catholic Standard*, February 19, 1887. This was in a speech before the Catholic Club of Philadelphia.

[41] *Herald*, February 8, 1887; *L'Événement*, February 17, 1887.

against efforts to procure a condemnation without letting the American bishops express their opinions.[42] Furthermore, Keane had enlisted the aid of Cardinal Manning against papal intervention in the labor and social question in the United States which threatened because of "the case of the disobedient and cranky priest." His request was for the English churchman to beg the Holy Father, "not to order or permit any overt decision of the American social questions at present, both because they have not ripened yet and taken shape, and because the action of the Holy See would hardly fail to be odious to the whole American public and to split up Catholic unity." [43]

Exactly what happened in Rome at that time cannot be fully recorded without the help of Roman documents or such sources as diaries of the participants.[44] As a matter of fact, only a portion of the episcopal correspondence in the case was available. Taschereau, for example, wrote to Legaré and remarked just incidentally how much the cardinals and Roman prelates were concerned with the question. The American bishops, he said, were giving the impression that they believed, what he hoped but did not anticipate that the Knights of Labor "will soon die out of itself." [45] In mid-February "the drift was towards condemnation, regardless of the widespread disastrous consequences that would inevitably have ensued." [46] Gibbons' first talk with the Holy Father and a little later with Cardinal Simeoni, at least as he reported them to Corrigan, were more concerned with getting McGlynn to Rome for the settlement of his case than with the Knights.[47] An act of obedience to the Pope's request on the part of Gibbons led to misunderstanding between himself and Corrigan, since the letter which was sent through

---

[42] ACUA, "Chronicles of the Catholic University of America from 1885."

[43] February 10, 1887, quoted in Shane Leslie, *Henry Edward Manning, His Life and Labours* (London, 1921), p. 360. No unpublished Manning papers were available, cf. p. 385.

[44] Cf. Essay on Sources, p. 382.

[45] Archives, Séminaire de Québec, IX, 3, Taschereau to Cyrille Legaré, Rome, February 17, 1887.

[46] Keane to Manning, Rome, February 28, 1887, quoted in Leslie, *op. cit.*, p. 361.

[47] NYAA, Gibbons to Corrigan, Rome, February 18, 1887.

Burtsell, the friend and adviser of McGlynn, was used to picture the cardinal as favorable to the rebellious New York priest.[48] But time was soon devoted to the case of the Knights of Labor and his attention was caught by the strong opposition of Taschereau. Gibbons called him "a very persistent man," who was "working very hard to have the Knights condemned in the United States, in order to save himself from the odium of undue severity." The Archbishop of Baltimore knew that he was trying to persuade the Holy Office "that the constitution now in force is substantially the same as that which was condemned, and that consistancy demands that the order in our country should be stricken down."[49] What Gibbons did not seem to know was the difficulty the Cardinal of Quebec had in pleading his case. A long conference with Cardinal Monaco revealed to Taschereau that this vice-prefect of the Holy Office knew nothing of his many letters to Simeoni on the subject. Monaco was very surprised to hear what Taschereau had to tell him.[50]

According to both contemporary and later accounts Cardinal Gibbons was far from inarticulate or inactive on the problem. His biographer, who drew on the cardinal's recollections as well as documents, said that along with Keane and O'Connell he "used argument and pressure in turn upon every member of the Congregation of the Holy Office to produce a change of view." Only after a "heated interview" in which he declared he would hold the commissary of the congregation, Vincenzo Sallua, O.P., titular Archbishop of Calcedon, responsible for the loss of souls in the United States if the organization was condemned, did he win a promise of reconsideration.[51] Yet Gibbons' method in Rome did not consist

---

[48] AAC, Gibbons to Elder, Florence, April 20, 1887.

[49] AAC, Gibbons to Elder, Rome, February 19, 1887.

[50] Archives, Séminaire de Québec, Taschereau to Cyrille Legaré, Rome, February 20, 1887.

[51] Will, *op. cit.*, I, 332-333. Years later Gibbons reminisced, "I can never forget the anxiety and distress of mind of those days. If the Knights of Labor were not condemned by the Church, then the Church ran the risk of combining against herself every element of wealth and power; . . . But if the Church did not protect the working men she would have been false to her whole history." He recalled, too, the "indomitable courage and perseverance of Cardinal Manning." "My Memories," *Dublin Review*, CLX (April, 1917), 170.

in conferences alone but in the composition of documents o
memorials on the pertinent problems of the American Church, such
as the writings of George, the nunciature, and the university. On
all of these, formal briefs were laid before the Roman officials. On
of these memorials was drawn up on the Knights of Labor,[52] o
whom he said, apparently with new realization gained in Rome
"They narrowly escaped condemnation in our own country when the
were condemned in Canada, which would have been disastrous t
many souls and have involved us in serious complications." An
he further informed his friend, the Archbishop of Cincinnati:

> I am preparing an elaborate paper showing the injustice, th
> danger and the folly of denouncing them. . . . We see the ex
> citement occasioned by the suspension of Dr. McGlynn becaus
> he is regarded as the friend of the workman—what a tumu
> would be raised if we condemned the laborers themselves.[53]

Nonetheless, it is impossible to attribute complete and sol
authorship to Gibbons of the fifteen-page French document whic
was addressed to Cardinal Simeoni under date of February 2(
the day after his letter to Elder.[54] This is so not only because
was completely finished and dated so soon after Gibbons' remar
that he was working on it, but also because it was in French. Th
cardinal did not write that language with sufficient ease to unde
take the task, and so the help of John Ireland, who had bee
trained in a French seminary, was undoubtedly called for at leas
to some extent. Moreover, Keane's testimony written some yea
later made himself a co-author. About the time he was removed b
Rome as Rector of the Catholic University of America in 189
he wrote quite plainly of his great friend, Cardinal Gibbons, "H

---

[52] Soderini, *op. cit.*, pp. 169-170, attributes to Pope Leo the advice to Ir
land and Keane, "let them prepare a Memorial to be studied by the Cardina
and Consultants of the Propaganda and Holy Office." This was before Gibbon
arrival and after the other two bishops found the Commissary of the Ho
Office, Vincenzo Sallua, O.P., inflexible on the Masonic and socialistic charact
of the Knights.

[53] AAC, Gibbons to Elder, Rome, February 19, 1887.

[54] BCA, 82-N-3, "La Question des 'Chevaliers du Travail.'" Cf. Append
III, pp. 365-378, for a full translation.

had us prepare a memorial on the whole labor question and on the Knights of Labor in particular, which he signed and urged with all his influence." [55] It is readily appreciated that while the busy Archbishop of Baltimore most likely did not personally compose the memorial it did incorporate his ideas and, more than that, it bore only his signature and thus placed solely upon him the full burden of responsibility for its contents.

The integral and accurate text of this statement which was undoubtedly the most important single factor in the settlement of the case, has not hitherto been revealed.[56] By way of introduction the memorial told of the meeting of the archbishops at Baltimore the previous October. Then in very orderly fashion it gave in nine sections (the last being a nine point summary of the arguments) the considerations which had influenced them to a favorable decision on the Knights of Labor. In the first place, the American Knights could not be classed among societies condemned by the Church since they had no oath, extreme secrecy, or blind obedience. Furthermore, the organization was not hostile to the Church and Gibbons cited the profession of devotion by Powderly as evidence. Neither did the Order intrigue against the State, as was shown by President Grover Cleveland's having told Gibbons of his long conference with Powderly wherein they discussed social problems and possible legislative measures to meet them.[57] As proof of the

[55] ACUA, "Chronicles of the Catholic University of America from 1885." Soderini, *op. cit.*, p. 170, is wrong in stating Gibbons merely put into French the Memorial which, while still at Baltimore, he had already drawn up in English, and which had been approved by his other colleagues of the American Episcopate, with only two exceptions." James Gibbons, *Retrospect of Fifty Years* (Baltimore, 1916), I, 190, later simply stated: "In preparing this Memorial, I gratefully acknowledge the valuable aid of the venerable Archbishop Ireland, of St. Paul, and of Rt. Rev. Bishop Keane, who were then in Rome."

[56] Soderini, *op. cit.*, p. 168, was given a copy by Gibbons (as well as information on the subject) but he did not use it fully. Will, *op. cit.*, I, 337, knew it existed but did not indicate the differences in it from the one he used.

[57] The Cleveland Papers in the Library of Congress revealed nothing of either of these interviews with Gibbons or Powderly. President Cleveland had made what a friendly biographer calls, "a notably liberal pronouncement," in his message to Congress of April 22, 1886, the first of such ever devoted entirely to labor. His suggestion of legislation to establish a permanent board for the

second point Gibbons cited the acknowledgement by the federal government of the existence of "grave and threatening social evils." Perhaps Cleveland had convinced the cardinal differently since that day on September 3, 1886, when his defense of the Knights of Labor had stated that the workers turned to the Church because the civil authority showed no interest. The remedy offered by the Knights, namely organization, Gibbons next pointed out, was both "natural and just." Catholic workmen, who as Powderly had testified, had avoided membership in the protective ranks of Masonry since it was forbidden by the Church, were naturally surprised to have their "only means of self-defense" threatened with condemnation.

The fourth consideration of this document disposed of some objections "made against this sort of organization." Rather than the Catholics suffering from contact with Protestants in this organization, an exact opposite and exaggerated picture was presented of Protestants benefiting by membership in an association of which "two thirds of the members and the principal officers are Catholic." Gibbons pointed out that what amounted to a Catholic union under the direction of the clergy was neither "possible or necessary" in the United States. The contacts with radicals within the Knights was merely another trial of faith for Catholics and the press and Powderly had testified how well they had stood up under the test. When there had been outbreaks of almost inevitable violence, very often the Knights were not responsible. They had not invented the strike, said Gibbons, and even when individual members had been at fault, the official position had always been to discourage it.

In a more philosophic vein, the fifth section of the memorial indicated the spirit of the new age of the people in which social questions would predominate—"the questions which concern the improvement of the condition of the great popular masses, and especially of the working people." Gibbons disclosed his agreement with Manning on the position the Church should hold in keeping

voluntary arbitration of labor disputes was never followed up by the divided Congress. Allan Nevins, *Grover Cleveland. A Study in Courage* (New York 1934), pp. 349-350; James D. Richardson, *A Compilation of the Messages and Papers of the Presidents* (New York, 1897), XI, 4979-4982.

the "poor multitudes" from extremes, "by bonds of affection, by the maternal desire which she will manifest for the concession of all that is just and reasonable in their demands, and by the maternal blessing which she will bestow upon every legitimate means for improving the condition of the people." If a contrary course were to be followed by the Church it would lead to the loss of her reputation as the "friend of the people," and it might leave her open to the charge of being "unAmerican," since organized labor had become so strong politically. In that age of unfettered big business Gibbons' citing of that danger was hardly based on reality, at least not so much as was the next reason he offered, namely, the loss of faithful Catholic workers to the Church. If any condemnation fell on the society they would consider it "false and unjust" and not respect it. Besides leading to the increase of Catholics in secret societies, such a step would result also in a situation in which, "The revenues of the Church, which, in our country, come entirely from the free offering of the people would suffer greatly, and the same thing would happen with Peter's Pence." Then as if to sum up this section—and here Gibbons' hand as revealed in his letter of February 19 to Elder is seen—the memorial read:

> In a word, we have seen quite recently the sad and threatening confusion caused by the condemnation inflicted by an Archbishop upon a single priest in vindication of discipline—a condemnation which the archbishop believed to be just and necessary, but which fell upon a priest who was regarded as the friend of the people. Now, if consequences have been so deplorable for the peace of the Church from the condemnation of only one priest, because he was regarded as a friend of the people, what will not be the consequences to be feared from a condemnation which would fall directly upon the people themselves in the exercise of that which they consider their legitimate right?

The closing paragraphs of the memorial brought home that besides involving dangers for the Church and being impossible to enforce, a condemnation of the Knights was unnecessary and would be wasted. This was so—and here the document revealed a good grasp of the American scene—because, as the press often insisted, the form of the Order had so little promise of permanence, "that in the estimation of practical men of our country it cannot last very many years." Gibbons utilized again one of his earliest observations on the matter when he repeated that the Holy Office need not be embarrassed by the Canadian situation since that previous judgment had been *juxta exposita*. The Holy Office would find in the present document, the cardinal maintained, the conviction of those most competent to advise on American affairs, for it was the agreed judgment of all but five (although the introduction said two or three) of the seventy-five members of the American hierarchy. There had been no poll taken of the bishops on this question, but the prelates in Rome were giving a highly probable estimate, if one may suppose that such men as Bishops Chatard and Healy were hostile enough to wish the extension of the Canadian prohibition of the Knights of Labor to the United States.

These "convictions of the Bishops of America," Keane announced a week later, had come to be accepted by the Holy Office as the safest guide. This he said after Gibbons' morning interview of "most gratifying results" with the officials of the Congregation of the Propaganda. The sentiments he had expressed, showing the weight of the whole American Church, had produced "an evident change of front." Keane took the occasion to tell Manning the good service that the latter's utterances, apparently those used in the memorial and likely also others sent privately to the congregation, had done for the Cardinal of Baltimore.[58] Gibbons in the flush of victory told Gilmour he had sent him a copy of the document and he added:

> I feel strongly on this subject. We must prove that we are the friends of the working classes; if we condemn or use them harshly we lose them, and they will look on us with as much hatred and suspicion as they do in the Church of France. They commit excesses now and then. Let us correct them, but they have also real grievances. Let us help them to redress them I would regard the condemnation of the Knights of Labor as a signal calamity to the Catholic Church of America.[59]

[58] Keane to Manning, Rome, February 28, 1887, quoted in Leslie, *op. cit.* p. 361.

[59] ADC, Gibbons to Gilmour, Rome, March 3, 1887.

Far from suffering a calamity, the Church was to be displayed to the world, even sometimes beyond its merits in this particular case, as the friend of labor. This happened through no devising of James Gibbons, but what has been aptly called the "happy zeal of a correspondent" [60] of the New York *Herald,* which on March 3 printed a truncated version of the memorial including in full the final nine points of summation. John Ireland, in soliciting from Gilmour a letter of approval of the document which Gibbons had sent to the Bishop of Cleveland, suggested an explanation:

> The document was intended only for private circulation among the Cardinals. The 'Herald' man evidently got it, as he indeed hints, by bribing some secretary. However, as it is now before the public we have only to make the best of the case. The Knights will not be condemned in Rome. This point is as good as settled. [61]

The man who administered the Archdiocese of New York during Corrigan's absence in the Bahamas was a pious man but he was laboring under no delusions, and his ideas agreed with Ireland's on the likely background of the newspaper story. Preston suspected that "the Herald *paid* no doubt a good sum." He forwarded the clipping to his archbishop and then, still wondering about its authenticity, he telegraphed Miss Edes as "most efficient to find out the truth." [62] Denis O'Connell knew, of course, of the origin of the memorial, but anxious about its leakage to the press, he called on "the Herald representative," who reassured him only to the extent that it had not come from anyone connected with the American College. The Roman rector told his New York friend and secretary to Corrigan that Gibbons knew of the publication only after he received a cablegram of congratulations. [63] This message from the United States proved to be but the first of many opinions expressed

[60] Leslie, *op. cit.,* p. 361.
[61] ADC, Ireland to Gilmour, Rome, March 6, 1887.
[62] NYAA, Preston to Corrigan, New York, March 4, 1887.
[63] NYAA, O'Connell to Charles E. McDonnell, Rome, April 14, 1887. The office of the *Herald Tribune* in New York, the successor of the *Herald,* knew of no records which might have elucidated this incident, nor of personnel files from that period.

on the case, for the Church in the role of "friend of the people" was kept before the public for several months by friend and foe alike.

It has been judged best to narrow down the widespread American reaction to this Roman story for the most part to the medium of the Catholic press. Therein was expressed in a not unintelligent and unlively way opinions which varied from high approval to incredulity. They revealed in the final analysis a popular social outlook not as far advanced as that expressed by their ecclesiastical leaders. This slowness in catching up to episcopal pronouncements certainly was not to be witnessed for the last time in American Catholicism. Some editorials reflected also the dominant notes in the secular and Protestant press during the weeks which followed the *Herald* "scoop." In every case the news was received *secundum modum recipientis,* and it was used to bolster all kinds of preconceived notions and prejudices. One generally accepted result of the "long-deferred and oft-reported action," as one labor paper put it, was to end the recurring reports of the "capitalistic press" that the Church had anathematized the American Knights.[64]

There was no reason for surprise at the friendly tone adopted by some of the Catholic papers. The *Pilot,* which claimed knowledge of the report as early as March 1, called it "good news" for Catholic workers and said it "practically settles the question." [65] Much more hilarious was the reception tendered it by the Brooklyn *Examiner* which reprinted in full the cabled version as given in the *Herald.* As befitted a loyal employee of that paper, Preston praised its "characteristic enterprise" and also the position it had taken in favor of the cause of labor. The second editorial in his Brooklyn paper was in praise of Gibbons' actions which, he claimed, were in perfect harmony with the constant policy of the *Examiner.* Here, too, he mentioned—contrary to actual fact—that the memorial to the Holy See had confirmed the "popular impression" that the two archbishops who voted for condemnation were from St. Louis and Santa Fe. Actually the disclosure of the names of Kenrick and

---

[64] Chicago *Knights of Labor,* March 5, 1887.

[65] March 5, 1887.

Salpointe was the *Herald* reporter's doing. With sharpened pen Preston then wrote of "Our Retrogressive Contemporaries," who he predicted, would turn out again in full array their vague platitudes about the Church's friendship for labor. He became very specific, mentioning the lately deceased James A. McMaster, editor of the New York *Freeman's Journal,* as a "fossiliferous remnant of a past age" who had been sure that the K. of L. would be condemned. Besides the editor of the *Freeman's,* his target included "a shallow imitator of his Quixotic genius, Mr. Sancho Pallen," who had denounced the "tyranny of organization" in "most windy sentences." Finally Hickey's *Catholic Review* was accused of a "retrogressive policy and a holy style" since it had advised the workers not to found their own political party, but simply, "Pray, Pray, Pray." [66] The following week, with less fire, the editor suggested that wires of congratulation should be sent to Gibbons to show the Holy See the support the cardinal enjoyed in the United States.[67]

The papers mentioned by the Brooklyn editor ran true to form only in their cool reception to the news from Rome. Maurice Francis Egan, the new editor of the *Freeman's,* was sure that if Gibbons had spoken well of the Knights, it was only because they had dropped "coercion and arbitrary boycotting." [68] After fuller reflection the editorial column, with a bow to Taschereau as well as to Gibbons, emphasized that the evolutionary character of the Knights had done its work by producing "the result of an effective revolution with comparatively little violence." [69] The St. Louis *Catholic World,* perhaps because it was changing ownership at the time, carried nothing on the memorial. It did, however, have an item on a recent speech of Powderly defending his Catholicism but stating that his fidelity to his religion did not imply that he was under the dictates of Rome in secular affairs.[70] A later editorial note did ask, "To Whom are the Knights Responsible?" A longer one undertook to answer Preston, saying, "We are not of the tribe of vulgarians who

[66] March 5, 1887.
[67] March 12, 1887.
[68] March 5, 1887.
[69] March 19, 1887.
[70] March 5, 1887.

bespatter their columns with vituperation for the purpose of venting a contemptible spleen or a shallow witicism." [71]   Pallen denied the charge of declaring war on the Knights for, "Henry Georgism is not to be identified with the Knights of Labor." [72]   The other Brooklyn editor, Patrick V. Hickey, who published, however, in New York, first warned against "Roman gossip," and then weeks later after some platitudes he counseled the Knights of Labor to give up its ways in favor of more conservative policies.[73]

Other Catholic papers, too, were definitely favorable in their reception of the report of the activity of Cardinal Gibbons in Rome. The *Catholic Knight* of Cleveland bragged of its prediction that Rome would not denounce the Knights, and it ventured further to prophesy "the friends of labor may possess their souls in patience. There will be no condemnation of the Knights of Labor this year." [74] The *Michigan Catholic* was ready to accept the substantial truth of the press item.   It stressed the fact that the action was what should have been expected from the American hierarchy and the Detroit weekly offered in explanation of the opinion of Archbishops Kenrick and Salpointe that the violence witnessed in their sections of the country had colored the prelates' views.   Powderly, for a change, received his meed of praise for his conservatism, which had helped to win favor for the Order in Rome.[75]   In Baltimore the *Catholic Mirror* supposed "some abrasion" in the text as a result of the translation and transmission of the report, but yet it felt all Catholics would be pleased.   Approval of the Knights' constitution by "so wise and discerning a person as Cardinal Gibbons" also spoke well, so the *Mirror* thought, for the conservatism of the Knights of Labor.[76]   A New York paper, the *Catholic Herald*, went further in referring to Gibbons' stand as outranking "all of his former claims" to the esteem of Americans.   This strongly pro-McGlynn weekly pictured the cardinal as the protector of those fighting in self de-

71 March 12, 1887.
72 March 19, 1887.
73 *Catholic Review,* March 5, 1887; April 16, 1887.
74 March 5, 1887.
75 March 10, 1887.
76 March 12, 1887.

fense against "the odious monopolies," and so "the Catholic Church in America no longer occupies the wretched position of appearing to be allied with the powerful corporation and wealthy monopolists." [77] Perhaps inspired by a news release in *L'Électeur* of Quebec, which was carried by many other papers, the *Catholic Herald* later defended Taschereau against inimical "labor editors" and spoke of him as really "broad-minded" and only following Rome's order in his early steps against the Knights of Labor. The Canadian item was displayed on the front page. It was believed to have been inspired by ecclesiastical authority, and it explained that there was no real difference of opinion between the two new cardinals and the ultimate decision would be adhered to by all.[78] The "future slanders" on the Knights which might have helped to make any judgment on them an adverse one had now been forestalled said the *Catholic News.* Again the Church was shown as "friendly to the great cause of the workingman" and Gibbons' words were considered a source of strength to the Order, "bracing it against the onslaught of the terrified monopolists." [79] It is not surprising that in one of the first reactions shown within the Knights, Powderly's veteran labor friend, Charles Litchman, should write the same thing, "That action of Cardinal Gibbons will surely help us." [80] A kindred notion that the inevitable papal "approbation" would swell the ranks of the society came from another New York paper, the *Tablet.* However, this weekly was extremely Irish in viewpoint, and it saw in the memorial as well a defense of the principle of home rule, since it had insisted on the competency of the American bishops in their own problems.[81] But even journals not too concerned with world problems, but designed for Catholic family consumption rendered editorial praise. The *Adam* of Memphis, Tennessee, commended Gibbon's boldness and the *Catholic Home* of Chicago expressed its con-

---

[77] March 12, 1887. Bell, *op. cit.*, pp. 95-98, has a one-sided brief notice of some of the trouble of this paper with Corrigan. Its editors were D. O'Loughlin and James Gahan.

[78] *Catholic Herald,* March 19, 1887.

[79] March 9, 1887.

[80] PP, Litchman to Powderly, Philadelphia, March 3, 1887.

[81] March 12, 19, 1887.

fidence in him.[82]   The *Illustrated Catholic American,* also edited by
Hickey, reflected the popular interest in the question by a drawing
of Gibbons on the front cover of the issue of March 12.[83]

The printing of explanatory and laudatory interviews showed
more strongly the position of some of the Catholic press.   The *Pilot*
carried an article by "Monsignor" Thomas J. Ducey, a New York
priest of the anti-Corrigan persuasion, and the *Catholic Mirror,* one
by Dr. Bernard O'Reilly, a clerical free-lance writer of these years
who spent much time in Europe.[84]   The Scranton Catholic paper,
which had only recently been established, reprinted reports of re-
joicing among labor supporters in New York who had feared that
the George-McGlynn issue and Taschereau's influence might have
prejudiced the Knights' case at Rome.   Added to this were the
interviews with Fathers E. F. Slattery of St. Patrick's Cathedral and
the well known John J. Riordan of the Rosary Mission at Castle
Gardens.[85]   The *Record's* own editorial summed up a Roman dispatch telling of an additional favorable report on the Knights of
Labor made by the former wandering and unwanted ablegate, Monsignor Germano Straniero.[86]

The news of Straniero's document was greeted with some of the
skepticism that had followed on the first news of Gibbons' work.
The *Freeman's Journal* classified these two reports made in Rome
as probably "appropriated" by the *Herald* correspondent.[87]   But it
was not alone in this doubting spirit about the memorial of February 20.   The *Colorado Catholic* suggested the later item of the
Associated Press was "merely guessing." [88]   Meanwhile the *Kansas
Catholic* promised to publish only "any official report." [89]   The
Wahrheits-Freund quoted approvingly the opinion of the St. Louis
German Catholic daily, *Amerika,* which held that the published version of Gibbons' views was not authentic.   The Cincinnati paper

---

[82] Both March 12, 1887.

[83] Cf. Frontispiece.

[84] April 9; April 16, 1887.

[85] *Catholic Record,* March 6, 1887.

[86] March 20, 1887.

[87] March 12, 1887.

[88] March 5, 1887.

[89] March 10, 1887.

continued with no trace of sympathy, "Even if the text agrees with the truth in its chief points one may not forget that the judgment of the Congregation of Propaganda and of Leo XIII has not yet been given." [90]   Both the *Catholic Universe* of Cleveland and the *Western Watchman* of St. Louis similarly questioned the authenticity of Gibbons' statement to the Propaganda on grounds of internal evidence.   He was thought to be especially out of character in raising the denial of Peter's Pence as a threat to the Holy See.[91]   The irrepressible Preston rushed to the cardinal's defense and told the St. Louis editor, who had said he would "never cease to be sorry" for Gibbons, if he had used that argument, "Tut! Tut! Tut! Father Phelan, you should not thus speak of the authorities of our holy church.   If your blood boils now, you will run the risk of evaporating in steam before Cardinal Gibbons gets through with his work."   He explained more calmly to Manly Tello that it was not a threat but "one of the prudential reasons' why a disciplinary measure should not be carried out." [92]   The *Western Watchman,* as was also true of the San Francisco *Monitor,* excused its own hesitancy by citing the *Herald* item of March 10, wherein the reporter admitted his information did not come from the cardinal.[93]   The latter Catholic paper had only a warning of the probable lack of truth in the original story.[94]

Other Catholic papers in Boston, Hartford, Troy, Baltimore, Washington, Louisville, and Chicago did not hesitate, however, to carry the news of Gibbons' plea, although for reasons best known to themselves, they made no editorial comment.[95]   One editor, Martin

[90] March 9, 1887.

[91] March 10; March 12, 1887.

[92] *Examiner,* March 19, 1887. To Catholic editors in general he said, "Wake up brothers! Cast aside puerile sneers and devote yourselves to the true sphere of Catholic journalism—the presentation of the progress of the Church, and an adhesion to all reform that will advance the liberties of the people."

[93] *Western Watchman,* April 9, 1887.

[94] *Monitor,* March 30, 1887. This was the only item of that paper available and was procured through the kindness of the Reverend Walter J. Tappe, editor.

[95] *Republic,* March 5; *Connecticut Catholic,* March 5; *Catholic Weekly,* March 5; *Katholische Volkszeitung,* March 12; *Church News,* March 6; *Central Catholic Advocate,* March 10; *Western Catholic,* March 6, 1887.

I. J. Griffin of Philadelphia who saw much of the religious press of his day, made the most pithy, if not the most exact comment on the situation; "When we read the report of Cardinal Gibbons to the Pope about the Knights of Labor we wondered if the cardinal ever read the Catholic papers. If he did he has not followed their advice given so often." [96] [Strangely enough, but perhaps with the hope of losing the favor of no one, the leading Catholic periodicals of a serious nature remained completely silent on the Knights of Labor throughout the year 1887. Although they did not neglect the social problem, the *Catholic World* of New York and the *American Catholic Quarterly Review* of Philadelphia were more concerned with the land question, and even that usually in its theoretical aspects.[97]

The task of rebuttal was assumed by other Catholic journals on this public issue. Gibbons' dictum, so the Denver paper thought —perhaps with its radical neighbor the *Labor Enquirer* in mind— would make some "worthy journals" to "crawl into holes." [98] In Philadelphia the *Standard* detailed the Holy See's systematic process of judging the question to refute those who considered it outmoded and its councilors, "Bourbons." [99] Later it rebuked the New York *Times,* which had sneered at the cardinal's "warm sympathy" for

[96] *I.C.B.U. Journal,* March 15, 1887. Besides being a leader in the Irish Catholic Benevolent Union, Griffin was largely responsible for the extensive newspaper collection of the American Catholic Historical Society of Philadelphia which was used for this study.

[97] Nonetheless, one New York priest did write, "If McGlynn's purpose was merely to improve the condition of the laboring classes by obtaining for them better wages or shorter hours where needed or to limit the power of corporations or control the influence of monopolies, no Catholic theologian would have spilled a drop of ink in trying to injure his cause. But he says that private property in land is the cause of poverty and is unjust." Henry A. Brann, "Henry George and his Land Theories," *Catholic World,* XLIV (March, 1887), 814. Another New York priest, John Talbot Smith, advocated specific and positive reforms, "The Eight Hour Law," and "Kitchens and Wages," *Ibid.,* XLIV (December, 1886), 397-406; (March, 1887), 779-786. Cf. also Reverend Edward McSweeney, "Social Problems," *Catholic World,* XLIV (February, 1887), 577-588; anonymous, "The State and the Land," XLVI (October, 1887), 94-102; Reverend M. Ronayne, S.J., "Land and Labor," *American Catholic Quarterly Review,* XII (August, 1887), 233-252.

[98] *Colorado Catholic,* March 12, 1887.

[99] March 12, 1887.

the workers, as just "shrewd policy." [100] The *Northwestern Chronicle* explained to the Chicago *Tribune* that no reversal of the Church's discipline on secret societies was implied nor had the Vatican come to think anathemas would be wasted on American Catholics, for the very joy of the workers at the news of Gibbons' defense of the Knights displayed their loyalty to the Church.[101] Least effective was the answer of the *Catholic Review* to the charges in the New York *Mail and Express* that the cardinal feared to confront the laborers with a choice between the Church and the Order.[102] The Pittsburgh *Dispatch* was given a lecture by the *Catholic* of the same city on the meaning of an *ex cathedra* pronouncement, and the *Catholic* was at pains to show that the condemnation of the Knights of Labor had certainly not been such.[103] It also remarked with great truth, "the Church is filling a rather large space in the public print just now. The names of Taschereau and Gibbons are unquestionably names to conjure with at present." [104]

This whole question of the handling of the Knights' case in Rome was a matter of concern to some Protestants as well. The *Catholic Mirror* thought it ludicrous when the *Morning Herald* maintained it was echoing the fears of the "great body of Protestants" at the aggressiveness of Rome in the United States.[105] The assertion that papal actions were impinging on political affairs in the United States was taken by the Cincinnati *Catholic Telegraph* as evidence of "Romophobia," and a want of appreciation of both the country and the Church.[106] Yet without missing the Peter's

---

[100] April 9, 1887.

[101] March 10, 1887.

[102] March 19, 1887.

[103] March 19, 1887.

[104] April 2, 1887.

[105] April 2, 1887.

[106] March 10, 1886. This was as close as the paper in Elder's archdiocese came to commenting on the issue except to gibe back at the New York *Herald* which thought it had outsmarted the Catholic press with its columns of the French memorial. April 7, 1887. On the *Telegraph's* attitude on labor in general, cf. Sister M. Stanislaus Connaughton, *The Editorial Opinion of the Catholic Telegraph of Cincinnati on Contemporary Affairs and Politics, 1871-1921* (Washington, 1943), pp. 165-202.

Pence clause and playing up violent strikes of the Knights of Labor, the Episcopalian *Churchman* of New York characterized the move of the "wily Cardinal Gibbons" as an inroad of Rome into American "social and political affairs."[107] The Philadelphia *Standard,* for one, answered in return that the Episcopalian paper had become "vulgarly abusive" in its malice.[108] The *Independent,* on the other hand, quite calmly pointed out how much better Gibbons had done by going to Rome, than had McGlynn who had refused. Concluding that the Catholic Church realized the new growth of the power of the people, it said: "Now this looks very much like the Church's being ready to patronize at least a mild form of socialism now that it has lost its hold on the dynasties and the civil power."[109]

The very impossibilty of any social harmony resulting was the note struck by the *Labor Enquirer.* It expressed disgust with the religious talk cluttering up the field of labor,[110] ignored Gibbons' action, and continued to insist that all religious groups were losing the masses by their alliance with the rich.[111] Other labor papers did not ignore the Roman memorial, even if it was only to consider it like Henry George, "The Rebuke to Archbishop Corrigan." George took almost the whole front page of the *Standard* for a signed editorial wherein he surmised the enterprise of the *Herald* was "facilitated, perhaps, by the shrewd sense of the cardinal."[112] The *Irish World* felt that such a report as Gibbons' memorial, coming while labor suffered at the hands of the capitalist press, should have been enough to kill the slander that the Church was "opposed to the just aspirations of the people."[113] In Chicago the *Knights of Labor* thought the memorial should also silence the "alarmist lies"

[107] March 9, 1887.

[108] March 26, 1887.

[109] April 7, 1887. The editor thought that Gibbons' mention of the "separated brethren" in his speech on taking possession of his titular church in Rome bespoke "the gentleman and the Christian." March 31, 1887. Cf. Will, *op. cit.,* I, 306-319.

[110] March 19, 1887.

[111] April 2, 1887.

[112] March 12, 1887.

[113] March 12, 1887. Ford had already sent a wire of congratulations to Powderly, PP, March 3, 1887.

about threatening ecclesiastical restaints.[114] The official organ of the Order did not consider the American clergy apt to be affected by such "newspaper vaporings" for the workingmen had always found in them "their best and wisest friends and champions." Like the rest of the labor journals, it showed no reluctance to print the phrase about the "transient form" of its own organization.[115] More respected and less given to partisan views was *John Swinton's Paper* which pointed out how Gibbons' document had outraged such capitalist papers as the New York *Post,* and called its comments on strikes "gall and bitterness" to such people. In sincere tribute he said:

> The arguments presented at Rome by Cardinal Gibbons of Baltimore in defense of the Knights of Labor, are as powerful as they are just, broad and liberal. If they should obtain the sanction of the sovereign authorities of the Church the latter will be planted upon grounds such as have never before been taken by any other ecclesiastical organization. In any event, his generous and manly voice will not fail of its efforts. . . .
> We thank Cardinal Gibbons for his report upon American labor, in which he utters as lofty sentiments as ever were heard in Rome.[116]

Cardinal Taschereau's position, on the other hand, received no journalistic support. Even in Quebec City only one important daily offered any consolation at all. An editorial in the conservative *L'Événement* deprecated the current scandal-mongering of the press, detailed the cardinal's earlier steps in the case, and pointed out that "a piece indelicately detached from a brief" did not amount to a whole juridical process. The zeal of Taschereau had begun the adjudication years before, and thus it was he who deserved credit.[117] Indeed, it was very true that Rome had not spoken and the case was far from finished. From the tone of his letter shortly afterwards, Taschereau would almost appear to have been opening it

---

[114] March 5; 12, 1887.

[115] *Journal of United Labor,* March 12, 1887.

[116] April 3, 1887.

[117] *L'Événement,* March 8, 1887. The *Irish Canadian* still spoke of the condemnation as if it had been Taschereau's idea, while praising the "illustrious Irish-American ecclesiastic." March 10, 1887.

anew. Spurred on by a telegraphic dispatch from Canada telling of the publication of the news there he brought forth more arguments for Simeoni. Cardinal Gibbons had assured him on March 6, that he knew nothing of the circumstances of the story's leaking out, but the Canadian still wanted to express his views on the association which now existed in his archdiocese as well as in the province and which he felt was dangerous in character. Without authority, he argued first that the "ostensible purpose" of the Knights was the living family wage, which in practice was impossible to maintain. Secondly, although the present leaders were well disposed, there was no way of being sure of their successors, who might not be able to prevent "the disorder, strikes, seditions, conflagrations and other troubles which the experience of these recent years shows us as the fruit of this association." The Cardinal of Quebec further accused the Knights of refusing to work for capitalists who had non-union help and of striking to protect workers who had been fired for good reasons. Taschereau's third point in this statement of position which he had never previously made, was to call it "a socialist fraternity," of evil forebodings. This charge was based on the fact that a Belgian socialist had been warmly received in the United States by the Knights of Labor and had returned to Europe hoping to spread its principles.[118] Displaying no doubts about the identity of the association in Canada and the United States, the cardinal concluded by asking Simeoni that the instruction that would be given to the American bishops be addressed also to the Canadians. He pointed out that on the basis of the earlier condemnation the Knights in his province who had refused to renounce membership were still being denied the sacraments and so an authentic declaration by the Holy See would be necessary if toleration were to be granted.[119]

[118] Although this foreign agitator was left nameless, some basis for such an accusation might be seen in a letter to the general assembly from the representative of an assembly in Belgium. A. Delwarte, writing from Charleroi, September 17, 1887, held up as part of their aim, "The land and the great instruments of labor belonging to all, and labor producing wealth to all." *Proceedings* (Minneapolis, 1887), p. 1742.

[119] AAQ, 35, 440, Taschereau to Simeoni, Rome, March 7, 1887, copy. *La Vérité,* August 25, 1894, omitted the arguments he used against the Knights of Labor.

None of this Taschereau side of the case, however, reached the public, although a representative of the New York *Herald*, through the cardinal's secretary, offered its wires for the publication of a statement or an interview on the matter.[120]

Publicity, nevertheless, did not hamper in any way the course of action of Cardinal Gibbons, or as Keane called it, the "no small venture" of uttering such sentiments "in an atmosphere like this of Rome." The publishing of his views without his knowledge had for a time made Gibbons' experience even more trying. As his fellow bishop further told Manning, "For a time the Cardinal was very apprehensive; but telegrams, and now newspaper comments, are coming in of a most cheering character, showing that the publication of the document has done great good among the people of America."[121] Its effectiveness was increased when Cardinal Manning penned a letter of endorsement, dated March 11, which likewise did not remain long unrevealed to the public. He wrote:

> I have read with great assent Cardinal Gibbons' document in relation to the Knights of Labor. The Holy See, I am sure, will be convinced with his exposition of the state of the New World. I hope it will open a new field of thought and action. It passes my understanding that officious persons should be listened to rather than official. Surely the episcopate of the world is the most powerful and direct instrument in the hands of the Holy See for gathering correct local knowledge, and enforcing its decisions. Who can know the temper of America, England, and Ireland as they who have its finger upon the pulse of the people?
> Hitherto the world has been governed by dynasties; henceforth the Holy See will have to deal with the people and it has bishops in close daily and personal contact with the people. The more clearly and fully this is perceived, the stronger Rome will be. Never at any time has the episcopate been so detached from civil power and so united in itself and with the Holy See. Failure to see and use these powers will breed much trouble and mischief.
> My thanks are due to the Cardinal for letting me share in the argument. If I can find a copy of my lecture on 'The Dignity and Rights of Labor,' I will send it to him. It will, I think,

[120] AAQ, CMR, VII, 204, C. Harry Meltzer to C. A. Marois, Rome, March 12, 1887.

[121] Keane to Manning, March 14, 1887, quoted in Leslie, *op. cit.*, p. 361.

qualify me for knighthood in the order. Bretano some years ago published a book on the guilds in which he proves that the association of labor and crafts goes back to antiquity. But there is this notable fact, in the English and Teutonic laws they were recognized, favoured and charted; in the Imperial and Latin laws they were rigorously prohibited.

The Church is the mother, friend, and protector of the people. As the Lord walked among them, so His Church lives among them. The Cardinal's argument is irresistible.[122]

Gibbons himself quickly acknowledged these warm words of the Archbishop of Westminster and took them, as well, for a mark of approval on his memorial of February 25 against the condemnation of the writings of Henry George, an action which succeeded in delaying for the time being a decision on that issue. He concluded: "We are indebted more than you are aware to the influence of your name in discussing these social questions and in influencing the public mind. We joyfully adopt your Eminence into the ranks of our Knighthood; you have nobly won your spurs!"[123] A month later Manning sent a word of exegesis to the American group in Rome,

> I carefully spoke of the "New World." And yet England and France are in the Old World. . . . The state of the "New World" is not the normal state of Christendom. But it is with the abnormal state that we have to do. We must deal with facts, not with memories, and lamentations. And to deal with facts we must go down into the midst of them. The Incarnation is our law, and wisdom.[124]

122 *Tablet,* May 7, 1887. It was so pubished because it had been "extensively but inaccurately produced on both sides of the Atlantic." It was described only as addressed to "a member of the American hierarchy." That member was Keane.

123 Gibbons to Manning, Rome, March 14, 1887, quoted in Leslie, *op. cit.,* pp. 361-362. The memorial on George was entitled, "La question des écrits de Henri George." Keane later wrote to Manning, March 22, 1887, from Rome, "The clear, strong, wise words of your Eminence will be a bulwark to the truth and a rebuke to mischief-makers." Quoted in Leslie, *op. cit.,* p. 362.

124 ADR, O'Connell Papers, Manning to [Keane], Westminster, April 15, 1887.

Another archbishop in another English-speaking part of the world also wrote his assent to Cardinal Gibbons. John J. Lynch's aid had not been solicited, but he would have willingly given it, if requested, since he sent his "most hearty accord." The Archbishop of Toronto recalled in a lengthy letter how he had examined the Knights and concluded not only that they were harmless, but even more, they were necessary for the oppressed workers. His hope was that the Knights of Labor was only a temporary remedy and that "capitalists will see the necessity as well as the advantage of fair dealing with the working men." An appreciation of the situation was shown in his final prayer, "that this very grave matter which involves the salvation or damnation of millions of souls may be settled as Christ wills it." [125] Agreeing with Lynch only on the need of Rome's decision, the Bishop of Portland, Maine, saw also that it was the time for explanations. Healy wrote, not to Gibbons, but to Cardinal Mazzella of the Holy Office. He, too, explained his previous position on the decree promulgated in Canada and he described it as a policy "of obeying first, and asking questions afterwards." [126]

The Archbishop of Baltimore while in Rome also heard directly from a number of American prelates, although the existing records do not indicate that very many of them wrote.[127] Even out of Corrigan's household a sample of American opinion on Gibbons' work was forwarded to him. This editorial from the *Nation* was hardly calculated to please the cardinal, for it indulged in some caustic comments on a reported interview from Rome in which Gibbons was quoted as considering himself an "enemy of plutocracy and of corporations of men with no souls." [128] Although it had made no remarks up to that time, this respectably conservative weekly thereupon spoke of Gibbons' "partaking freely of the labor beverage"

[125] AAT, Lynch to Gibbons, Toronto, March 23, 1887, copy. He thought the majority of the Knights were Irishmen and "good conscientious Catholics."

[126] ADPM, Healy to Camillo Cardinal Mazzella, Portland, March 15, 1887, copy.

[127] The absence of the archbishop from his own see might help to explain to some degree the lack of such letters. Similarly, originals of the Manning correspondence are notable among the missing items in the Gibbons Papers.

[128] *Irish World*, March 19, 1887.

and of the "terrible loss" sustained by politics when he entered the
Church. The *Nation's* hope was that he would defend the freedom
of the workers who did not belong to the Knights of Labor, which
it dubbed "the most soulless corporation" in existence.[129] All of
this Gibbons had already read, and so New York's thoughtfulness
was of no avail.[130] Seemingly in a pull away from the Corrigan
camp, word came from Bishop Gilmour agreeing with the Baltimore
cardinal on the Knights and even saying, "The few illegalities, so
far committed only show the inner spirit of justice in the boom." [131]
Bishop Edward Fitzgerald of Little Rock, in thanking him for copies
of the two memorials on the social question, declared condemnation
would be neither justified nor expedient.[132] From Corrigan's
jurisdiction came Burtsell's congratulations with a note of thanks
for the cardinal's letter of February 18, which he characterized as
"the very gratifying proof of your sympathy with Rev. Dr. Mc-
Glynn." [133] The case of the unruly priest was the chief concern of
Archbishop Ryan of Philadelphia in welcoming home the Archbishop of New York, but he did remark the publication of the
names of Kenrick and Salpointe as if Gibbons were responsible,
"It was not necessary for his purpose, and was unfair to these prelates." [134] Ryan had earlier mentioned this same thing to the
cardinal as regrettable, and Cincinnati's archbishop concurred in
that opinion. Elder, after referring to the "luminous report," cited
for Gibbons the similar case of the private *Acta* of the council of
1884, which had also found its way into the press, and he urged a
protest at Propaganda. His reason was: "It will destroy all freedom
in our deliberations if our confidential conferences can thus be
reached by newspaper reporters, and if we can be exposed to public
odium for uttering our sentiments." [135] Both Ryan and Elder had
received copies of the memorial on the Knights of Labor from Rome

[129] March 17, 1887.

[130] NYAA, O'Connell to Charles McDonnell, Rome, April 14, 1887.

[131] ADC, Gilmour to Gibbons, Cleveland, March 16, 1887, copy.

[132] BCA, 82-N-10, N-11, Fitzgerald to Gibbons, Little Rock, March 20,
1887.

[133] BCA, 82-N-6, Burtsell to Gibbons, New York, March 8, 1887.

[134] NYAA, Ryan to Corrigan, Philadelphia, March 23, 1887.

[135] AAC, Elder to Gibbons, Cincinnati, March 22, 1887, copy.

and the latter showed his to the visiting Bishops of Covington, Louisville, and Grand Rapids (Maes, W. McCloskey, and Richter), while Ryan had undertaken to send word to Powderly "through an intimate friend of his" that the cardinal wanted a copy of the constitution of the Knights as revised at Richmond.[136] Gibbons' secretary had also been at work on this project and had enlisted the aid of Powderly's parish priest in Carbondale. Father Carew, in turn, had the labor leader's brother report the cardinal's message and say that "it was absolutely necessary for him to have it." [137]

Neither the archbishop nor the priest could have been successful in their quest since no such recently-revised edition of the constitution existed. It was only in May that even the proposed emendations were submitted to a membership vote of the Knights.[138] Hence the constitution which Rome was interested in re-examining in mid-March was no different from that first handed in by Gibbons' group. Taschereau, while still in Rome, was informed that the Holy Office was again studying the Knights of Labor, "the constitution of which apparently has been changed since the issuance of the decree of 1884, given in response to my consultation." [139] He then requested

[136] BCA, 82-N-8, Ryan to Gibbons, Philadelphia, March 15, 1887. Powderly at this time had plans to discuss the McGlynn case with the Archbishop of Philadelphia some evening. He had already had an "animated" talk with Dr. Ignatius Horstmann of the same archdiocese who had called at the Knights' new headquarters on Broad Street. Powderly's impression of the latter was: "He is a crank on Arbitration, a theoretical one, in fact, a visionary or more properly speaking, a Doctrinaire. . . . I detest him for he is an Aristocrat and he hates the Irish. . . ." PP, Powderly to Maggie Devers, Philadelphia, March 21, 1887.

[137] PP, H. [?] Powderly to T. V. Powderly, Carbondale, March 8, 1887.

[138] *Proceedings* (Minneapolis, 1887), pp. 1864-1865, Circular letter of May 17, 1887, from Charles Litchman.

[139] There had, of course, been revisions at the regular sessions of the general assembly; at Philadelphia in 1884, at Hamilton in 1885, as well as the beginning of a new one at Richmond in 1886. Since the condemnation of 1884 had been based on an examination of the society's "principles, organization and statutes" these minor changes could hardly have been reasonably expected to make a difference. As a matter of fact, the only section specifically singled out as suspect by American theologians and later by the Holy Office had come into being only in 1884 at the Philadelphia convention, *Proceedings* (1884), p. 780.

from Vincenzo Sallua, O.P., a revision of the status of the question in his jurisdiction. The archbishop thought that the bishops who had enforced the decree against the Knights should be allowed to permit their priests to receive back to the sacraments those members "who promise sincerely to obey the decision which the Holy See will give when the examination of the new constitution will have been completed." Since the time for the Easter confession was approaching and he was leaving for Quebec, the Canadian cardinal hoped the Holy Office would give him a favorable answer by the end of that week.[140] As he later explained to Gibbons in writing to him from Paris, Taschereau during his stay in Rome had been seeking authorization to make such an announcement publicly, but Sallua informed him that "the Pope authorized me to give this instruction to the confessors, but *privately* and not through a public document." On the day he left Rome, March 20, just three days after they had both received the cardinal's hat, Taschereau was still hopeful and he obtained Gibbons' promise to let him know by wire if his request was granted.[141] On March 22, "for fear of any misunderstanding" he wrote Gibbons a résumé of his dealings with the Roman officials since 1884 which had been prompted by a desire to end the scandal. He concluded that the permission granted by Sallua would not be very helpful, "since the secret will not be able to be kept and the public once it finds out will not fail to make comments which will contravene the true sentiments of the Holy See." If the request to allow the public change of policy was not answered, he would keep silent and there would be no need of Gibbons' telegram.[142] Before the Archbishop of Baltimore could possibly have done anything, another response went out from the Holy Office to confuse Taschereau. This time Cardinal Monaco announced that an answer to his question had been reached on March 10 and it read, "The decision already given is to be abided by. When indeed the new statutes which are to be sent have been examined his Eminence the Archbishop will be notified of the

140 AAQ, 35, 441, Taschereau to Sallua, Rome, March 15, 1887, copy.

141 This last conference probably took place at the dinner in Gibbons' honor at the American College. *Tablet*, April 2, 1887.

142 AAQ, 35, 442, Taschereau to Gibbons, Paris, March 22, 1887, copy.

result." [143] Taschereau's marginal notes show he understood the "decision already given" to be that of October, 1884, and so the communication completely ignored the permission granted by Leo XIII by which Taschereau could change the procedure in his archdiocese, although only privately. The next meeting of the congregation on March 30, apparently resulted in re-established harmony, for their decree emerged bearing Sallua's name:

> Those members of the Knights of Labor in Canada can be admitted to the Sacraments who declare themselves disposed to stand firm in the precept which the Holy See will issue after the examination of the modifications which the Society has introduced or intends to introduce in its statutes. Cardinal Gibbons shall make this known to his Eminence, the Archbishop of Quebec to whom also there is given the faculty of publicizing this decision.[144]

The wire was sent promptly from one cardinal to the other as prearranged, "Pope grants your petition fully." [145] It would seem, therefore, that Leo XIII himself as prefect of the Holy Office, was responsible for this step, but what part Gibbons played in influencing him is not evident. The cable he sent, however, was also at the bidding of the congregation, and more than the fulfillment of a promise, it was the announcement of a directive of the Holy See.[146]

While Gibbons remained in Rome, at least one other negotiation was conducted with the Holy Office in the form of a brief petition in favor of the Knights.[147] It explained that the American bishops had not followed the ban decreed by the congregation on August 27, 1884, "at the instance of the Archbishop of Quebec," because they had not even a "reasonable suspicion" against the society as they knew it. Not using the usual argument that the former decision had been *juxta exposita,* the defendant relied solely on the

[143] AAQ, CMR, VII, 191, Monaco to Taschereau, Rome, March 23, 1887.

[144] BCA, 82-P-3, Sallua to Gibbons, Rome, March 30, 1887; also to Taschereau, AAQ, CMR, VII, 194.

[145] AAQ, 35, 443, Gibbons to Taschereau, Rome, March 31, 1887.

[146] AAC, Gibbons to Elder, Rome, March 31, 1887.

[147] BCA, unclassified, "Draft. Petition to Holy Office. Knights of Labor. Filed April/87."

harmless character of the Knights.[148] The petition faced a possible objection also:

> But if nothing positive about religion is found in these Statutes, or even if non-Catholics are found among the members, this is to be expected from the nature of the society. It is really only a civil society and concerns the workers, craftsmen and merchants only in what pertains to their trade or work for the sake of mutual help especially in the case of sickness or incapacity.

Without giving any supporting evidence, Gibbons repeated the fear of the bishops that a condemnation would mean a drifting of Catholic members to Masonic groups. They were meanwhile depicted as the type of faithful, "who frequent the sacraments, perform works of piety and religion and freely support and aid churches and the sacred ministers." For this reason there was no doubt, "that the statutes already proscribed by the S. Congregation will be emended." With a promise of vigilance over all such societies Cardinal Gibbons in the name of "almost all" the bishops of the United States asked that "nothing be changed" concerning the status of the Knights of Labor in their country "lest there result great disturbance among the people and harm to religion."

All this transpired while reports from the other side of the Atlantic kept telling Gibbons of the great commotion his Roman doings had caused. Abbé Alphonse Magnien, S.S., superior of St. Mary's Seminary in Baltimore, supplied him with favorable evidence, but his inclusion of a sample of what he called, "the few discordant voices . . . prompted by bigotry, or jealousy," indicated there was not unanimous approval.[149] An evidence of the concern of big business over the affair was recounted by the Bishop of Wheeling, John J. Kain, as "no outspoken protest," but yet, "some mutterings of dissatisfaction." He specifically mentioned an employee of the St. Louis paper, the *Age of Steel,* who had been instructed to produce

---

[148] John Ireland, in an exclusive Roman interview, had pointed out that the prohibitory decree was local but also that Gibbons' action was merely in favor of non-condemnation, not approval. *Pilot,* April 2, 1887.

[149] BCA, 82-P-2, Magnien to Gibbons, Baltimore, March 29, 1887.

an article showing the inferences in Gibbons' statement that were hostile to capital. "The purpose," the prelate said, "was to put into words what 'Puck' had tried to delineate by cartoon." [150] This man, whom Kain knew, had refused the task, but he reported that other business men also regarded the cardinal as biased. Kain suggested, "If, in the future discussion of this knotty and delicate question, opportunity offers, a word more strongly condemnatory of the unjust methods practised by the Knights of Labor and kindred societies, would be well received." [151] On the other side of the picture, however, was the Coadjutor of Pittsburgh, Richard Phelan, who praised Gibbons' action as the salvation not only of the Knights of Labor but of the trade unions also. His appreciation of labor societies which "have certainly alleviated the condition of laborers," concluded:

> Among large bodies of men abuses are inevitable. This state of things can scarcely continue. Legislation, State and National, will probably settle it in time. There are signs of it now. It would, I venture to think, be better for the Church not to commit herself by seeming to take sides in favor of capitalists. The time has scarcely come to approve or condemn them. The man who can protect laborers without infringing on the rights of others will be a benefactor of his race and country.[152]

From the Bishop of Omaha came praise of a defense that was "timely and most judicious," and that would make easy any future rebuke of the Knights of Labor that might be necessary.[153] The Archbishop of Philadelphia, although he had always been friendly to the Knights, did not express any opinion that is extant. Probably his closeness to Corrigan and the fear of seeming to mix in what touched that archbishop's business led him merely to assure Gibbons,

[150] Cf. illustrations from *Puck,* pp. 275, 313.

[151] BCA, 82-P-5, Kain to Gibbons, Wheeling, April 4, 1887.

[152] BCA, 82-P-6, Phelan to Gibbons, Allegheny, April 5, 1887.

[153] BCA, 82-P-14, James O'Connor to Gibbons, Omaha, April 20, 1887. Francis Janssens, Bishop of Natchez, had the same notion. He also praised Gibbons' action for preventing a situation wherein, "our laborers would have lost confidence in their Church and ranked her on the side of capital against the poor." BCA, 82-R-10, Janssens to Gibbons, Natchez, May 30, 1887.

whimsically, "On your return the Knights of Labor (the male portion) will receive you with 'open arms.' " [154]

The Baltimore cardinal used a day's holiday outside Rome to try to pave the way for a friendly reception from the Archbishop of New York. His letter told Corrigan that matters looked hopeful on the nuncio question.[155] He reported on the recent Roman discussions concerning the transfer and removal of parish priests and he included an avowal of having made no further move in connection with McGlynn. Of him he remarked wisely, "it is unfortunate that his case has been mixed up with the labor question." Professing ignorance of how his memorial leaked out and grief because of the revelation of the names of the two dissenting archbishops, the cardinal said, "The publication of my paper on the Knights of Labor by the *Herald* gave me exceeding pain. . . . It has been published more fully since then in the *Moniteur de Rome,* as the N. Y. publication left out some important points." [156] What Gibbons did not seem to know was that Archbishop Corrigan and his friends were aware of other points left out of the *Moniteur* version also, namely, the paragraph on McGlynn. McQuaid alluded to the *Moniteur's* account as the "expurgated edition of the Cardinal's private document from which is omitted his reference to your affairs." The Bishop of Rochester went on to explain, "The *Herald* evidently had possession of the original. It accords with the first edition for private circulation. His Eminence put his foot in it badly." [157] Corrigan, nevertheless, diplomatically acknowledged Gibbons' "kind letter of March 29," and thanked him for defending the interests

154 BCA, 82-P-11, Ryan to Gibbons, Philadelphia, April 10, 1887.

155 Gilmour said of Manning's letter of March 11, "I see Cardinal Manning has spoken on this nuncio business, taking the K. of L. as the pretext. . . . I am glad he has spoken." AAC, Gilmour to Elder, Cleveland, March 31, 1887.

156 NYAA, Gibbons to Corrigan, Anzio, March 29, 1887. O'Connell, a newly-named monsignor, thanked Corrigan's secretary, McDonnell, for his congratulations and told him the same story. NYAA, Rome, April 14, 1887.

157 RDA, McQuaid to Corrigan, Rochester, April 12, 1887, copy. It can only be surmised that they came to know the original document from some bishop, most likely Gilmour, who received a copy, or from Miss Edes. Apparently the prelates in Rome chose to send it only to certain bishops.

of the American bishops "in the recent important issues." The
McGlynn affair he described as in the phase of "organized opposition
to Episcopal authority." Furthermore, his troubles with the Knights
of Labor had now passed out of the realm of the theoretical:

> The Knights continue to be quite exorbitant in their demands.
> E.g., we have 150 men working steadily in our Cemetery and
> receiving larger wages than are given in any other Cemetery
> in the neighborhood. Now these Knights have not only asked
> me, as chairman of the Board, to raise their wages still higher,
> but they also insist that we must neither employ nor discharge
> a single workman without their previous knowledge and
> consent.[158]

The issuance of Taschereau's final circular on the Knights was
related to Gibbons by Corrigan as well as by the Quebec prelate
himself, although the former did not mention Taschereau's ironically
expressed hope, "that it will be found orthodox." [159]

Cardinal Taschereau had hardly returned to his see and the
welcoming celebration that awaited him when he had to prepare
two letters. One was to *Le Canadien* of Quebec denying completely
the truth of a ship-side interview which they had republished from
the New York *World,* allegedly giving inner details of the Roman
story. Nevertheless, he did not indicate any change in his position
on the Knights.[160] Of much more importance was the circular
to the clergy, printed in French and English, dated April 5, 1887,
and marked, "To be read only in the parishes where there are
Knights of Labor." It stipulated:

> After representations made by their Lordships the Bishops of
> the United States, the Holy See has suspended, until further
> orders, the effect of that sentence. [In his circular of February
> 2, 1885].

[158] BCA, 82-P-12, Corrigan to Gibbons, New York, April 12, 1887. The
board of arbitration of District Assembly 49 had approached him as chairman
of the Calvary Corporation, speaking of the "many grievances" of the employees. NYAA, H. B. George to Corrigan, New York, March 18, 1887.

[159] NYAA, Taschereau to Corrigan, Quebec, April 7, 1887; BCA, 82-P-9,
Taschereau to Gibbons, Quebec, April 7, 1887.

[160] *Le Canadien,* April 9, 1887.

In consequence, I authorize the confessors of this diocese to absolve the Knights of Labor, on the following conditions, which it is your bounden duty to explain to them, and to make them observe:

1° That they confess and sincerely repent the grievous sin, which they committed by not obeying the decree of September 1884;

2° That they be ready to abandon this society, so soon as the Holy See shall ordain it;

3° That they sincerely and explicitly promise absolutely to avoid all that may either favor masonic and other condemned, societies, or violate the laws either of justice, charity, or of the state;

4° That they abstain from every promise and from every oath, by which they would bind themselves either to obey blindly all the orders of the directors of the society, or keep absolute secrecy even towards lawful authorities.

In behalf of those penitents only, and by virtue of an indult, I prolong the time of the paschal communion until the feast of the Ascension inclusively.[161]

Copies were duly sent to Simeoni and Sallua in Rome, and Taschereau noted for Gibbons that the last three points were based on the Second Plenary Council of Baltimore.[162] This same message and directive were sent by Archbishop Fabre to his priests on April 9.[163] At least in the Quebec parishes, the reading of this letter resulted in reports of great jubilation among the Knights. The only editorial remark that seems to have been made in that city was by the English paper. It detailed the "onerous conditions" and said, "one other such 'Victory' and the Knights of Labor would indeed be undone." [164]

During the month of April, 1887, the Quebec revocation and the version of the memorial from the March 28 *Moniteur de Rome* appeared frequently in the American and Canadian press. Apart from keeping the question a while longer in the public eye the newspaper comments at this point added little of importance to

[161] Têtu-Gagnon, *Mandements,* II, 613-614.

[162] BCA, 82-P-9, Taschereau to Gibbons, Quebec, April 9, 1887.

[163] *Mandements, lettres pastorales, circulaires et autres documents publiés dans le diocèse de Montréal depuis son érection,* X (Montreal, 1893), 332-336.

[164] *Morning Chronicle,* April 12, 1887.

the story of the Church's relations with the Knights of Labor. Many papers carried the texts, and some few unfriendly journalists made their usual gibes.[165] The *Churchman,* for example, spoke of the inconvenience of "papal infallibility." [166] Powderly's efforts to suit Gibbons were called a "cold and frozen fact" and the Knights were warned of the experience of the Crispins which had been killed by Church interference.[167] In Catholic circles, the *Kansas Catholic* published the *Moniteur* version of the Roman document, explaining it had refused to use the first one, "as its crude utterances and style made us believe there was something amiss with it" [168] Some Catholic papers like the *Western Watchman* boasted of their copy of the "correct text" as coming direct from "the Propaganda press," but the fifteen-page booklet issue of it found only in the archives of the Diocese of Cleveland shows no indication of origin, but it may be safely presumed it was prepared in Rome by those most interested in the question.[169]

Two Catholic journals claimed to have secured unique news items during these weeks, but only one of them had, so far as it can be ascertained, the true facts. The *Catholic News* of New York, not reluctant to feature something that might help its budding circulation, announced in a Roman note of April 16 that the Holy Office had decided in favor of the Knights of Labor.[170] A cablegram from its correspondent in Rome, Francis A. Steffens, told of the Pope's approval. This was supplied to the press of the United States and so the paper claimed to have beaten even the Rome, Paris, and London dailies which later carried the item.[171] This notice at-

[165] The Quebec edict appeared in such papers as the *Canadian Freeman* (Kingston, Ontario) April 13, 1887; *Irish Canadian,* April 14, 1887; also *Pilot,* April 5; *Catholic,* April 17; *Catholic News,* April 17; *Church News,* April 17, 1887. The *Moniteur* version was reported in such as *Examiner, Irish World, Western Catholic* on April 2, 1887; also *Church News,* April 3, *Catholic World,* April 16; *Catholic Standard,* April 23; *Catholic Review,* and *Freeman's Journal,* April 30, 1887.

[166] April 16, 1887.

[167] *Labor Enquirer,* April 23, 1887.

[168] April 14, 1887.

[169] April 23, 1887; similarly *Connecticut Catholic,* April 23, 1887.

[170] April 17, 1887.

[171] April 17, 24, 1887.

tracted Taschereau's attention and he quickly sent Corrigan a copy of the Holy Office's decree of March 30, which had anticipated a change in the Knights of Labor, but had not given approval on the condition of *nihil innovetur* as the press was stating.[172]

Thomas Preston really had a more substantial story, for he attacked the *Moniteur* version as a "doctored" report. On the basis of the "document in the original French" as it was presented to Propaganda he boldly asserted this had been done "shamefully" by suppression of parts of the original, by addition to it, and by interpretation which toned down its strength. The outstanding item was the passage on McGlynn which like the other omissions was given in both French and English, but this alone was doubled in size and shade of print.[173] Preston was not easy on the "gullible Catholic journals," and so the battle was joined again. The official statement was upheld by the *Catholic Mirror* and the *Freeman's Journal*, which even referred to the "God-forsaken little panderer to the Herald's anti-Catholic prejudices." [174]

These more respectable members of the Church press were wrong about the authentic reading of the memorial, but they were correct in insisting that the Holy See had granted only a temporary toleration of the Knights of Labor. The rebellious *Catholic Herald* of New York reflected with bitter humor this situation:

> The goody-goody editors of the Pallen-Egan-Hickey stripe are trying to hedge on the Labor question. Now *they* tell us that the Pope has not approved of the Knights of Labor, that he merely permits them to continue on their present lines. Well, no one asked for his approval. The Knights simply wish to be let alone. But the hearts of the editors are scalded because the Pope did not *condemn* the great labor organization. Poor fools! They are neither fish, nor flesh, nor even passable salt herring. God reigns, Cardinal Gibbons lives and Labor thrives.[175]

---

[172] NYAA, Taschereau to Corrigan, Quebec, April 20, 1887.

[173] *Examiner*, April 23, 1887.   The variant readings are noted in the translation in Appendix III.

[174] *Catholic Mirror*, April 30, 1887; *Freeman's Journal*, May 7, 1887. In a similar manner, the *Catholic World*, and *Western Watchman*, May 7, 1887.

[175] May 21, 1887.

It was little wonder that Archbishop Corrigan had put both the *Examiner* and the *Herald* on the agenda for discussion by the bishops of the Province of New York.[176]

Among the more moderate papers was the *Catholic Standard* of Philadelphia. It even received a letter of congratulations from Bishop Keane for its understanding and exposition of Gibbons' work. It was printed immediately beneath an editorial on that bishop's election as first rector of the new university. As he put it, the cardinal thought that the task of dealing with such labor organizations should be "left to the conservative good sense of the American people, to the strong legal authority of our country, and to the patient prudence of our Hierarchy." He wanted, moreover, to impress the rulers of the Church with the way of gentleness and justice in dealing with the "toiling millions" and to demonstrate the difference between "our American assertion of popular rights" and European forms of "social dissolution." Keane testified to the cardinal's distress at the presentation to the world of what was meant "only for the eye of ecclesiastical authority." Yet it had all been for the good since it had convinced millions of the Church's friendship for the workers, produced a profound impression in Rome, and so far as Europe was concerned the press had been "simply enthusiastic;" in fact, it had "poured oil on troubled waters in more countries than our own." [177]

Even a reflection of the European press in the American Catholic papers showed how widely the story of the Roman activities had been circulated and how favorably received. This was principally due to the fact that Cardinal Manning had come to the support of the cause. His letter of assent of March 11 went into the *Moniteur* with the approval of the archbishop secretary of Propaganda, Domenico Jacobini.[178] The memorial on the Knights of Labor was

[176] AAC, Corrigan to Elder, New York, Low Sunday, 1887.

[177] *Catholic Standard,* May 14, 1887, letter of April 21, 1887 from Rome. The *Standard,* against a New York *Times* tirade, had previously estimated from the press reaction that in the United States nine-tenths of the people were in accord with Gibbons. April 30, 1887.

[178] Keane to Manning, Rome, April 23, 1887, quoted in Leslie, *op. cit.,* 363. The *Tablet,* April 16 and 23 carried the *Moniteur* version with edi-

thought by the Roman correspondent of the Liverpool *Catholic
Times* to have been more than just noticed in "the highest quarter
in Rome."[179] Both the Paris *Univers* and the London *Chronicle*
carried the false report of papal approval in mid-April.[180] But the
most remarkable European item was Manning's long letter to the
Tablet in which he strongly and publicly took sides on a question
which did not enjoy the complete agreement of the American
hierarchy. He summarized and supported Gibbons' stand, arguing
it was the office of the Church to protect the poor. He said, "The
Knights of Labor and the English trade unions represent the right
of labor and the rights of association for its defense."[181] Meanwhile
his briefer and originally private document of the month previous
found its way into the *Unità Cattolica*, the *Germania*, the *Reich
zeitung*, all of which saw the foreshadowng of an alliance between
the Church and the popular movement. The *Vaterland* of Vienna
took it as a sign that "the old principles of Christian morals are
to serve social justice."[182]

It was no more than fitting, therefore, that Gibbons should not re
turn home without visiting his co-laborer, the Archbishop of
Westminster.[183] Before the trip to London and while still in Paris
he had written again to Corrigan admitting a mistake in judgment in
ever letting Burtsell receive the letter that had been used to make
Gibbons appear an interferer in the McGlynn issue. Likewise, al
though the paragraph on the single tax priest had been used against
Corrigan, it had been deliberately omitted in the *Moniteur* pub
lication, "not because it contained any argument against your
Grace," but lest his enemies should have distorted it. Gibbons hoped
the paragraph printed in the original French in the *Herald* had
"escaped observation." He said further that boycotting was con
demnable, and referring to the cemetery workers, he remarked, "it

torial thanks for a contribution to the Christianizing of the new democrat
power.

179 *Catholic World*, April 23, 1887.
180 *John Swinton's Paper*, April 24, 1887; *Catholic News*, April 24.
181 *Tablet*, April 30, 1887.
182 *Catholic Mirror*, May 21, 1887.
183 Leslie, *op. cit.*, p. 363.

vident there are some bad Knights in New York." [184] The Archbishop of New York answered in the hope of catching the cardinal
embarking at Queenstown. He informed him of how the fatal
passage had not escaped the *Examiner,* "a journal owned and controlled by Priests." He was, however, beyond being surprised or
disturbed by an "unprincipled Press." In the socialistic papers,
especially, he found calumnies abounding, "as a rank field in poison
mushrooms." Corrigan expressed his regret "that Y. E. has been
so badly repaid for your kindness towards me in Rome, and for
your efforts, (for which I am sincerely grateful) in the sacred
interests of Religion and legitimate authority" [185]

Preparations for the homecoming of the second cardinal of the
United States went forward under the direction of his secretary,
Father Foley, and Abbé Magnien. The latter reflected how cautious-
ness ruled when he told of their plans to give the reception "as canonical a character as possible." He feared a "wrong interpretation"
might be put on it if labor groups took part officially. They would
have other opportunities to show their gratitude.[186] Corrigan found
evidence of a spirit which would have worried Magnien, although
he had heard, too, that the "Flying colors" of Gibbons' departure
from Rome contrasted with the current "sadly demoralized condition" of the Knights.[187] The superintendent of the cemetery
rebels told the archbishop of the assessment of a dollar laid on the
50 or so Knights for a procession on June 18 in honor of McGlynn,
and beyond that, "they want a contribution of two dollars per capita
more, to charter a steamer and escort His Eminence to the Cathedral,
adding that I am to be thrust out of the See, and Dr. McGlynn
installed in the adjacent residence by the Cardinal as Vicar General
and Rector of the Cathedral." Although it is difficult to say who
was being fooled, Corrigan concluded, "So they delude and impose
on our poor people." [188]

Even on his leisurely journey home Cardinal Gibbons did not

[184] NYAA, Gibbons to Corrigan, Paris, April 30, 1887.
[185] BCA, 82-Q-5, Corrigan to Gibbons, New York, May 16, 1887.
[186] BCA, 82-Q-2, Magnien to Gibbons, Baltimore, May 14, 1887.
[187] NYAA, Healy to Corrigan, Portland, April 29, 1887.
[188] AAC, Corrigan to Elder, New York, June 2, 1887.

get out of touch with the case in Rome, nor did his agents cease
their work. Keane gave the Holy Office and the Propaganda French
translations of all the letters of endorsement of the memorial. A
large compilation of newspaper extracts, annotated in French, were
sent through Jacobini to Cardinal Monaco. After consultation with
O'Connell, Keane himself also gave Monaco the volume of the Rich
mond *Proceedings* of the Knights of Labor and the constitution
with the explanation that the former commented on the latter. The
sub-prefect of the Holy Office was further instructed that "these
though the *latest* documents, are not *final,* as the constitution thu
amended must be submitted to the local assemblies for adoption."
The American case seemed to rely on sheer bulk, for Keane re
marked, "They will be apt to see that the mass of English prin
is an elephant on their hands, and they will be very slow to touch
the matter again—Cardinal Monaco intimated as much." [189] Arch
bishop Williams of Boston had arrived in Rome and had been in
structed on how to follow up the various questions originally under
taken by Gibbons. He was in thorough agreement with the cardina
and although he only expressed his "strong views" when asked, i
O'Connell's opinion he did so "bravely and unhesitatingly." [19]
Referring to the triumvirate of the American hierarchy in Rom
through the spring of 1887, Williams had been told by Vladimi
Cardinal Czacki, a member of the Congregation of the Propaganda
that "the two bishops and the Cardinal made a very deep an
favorable impression." Further encouragement for Gibbons cam
in the Roman rector's view that the sad experience of nearly creatin
trouble, and the huge task of translation would discourage the Hol
Office from any reversion to a judgment of condemnation. H
impression of the whole affair was:

> the authorities of the Church have been drawn nearer the peop
> by the publication of that document, and the people too to th
> Church. All counter-representations amount to little since Card
> nal Manning has spoken so bravely. Representations may b
> made to show you have not much influence nor regard in th

---

[189] BCA, 82-Q-1, Keane to Gibbons, Rome, May 14, 1887. Concluding
postscript he said, "What splendid work Cardinal Manning has done for us."
[190] BCA, 82-V-4, O'Connell to Gibbons, Rome, June 24, 1887.

U. S., but that will be a personal concern aimed more against you than the cause.[191]

On arriving back in the United States at the beginning of June, 1887, Cardinal Gibbons hoped to remove the impression that had been fostered by some to the effect that he and the Archbishop of New York were personally at odds. This was alleged to have been his reason for going directly from the pier to the archiepiscopal residence when he landed in New York.[192] It was certainly true that events in Rome had shown their positions as agreed on the German question, in opposing a nuncio, and in strengthening the position of the bishop in relation to the parish priest. They had just as definitely been already revealed as on opposite sides about the university and the condemnation of George's book. On the Knights of Labor the lines had not been so clearly drawn and certainly it was Taschereau, not Corrigan, who led the opposition to Gibbons' position. No extant evidence has shown that Corrigan ever changed from the position he assumed in October, 1886, when he voted to let Rome decide the question. That he was definitely unfriendly to the Knights there can be no doubt, especially since they were inextricably tied up with his great cross, the McGlynn case. On this last problem, too, it would seem New York and Baltimore suffered the beginnings of a rift due to the way Gibbons was misrepresented, even though he tried to stay clear of being implicated. Just as their letters more frequently spoke of those subjects on which they were agreed, so must it have been at the cardinal's New York reception, for Corrigan wrote later, "He made no allusions to the Knights of Labor, directly, and I did not like to ask questions."[193]

The "few discursive remarks" the cardinal made on his return in his cathedral at Baltimore about his trip abroad contained a mention of labor only to praise the happy state of the American workers as compared to those in Europe. He concluded with a warning against anarchists and nihilists who would "pull down the fabric

[191] BCA, 82-Q-10, O'Connell to Gibbons, May 18, 1887.

[192] NYAA, John D. Keiley, Jr. to Corrigan, New York, June 1, 1887; also John Foley to Corrigan, Baltimore, May 31, 1887.

[193] AAC, Corrigan to Elder, New York, June 5, 1887.

of our constitution." [194]   Gibbons did not tell the faithful what had happened in Rome where affairs were now quiet, for even his adjutant, the Archbishop of Boston, had gone home and a harbinger of his greatest victory was on its way, "nothing would be done in the Knights of Labor question." [195]

[194] *Freeman's Journal,* June 18, 1887.   Ireland's sermon on his return advised the Knights of Labor to keep away censure thus: "In protecting their rights they must not infringe on the freedom of labor, they must not by force induce others to strike; they must not deny to others not members of their society the right to work." *Northwestern Chronicle,* May 19, 1887.

[195] BCA, 82-V-4, O'Connell to Gibbons, Rome, June 24, 1887.

VOL. XXI (March 23, 1887), 60-61

PUCK

CHAPTER VIII

THE REACTION IN THE UNITED STATES

EVEN as Cardinal Gibbons' Roman negotiations were being carried on in their favor and the restriction on Catholic members in Canada was being lifted, the Knights of Labor in the United States were losing ground. This fact has been attributed to the continuing hostility of organized employers and to the ineptitude of the leaders of the Knights themselves. The latter element was shown especially in the Chicago meatpackers' strike late in 1886 and early in the next year in the even greater fiasco on the New York waterfront under the direction of the District Assembly 49.[1] Beyond the rather improbable effect of the action of one priest in the Chicago strike no debilitating incident can be attributed to the influence of the Church. One may, perhaps, see the effects of closer contact with conservative ecclesiastics in Powderly's continued refusal to allow an official expression of sympathy for the condemned anarchists of the Haymarket trial and this did, in turn, alienate some elements of organized labor.[2] Moreover, the much discussed news, which in its truest and mildest form was that the Holy See was considering the arguments against condemnation as presented by Gibbons, certainly did not appreciably help the progress of the Order. On the contrary, the renewed arousing of the capitalist press against what looked like fresh strength for the Knights of Labor, the attacks on Powderly for "selling out" to Rome, and the general "religious firebrand" thereby thrown into the field of labor could not help weakening the organization. The publicity from Rome apparently did not even add to the Catholic membership, for they belonged to a predominantly urban religious group, and in the large cities the falling off of the Knights in the year ending July 1, 1887, was 191,000, or the approximate total of the loss throughout

---

[1] Commons, *History*, II, 420-422.
[2] David, *op. cit.*, p. 536.

the whole Order.[3]   It should be remembered that although the Catholic press had been uneven in its appraisal of the Knights, no paper had gone so far as to urge its readers to join the association.   One of the Catholic weeklies indicated the loss of one-third of the Knights of Labor membership since the Southwest strike and attributed it to the unwillingness of conservatives to remain in an organization controlled by radicals.[4]

Nonetheless, among the leaders of the Knights hopes had generally risen at Gibbons' efforts in their behalf.   Litchman thought the cardinal's stand would be good for the Order.[5]   Not unexpectedly, however, Joseph R. Buchanan proclaimed they were not concerned with Rome's position since it would have no practical effect on them.   Only about fifteen per cent of the Knights were Catholic, he said, and "most of these hold the opinion that the Church has no right to interfere in the matter." [6]   While on an organizing trip through the South Thomas O'Reilly sent Powderly congratulations saying, "The Cardinal has stood our brave friend to the end!" [7]   From Toronto came news of growing political strength, but on the ecclesiastical side there was only O'Donoghue's note of personal triumph, "Well, *you* beat Cardinal Taschereau!   How rarely a layman can say as much for himself." [8]   For a time at least Powderly, perhaps encouraged by local sentiment, felt a demonstration for Gibbons on his return might be in order and he sought the opinion of a non-Catholic brother on the matter.[9]   At least one assembly passed a vote of thanks to the churchman and sent it to the general master workman to forward to Baltimore if he saw fit.[10]

An event of the next month, however, was to indicate the growing discomfort that Powderly was to suffer from his identification

3 Commons, *History*, II, 422, 423.

4 *Connecticut Catholic*, June 4, 1887.

5 PP, Litchman to Powderly, Philadelphia, March 3, 1887.

6 St. Louis *Catholic World*, April 30, 1887. This paper called him "not only an ignorant, but an impertinent Catholic."

7 PP, O'Reilly to Powderly, Macon, Georgia, received March 7, 1887.

8 PP, O'Donough to Powderly, Toronto, April 17, 1887.

9 PP, Powderly to William Yuill, April 13, 1887, copy.

10 PP, G. H. Sturdwart [?] to Powderly, Jerseyville, Illinois, April 8, 1887.

with the Church.   In May, in response to many pleas, he undertook a trip to Denver, a center of opposition to his own leadership.[11]
On May 10 he lectured before a large crowd with the governor, the
mayor, and Bishop Joseph Macheboeuf on the platform.   He denied
he had "betrayed the secrets of my order when I held my interview
with Cardinal Gibbons and other dignitaries of my church. . . ."
At the same time he admitted having held a red card of the Socialist
Labor Party, but he said that had been merely out of friendship
for Philip Van Patten.[12]   It was much more unpleasant for the
general master workman the following evening, for then he faced
his enemies of District Assembly 89 in a secret meeting.   He was
asked to answer fifty questions on his activities of the previous year
which had been drawn up by Burnette G. Haskell and published
in the *Labor Enquirer* on May 7, 1887.   Powderly was accused, to
put it briefly, of attempting to lead the labor movement toward
"absolutism and imperialism."   It was several months after the
actual session that a report of his responses was sent abroad by
District Assembly 89 to all its own locals and to all the district
assemblies of the Order.[13]   It claimed the G. M. W. had been
responsible for the secrecy of the matter, and even then the
report noted that the answers contained therein should not be
publicized.   Although they carried a certificate of authenticity in
the form of ten signatures, these replies tended to show Powderly
at his worst.   The following October, at the general assembly in
Minneapolis, he protested that they "were forgeries in nearly every
instance." [14]   Several sections of this circular are of interest in
showing how the religious issue was to affect Powderly.   At the

[11] PP, Thomas Neasham to Powderly, Denver, January 10, February 28,
March 29, April 24, 1887. This knight represented the friendly D. A. 82.

[12] *John Swinton's Paper*, May 22, 1887. The *Colorado Catholic* was very
impressed with his public appearance and thought the whole community felt
the same, May 7, 14, 1887. The House of the Good Shepherd was to share in
the proceeds of the public meeting. April 30, 1887.

[13] Wisconsin State Historical Society, Manuscripts, Knights of Labor,
Circular of July 15, 1887, from District Assembly 89, Denver.

[14] *Proceedings* (Minneapolis, 1887), p. 1511. The questions were reprinted
therein (pp. 1506-1511) and Powderly offered to give the answers if the delegates desired it, p. 1506.

outset he denied the story of the influence of Father Flannigan in the meatpackers strike as "an absolute lie." [15]   His connections with the socialists were explained as nothing but the holding of an honorary card.   In Buchanan's comments, which were added to the document, it was retorted that he had paid dues for "more than two years." [16]   A later exchange brought Powderly's profession that he was not a socialist in the "red flag and dynamite" sense, and this led Buchanan to remark that some day he would "open up on this . . . in a way that will make *Rome* howl."

Several other queries touched on Church affairs.   When asked if he approved of the "Church's persecution" of Edward McGlynn, Powderly simply responded, "I believe Dr. McGlynn should have gone to Rome."   On the charge of revealing the "Secret Work" to Gibbons and promising any alterations desired by the Church, the head of the Order replied, "He never saw the secret work nor did I ever say anything of the kind to him."   The Denver knights went so far as to accuse Powderly of attending Mass on occasion three times a day, of confessing all their secrets to the priests, and of pledging to bind the Order to the will of the clergy.[17] Powderly's reply to this was stated to be: "It is an insult to ask such a question. . . ."   Haskell retorted, to the applause of the assembled brothers, that it was necessary for their own safety to know "how far your bigotry extends."   Powderly was pictured in this not unbiased account, as pausing and grasping his heart, and being rescued by the interruption of the friendly Thomas Neasham. The appended commentary to the Denver documents by Buchanan opined that Powderly lied about Church affairs since Gibbons could not have decided that there was nothing objectionable in the Knights of Labor unless he knew its inner workings from a consultation with him.   Actually, it has not been discovered that the cardinal knew any more of the Order's literature than the constitution, and even the *Adelphon Kruptos* is mentioned only in connection with the

[15] Circular, p. 3.

[16] *Ibid.*, pp. 14, 16. Buchanan's comments on Powderly's answers ran from p. 12 to p. 17.

[17] The *Catholic Universe* had seen the questions and wondered if the Denver group knew "a mass from an organ rehearsal." May 18, 1887.

meeting of the archbishops where John J. Williams of Boston read from it. This hectic secret session in Denver came to a close with Powderly's friends succeeding in the passage of a vote of confidence in him, although other resolutions opposing the *Labor Enquirer* and expressing confidence in the whole executive board were tabled.

Quite different in character was Powderly's reception in the city of Boston on June 11, where he undertook to expose once more his official relations with the Church. His purpose in all his moves had been, he said, not to use the Order in the interest of any organization but merely to clarify its make-up for leading churchmen, even as he claimed his predecessor, Uriah S. Stephens, had done. To a very friendly audience of about 400 which received him enthusiastically he said:

> Dishonest men have gone before priest, bishop, cardinal and minister and have said that our organization was not a lawful one, and I have had to follow after them to undo the villiany they have done. It has been said that the church turns her ear to the capitalist, and is indifferent to labor. My experience has taught me that it is not so.

He then waxed eloquent on the evils of drink and was described once again, undoubtedly for a different reason than in Denver, as clutching his breast and being unable to finish.[18] This was but one example of Powderly's forceful position on temperance, which helped to endear the labor leader to many clergymen.[19]

After these public testimonials to the compatibility of his religious loyalty with his labor activities, Powderly undertook to make a private gesture of gratitude toward Cardinal Gibbons. To this end Father Cornelius O'Leary again came into the picture. The Missouri pastor, who felt very friendly toward McGlynn and impatient toward many bishops for their ignorance, "not only of the social science, but even of theology and ecclesiastical history," had been compared by some to his eastern prototype and like McGlynn

---

[18] *Pilot*, June 18, 1887.

[19] Ware, *op. cit.*, p. 88, considers this perhaps his strongest conviction, and rabble-rousing his greatest strength.

he, too, had been suspended.[20]   Archbishop Kenrick allegedly took
this action because of O'Leary's adherence to the Knights of Labor,
especially in testifying before the Curtin Committee a year previously; and if he needed further reason there was the priest's charge
that his ecclesiastical superior's opposition to the Knights resulted
from the prelate's connection with Hoxie the railroad man.[21]   Powderly was aroused by the injustice which he maintained had been
practiced "for no other reason than because you practiced what you
preached."   He told the priest of the "growing feeling of unrest
and even contempt" among many Catholic laymen.   It was not reflected in any lessening of religious fervor, "but they do speak plainly
and boldly against the tyrannical edicts that are frequently sent out
against those among the clergy who are warmly welcomed among
the poorest of God's poor."   Obviously his sympathy was with Mc-
Glynn, although he considered his refusal to go to Rome a mistake.
Powderly's feelings in the O'Leary case were shown by the enclosure of a check for $400 as a "start" in paying a debt owed to
the priest for assistance to the striking railroad men the year before and by the vote of the executive board asking him to become
a contributor to the *Journal*.[22]

Father O'Leary and Powderly met at the Bingham House in
Philadelphia near the end of June and a few days later the former
went to Baltimore.[23]   He carried a letter of introduction and a
communication from the head of the Knights, "containing an earnest,
though somewhat tardy, expression of my personal gratitude for
the friendly attitude adopted by your Eminence while in Rome
toward the K. of L."   The general master workman wrote further
in this letter, "Words are inadequate to express our gratitude to
the good God in protecting you during your travels and in returning you once more to your faithful and loving people."   For the
most part, however, he presented a brief plea for Gibbons' "kind

[20] PP, O'Leary to Powderly, Webster Groves, January 23, 1887: "A
McGlynn Case in St. Louis," New York *Sun,* April 5, 1887.

[21] Chicago *Knights of Labor,* April 9, 1887.

[22] PP, Powderly to O'Leary, April 8, 1887, copy.

[23] Hayes was directed to secure hotel rooms for the two of them. PP,
Powderly to Hayes, June 25, 1887, copy.

intercession in behalf of the Reverend bearer of my letter." Although the priest would himself tell of his "persecution," Powderly pointed out his service to "the cause of law and order," and he took the blame on himself, "for the troubles which surround Father O'Leary," since the priest had entered the strike scene at his request. His final petition was rather indefinite, "I respectfully crave for him a hearing, and pray that Your Eminence will give him good cheer, and let not a true soul labor under a despondent heart." [24]   The extant ecclesiastical records do not reveal what Gibbons did, but since he was always wary of overstepping jurisdictional lines on his own initiative and had recently had such a sad experience with McGlynn, it is doubtful if he did more than to give O'Leary some good advice. At any rate, the next year the priest was back in a St. Louis parish after a trip to Ireland. He was still interested in labor, but confided to Powderly, "My friends here have corrected their errors and I forgive them." [25]

The expression of the indebtedness of the Knights of Labor which O'Leary carried to Cardinal Gibbons has remained unpublished since that time, either in the *Proceedings* of the general assembly or in the personal recollections of the leader of the Order.[26] Under the elaborate letterhead of the Knights it read:

Your Eminence:

It is nothing but diffidence in addressing you, that has so long prevented me from giving some expression of my deep appreciation of the great benefits you have conferred on our Order by your friendly presentation of its merits before the Roman Court and the world at large. I have especially been overwhelmed with a sense of profound gratitude for your kindly reference to my unworthy self. I cannot half express my thoughts and feelings on this subject.

Indeed we all felt that the order was in the safest hands when your Eminence undertook to be its champion, and our hearts— a million hearts, went out to you on reading your lucid and forcible report in which you stated our real aims and objects—the amelioration of the toiling masses and the building up of human society by fostering the reign of justice and humanity.

[24] BCA, 82-W-9, Powderly to Gibbons, Scranton, June 30, 1887.
[25] PP, O'Leary to Powderly, St. Louis, June 4, 1888.
[26] Cf. *Proceedings* (Minneapolis, 1887), pp. 1644-1648; *Path,* pp. 354-355.

God knows our sincerity in the work we have begun and that sinister motives or ulterior objects are foreign to us.

Your Eminence has placed us under many lasting obligations and let us hope that we will continue to merit your good will and favorable opinion as well as the toleration of our mother Church.

Pardon me if I presume to tell you how my heart swelled within me when I read the grand and lofty sentiments to which you gave utterance while abroad in reference to our Country and her institutions. The patriotic words you spoke have won, not alone for yourself, but for our Church, the respect and esteem of Protestant Americans everywhere. I who meet with so many men of all shades of religious and political belief bear cheerful testimony to the truth of the assertion that 'the defense of his country's institutions has won friends for his Church.'

With profound respect and esteem I am

Your most obedient servant,[27]

It is indicative of Powderly's future state of mind that this quite justifiable letter, which could be considered too obsequious only by those unfriendly to the Catholic Church, was not even mentioned in his autobiography published about thirty years later. It would even seem that he attempted to cover his tracks from the historian by removing his own copy and O'Leary's letter of introduction from his copybook.[28]

There was a further indication of approval of Gibbons, however from a higher quarter than Powderly's. President Grover Cleveland,

---

[27] BCA, 82-W-10, Powderly to Gibbons, Scranton, June 30, 1887. Part of the "patriotic words" spoken in Santa Maria in Trastevere were, "There are, indeed, grave social problems now employing the earnest attention of the citizens of the United States, but I have no doubt that, with God's blessing, these problems will be solved by the calm judgment and sound sense of the American people, without violence or revolution, or an injury to individual right." Will, *op. cit.*, I, 310.

[28] The index of Letterbook, April-August, 1887, shows on p. 5: "Gibbons, Cardinal James, Baltimore, Md. 179, 179½." Above these page numbers is written, "Between 178½ and 179 (3 pages)." Within the book are found p. 178, dated June 23, 1887 and then the next page is 181, dated July 31, 1887. Inside the front cover is noted, "Read to page 261—Dec. 9, 1919. T. V. P."

whose name the churchman had used to bolster his case in Rome, received a copy of the cardinal's "communication to the Holy See upon the subject of the Knights of Labor, which was forwarded to me by Colonel Keiley." In thanking him for the document the President expressed the desire to have the cardinal call at the White House while he was in Washington.[29] About a month later, in writing to the Rector of the American College from St. Mary's Seminary, Gibbons commented on what he feared would be the dire consequences of the McGlynn excommunication of the previous week, and he told O'Connell of his call on Cleveland:

> Yesterday I had a long and pleasant conversation with the President and his wife. While we were alone, he was quite communicative. He expressed his strong sympathy for me on account of the attacks on me by the New York *Times* made some months ago, and he declared them unwarranted and unjust. He is a candidate for a second term.[30]

Whether or not the two ecclesiastics suspected the President of mere political expediency, O'Connell used the incident for their cause by telling it to the Cardinal Prefect of Propaganda, who "laughed pleasantly at it." [31]

The Knights still meant work in Rome for Monsignor O'Connell. He was translating and handing in letters to Simeoni on the Knights of Labor, and also keeping in touch with official sentiment on the question. He reported further: "I heard some say that in view of the turn Dr. McGlynn's course took, the appearance of your [   ] about the Knights was a Providence. Some wish to say you changed after your return. It is very doubtful if any action will be taken on them. Boston corroborated your views." [32] In the United States, the Bishop of Cleveland for one was aware that the question was not yet solved. In commenting on the German issue and lamenting McGlynn's fate, he added his thanks to Gibbons, "for the results of

[29] BCA, 82-S-2, Cleveland to Gibbons, Washington, June 7, 1887. This John D. Keiley, a close friend of Gibbons, had been the cardinal's host in Brooklyn before his departure for Rome.

[30] ADR, Gibbons to O'Connell, Baltimore, July 15, 1887.

[31] BCA, 83-D-12, O'Connell to Gibbons, Rome, July 31, 1887.

[32] *Ibid.*

your efforts on the Knights of Labor question." [33] Gilmour was privately more friendly than his previous public statements would indicate, for in writing Elder about his hesitancy to condemn a secret society he observed:

> This network of societies that now covers the land forebodes no good and shows the feeling on the part of labor that capital is driving it to the wall.
> Labor has much on its side to complain of. The systematic combination of capital must be met by combination of labor, and the end is—riot, loss of life, and yet even these are sometimes necessary to cure evils.
> We have a difficult problem to deal with.[34]

Gilmour's further linking the Knights with the McGlynn case was in no way unique with him, or with gossiping Romans. The New York *Times* featured a story from Rome which had appeared in a London paper. The item remains otherwise unverified, but it was to the effect that the Pope thought Dr. McGlynn had missed his best opportunity "by not coming to Rome when Cardinal Gibbons was there." The paper snidely agreed "an infallible pontiff" could have done little against the priest and his "communistic theories" while the Church gave "the weight of its authority to the performance of the Knights of Labor." [35]

Yet the leader of the Knights did not support McGlynn at this time, and various groups within the Order were themselves divided on the support of this clerical advocate of the single tax. The radical *Labor Enquirer* attacked Powderly for not backing McGlynn while the *Examiner* took the advice of one of his circulars to the membership telling them not to neglect the land question as evidence of his sympathy with the George movement.[36] The general master workman, however, did not show his hand, and he refused to take part in the Union Square demonstration of June 18, "to protest against interference from abroad with the rights of American citizens as exemplified in the case of Rev. Edward McGlynn D.D." The

[33] BCA, 83-C-6, Gilmour to Elder, Cleveland, August 14, 1887.
[34] AAC, Gilmour to Elder, Cleveland, August 14, 1887.
[35] July 16, 1887.
[36] April 30, 1887: "Powderly's Sage Advice," *Examiner*, May 21, 1887.

demonstration had been arranged by a joint committee of the Central Labor Union, District Assembly 49 of the Knights of Labor, and a Catholic committee. Powderly noted on the invitation to speak, "No interference yet. Let him obey, and find out whether he has been interfered with as a priest of the church or as an American citizen." [37] Nonetheless, Archbishop Corrigan's scrapbook soon included the editorial item from the Philadelphia *Times,* which pointed out that a revolt against Church authority was being made under the banners of the Knights whom Gibbons had assured the Holy See were most obedient sons.[38] The suspended priest's lectures in Rochester and Lockport, New York, were sponsored by the Knights of Labor, although they were reported as very unsuccessful by Bishop McQuaid.[39] In planning a speaking trip to St. Louis for McGlynn the Knights there hoped to keep their connection with the tour quiet until it was over, while in Chicago his coming was unsuccessfully opposed by Catholic members of the Knights of Labor.[40] In Erie, Pennsylvania, Henry George, against the better judgment of many Catholics, was invited to speak, and the result was uproarious and harmful to the Knights when protests were made to his reference to the then excommunicated priest in his remarks.[41] The *Standard* reported several cases of county and local assemblies passing resolutions in favor of Dr. McGlynn, but at the same time the *Catholic News* was coming to the conclusion that the priest had ceased to be a picnic attraction for the Knights since Catholics would not attend if he were to speak.[42]

By July, 1887, two of the Catholic papers in New York which had been most active in confusing the two issues and in making Gibbons' action equivalent to a blessing, not only of the Knights but of the land movement, suffered crises. While the *Freeman's*

[37] PP, John McMackin to Powderly, New York, June 11, 1887.
[38] Corrigan Scrapbook, p. 94, Philadelphia *Times,* June 20, 1887.
[39] NYAA, McQuaid to Corrigan, Rochester, June 12, 1887; June 23, 1887.
[40] PP, S. M. Ryan to Powderly, St. Louis, May 31, 1887; *Michigan Catholic,* June 16, 1887, New York *Times,* June 26, 1887.
[41] PP, James N. Lanagan to Powderly, Erie, June 24, 1887; July 26, 1887. Corrigan Scrapbook, n. p., New York *Mail and Express,* July 14, 1887.
[42] *Standard,* July 9, 1887; *Catholic News,* July 17, 1887.

Journal gloated, the Brooklyn *Examiner* changed ownership and the *Catholic Herald* failed completely and discontinued publication.[43] About the only phase of the Knights of Labor on which all the Catholic press and the non-Catholic religious press really did continually agree was their advocacy of temperance.[44] The *Freeman's* took up another constant theme of the Knights when Egan lectured Powderly on the necessity of training in Christian morality in order to bring about an end to violence in the labor movement. Beyond that he persisted in showing the distinction between Gibbons' toleration and full approbation.[45] Even apart from its historical position Egan found it unnecessary for anyone to put the Church on the side of labor in the United States when, "its Bishops, its priests, the majority of its members come from the class which Our Lord most loved." With the accent on the Church's desire to protect the rights of the individual, he interpreted Gibbons' action as securing an extension of time within which the Knights might prove themselves. The editor judged: "His kindness has perhaps strengthened what is good in the order; as yet, however, it has not subdued what is bad." He suggested public opinion and the law as means of wiping out the abuses he recognized as "the oppression of capital and of unrestricted land-lordism." [46]

Like the New York editor, Cardinal Gibbons in responding to Powderly's letter of June 30, recognized imperfections in the Order, but unlike Egan he found some hope in the organization of workers. He wrote to the labor leader:

> My dear Sir:
> I thank you for your leter in which you are so [   ] in your expression of gratitude for my efforts while in Rome in behalf of the Knights of Labor and the cause of organized labor generally.

43 *Freeman's Journal*, July 2, 1887; *Catholic Record*, July 16, 1887; New York *Tribune*, July 6, 1887.

44 E.g., *Northwest Chronicle*, July 7, 1887.

45 Other evidence that there was a widespread notion that the Church had given its "seal of approval" is found in such items as an "Oration by Charles Halsey Moore of Plattsburgh, N. Y., delivered before the Knights of Labor of Saranac, N. Y., July 4, 1887" (19 pp.) p. 14. Widener Library, Harvard University.

46 *Freeman's Journal*, July 9, 1887.

In return I desire to acknowledge my grateful sense of all you have said and done in trying to purge the association from anarchy and all other dangerous affiliations. No effort should be spared to improve the society and to eliminate every objectional [*sic*] feature from it so that it may fully command the sympathy and respect of the Church and of all conscientious men.

I have watched the society with profound interest and not without some anxiety, fearing lest it might be made the tool of selfish and designing men, political demagogues, or that it might be degraded in countenancing anarchical and revolutionary sentiments. The enemies of the Order are always very industrious in commenting upon every disloyal sentiment or breach of law perpetrated by some of the members in the name of the order. I should rejoice exceedingly if you would continue to use all your efforts in abolishing or reducing to a minimum the number of strikes which paralyze labor and industry and nearly always result disastrously to the workman. My earnest desire in the interest of tranquility and of the workmen themselves is that the system of arbitration happily introduced into certain quarters, should be generally followed in settling the price of wages and in arranging the misunderstandings sometimes arising between the employer and the workmen.

God grant that your order may contribute to the material and moral well-being of the laboring classes who are so dear to my heart.[47]

The cardinal's recommendation and good wishes remained known apparently only to Powderly. On the other hand, within a week there appeared a public diagnosis of labor's crisis as seen by an outstanding Catholic observer, "Phineas," of the Boston *Pilot*. He saw the dark day for organized workers in the middle of 1887 to consist in the attempts to cause division along lines of religion. The charge was made, "There are labor papers published in nearly every city in the Union, and there are labor leaders in every locality who are preaching the doctrine of disunion and discord." "Phineas" argued that such men as these had been fooled by the favorable position of the Church on the Knights and so had attacked Powderly for his efforts toward peace with it. Likewise they sought to make

[47] BCA, 83-B-4, Gibbons to Powderly, Baltimore, July 9, 1887, copy. This is not found in the Powderly Papers nor in any published form.

more of the McGlynn affair than was warranted and to interfere between a priest and his superior. On this he commented:

> The labor movement is too large and too great to be tied to any man's coat-tail. The fact is these 'labor leaders' think less of advancing the labor movement than of breaking the power of the Catholic Church in America. . . . They will do the Church no harm but they are doing the labor movement incalculable injury.

This commentator blamed petty bigotry for the loss of support to the movement from other citizens as well as Catholics outside labor's own camp. Of the workers themselves, he wrote:

> There are tens of thousands of Catholics within the labor camp who have nobly borne their share of the trials and struggles of the past ten years. They have endured the black-list, faced starvation and were always ready to make sacrifices for the common cause. They have proven themselves good and faithful soldiers. Yet today these very men are staggering away from the ranks because of the foul attacks which have been made against their holy religion.[48]

This suggestion of a Catholic exodus may have been a bit exaggerated, but it was, indeed, true that the ranks of the Knights of Labor thinned out from the maximum of 700,000 members to 510,351 by July, 1887. The religious issue has not previously been considered as attributing to this decline, but without doubt it had an influence, although hardly the predominant one attributed to it by "Phineas." Part of the retrogression was the national falling off due to the fact that such numbers of unskilled workers had joined the Order in the troublesome days of 1886 that it was impossible to make them really organization-minded and to instruct them in the principles and procedures of the Knights. A more powerful cause, however, was the associations of employers which sought simply to eradicate the Knights of Labor, whose brief threat had alerted them. Consequently the method of arbitration, for which Cardinal Gibbons hoped, and of the trade agreement could not compete in popularity

[48] *Pilot,* July 16, 1887.

with the tried techniques of the blacklist, the iron-clad, and the Pinkerton labor specialists. The leaders of the Knights had shown faith in the trade agreement, however, and by 1887 there was an increase in its use; yet the general rule was still the lockout and the strike.[49]

Faced, then, with a crisis of this kind the Knights of Labor prepared for the eleventh regular session of the general assembly which was to be held in Minneapolis in the fall of 1887. There again the relations of the Order and the Catholic Church were to be aired, and for the first time within the organization in a formal way. Powderly took no chances but set the scene carefully. As early as July he expressed the desire that the assembly take action by "drawing up suitable resolutions expressive of our appreciation of the great service rendered the cause of labor by the Cardinal." [50] The action which did eventually result was the work of the general master workman and his assistant, in ecclesiastical matters, Thomas O'Reilly. The latter seemed sincere when a premature report of Roman endorsement on July 27 prompted him to credit it to "the earnest and intelligent advocacy of our cause by our good friend Cardinal Gibbons." He reminded Powderly of their obligation not "to falsify the excellent character given our organization by the American Prince of the Catholic Church."[51]

O'Reilly's sincerity, nevertheless, was not beyond some question. It is highly probable that at this time he undertook with Powderly to bring into being the committee which was to be represented as having called on Cardinal Gibbons in October, 1886. No doubt after some preliminary arrangements made personally or by non-extant correspondence, he wrote Powderly around August 15 about affixing the date of October 25, 1886, to a letter calling him to Baltimore.[52] Not satisfied with that he continued,

---

[49] Commons, *History*, II, 414-416. A French observer, E. Levasseur, thought Powderly's clerical connections had helped to weaken his influence. *The American Workman* (Baltimore, 1900), p. 202.

[50] PP, Powderly to Milt Hawkins, July 19, 1887, copy.

[51] PP, O'Reilly to Powderly, n.p., received July 28, 1887. Denials of the report followed quickly, e.g., *Catholic Review*, July 30; August 20, 1887.

[52] *Vide supra,* pp. 208-210.

The letter instructing me to proceed to Canada and see Cardinal Taschereau should be dated March 28th, 1887.

In the latter communication, instruct me to make a careful examination of the French edition of the constitution, and express the fear you entertain that some ill-advised sentiment has been introduced in the translation, provoking the present ecclesiastical hostility. Don't put these letters in your copying book. You understand.[53]

It is uncertain whether this device was intended to preserve a fairer reputation for themselves—which is unlikely—or to show a more ambitious and systematic handling of the Church problem than had actually been the case. Perhaps they hoped thereby likewise to bolster their right to spend more of the society's funds, but at any rate Powderly complied. Yet again, he made the mistake of leaving a copy in a letterbook.[54] This record tells of Canadian trouble when no other sources give even an inkling of it and, moreover, Powderly used an unnamed Quebec priest as his informant that the A. K. contained an oath, and the translation was also otherwise garbled so as to give the impression of a revolutionary society.[55] Thomas O'Reilly carried through his part of what now appears to have been a sham by answering in two letters which—with a thoroughness that was not characteristic—bore both an indication of place and dates. The former announced his start, and the second told of his return to New York on "April 10th" because of ill health. The fact that he had learned "on reliable authority" that all was quiet in Canada led him to suggest the suspension of the mission. This decision, supposedly made several months after

---

[53] PP, O'Reilly to Powderly, n.p., received August 15, 1887.

[54] However, it was in the letterbook, January-March, 1886, on p. 322. The original was in a batch of O'Reilly correspondence preserved as a unit within the Powderly Papers.

[55] The only other mention of complaint against the French version of any book of the Order was about the constitution and on linguistic grounds. It came from a Canadian local, and the G. M. W. gave permission to change it at their own expense, and observed that the Belgian Knights had no complaint. PP, George S. Warren to Powderly, Montreal, December 7, 1885, with Powderly's intended answer scribbled at the bottom.

Taschereau's widely-publicized retraction, made no mention of the Quebec cardinal's action.[56]

Shortly after dreaming up this French Canadian hostility Powderly found himself under brief but less imaginary fire from the organized German Catholics in the United States. In early September the German Roman Catholic Central-Verein met in convention at Chicago. Delegate George Mitsch of St. Paul introduced a resolution identifying the Knights of Labor with anarchists, socialists, and prohibitionists.[57] Powderly was quick to go to the defense of himself and to indicate not too subtly what he thought the heart of the difficulty was. "I am not an enemy of the Germans," he wired the convention, "and nothing in my career can be so construed unless my advice to all workingmen to be sober and temperate can bear that construction." [58] The press did not report a ready willingness to drop the resolution but, after Powderly's message arrived, it told of one delegate's wanting to rebuke him for even thinking the group would oppose the Knights.[59] Mitsch explained his position as amounting to hostility to anarchism and revolutionary socialism, and the president telegraphed an explanation to Powderly relating how promptly the measure had been tabled.[60] This action was in conformity with the general attitude expressed by the Hartford Catholic paper, which eulogized Powderly since, "not only the body of the Knights of Labor have confidence in his

[56] PP, O'Reilly correspondence, O'Reilly to Powderly, New York, "March 30, 1887"; "June 15, 1887."

[57] Sister Mary Liguori Brophy, *The Social Thought of the German Roman Catholic Central Verein* (Washington, 1941), pp. 72-73. The press, not always a reliable source, included another charge which is interesting in the light of the ecclesiastical trouble of Cahenslyism, "The Germans ought to consider it a disgrace to be ruled by Irish ignoramuses." New York *Sun*, September 6, 1887.

[58] PP, Powderly to President P. J. Spaunhorst, September 6, 1887. The Catholic paper of St. Paul defended Powderly and regretted the action of its native son, Mitsch. *Northwest Chronicle*, September 8, 1887.

[59] St. Louis *Republican*, September 6, 8, 1887, in Collection of Clippings relating to German Catholics in the United States, New York Public Library.

[60] PP, Spaunhorst to Powderly, Chicago, September 8, 1887.

integrity, but the public generally look upon him as an honest conscientious worker for the interest of the working man." [61]

While O'Reilly commended Powderly for this assiduity in watching the interests of the Order, he showed wisdom himself in guiding the Knights of Labor away from any public affiliation with the forces of Henry George lest they agitate the Church.[62] O'Reilly cited the example of Catholic indignation in Detroit because McGlynn had been invited to address another association there. In view of such a state of affairs he told his friend Powderly, "the Knights cannot very well identify themselves with the Doctor." [63] Hence he took steps with Powderly's strong backing to prevent what had been proposed, but which he knew would have "distressing results," namely, "the introduction of the Doctor or Mr. George to a Minneapolis gathering at the particular moment of the General Assembly meeting." [64] Furthermore, shortly after seeking a letter of introduction to the cardinal from the general master workman, O'Reilly was approached by the United Labor Party in New York to stump the state with McGlynn in preparation for the coming elections.[65] Although moving among the pro-George members of District Assembly 49, he refused the offer partly, at least in his own mind, because, "I could not accompany Dr. McGlynn and at the same time go and solicit a favor for the Order at the hands of his Eminence the Cardinal." [66]

What Powderly's "friend and confidential adviser" sought from the Archbishop of Baltimore, according to the letter he bore, was "an expression of your sentiments to be read before our convention

---

[61] *Connecticut Catholic,* August 27, 1887.

[62] PP, O'Reilly to Powderly, n.p., received September 9, 1887.

[63] *Ibid.,* received August 15, 1887.

[64] *Ibid.,* August 16, 1887. Powderly to P. J. McGaughey, August 15, 1887. The G. M. W. arguing for "harmonious relations between the Church and the order," asked, "Can we act honestly in disciplining a refractory Assembly or District Assembly and at the same time honor a man who, no matter how much good he has done in the past, now stands before the American people as the apostle of disobedience to his superiors?"

[65] *Ibid.,* New York, received August 29, 1887; n.p., received September 11, 1887.

[66] *Ibid.,* n.p., received September 13, 1887.

in October." [67] Several days before his visit to the prelate O'Reilly had finished his own report for the convention on "The Order and the Church," which he offered to read to Powderly and John Hayes, the two other members of the reported ecclesiastical committee.[68] The Baltimore meeting took place on September 20 and O'Reilly fretted for several days about whether the requested letter had been sent to Powderly.[69] Although he felt he had "made sure when with him, that he wd not forget it," yet he was relieved to hear of its arrival.[70] Gibbons was actually very prompt in replying to their petition, and it would seem he had been shrewdly advised of the public use to which his answer was to be put. His letter made no allusion to O'Reilly's special mission, although in fact he spoke of the coming convention as being on the fifth of the next month and this he had learned only *viva voce*. This statement, with its plea for conservatism and especially its insistence on the inter-dependency of capital and labor, foreshadowed many an official Catholic utterance in the years ahead. The cardinal's true copy read:

My dear Sir:
    Your letter was received yesterday informing me that the next convention of the K. of L. was to be held at Minneapolis on the 5th prox. When absent from America, I did not hesitate to advocate the just rights of the laboring classes, and to point out the wrongs they were suffering. Now that I am again at home, I may be permitted to speak, in a friendly spirit of the duties and responsibilities which they owe to themselves, to their country and to society. I entertain the hope that good counsels will prevail in your deliberations, and that a calm conservative spirit will control all your proceedings. It is self evident that there should be no conflict between Capital and Labor, since both are necessary for the commonweal, and one cannot subsist without the other, and, therefore, no measures should be countenanced which do not provide for the protection of both.

[67] BCA, 83-M-10, Powderly to Gibbons, Scranton, September, September 12, 1887. The cardinal noted on it, "Convention meets at Minneapolis Tuesday Oct. 5, 87."

[68] PP, O'Reilly to Powderly, n.p., received September 19, 1887.

[69] *Ibid.*, n.p., n.d. (Friday); n.p., September 27, 1887 (Sunday).

[70] *Ibid.*, n.p., n.d. (Tuesday).

Experience has proved that strikes are a questionable remedy for the redress of your grievances. They paralyze industry; they often foment fierce passions, and lead to the destruction of property; and above all they result in inflicting serious injury on the laborer himself by keeping him in enforced idleness during which his mind is clouded by discontent while brooding over the situation, and his family not unfrequently suffers from the want of even the necessaries of life. Strikes therefore, should be rarely if ever resorted to. Boycotting, as far as I understand its methods, infringes on the just rights of others, and will therefore never meet with approval from an observing public.[71]

Remember that the eyes of our countrymen are upon you, and that they will watch your proceedings with the deepest interest. As a law-abiding and industrious body seeking by honorable means, to improve your conditions, you owe it to yourselves, and to the good name of your order to set your face against Anarchists, Nihilists and other dangerous associations, which are guilty of the base ingratitude of attempting to undermine the Government that protects them, and the Temple of the Constitution that shelters them. Do not permit your reputation to be tainted by any morbid sympathy for men who have not substantial grievance to redress, and who strive to make their cause respectable by obtaining the connivance, if not the sanction of your powerful organization.[72] But, for my part, I have no fear that they will succeed in infusing the leaven of their poison into the ranks of the honest sons of toil: 'For what concord hath Christ with Belial, or what participation hath justice with injustice, or what fellowship hath light with darkness?' My only

---

[71] This was stronger than later moral theologians were to hold on boycotting, when proportionately grave reasons existed. (Cf. John A. Ryan, "Moral Aspects of Labour Unions," *Catholic Encyclopedia*, VIII [New York, 1910], 726-727.) At this point in the text a sentence was added by the cardinal's hand in pencil with no indication of the time when it was done or whether it was in the letter sent to Powderly. It read, "A non-union man should be free to enter, or not. He should not be persecuted if he refuses to enter." This is the only difference from the published version, *Proceedings* (Minneapolis, 1887), p. 1647. Commons, *History*, II, 416, points out that the trade agreements of that day "included no closed shop provision."

[72] Whether Gibbons had the Chicago anarchists in mind or not, it was Powderly's argument at the convention of 1887 that the Order as such should show them no sign of sympathy, and this view won out, although at Richmond in 1886 they had passed a resolution asking mercy. David, *op. cit.*, pp. 413-418.

motive in offering these suggestions is my sincere affection for the laboring classes, whose sterling virtue I admire; my sense of the dignity of their calling and of their influence in the future well being of our country, as well as my ardent desire for their material and moral elevation. God grant that your deliberations may be marked by a wisdom and discretion and a spirit of true patriotism which seeking to advance your temporal interest, will merit the approval of heaven as well as of your fellow citizens.

Permit me in conclusion to express my appreciation of the successful efforts you have personally made in fulfilling the delicate and arduous duties which have devolved upon you as President of the Knights of Labor.[73]

Powderly's duties at Minneapolis in October, if not arduous, were at least fulfilled in a long-winded way. Against his enemies such as Thomas B. Barry, a member of the executive board, he gave in his report a review of his part in the Chicago strike replete with documents. Of interest for its ecclesiastical aspects was his argument:

> The charge that I was acting under church influence was circulated by no friend of the Order and is without shadow of foundation. When I heard of it I did not reply to the very courteous and well intentioned dispatch from Father Flanagan. I made up my mind not to place him in the position of interfering in the matter, although I believed, and still believe, that he described the actual situation in his dispatch. For those who set in circulation the rumor that he was using the power of the church to influence me I have no reply.[74]

He reviewed, too, his connections with anarchists and his relations with the clique in New York known as the Home Club. In doing so he denied the truth of the answers supposedly given by him to his Denver interrogators, and explained that he had gone to New York to give his support to George, not because of the club, but to fulfill a promise made to O'Reilly and James Archibald at Richmond. Further irritants to the radical element came in the refusal to seat Joseph R. Buchanan and to vote a petition of clemency for

---

[73] BCA, 83-N-10, Gibbons to Powderly, Baltimore, September 21, 1887, copy.

[74] *Proceedings* (Minneapolis, 1887), p. 1496.

the convicted Chicago anarchists.[75]   Moreover, Powderly reminded
the gathering that it amounted to a "constitutional convention"
able to change the laws in any way, and he indicated, "There are
many things in the constitution which, to my mind, should be
changed." [76] The report of General Secretary Litchman, however,
on the acceptance of the revised constitution, effective July 11,
1887, showed no indication that anything had been done which
could be attributed to ecclesiastical pressure.[77] The major change,
in which the future shape of organized labor was predicted, was
the strengthening of the position of the national trade assemblies
of the Knights of Labor, wherein the locals of bookbinders, hatters,
plumbers, etc. were organized pretty much along regular trade union
lines.[78]

At the afternoon session on October 6, after submitting his annual
report, the general master workman made his official public gesture
on the question of the Church and the Order. He asked for consideration, in executive session, of a special "report in manuscript"
on the matter. This represented that the ecclesiastical authorities
had been bombarded with the charges of the Order's enemies about
the pernicious and revolutionary character of the Knights of Labor.
The synopsis of what the labor leaders said during the interview at
Baltimore was presented in the report after it told of Powderly's
invitation from the cardinal and the supposed selection of O'Reilly
and Hayes to accompany him. The substance of the "official" version
of what Gibbons responded has been seen.[79] The rest of O'Reilly's
report contained an unique version of Gibbons' memorial, plus the
letter of Cardinal Manning's assent, and in the printed form only,
Gibbons' letter of September 21 to Powderly. The Roman document,
although given as a direct quotation, included only a paraphrase
of the first part which related the society's lack of hostility to religion
and to the state. In this reproduction of the memorial explanations

[75] *Ibid.*, pp. 1511, 1525.

[76] *Ibid.*, pp. 1538-1539.

[77] *Ibid.*, cf. pp. 1780-1783; the position on land in the preamble remained
the same, p. 1782; pp. 1789-1790.

[78] *Ibid.*, pp. 1555, 1864-1865; Commons, *History*, II, 498-499.

[79] *Vide supra*, pp. 213-214.

were said to have been made to the archbishops by the "principal
officers," and the promise of such modifications of anything offensive
to the Church had been given not only by Powderly but also "their
most zealous officers." This was an exaggeration of the phrase of
the "official" episcopal text, "he and several of the principal members, devout Catholics." [80] Such things as might have proven em-
barrassing were omitted, even though found in the well known
Moniteur edition. Hence the fact that although the archbishops
were opposed to a sanction on it, they yet found in the Order "things
that we would not approve," and also Powderly's declaration of
his devout Catholicism were passed over in silence.[81] Without any
indication of elision, this report at Minneapolis went immediately
to the better known eight-point version of the conclusion in which
it did not seem to be worthwhile to eliminate the reference to the
"transient form" of the Knights.[82]

The comment was interspersed before Cardinal Manning's letter
that after this "forcible plea" the Holy See's bearing was now
"friendly and conciliating," for Leo XIII had "wisely determined
not to provoke an antagonism between the church and the mighty
industrial power that is now making itself felt throughout this free
land of ours." [83] The private copy of the document contrasted the
Archbishop of Quebec with the Pope who had been neither "rash
nor illiberal." It said further, "we regret exceedingly that Cardinal
Taschereau did not see the question of the Knights of Labor from
a universal standpoint, but only from a very restricted space around
his eyeglass, which did not reach beyond Canada." [84] Although
O'Reilly's manuscript did not contain it, the document in the *Proceedings* over Powderly's name showed the insertion of Gibbons'
letter of September 21 with no indication that it had been solicited
by the G. M. W. The conclusion read:

[80] Gibbons, *Retrospect,* I, 193.

[81] *Ibid.,* I, 192-193.

[82] *Proceedings* (Minneapolis, 1887), p. 1646. Some months later when
reading the printed minutes Robert Layton expressed disbelief that Gibbons
had put "the points" in that way, "as it implies endorsement of the Order
through fear." PP, Layton to Powderly, Pittsburgh, April 19, 1888.

[83] Manuscript, p. 12; Printed, p. 1646.

[84] Manuscript, p. 12.

There is no reason to fear that the Order, as an association will falsify the good character given it by the American prince of the Church. Our organization is entirely free from the elements of sectarian, religious or irreligious discussion, and its fundamentals are of a kind to guard it against disturbing influences outside of the sphere for which it was created.[85]

The general assembly came back into regular session and voted approval of Powderly's action with regard to the Catholic Church as he had related it. Furthermore, on Litchman's move Powderly was instructed to prepare for publication in "the revised Proceedings" whatever part of it "as in his judgment he deemed proper." [86] The difference between the manuscript and printed form of the above document may, therefore, amount to what Powderly wished to remain for all the members and posterity to read, rather than a mere pruning off of what he judged it were better not even to present orally to the delegates, because it was either too obsequious or too harsh on churchmen.

In an interview given to the Catholic paper of St. Paul, Powderly showed a tendency to tone down the influence of Catholicism. He was reported as saying he did not think the Knights would avoid trouble with the Church solely because so many of the members were Catholics. That end would be attained, he alleged, rather because "the vast majority of the members, Catholics and Protestants, are very conservative in their views, and are sternly opposed to the introduction of any element of disorder, or of any of the wild theories of anarchists and so called socialists, into the Order." He explained the last expression by answering, "I and the majority of the Knights are socialists in the proper sense of the term." More pleasant and less mystifying to readers among his coreligionists must have been his affirmation that his convictions on temperance grew ever stronger and that there was no danger of radicals taking control.[87]

85 Manuscript, p. 14; Printed, p. 1648.

86 *Proceedings* (Minneapolis, 1887), p. 1644.

87 *Northwestern Chronicle,* October 6, 1887. This article included a description of the "uncrowned king." Cf. also Ware, *op. cit.,* p. 83, quoting Swinton's description of October 17, 1886, which emphasized that he looked more like a poet than a leader of "horny-fisted sons of toil."

The head of the Knights was not, however, left at peace by such members and within a week battle was joined on the floor of the Minneapolis meeting hall. The *Proceedings* themselves are rather non-committal as to the details of the controversy. On the morning of Saturday, October 15, Brother Barry undertook "to severely criticize the actions of his colleagues· upon the General Executive Board, as well as those of the General Secretary." The time for debate was extended, and the afternoon was given over to answers from the accused parties. The session ended with Powderly's disputing the position of Barry, and explaining "the reasons for actions taken during the year." William H. Bailey took up the cudgels on the following Monday, and Litchman answered.[88] Powderly later asserted that the two of them were simply bringing out into the open the fight they had lost at the July meeting of the executive board when Powderly's use of O'Reilly had been approved against Bailey's protest that the money to pay him had been "misappropriated."[89] The burden of Bailey's barrage at Minneapolis was given in the press as an attack on the "political plotting" of the head officials of the Order. He accused Powderly of an alliance with "the Church of Rome" as shown by his "employing men to work for Church interests without the knowledge and sanction of the other officers of the order and paying them out of the funds of the order." One Catholic paper which carried this story attributed the enmity among the delegates to their presiding officers willingness to take advice from Cardinal Gibbons.[90] Powderly put it on the basis of his opposition to anarchist influence in the Order.[91] That afternoon the general assembly voted to ask for the resignations of the general officers of the Knights of Labor, and all but Barry and Bailey complied. For a while the regular order of business was resumed, and then the delegates returned to the more lively question. They sustained Powderly, not only by refusing to accept his resignation, but by endorsing his action during the year,

[88] *Proceedings* (Minneapolis, 1887), p. 1787.
[89] PP, Powderly to Thomas McQuade, November 24, 1887, copy.
[90] *Michigan Catholic*, October 20, 1887.
[91] Powderly, *Thirty Years*, p. 646. This book was written during the year 1888.

including his "securing the services of Thomas O'Reilly in service of a secret character." They considered "his action in this matter far-seeing and wise and the money expended well used." Even beyond that they refused to hear of his reimbursing the Knights of Labor as he had offered to do.[92]

After leaving Minneapolis the re-elected general master workman was unapologetic for what, as he put it, he was "as proud of as any work of my life." In an effort to spike rumors Powderly claimed he had already spent $216 of his own money for the expenses of his agents for ecclesiastical business that he could not tend to personally.[93] There was no evidence found to establish the reliability of this statement, any more than for the one that was circulated in the Order that he had used $3,700 of the Knights' money for bribes and presents in order to win the favor of Catholic churchmen.[94] To Powderly's mind the whole upheaval had a simple explanation:

> These men oppose me because they could not lead. And in the hope of enlisting the sympathy of Protestants and non-believers attacked my position on the church question, and discovered their mistake when too late. I am too well fortified and too practical a Catholic to allow any mistakes or blunders to show on the surface as a result of my work in that direction. Patrick Ford is not the only one who swings his anchor on the church question. I am glad I never had to do so. I have always been too steadfast in my observance of the rules of 'Mother Church' to allow myself to drift for one moment away from her influence Cum grano salis [The last phrase looks like an addition of a later date.] [95]

Terence V. Powderly was also a name synonymous with devotedness to the Church according to the Catholic press in the fall of 1887. His gesture toward Gibbons further helped his cause in those circles. Even before the convention in Minneapolis he was defended as having no part in any new "Knownothingism" and a

92 *Proceedings* (Minneapolis, 1887), pp. 1787-1789, 1791.

93 PP, Powderly to McQuade, November 24, 1887.

94 PP, Powderly to D. W. Daley, November 27, 1887.

95 PP, Powderly to F. W. Jackson, Philadelphia, November 5, 1887.

being invaluable to the Knights of Labor.[96] The Detroit paper went on record to the effect "On the whole we think he is a Godsend to the labor movement." [97] An earlier editorial—unlike the *Pilot* a few months before—considered the Church's stand on the recent social trouble as one of the reasons for the lessening of prejudice which had been exemplified by Gibbons' reception at the celebration marking the centennial of the Constitution in Philadelphia the previous week.[98] Powderly's influence, according to the St. Paul newspaper was due to the fact that he was "a docile and filial son" of the Church, which was the great friend of the workingman, and Ireland's weekly did not hesitate to recommend reforms especially with regard to the boycott and the sympathetic strike.[99] Some of the Catholic papers which took notice of the Knights' convention pointed out how any growth in radical tendencies would weaken the Order before the public.[100] Even stronger than others was the sentiment of the *Freeman's Journal* which had faith in but one social remedy put forth by Powderly, namely, his temperance principles. Egan showed that unlike the medieval guilds in modern organization, "the employers are either left out or they will not go in." He concluded on a half truth, "While the employers hold aloof, while the power of corporations is practically unlimited by honest legislation, while rents are increased and wages decreased by outrageous taxation, labor reformers waste their breath." [101] With obvious approval the document submitted to the general assembly was brought to the attention of the Catholics of Baltimore, Philadelphia, and St. Louis.[102] In New York the *Catholic Review* advised the Order that it held its future in its own hands, but much more enthusiastic was the *Irish World*.[103] To Patrick Ford the action taken at Minneapolis made doubly clear the position of the hierarchy, and with an eye on the McGlynn trouble he considered

[96] *Church News*, September 11, 1887; *Catholic News*, September 11, 1887.
[97] *Michigan Catholic*, October 6, 1887.
[98] September 22, 1887.
[99] *Northwestern Chronicle*, October 6, 1887.
[100] *Catholic Knight*, October 8, 1887.
[101] October 15, 1887.
[102] *Catholic Mirror, Catholic Standard, Catholic World*, October 15, 1887.
[103] *Catholic Review*, October 22, 1887.

it inconsistent and ungrateful, "to magnify a local grievance into an excuse for attacking the Church in the name of labor." With not quite as much penetration he foresaw the Order's going on to future success.[104] The Pittsburgh *Catholic* at least felt sure that the Knights of Labor would now avoid anarchist principles. It thought it an honor to the Church to have within its membership men found on the side of labor, like Gibbons and Powderly, and also Michael Davitt, who had addressed the G. A. In concluding it said:

> We must be a great people when the humblest and poorest of us are more anxious than the rich and learned to preserve the government and the laws of God, even in the moment when we suffer from the heartlessness of men who know no God but mammon and self.[105]

While the Catholic press and the Church in general found in the action of Cardinal Gibbons a certain amount of agreement and a point of departure for differences of opinion, American Protestant reaction to the Knights of Labor had no basic position. Some of the trimmings of fraternal and semi-secret lodges may have abetted the feeling among Protestant leaders that the society was providing a substitute for church-going.[106] In fact, blindfolding and regalia and funeral ceremonies were not as universally outlawed as the Order's laws required.[107]   Robert Layton, however, attributed the falling off in the proper execution of "our sign manual" to the Catholic element which had no contact with secret brotherhoods. Among his Masonic friends he had heard comments on the slovenly way of conducting "the floor work of an A." In his suggestion was found an unconscious tribute to a Catholic contribution to American unionism. He said, "Intelligent instructions only will prevent a session from degenerating into a common trade-union or worse."[108]   The book for such a meeting, namely, the *Adelphon Kruptos,* and the "Secret

104 *Irish World,* October 15, 1887.

105 October 22, 1887.

106 Macdonald, *op. cit.,* p. 209.

107 PP, Powderly to H. O. Watrous, March 15, 1887, copy; Patrick Rooney to Powderly, Newcomb, Tennessee, September 7, 1887.

108 PP, Layton to Powderly, Sewickley, Pennsylvania, April 22, 1888.

Work" were, according to a decision of the general assembly, permitted to be shown to the authorities of the Swedish churches opposing the Order in Rockford, Illinois.[109]

Less official recognition was given to other examples of the Protestant attitude toward the Knights. It is hardly possible to say here how Protestants divided on the question or how many ministers supported the Knights. It is true some of the non-Catholic clergy entered the Knights of Labor and even contributed to the leadership on the lower levels.[110] On the other hand, in some of their organized expressions Protestants were not so quickly found on the side of the Knights of Labor. The *Wesleyan Methodist*, for example, was credited with calling labor unions, "the dark dens of secret demonism." [111] The Missouri Synod of the Lutheran Church had a committee work over the problem for a year. Its report favored the ends or purposes of the Knights of Labor, but on the means employed, especially the boycott and the conduct of strikes, it demurred and so the synod issued a warning against joining the Order.[112] Powderly expressed an awareness of this difficulty as the only "fight with a church of any kind" that engaged their attention, but he hoped for an early settlement.[113] A Catholic paper found fault with a group of Congregationalists in Chicago for giving an extreme picture of the demands of the working class and indicated that it thought its proposal of accomplishing social reform through a Sunday school program rather long-ranged.[114] In Dubuque, Iowa, it was said that only through the "unwitting instrumentality" of the Universalist Church did a lecturer who was also a knight find sponsorship.[115]

But on the American religious scene by the latter part of 1887 it was again the Catholic Church which was most intimately involved in the labor question. This was particularly true because

---

[109] *Proceedings* (Minneapolis, 1887), p. 1220.

[110] E.g., T. S. Epps to Powderly, Scottsburg, Virginia, April 1, 1887.

[111] *Enquirer*, January 1, 1887.

[112] *John Swinton's Paper*, May 22, 1887.

[113] PP, Powderly to Thomas McQuade, November 24, 1887, copy.

[114] *Western Catholic*, October 22, 1887.

[115] PP, Pamphlet, James K. Applebee, "The Labor Problem and Its Solution," (November 12, 1887).

of labor's political activity in the State of New York. Out of George's mayoralty campaign of 1886 had come the United Labor Party, but its unity was not to last long since the increasing emphasis on its land platform, to the neglect of labor reform, led to the alienation of the socialists and the tension resulted in the latter's rejection at the Syracuse convention in August, 1887.[116] Meanwhile Dr. McGlynn continued as an active force for Georgism in Archbishop Corrigan's territory, especially through the Anti-Poverty Society of which he was president. This means of popularizing the cause had been set up in March, and the society began to hold public meetings by May, 1887. Apart from his regular Sunday evening addresses, which were long and spell-binding, McGlynn was asked amid much ecclesiastical furor to address the Ancient Order of Hibernians in Brooklyn, where the Reverend Sylvester Malone was his chief lieutenant.[117] McGlynn did not fail to remind the Ancient Order of Hibernians of the suspicion churchmen had had of them. He also ridiculed how "some small narrow, bigoted, antiquated ecclesiastics in the city of Rome" had thought that in place of the Knights of Labor there should be "the holy guild of shoemakers" or "the sanctified confraternity of stone cutters." [118] As the election campaign continued, the press in general opposed those running for state officers on George's ticket, and, while one paper thought the excommunicated priest a liability to the party, another believed his lost allegiance would indicate to the Church how the laity would decide, if they must choose between membership in the Knights and good standing in their religion.[119] Indeed, among McGlynn's supporters the Knights of Labor were one of the predominant elements, for they not only turned out for his as well as for George's speeches, but they often arranged the meetings and had official representatives on the same platforms.[120] Hence in

---

[116] Commons, *History*, II, 454-460.

[117] Bell, *op. cit.*, pp. 161-162. Within the year even Powderly could write to Michael Davitt, ". . . Anti-Popery is what it ought to be called. I don't think McGlynn is all there." April 6, 1888.

[118] *Standard*, September 3, 1887.

[119] Corrigan Scrapbook, p. 137, New York *Daily Tribune*, August 9, 1887; p. 222, *Times*, September 11, 1887.

[120] New York *Herald*, October 1, 1887; *Standard*, October 15, 22, 29, 1887.

Rochester Bishop McQuaid took the pulpit against the wayward cleric and the party he supported.[121]

At this time, in Powderly's phrase, Patrick Ford "swung his anchor" and announced his split with George, not only because of disagreement on the single-tax doctrine and on free trade, but chiefly because of George's war on the Catholic Church. As one who wished well to the labor movement and to the Church he felt he could finally speak out. He said, therefore, "Dr. McGlynn's terrible resolution escorted by an equally terrible temper has landed him outside the pale of the Church. All controversy therefore is at an end, and with it the utility of further silence is also ended." [122] Again editorially he pointed out how the Labor Party had been demoralized by the introduction of the religious issue. Then after quoting Gibbons in contrast to the very first editorial ever to appear in George's *Standard,* which foresaw no help from the Church, Ford included also quotations from Henry Ward Beecher, the recently deceased popular Protestant preacher who had been so admired by McGlynn. The first was from Beecher's "Bread and water sermon" of July 28, 1877, in which he maintained a dollar a day was enough for any worker, and the other was from an address of February 4, 1887, referring to the Knights of Labor as an "abomination." [123]

Among vocal Catholic laymen, on the other hand, Thomas Preston remained strongly behind George and wrote for the *Standard* before the election to explain, "Archbishop Corrigan's Mistake." He told the prelate again that he and Monsignor Preston ("who is undoubtedly the chief adviser of the archbishop and the real head of the diocese") that they had missed the point by giving George's books to theologians who could find and condemn statements out of context, some of which "might be interpreted as tending to deny the right of individual possession of land." He used once more the McGlynn reference in the Roman memorial of February 20, 1887, as an indication of how correct Gibbons' ap-

[121] Zwierlein, *op. cit.,* III, 45-46.

[122] *Irish World,* October 22, 1887.

[123] November 5, 1887.

proach had been. Preston predicted no trouble from the Church, as such, but from individual churchmen like his uncle, yes, and he added, "The memory of the events of the past year will be likely to bring a sore feeling to the hearts of Catholics for many generations." [124] The vicar general did not miss these words of his "self-willed nephew" and he told Corrigan of his grief especially, "for his insulting words of you." [125]

The month of November saw two signs of victory for the conservative forces in the United States, one the defeat of Henry George's political hopes in New York and the other the hanging of the four men convicted for the Haymarket killings in Chicago. Only the former aroused any sense of satisfaction among some Catholic observers. The Catholic press rather considered the executed anarchists victims of a misplaced zeal for their fellowmen.[126] Powderly, however, confessed that as a result of the execution he had "never felt so stirred before," but this feeling of the mercurial labor leader soon ceased when his erstwhile friend, Joe Labadie, spread the report that the general master workman was responsible for the hangings.[127] He confided to Hayes at the same time that he was glad he had not gone to New York to talk for Henry George since he "fell so flat." The "war on the Church" and the consequent opposition of the *Irish World* were generally given much credit for George's defeat.[128] The result was considered important enough by Archbishop Corrigan's friend, Bernard N. Farren, to warrant a speedy letter of congratulations from abroad, and even Archbishop Ireland mentioned in passing how he rejoiced at the "political over-

---

124 *Standard,* November 5, 1887.

125 NYAA, Preston to Corrigan, New York, November 4, 1887.

126 *Catholic News,* November 16, 1887, called it a "pitiful spectacle." Also *Irish World,* November 19. The *Pilot* said, "Of their moral guilt there is no doubt. Of their personal responsibility for the awful Haymarket tragedy there is less certainty. Of their sincerity there is no question whatever." November 19, 1887.

127 Hayes Papers, Powderly to Hayes, Scranton, November 12, 1887 and PP, Powderly to Emma Fichenscher, n.p., November 23, 1887.

128 *Irish World,* November 19, 1887.

throw of George and his friends." [129] A short time later the Bishop of Rochester expressed his pleasure to his metropolitan thus:

> How does his Eminence feel now about his pets, the Knights of Labor?
>
> They are evidently breaking to pieces and are getting many more kicks than kisses. . . . For the countenance his Eminence gave them, he will have to suffer. He exceeded his instruction and must bear his burden.[130]

Corrigan's reaction, rather contrariwise, was to mention to McQuaid the anxiety about the Order reported by Cardinal Taschereau. Since many Catholics had taken advantage of the Holy See's permission and joined the Knights of Labor its dangers were becoming more apparent. Taschereau had, moreover, lately received "the complaints of several capitalists," and he feared his worst forebodings would be realized.[131] The year 1887 thus ended with Quebec and New York seeing eye to eye, but within the jurisdiction of Corrigan two important papers were still able to disagree. The *Freeman's* decried the sad results of the Philadelphia and Reading Railroad strike and persisted in arguing that the Holy Father had not *approved* the Knights of Labor,[132] while Ford's paper publicized Leo XIII's jubilee by praising his "sort of tacit approval" of the Order.[133]

In one way the Catholic friends of the Knights were to do them a disservice in stressing papal friendliness even while a definite answer was awaited from Rome. McGlynn caused a temporary flurry of excitement by attacking Powderly in his Anti-Poverty Society speech, "The Church and the Labor Movement," for sending an ambassador to the Vatican on Knights of Labor funds.[134]

---

[129] NYAA, B. N. Farren to Corrigan, Paris, November 10, 1887; John Ireland, St. Paul, November 12, 1887, said further, "Their defeat will be their death knell: anything seeming like victory would have given them fresh courage."

[130] NYAA, McQuaid to Corrigan, Rochester, December 28, 1887.

[131] NYAA, Taschereau to Corrigan, Quebec, December 23, 1887; RDA, Corrigan to McQuaid, New York, December 29, 1887.

[132] December 31, 1887.

[133] *Irish World*, December 31, 1887.

[134] The full text is in the *Standard*, February 4, 1888.

The doctor's flippancy went beyond the picturing of a democratic Pope in a stove pipe hat walking down Broadway, to a suggestion of bribery in Rome.[135] Powderly was angered and rushed to telegraph a brief denial to the *Herald* and a longer accusation of slander to the *World*.[136] His emotional reaction was expressed to O'Reilly:

> Is there an honest impulse in the Dr. or has he thrown off all semblance of the gentleman as well as priest. I now regard McGlynn as a villain and liar of the worst type. He is acting at the dictation of George in this slander and I do not intend to deal out any mercy when the time comes, the infamous rascal.[137]

The *Herald* followed up with a retort from McGlynn, while the *World* thought McGlynn sadly imposed upon.[138] The latter paper found the priest too vague about naming the so-called papal emissary and it, therefore, concluded, "Judgment for Powderly." [139] The labor leader considered his accuser a "damn lier" [*sic*] and threatened to "open on him with a vengeance if he don't let up for he himself offered to go to Cardinal Gibbons for me if I desired it." [140] When O'Reilly admitted to the press that he had worked in the United States to fend off Rome's condemnation, McGlynn took that as a justification of his position.[141] Henry George meanwhile considered Powderly's Church contacts of small concern, in comparison with his pussy-footing about the land problem.[142]

The general master workman apparently could not resist the temptation to be humorous over the whole situation. Part of his remarks, however, seem to have been given a serious coloring since they resembled some of the popular anti-Powderly charges made

135 New York *World,* January 30, 1888.

136 PP, Powderly to New York *Herald,* January 30, 1888; to J. T. McKechnie, January 30, 1888, copies.

137 PP, Powderly to O'Reilly, January 30, 1888, copy.

138 January 31, 1888.

139 *World,* February 1, 1888.

140 Hayes Papers, Powderly to Hayes, Scranton, January 31, 1888.

141 PP, Powderly to O'Reilly, January 31, 1888; *Standard,* February 11, 1888.

142 *Standard,* February 11, 1888, in a signed editorial.

by bigots at a later day. In a variation on the theme of several letters, he wrote:

> I will never forgive McGlynn, he gave the whole thing away on me. If he kept still I would have secured the Vatican for a headquarters of the K. of L. Now my little game is up and we wont get a chance to 'wade knee deep in the carpets' at the Vatican. Now that it is all over I will let you into the secret; in consideration of the valuable concession which the Pope was to make in giving up the lease of the Vatican to me, I had agreed to make Leo, Master Workman of the Italian District Assembly. Of course the honor which I conferred on the old 'bag of bones' tickled him to death and he at once asked me who I would select to take Taschereau's place over in Quebec; I promptly said 'Tom O'Reilly.' . . .[143]

The more serious defense which he made of himself revealed not only the fact that the Canadians had failed years before in trying to get him to go to Rome, but also the new claim that he had "sent a messenger on two occasions to Canada" to study the Church's attitude at an expense to himself of $198.[144] Powderly began to gather material for what he thought might be another public altercation with McGlynn, but then he decided to treat him, "as the Irishman served the woodpecker—let him alone and he will knock his own brains out." [145]

Yet in Church circles the leader of the Knights could not be completely disassociated from the head of the Anti-Poverty Society. An interview was published in the New York *World* of March 25, 1888, purporting to be the opinion of Monsignor Preston, that Catholics were forbidden to attend McGlynn meetings, but since his break with George the Church had no theological quarrel with the land doctrine. Powderly, it also maintained, had fallen in the

---

[143] PP, Powderly to O'Reilly, February 14, 1888; also to David Healy, February 7; to Miss A. A. Wright, February 9, 1888, copies.

[144] PP, Powderly to John J. Johnson, March 1, 1888, copy.

[145] PP, Powderly to Messrs. Handy and Mahony, January 30, March 6, 1888, copy. He procured a copy of an article by McGlynn which would have been very appropriate: "The Bugbear of Vaticanism," *American Catholic Quarterly Review,* I (January, 1876), 73-99. It was a review of Gladstone's pamphlet on the decrees of the Vatican Council.

Church's eyes since he had not carried out the promises to Gibbons to submit the constitution for ecclesiastical approval and, therefore, the Knights of Labor was still under ban as a secret society.[146] In the New York papers the next day the archbishop and his vicar general denied ever having issued such a statement.[147] Powderly remarked, "Aint the *World* and Corrigan having lots of fun. More power to them." [148] The Archbishop of Baltimore, informed of the New York ruse by one of the staff of the *Catholic Mirror,* expressed his regrets to Corrigan that the culprit, Hugh P. McElrone, who was formerly with the Baltimore paper and whom Gibbons had recommended to him, should have abused his confidence and kindness.[149] Corrigan, in turn, explained this false newspaper report to Bishop Healy of Portland, Maine, who regretted that the retraction had not been spread as widely by the press associations as the original "forgery." [150] Healy's low opinion of Powderly and the value of his word or promise had not changed, yet he felt that any attempt to enforce a hostile Roman decree would mean, "the wave that we have either helped to swell or allowed to swell into monstrous size will sweep away thousands of souls." His viewpoint remained unaltered, "Temporising has its comforts but in the long run, it seldom pays." [151] This case of newspaper sensationalism gave occasion again for Cardinal Taschereau likewise to show his immutable views. His inquiry about the foundation of the rumor of Roman condemnation was addressed to Gibbons, and though he pointed out the Order had become quieter and more weakened in numbers, he hoped there would be an eventual "opening of the eyes of our poor workers." [152]

The general master workman congratulated himself on not having "gone off half cocked," by sending to the press the answer

[146] Also in the Philadelphia *Press,* March 25, 1888, Collection of Newspaper Clippings relating to the situation of the Roman Catholic Church in America, New York Public Library, I.

[147] *World,* March 26; *Herald,* March 26, 1888.

[148] Hayes Papers, Powderly to Hayes, Scranton, March 27, 1888.

[149] NYAA, Gibbons to Corrigan, Baltimore, March 27, 1888.

[150] NYAA, Healy to Corrigan, Portland, March 30, 1888.

[151] *Ibid.,* March 27, 1888.

[152] BCA, 84-H-8, Taschereau to Gibbons, Quebec, April 9, 1888.

which he had already drawn up.[153] O'Reilly assured him that he would have caught any such statement since he suspected the veracity of the bogus interview written by a "religious hypocrite." [154] Powderly did undertake to write an explanation to one mid-western brother who had sent on a clipping of the story. His answer read:

> At any rate, brother Bannan, if I have not kept my promise with the Cardinal, neither Monsignor Preston or Archbishop Corrigan has any right to say anything about it. I made no promise to the Cardinal that I would not make to a clergyman of any other denomination and I have faithfully kept my word as well as my pledge of Knighthood. So far as my failing in the estimation of the church is concerned, that is not the question for either Monsignor Preston or any one else to discuss in public. I never posed as a Saint and not yet a devil, but if I keep my vow as a Knight of Labor and do my duty to my fellow-men as nearly in accord with the golden rule as possible, I will take my chances in the next world with the rest of the lambs and goats.[155]

Powderly and the Knights of Labor, however, still had to face the judgments of churchmen in this world since Rome's definitive answer was yet to come. While there were some signs of a more friendly relationship between the Church and organized labor, Bishop Gilmour saw in the strikes and the popularity of George's

153 PP, Powderly to O'Reilly, April 12, 1888, copy.

154 PP, O'Reilly to Powderly, n.p., April 5, 1888.

155 PP, Powderly to J. M. Bannan, April 7, 1888. Cf. *Path,* pp. 354-355. This is Powderly's account of a betrayal of confidence by Corrigan who, it was said, gave the New York *Sun* the story that Powderly had promised Gibbons he would change the constitution to suit the Church. Powderly and Gibbons, at a meeting "early in 1887"—the former maintained—had agreed to secrecy about the labor leader's proposal to submit suggested constitutional changes to the Minneapolis convention of the G. A. Corrigan's distorted version must, therefore, have been a betrayal of Gibbons' trust in him, Powderly reasoned. Shortly after this event a purported violent session with the Archbishop of New York was held, which was recorded in *Path,* pp. 356-359. The incident of the alleged Preston interview in the *World* of March, 1888, is the closest thing to what the autobiography contains. Gibbons returned from Europe only in June, 1887, and the files of the *Sun* from June to December, 1887, did not disclose anything of Corrigan's alleged action, nor is there any indication in his records that he ever met Powderly personally.

theories, "ominous risings of the poor for bread and butter," and an indication of a revolutionary current.[156] It was something new, nevertheless, to have Bishop John J. Kain make an anonymous donation to the fund for striking miners and for Bishop William O'Hara to invite Powderly to the laying of the cornerstone of St. Thomas College in Scranton.[157] Although Powderly ignored his own bishop, he did not remain unmoved by reports from the old trouble spot, Schuylkill County. This time it was Father Peter C. McEnroe, of Mahanoy City, who was reported to be opposing the work of a woman organizer for the Knights of Labor, Mrs. L. M. Barry, with such ungentlemanly epithets as "Lady Tramp." [158] It was still true that priests followed no standard pattern of social thought and had no norms to guide them, so that one in Pennsylvania opposed a lecturer as anti-religious, while a priest in the Dakotas was very pleased with the same man.[159]

By the spring of 1888 the Congregation of the Holy Office had been considering for a year the American presentation of the problem of the Knights of Labor. As the importance of the Order declined in the United States, there was not so much interest as formerly in the Church's attitude toward them. Nonetheless, Rome's final decision and the aftermath of the question were to be of immense importance for the whole Catholic Church as well as for the American labor movement.

[156] NYAA, Gilmour to Corrigan, Cleveland, February 28, 1888.

[157] PP, Powderly to Kain, March 14, 1888, copy; O'Hara to Powderly, Scranton, August 6, 1888, stamped, "No answer required."

[158] PP, Powderly to Julie A. Coyle, February 27, 1888; to Mrs. L. M. Barry, February 27, March 23, 29, 1888, copies.

[159] PP, Powderly to J. J. Dunn, March 26; to R. W. Haire, March 27, 1888, copies.

VOL. XXI (April 13, 1887), 114-115

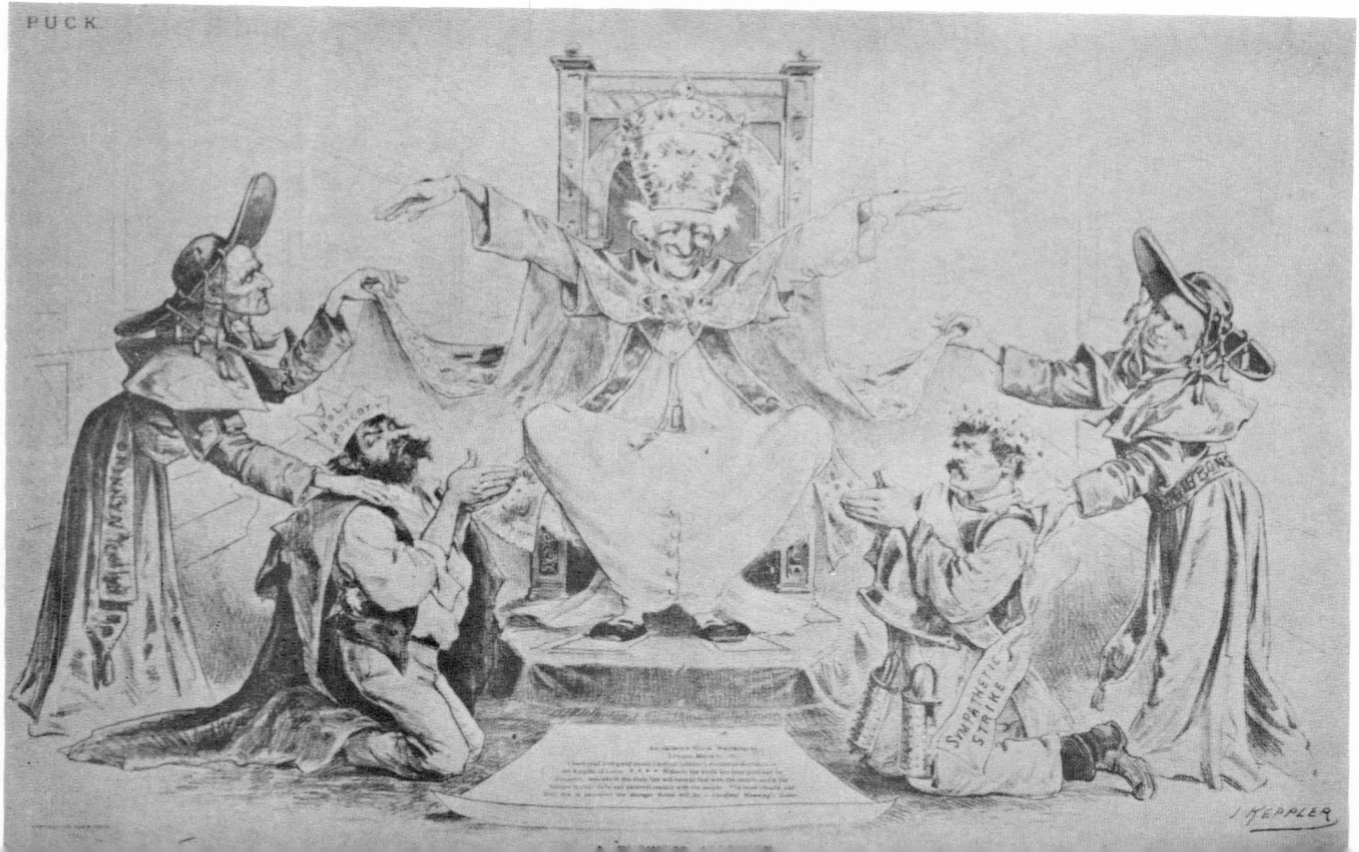

CHAPTER IX

AFTERMATH

As the Catholic hierarchy of the United States had been brought face to face in a forceful way with the question of the Knights of Labor so, too, in other countries the Church had become increasingly aware of the problem of labor. As a matter of fact, European Catholics had already taken up the challenge of applying their moral principles to the mal-functionings of modern society. In France and Germany especially the Catholic social movement had been growing for decades and by the end of the 1880's it was ready to receive the crowning endorsement of its efforts in a papal pronouncement. The Knights of Labor and the Henry George issues were the two American contributions toward hastening that action. They did this, not so much by giving Pope Leo XIII a precedent in Catholic social thought, as by pointing up the urgent necessity for an authoritative statement of principles. Thus the final decision on the American workers' organization was a part of a broad panorama of events within the Church which led to *Rerum Novarum* in 1891.

With their own increased advertence to social problems during the years of the 1880's American Catholics also became attuned to the rumblings of social Catholicism in Europe. The Knights of Labor agitation in the United States led the Catholic press to note such things as a letter of Leo XIII to the Hungarian bishops telling them of the need of the application of the gospel precepts to prevent socialism.[1] Especially popular copy for Catholic editors was the recurring rumor that the Pontiff was preparing a new encyclical, and one paper went so far as to predict, "He will treat concisely of special problems distinguishing good and lawful from unChristian combinations." [2] A good part of the religious press reprinted a story from Rome in the Liverpool *Catholic Times* to the effect that

---

[1] *Catholic Standard,* September 25, 1886.
[2] *Catholic Telegraph,* March 10, 1887.

Pope Leo would naturally be influenced in such a document by his consultation with the American prelates, especially Gibbons and Ireland.[3] As might be expected, apart from the Catholic German language papers which naturally carried current news of the homeland, the Catholic social movement in the German Empire was not noticeably publicized in the Church papers of the United States. Such men as Adolphe Kolping (1813-1865) had built up strong Catholic associations of workingmen, but more for mutual charity and moral well-being than for economic reform.[4] More important was the nobleman and bishop, Wilhelm Emmanuel von Ketteler, who was not without predecessors as a Christian social philosopher but who was the first among modern German prelates, "to leave the purely theoretical field to attempt something practical." [5] He died in 1877, but the annual national Catholic congresses on social problems continued. The one held at Breslau in 1886 was made known among American Catholics, for their press contained the address of Franz Hitze, a member of the German Reichstag, who was a moving spirit behind worker societies and who had long sought for the alleviation of labor's ills through legislation.[6]

It was through Cardinal Gibbons, however, that the American Church had its closest contacts with the social Catholicism of the continent. This came about as a result of his trip to Rome in the early months of 1887. In Italy he became friendly with Eduardo Soderini who, although not a leading light such as his fellow-Italian layman, Guiseppe Toniolo, was very close to Pope Leo XIII and vitally aware of the new role which the Church was called on to play in the world.[7] Before Gibbons' return to Baltimore he visited

[3] E.g., St. Louis *Catholic World*, April 23, 1887.

[4] Robert Kothen, *La pensée et l'action sociales des catholiques (1789-1944)* (Louvain, 1945), pp. 195-200.

[5] William E. Hogan, *The Development of Bishop Wilhelm Emmanuel von Ketteler's Interpretation of the Social Problem* (Washington, 1946), p. 105.

[6] E.g., *Northwestern Chronicle*, November 24, 1886.

[7] BCA, 84-P-13, Soderini to Gibbons, Rome, June 20, 1888. Of Toniolo it has been said, "A close friend of Leo XIII, Toniolo was consulted, as an economic expert more than once by him on the eve of the promulgation of the Encyclical *Rerum Novarum*." H. L. Hughes, *The Catholic Revival in Italy, 1815-1915* (London, 1935), pp. 76-77.

France and while there the cardinal met with those who carried on the tradition of such men as Vicomte Alban de Villeneuve-Bargemont, who in an earlier period had accepted the new liberty as compatible with the Church and her mission.[8] In this sense they were liberal Catholics, and not because of any agreement with the classic economists who held that there was no place for the intervention of moral considerations in economic and political life.[9] The outstanding men of this group in late nineteenth-century France were Léon Harmel, René de la Tour du Pin, and Albert de Mun, whose ideas of social reform are said to have been related to Ketteler's by way of Baron Charles von Vogelzang, the Christian Democratic leader in Austria.[10] When Gibbons visited Harmel's model factory, "conducted on strictly Christian lines," in Val des Bois, his host was the Archbishop of Rheims, Benoît Cardinal Langenieux, with whom he had received the red hat. Comte de Mun, founder of the Cercles catholiques d'ouvriers, was also present to assist in explaining the various workers' clubs, co-operatives, and pious associations which had made the mill a master pattern for about fifty other French firms. Gibbons, it was duly reported, was deeply impressed.[11] Archbishop Ireland not only told of the "enthusiastic cheering" of the workers for Gibbons on this visit, but he went so far as to report from the pulpit of his cathedral that Gibbons had found de Mun's associations the ideal of what he would like to see established in the United States.[12] If the Archbishop of Baltimore expressed such sentiments—possibly he did so out of politeness—he never showed any sign of inaugurating such a work at home. Only one Catholic paper seems ever to have proposed that he undertake with the rest of the hierarchy to set up under their supervision "trades guilds" on the European Catholic model.[13] Yet Gibbons must have been influenced by what he witnessed and learned in

---

[8] Cf. Sister Mary Ignatius Ring, *Villeneuve-Bargemont, Precursor of Modern Social Catholicism, 1784-1850* (Milwaukee, 1935).

[9] Kothen, *op. cit.*, pp. 156-157.

[10] *Ibid.*, p. 213.

[11] *Catholic Review*, June 25, 1887.

[12] *Northwestern Chronicle*, May 19, 1887.

[13] Troy *Catholic Weekly*, June 4, 1887.

the chapel-equipped factory, for after his return from one of the most memorable trips of his crowded life he characterized his visit to the French factory as "among the most precious memories of my voyage."[14]

Yet due probably to the great differences of their respective environments the two neophyte cardinals, of Baltimore and Rheims, maintained only a brief correspondence on social affairs. Langenieux told Gibbons of two outstanding events in the European movement, but only after saying how they had "partaken of the joys of the triumph which was tended you on your return from Rome, not only by Catholics, but by all the American people." He mentioned the Congrès de oeuvres sociales held at Liége in Belgium under Bishop Victor Doutreloux, only to remark that the mention of the name of Gibbons had brought a unanimous applause from an audience that was somewhat international in character.[15] Langenieux himself at this time was about to undertake a pilgrimage, a peculiarly French manifestation of the loyalty of the workers to the Holy See, in its unhappy position vis-à-vis the Italian government. The expected 1,500 pilgrims with whom he was to make a pilgrimage in a few weeks did go to Rome and received the papal blessing and admonitions.[16] The Archbishop of Rheims did not stint in praising his American colleague in the College of Cardinals. He said of Gibbons' efforts in "the great cause of the workers,"

> What an honor it is for the Church which finds itself so officially and publicly become again the protectress of the humble and the poor, of those above all whom modern industry has thrown so cruelly into wretchedness through the excesses of

14 BCA, 83-U-3, Gibbons to Langenieux, December 3, 1887, Baltimore, copy.

15 The American Catholic press did not know as much but they featured the congress and the letter of approval from Leo XIII as further evidence that the Church was "friend, counsellor and guide to the laboring classes." *Catholic News*, September 4, 1887; also *Northwestern Chronicle*, September 22, 1887.

16 *Catholic News*, October 23, 1887. The reply of the Pope to a similar pilgrimage of workers the following year has been called, "the prelude of the Encyclical *Rerum Novarum*." Edouard Lecanuet, *Les premières années du pontificat de Léon XIII, 1878-1894* (Paris, 1931), p. 450.

its prosperity. The Holy See, it is said, should soon give us an instruction which will be the guide for all, but Your Eminence will have been on the attack at the first hour and your word is a preparation for that of the Supreme Pontiff.[17]

The Baltimore cardinal was touched by this approbation—as well as thankful to his brother of Rheims for the champagne that had accompanied it. In solving the labor question on Christian lines, he pointed out in response, "our union will be our strength and the teachings of Leo XIII will become our light." The common aim of all was "to maintain or to revive the former Christian spirit of our workers, and through them to bring society back to those principles of order and Christian liberty which the Church has always taught and which her influence alone can reestablish in the world." [18]

Gibbons' contacts, however, with the outstanding proponent of social Catholicism in the English-speaking world had already moved beyond the stage of mere mutual respect and exchange of generalities into the field of practical issues. Just as he had called on Cardinal Manning for aid in the case of the Knights of Labor, so did he turn to him again in 1888 when the closely related issue of Henry George's writings was raised in Rome for the second time. As Gibbons put it: "Your Eminence's Knightly help to me last year prompts me to call on you again." [19] The Corrigan forces were once more bringing pressure to bear to have the works of George put on the *Index of Prohibited Books*. The American cardinal considered the move highly inexpedient since the waning popularity of George's *Progress and Poverty* would thus be revived, George himself would be given new prominence, Protestants would be excited against their Catholic neighbors, and bigots would hail it as a new example of the Church's opposition to free discussion. Moreover, he told Manning, who was a member of the Congregation of the Index, that the errors in the book had been "amply refuted by able theo-

[17] BCA, 83-N-9, Langenieux to Gibbons, Rheims, September 21, 1887.

[18] BCA, 83-U-3, Gibbons to Langenieux, Baltimore, December 23, 1887, copy.

[19] Gibbons to Manning, Baltimore, March 23, 1888, quoted in Leslie, *op. cit.*, p. 365.

logians." [20]   It was two months later that Gibbons thanked the
English cardinal for the reassurance that George's writings would not
be prohibited.[21]

In the meanwhile the Archbishop of Baltimore had not been
idle, but with the help of John Ireland and Denis O'Connell he
had drawn up an array of American bishops who were urged to
present to Rome opinions confirmatory of his own on the George
question.[22] For the first time the hierarchy showed interest in having
the Supreme Pontiff clarify the issues involved and thus they were
in effect petitioning for what finally appeared as the encyclical,
"On the Condition of Labor." Even McQuaid, who was poles
removed from Gibbons' position, had an "impression" that the Pope
would "settle George's theories" by covering in his next encyclical,
"the whole doctrine of property as to the right of ownership." [23]
Gibbons, however, went so far as to ask for such a papal statement:
"Instead of a condemnation—I wd recommend an Encyclical from
the Holy Father on the social question of the day. . . . If your
Grace entertains these views as I believe you do, I hope you will
espouse them strongly and speedily to the Holy See." [24] Besides
Archbishop Ryan, to whom Gibbons had written, another bishop
who favored dropping the George matter was Camillus P. Maes of
Covington, who had been in communication with Bishop Keane of
Richmond. Keane strongly sided with Gibbons, and he left Maes
with the notion that Baltimore had been consulted by Rome "on
the propriety of acting upon our suggestion of a condemnation of
general propositions." [25]

Although the original of this collective opinion of some of the
bishops of the Province of Cincinnati, which Maes called "our
suggestion," was not found, it apparently was not inconsistent with

[20] *Ibid.*

[21] *Ibid.,* May 23, 1888.

[22] BCA, 84-F-11, Ireland to Gibbons, St. Paul, March 26, 1888.

[23] McQuaid to Corrigan, Rochester, January 14, 1888, quoted in Zwierlein, *op. cit.,* III, 58.

[24] BCA, 84-H-2, Gibbons to Ryan, Baltimore, April 3, 1888.

[25] AAC, Maes to Elder, Covington, April 13, 1888. Keane had adduced
the additional reason that a condemnation "might have a baneful effect on
Catholic workingmen."

the cardinal's approach. Their ideas were contained in what Elder later referred to as his original "letter of last December (16th I think) to Cardinal Simeoni on the same subject." [26] Gilmour, as an individual, also co-operated with Gibbons, saying the George issue was dead and "the Knights of Labor are breaking up." To presume to speak on account of the Catholic membership in these social movements, the Bishop of Cleveland thought, was to act like a prelate trying to stop a riot. Such a man would be branding most of the rioters as Catholics—or else he had no business there. He thought, "We had better not exaggerate either our influence or feed the idea that Catholics are the only persons who need regulating." [27] Obviously unaware of or forgetting the previous action of Elder, Gilmour somewhat hesitantly suggested to his metropolitan that he should also write to Rome to avoid letting the Church appear hostile to the workers, whose bitterness might turn them against it. This "siding with wealth" had wrought havoc formerly in France, Spain, and Mexico, he claimed, and "now in Italy." He was not enjoying ease of mind on the Church in the United States either, for he went on to say:

> Here in America we are drifting with a large, large [sic] stream into the ranks of wealth, and when we speak it is timidly in the face of capital. Seldom is there a word for the poor, and when we have outbursts and bishops appear there is no word against the cause which called forth the outburst, but an appeal for peace—Such the whole field looks to me. Now to condemn George's book will be turned to look as if the Church sided with capital and was against labor. Besides, it is a purely economic question, and to me it looks as by far best to let it alone.[28]

Elder did not question the reason put forth by Gilmour for letting well enough alone, but he was quick to respond that he had not noticed any trend toward powerful wealth on the part of the Church in the United States. He assured his suffragan of Cleveland, too, that he had already requested "the true doctrine set forth by authority,

[26] ADR, Elder to O'Connell, Hot Springs, North Carolina, April 26, 1888.
[27] BCA, 84-I-7, Gilmour to Gibbons, Cleveland, April 16, 1888. He may have had Bishop Tuigg's experience of 1877 in Pittsburgh in mind.
[28] AAC, Gilmour to Elder, Cleveland, April 17, 1888.

in sound forms of words, which we could all use with confidence in our instruction to the people." [29]

As middleman in Rome, O'Connell received the reports of many American bishops and in all it was later said that twenty-three had protested the threatening condemnation.[30] Some, the monsignor thought, resented any atempt to take action on the George question without consulting them. Nevertheless, he felt there was not so much difference of opinion that all could not agree on "an expression of Catholic doctrine without any allusion to George." So sure was O'Connell of success that he considered the only point to be settled was whether it would be wise to have the pronouncement made before or after the presidential election in the United States.[31] Elder was likewise asked by Gibbons to write his opinion a second time and to send it through O'Connell for presentation to the Holy See. This he did while the two archbishops were enjoying a holiday together. Elder felt his letter had the general backing of all his suffragans, except possibly the three with whom he had not had occasion to confer, namely, Bishops Watterson of Columbus, Richter of Grand Rapids, and Borgess of Detroit. On this occasion the Archbishop of Cincinnati made the most explicit statement of the kind of elucidation that most of the American hierarchy desired from Pope Leo XIII on the social question:

> It is desirable to have a clear statement of Catholic doctrine on all these questions of rights and duties in regard to property— labor—wages etc. Many Catholics do not know what to believe. Some have correct opinions but not certain convictions; and some who know what is right, yet hesitate to condemn opposite errors, as long as the Church has not spoken distinctly. But such exposition of doctrine ought to embrace the various questions —of property—real and personal—labor-wages etc.; and only treat George's particular notion as an incidental part and without reference to his name or his book.
>
> Moreover, it ought to be carefully noticed that there are errors on both sides. Property owners and employers have false notions

[29] ADC, Elder to Gilmour, Cincinnati, April 20, 1888.

[30] McQuaid to Gilmour, Rochester, January 22, 1890, quoted in Zwierlein, *op. cit.*, III, 66.

[31] AAC, O'Connell to Elder, Rome, April 19, 1888.

about their rights and many have *no notions* about their duties. And indeed the very root of these difficulties out of which the dissatisfaction and extravagance of the poorer classes grow is the unchristian spirit of the rich. Their errors may perhaps be summed up in the axiom: 'A man has a right to do what he likes with his own,' and 'Every man has a right to get the highest price; and pay the lowest price he can.' [32]

But Elder was far from alone in supporting Gibbons. Denis O'Connell preserved the records of such unexpansive endorsements of the cardinal's arguments as those of Archbishop Michael Heiss of Milwaukee and Bishop Francis Janssens of Natchez, the latter to become in a few months Archbishop of New Orleans.[33] The Baltimore suffragans, Henry P. Northrup of Charleston and Leo Haid, O.S.B., Vicar Apostolic of North Carolina, penned their agreement with their metropolitan.[34] More outspoken than these was Bishop Kain of Wheeling who expressed his fear that the few bishops who favored George's condemnation were,

actuated too much by local considerations and that unconsciously perhaps they are narrowing their views on this subject to the horizon of their own immediate surroundings, instead of extending them so as to embrace the best interest of the entire Church of America for the future as well as the present.[35]

The folly of condemnation was re-echoed from Omaha where Bishop O'Connor found socialism's only danger to lie in exciting urban labor troubles. His sympathies seem to have been revealed when he pointed out that even this possibility was lessened since big business was uniting against labor, and "when American capitalists combine to accomplish anything that touched their pockets, they are pretty

[32] ADR, Elder to O'Connell, Hot Springs, April 26, 1888. He cut himself off with the remark, "But I am getting into a dissertation."

[33] ADR, Heiss to Gibbons, Milwaukee, May 6, 1888; Janssens to O'Connell, Richmond, April 30, 1888. He said, "independently of his [Gibbons'] request I fully share his views on this question."

[34] ADR, Haid to Gibbons, n. p., April 30, 1888; Northrup to Gibbons, Charleston, May 11, 1888.

[35] ADR, Kain to O'Connell, Wheeling, April 23, 1888.

sure to succeed." [36]   As might have been expected, it was Archbishop Ireland more than any other who backed Gibbons strongly in this episode. He not only wrote in "strongest language" for Roman eyes in the *Moniteur,* but he sent an emphatic note of congratulations to "our friend," the newly-named Prefect of the Congregation of the Index, Placide Schiaffino. Of him he said, "I have confidence in Cardinal Schiaffino." [37]

This campaign under the leadership of Gibbons met with at least temporary success since nothing was forthcoming from Rome about George. The first inkling, however, that the Holy See had not forgotten or had not been completely overwhelmed by documentary material on the Knights of Labor did leak out.[38] In mid-June of 1888 O'Connell said in a communication to the cardinal in Baltimore, "The final decision on the Knights of Labor by H. Of. arrived at a short time ago, was: 'Tolerari possunt.' " [39] It was hardly surprising that a few weeks later the press had such a story. The *Irish World* announced a coming papal communication which assured Catholics "through the bishops of their full permission to join the Order." Ford, the editor, received this as good news for the conservative members under Powderly who had feared the strain put on Church relations by the public utterances of ill-advised Knights. The *Irish World* linked it further with the recently published "declaration by the Knights of Labor in favor of the educational and constructive policy" as a sign of assurance to all "that the sympathies of the Church are with them in their efforts to better their condition." [40]   On the other hand, an unfriendly journal considered the reported "tolerari possunt" not at all complimentary to the Knights. It maintained it was another example of "how Rome creeps out of a difficulty by using some heathenish phrase." Credit was given to the "bland, insinuating, persuasive power" of the Arch-

---

[36] ADR, Gibbons to O'Connell, Baltimore, April 24, 1888, enclosing James O'Connor to Gibbons, Omaha, April 24, 1888 [*sic*].

[37] BCA, 84-K-4, Ireland to Gibbons, St. Paul, May 7, 1888.

[38] No indication was found that Vatican officials had received the newly revised constitution.

[39] BCA, 84-P-7, O'Connell to Gibbons, Rome, June 17, 1888; also ADC, O'Connell to Gilmour, Rome, June 20, 1888.

[40] July 7, 1888.

bishop of Baltimore by saying the "blarney of Gibbons was an over-match for the Italians in the Vatican." [41]

Such reports may have aroused some little hope among those in the United States who were well disposed towards the Knights, but they were without foundation. O'Connell wrote in explanation of his note of a month before: "It is certain that the Holy Office arrived at the decision that I wrote about the K. of L., but they do not care about publishing their contradiction." The Rector of the American College took occasion to add this judgment, "You never did anything that so added to your prestige in Rome as that action of yours in regards to the Knights." O'Connell quoted directly the words of Archbishop Francesco Satolli, who in 1893 was to become the first permanent apostolic delegate to the United States, but who then was a member of the Congregation of the Holy Office and, as O'Connell thought, an "intimate friend of the Pope." Satolli compared the Irish bishops unfavorably with the Americans, and he said:

> But they are not wide awake as the American Bishops. There the Holy Office wished to condemn the Knights of Labor, and the American Bishops opposed it, and Cardinal Gibbons, 'great statesman as he is' laid the matter before the Holy See, and showed that in Canada the Knights had been condemned for an accidentality, and thus saved the commission of a great mistake.[42]

The details of the authentic and official copy of the final Roman decree on the Knights of Labor showed that Gibbons' Roman agent had been wrong, not only on the time of the judgment but also in omitting the condition placed on their toleration. The communication to Cardinal Gibbons from the Prefect of Propaganda, dated August 29, 1888, read:

[41] *Protestant Standard,* July 26, 1888, "Mr. Leo and the Knights of Labor." Collection of Newspaper Clippings Relating to the Situation of the Roman Catholic Church in America, II, New York Public Library.

[42] BCA, 84-V-6, O'Connell to Gibbons, Rome, August 14, 1888. The Irish hierarchy at least was not heeded as much by Rome on the land problem. Cf. Walsh, *William J. Walsh, Archbishop of Dublin,* "Condemnation of the Plan of Campaign," pp. 317-370.

I think it my duty to inform your Eminence that the additional documents regarding the Society of the Knights of Labor have been examined in the General Congregation of the H.[oly] R.[oman] and U.[niversal] I.[nquisition] held on the 16 of August—Thursday instead of Wednesday. After thorough consideration of the same, it was decreed that the following answer should be given: In view of the latest statement of the case, the Society of the Knights of Labor may be allowed for the time being, provided whatever in its statutes is improperly expressed [minus recte dicta] or susceptible of wrong interpretation shall be corrected. Especially in the preamble of the constitution for local assemblies words which seem to savor of socialism and communism must be emended in such a way as to make clear that the soil was granted by God to man, or rather the human race, that each one might have the right to acquire some portion of it, by use however of lawful means and without violation of the right of private property.

It gives me great pleasure to inform your Eminence that the intention of the Ordinaries of your country to watch diligently with yourself, lest anything should creep into this and other similar societies which deviate from the straight path of justice and morality and which do not conform with the instruction, De Secta Massonum, issued by the Supreme Congregation, has been found worthy of high approbation.[43]

This decision of the Holy Office, in reply to Gibbons' petition of a year and a half before, was sent to Baltimore by Simeoni on his own judgment. It certainly showed no outright approval of the American labor organization, but was rather in essence a conditional toleration. Furthermore, it was based strictly on the application of the principles long before formulated by the Congregation of the Holy Office on secret societies, especially those which contained elements destructive of the existing social order. Its emphasis was definitely anti-socialistic, rather than on the positive necessity and the good to be derived from such a labor association. The only change specified was in precisely the paragraph pointed out both by Robert Fulton, S.J., to Archbishop Corrigan and Paulinus Dissez, S.S., to Cardinal Gibbons, as obscure and open to misinterpretation. All of this arouses a strong but unsatisfied curiosity about the basis of the two condemnatory judgments which had been handed down

---

[43] BCA, 84-Y-3, Simeoni to Gibbons, Rome, August 29, 1888.

by the Holy Office to the Archbishop of Quebec. Even at the end, Soderini reported, the Roman officials remained so doubtful about the whole case that only the personal intervention of the Pope prevented the further prolonging of the discussions.[44] In what the ecclesiastical historian, Fernand Mourret, S.S., considers practically the memoirs of Pope Leo XIII one reads that the declaration of toleration showed that the Holy See would not condemn in principle any attempts of labor to organize, even if outside its own control, and that, "it is far from putting its strength at the service of capital against the claims of labor." [45]

The same mail that brought this Roman news to Baltimore carried a letter from Powderly to Gibbons asking his "good offices" in behalf of one James Lonergan.[46] The cardinal's reply informed Powderly of Simeoni's message and said of the "few verbal changes" that had been demanded, "This being done, I believe that the good standing of the Knights will be fully recognized by the Holy See especially so long as the organization is under your wise control." He requested the labor leader to call at his residence for a conference any day, except Sunday, of that current month so long as he informed him beforehand when he was coming. He was also reminded to bring a copy of the latest constitution. The archbishop did not forget to assure Powderly that they would talk over his request for his friend Lonergan at that time.[47] Gibbons was determined to handle the situation alone, and so for the time being the Propaganda communication was not sent out to the other archbishops.[48] Powderly, moreover, at this time was not parading his Catholic connections. He refused an invitation to speak under Catholic auspices in Cincinnati lest he arouse the anti-Catholic charge of running the Order for the Church's interest. This explanation was offered:

[44] Soderini, *op. cit.,* p. 176.

[45] Charles de T'Serclaes, *Léon XIII, son action politique, religieuse et sociale* (Lille, 1894), II, 43, quoted in Fernand Mourret, *Histoire générale de l'église* (Paris, 1923) IX, 407.

[46] PP, Powderly to Gibbons, Scranton, September 7, 1888, copy.

[47] BCA, 85-B-2, Gibbons to Powderly, Baltimore, September 11, 1888.

[48] AAC, Gibbons to Elder, Baltimore, September 15, 1888.

> I wouldn't care so much if the damned rascals who belong to the Church would only stand by the Order, after I won the favor of the Church for them, but they, like cowardly dogs, are slinking out with the rest and some of them snarling as they go, about being good Catholics but they don't believe in a G. M. W. that sells out to the Pope, and a load of such rot as that. . . .[49]

Hence his proposed visit to Baltimore was to be kept "an absolute secret" between himself, Hayes, and O'Reilly.[50] If it had been up to Powderly, even his acceptance of the cardinal's invitation would likewise have remained hidden for it was removed from his records.[51] Gibbons, however, had received it by September 20, and was expecting him the following Monday.[52]

The events leading up to the second meeting of Gibbons and Powderly seemed to augur a pleasant outcome. The story from Rome had broken in the press in a way that would naturally have cheered the labor leader. The cable dispatch to the New York *Catholic News* announced a favorable decree, and it concluded, "It settles for good the question as far as Rome is concerned, provided, of course, that the constitution and aims of the order remain the same."[53] This distorted report was spread also by the *Irish World,* which saw it as another vindication of a growing public favor toward labor. This paper expressly hoped in addition for an increased interest on the part of the general assembly in such matters as southern labor and women workers.[54] The Knights of Labor paper, although it cautiously remarked, "If the information furnished by the *Catholic News* is correct," was quick to call it "gratifying" and "just what

[49] PP, Powderly to Hugh Cavanaugh, Scranton, August 29, 1888, copy.

[50] PP, O'Reilly to Powderly, n.p., September 14, 1888; Powderly to Hayes, Scranton, September 12, 1888, copy.

[51] Letterbook, June-September, 1888, in its index shows that besides the letter of September 7, the copy of which is on page 264, another letter went to Gibbons, but page 297 where it should be, is torn out. It followed one dated September 17.

[52] ADR, Gibbons to O'Connell, Baltimore, September 20, 1888.

[53] *Catholic News,* September 16, 1888; in *Catholic Mirror,* September 22.

[54] September 22, 1888.

we anticipated." [55] At the same time Powderly seemed to be mellowing when he denied that there had ever been more than individual cases of hostility to the Order from priests in the Pennsylvania coal regions; and these, he said, often had occurred because of the faulty representation made to the clergy by the Knights. He asserted further that in the past, "there was no such action as leaving the Church in a body, and at the present time our Order need fear no opposition from the Church so long as its principles and laws are respected by members of the Order." [56] Meanwhile, awaiting Powderly's promised call, Gibbons not only remained well disposed toward him, but was shrewdly prepared to satisfy Rome. He told O'Connell of Simeoni's letter, saying:

> The decree is in substance that 'tolerandi sunt,' provided some verbal changes are made in the constitutions of expressions which might be distorted into a bad sense. The particular expressions are not even indicated. Hence I infer that the emendations are suggested to save the H. Off. from a charge of inconsistency, and to get out of the difficulty as quickly as they can.

The cardinal proposed to let the letter be publicized "even to the Bishops" only after he "had taken the little sting out of the Decree— by being able to produce together with the letter Mr. Powderly's entire willingness to make the corrections which I have no doubt he will do." Gibbons concluded the matter with a rather fervent, "I can now breathe freely. Thanks to God, and to your vigilance." [57] The very cordial conference between Gibbons and Powderly took place on September 24. The first report of it was that Powderly "cheerfully promised to make the emendations required by the Holy Office, and expressed his readiness to comply at all times with the wishes of the ecclesiastical authorities." [58] That was the

[55] *Journal of United Labor,* September 20, 1888.

[56] PP, Powderly to James McFeely, Scranton, September 20, 1888, copy.

[57] ADR, Gibbons to O'Connell, Baltimore, September 20, 1888. Meanwhile the usually vigilant O'Connell just back from a trip out of Rome was assuring the cardinal the report of toleration was certain, BCA, 85-C-3, September 17. Gibbons told Ireland also, "I attach little or no importance to the conditions imposed by the H. Office. Sept. 17, Papers in possession of James H. Moynihan.

[58] BCA, 85-D-2, copy of letter sent to Archbishops, Baltimore, September 25, 1888.

covering message that went out to all the American archbishops with copies of Simeoni's letter of August 29. Gibbons conveyed to Rome the same news, along with the account of his own action in notifying the other metropolitans. He offered even stronger assurances that Powderly and the Knights were "prepared to correct and change anything in the statutes which the ecclesiastical authority might in the future judge necessary." Simeoni was further informed:

> I am very glad that the Holy Office has settled the affair with such an opinion, for it brings peace to souls, preserves the authority of Holy Church and aids the salvation of many in our United States.
>
> While in Rome in February, 1887 in my letter to the Sacred Cong. concerning these Knights, I said this society for various causes would soon lose many of its members. Events have proved the truth of that statement for then this society numbered 700,-000 adherents now it contains scarcely 350,000.[59]

This little note of appreciation of his own acumen might have been inspired by the receipt of word from Denis O'Connell that Camillo Cardinal de Rende, Archbishop of Benevento, had mentioned Gibbons' "rare judgment" to him and cited as an illustration his speaking to the American cardinal in Paris about the Knights of Labor, and how, "since then everything has transpired exactly as he foretold." [60]

The significance of this latest victory for the Archbishop of Baltimore on the question of the Church and the Knights of Labor did not go unnoticed. Corrigan's congratulations on the "happy termination" were not lacking in a suggestion of self defense and an awareness that the really final step now lay with the labor organization. He wrote:

> Apart from the wise and considerate action of the Holy See with regard to the Knights of Labor, I am very much gratified to find, unexpectedly in such a document, an authoritative decision with regard to the right of ownership and private property.

[59] BCA, 85-D-10, Gibbons to Simeoni, Baltimore, September 28, 1888, copy.
[60] BCA, 85-C-3, O'Connell to Gibbons, Grottaferrata, September 17, 1888.

Nothing could be clearer or more significant than the concluding phrases of the first paragraph of Cardinal Simeoni's letter, or rather the response of the Holy Office itself. . . . I trust that the promise made by Mr. Powderly to Your Eminence will be duly and faithfully accepted by the organization of the Knights of Labor at large, and put into practice.[61]

The qualified joy of New York was reflected in Rome whence it was reported, that except for the New York agent, Miss Edes, "Everybody else seemed glad," about the decree.[62] Real delight, however, was expressed by Archbishop Ireland who was then much concerned with the German question. With typical pugnacity he added, "The delay, I presume, was caused by Quebec intrigues." [63] Yet on the basis of available evidence, the Canadian cardinal by this time was out of the picture, except that Powderly—the unpredictable —was planning to send both to him and to Gibbons with his compliments a bookmark bearing a likeness of Pope Leo XIII.[64] The general master workman wanted this gesture to be kept confidential, just as he felt that Gibbons at least for a while was adverse to publicity on the relations of the Church with the Knights. The cardinal, he said, had not been pleased the previous year at the public notices given to Tom Barry who had brought up the charges of ecclesiastical influence on Powderly.[65]

Two suggestions of opposition to the final decision, nevertheless, did come from Rome. They were both rather veiled in nature. One of Gibbons' subjects told him of the great esteem in which a "Monsignor Vaga" of the Vatican held him. The Roman prelate was quoted as having said his defense of the Knights of Labor had made a "profound impression" and that in Rome he was regarded as "the St. Bernard of America." Beyond that he told

---

[61] BCA, 85-D-11, Corrigan to Gibbons, New York, September 29, 1888.

[62] BCA, 85-F-4, O'Connell to Gibbons, Grottaferrata, October 8, 1888. He explained he had just left for vacation when the Holy Office's statement was issued.

[63] BCA, 85-F-13, Ireland to Gibbons, St. Paul, October 12, 1888.

[64] PP, Powderly to John Hynes, Scranton, October 2, 1888, copy.

[65] PP, Powderly to Patrick Ford, Scranton, October 11, 1888. Barry was said sarcastically to have become, "so advanced in thought and science as to no longer have any use for the Catholic religion. . . ."

the cardinal of "one of two English prelates" who had tried to influence Pope Leo against him on the grounds that he "endorsed the doctrine of socialism." [66]   The rector of the American College, in a similarly mysterious vein, wrote of his "young friend" who might have been able to inject "a little animadversion on the George question" into Simeoni's letter on the Knights.   O'Connell observed that the original of the decision had not been sent and this unidentified person had previously worked for the condemnation of Georgism to the extent of building up a great fear of it in the cardinal prefect's mind.   He said further, and in part just as cryptically:

> It may be that this communication is the quiet ending of those two great questions, that some tried to make appear as one, and if so, it is a singularly quiet and happy ending of much fuss and danger.   Your triumph is complete, and you owe nothing for it to those false friends, who drew you into their arms, and then did everything in their power to make you appear here a mass of weakness and inconsistency, to the peril of your cause and the grief of your supporters.[67]

It was very true that the Roman decision was close to being the "quiet ending."   It went practically unnoticed even in the Catholic press in contrast to the furor which blew up in the spring of 1887 over the Knights.   Yet an article in *Observateur Français* of Paris on the question was reported as having been "copied by the European press generally." [68]   Perhaps because of Archbishop Ireland the *Northwestern Chronicle* was able to claim a paraphrase of the item together with a translation of the decree as a special feature. Its postulate was that the Church was "anxious to help on the amelioration of the lot of the landless and poor workingmen with-

---

[66] BCA, 85-F-3, Richard B. MacCarthy to Gibbons, Rome, October 8, 1888. He remarked of the compliments, "Monsignor McColgan will be glad to hear this," "Vaga" could not be identified from *La Gerarchia Cattolica* (Rome, 1888).

[67] BCA, 85-G-2, O'Connell to Gibbons, Grottaferrata, October 17, 1888. If he was referring to Corrigan and his friends, what they did in Rome along these lines has not been further uncovered.

[68] BCA, 85-G-13, O'Connell to Gibbons, Rome, October 31, 1888.

out encroaching upon the rights of property, such as centuries have constituted it." [69] The English version of Simeoni's letter gradually found its way into the secular and religious papers, and Bishop Francis Chatard who had read the original on his way through New York, found it was "not faithfully represented by translation." [70] The *Catholic Standard* of Philadelphia a few days later also recognized this fact and with the help of one qualified by his experience in English and "pure Latinity," presented an accurate translation.[71]

The European publicity meanwhile resulted in a warm but penetrating expression of congratulations from Gibbons' fellow cardinal, the Archbishop of Rennes, Charles P. Place, a leader in the Catholic social movement in France. The results of the American prelate's effort, said Place, was of interest to the whole world. His long and very quotable reasoning followed:

> The Church cannot remain indifferent to the great debate over the organization of labor; justice and morality, of which she is the guardian, are involved in it and it is a question of injustice to the great masses who pay with their sweat for their daily bread. Therein lies a cause for the Church, *the constant friend of the people,* as your Eminence so correctly and eloquently remarked. If the Gospel could have been partial it would have been in favor of the weak, the worker.
>
> I believe with you, that one of the titles to glory of the Church in the past and one of the conditions for her strength in the future is this solicitude for the interests and rights of the people. . . .

Cardinal Place appreciated the plight of the workers and rejoiced that Catholics were more and more giving their attention to "the grave problem of the relation of capital and labor." In conclusion he told Gibbons:

> Little by little, I hope, the light will dawn and the people whose suffering the enemies of the social order exploit will recog-

[69] November 16, 1888; also the Pittsburgh *Catholic,* December 8, 1888. Neither carried any editorial comment of its own.

[70] NYAA, Chatard to Corrigan, Indianapolis, December 2, 1888.

[71] December 8, 1888.

nize that, even from the viewpoint of their temporal condition, there is no salvation and redemption, except in putting into practice the liberating doctrines of the divine worker of Nazareth, doctrines which you have explained so correctly and eloquently in your work.[72]

At the same time a mere chance remark of an Italian cardinal showed a similar, albeit more succinct, approval. When Mariano Rampolla, Secretary of State to Leo XIII, was reproached for the leakage of such documents as Gibbons' memorial on the Knights from Roman congregations, he promptly retorted, "Oh, but that did a great deal of good."[73]   It was probably this new flurry of attention in the press which prompted, too, the request made to Gibbons to endorse a campaign against unnecessary work on Sundays with which he complied.[74]   Finally the story of Rome's judgment in its entirety was put before the general public when such a paper as the *Irish World,* with its labor as well as Catholic readers, reprinted from the Cleveland *Catholic Universe* the letter of September 25 from Gibbons. It was cited as having been received by Archbishop Elder of Cincinnati, but with no explanation of how it got into the paper. Patrick Ford's editorial praised Gibbons, but more particularly, Powderly whose past action was such, "that there can be no friction caused by the courteous and judicious manner in which he has avoided any possible misunderstanding with the Church authorities as to the proper interpretation of clauses in the official declarations of the order which were regarded as obscure."[75]

The truth of the matter was that Powderly had already shown signs of giving up any attempt to clarify even modes of expression which might lead Catholic churchmen to misinterpretations. At the Minneapolis session of the general assembly in 1887 an unsuccessful attempt to align the Knights with the single tax movement was made. An amendment to the constitution, which would have made the fourth article of the preamble declare that all land should

[72] BCA, 85-I-1, Place to Gibbons, Rennes, November 21, 1888.

[73] BCA, 85-I-7, O'Connell to Gibbons, Rome, November 23, 1888.

[74] BCA, 85-K-1, Reverend Wilbur F. Crofts to Gibbons, New York, December 1, 1888; Gibbons to Crofts, Baltimore, December 4, 1888, copy.

[75] December 22, 1888.

be taxed to its full rental value, was defeated.[76] The next fall at Indianapolis, a few months after his call on Cardinal Gibbons, the general master workman recommended that they concentrate their agitation on certain more important sections of the preamble. He thereupon singled out their monetary aims, the government owner-ship through purchase of some public utilities, and their land tenet,[77] which read: "That the public lands, the heritage of the people, be reserved for actual settlers; not another acre for railroads or spec-ulators, and that all lands now held for speculative purposes be taxed to their full value." [78] Among the many resolutions offered at this Indianapolis gathering, including even proposals to return to their early secrecy, there were renewed attempts to inject the ideas of Henry George. Exactly the same proposal for rewording the fourth section of the preamble as had been made a year before was again dismissed.[79] Likewise the substitution, "The appropriation of the economic rent of land and natural opportunities for all governmental uses in lieu of all other taxes" was judged "inexpedient to legis-late." [80] Similarly the proposal to substitute "a single land value tax" for "a graduated income tax" as the thirteenth in their official list of demands made no progress.[81] Powderly's suggestion that they concentrate on the land clause as it stood did, however, succeed in being referred to the general assembly, but nothing was de-cided at that session.[82]

In the face of far more vehement sentiments on the land ques-tion than his own, Powderly made no effort to procure changes in any part of the constitution which smacked of communism or social-ism. More than that, he preferred to find in the ecclesiastical ob-jection to part of the preamble of local assemblies no reference to questionable words on private property. Simeoni's letter was clear on that point, and Corrigan had stressed it to Gibbons, so it is hardly

---

[76] *Proceedings* (Minneapolis, 1887), pp. 1729, 1781, 1782.

[77] *Proceedings* (Indianapolis, 1888), p. 7.

[78] *Constitution* . . . (approved 1885), p. 3.

[79] *Proceedings* (Indianapolis, 1888), pp. 31, 40.

[80] *Ibid.*, pp. 46, 92.

[81] *Ibid.*, p. 21.

[82] *Ibid.*, pp. 13, 40.

possible that the Baltimore prelate did not point it out in consulting with Powderly. Still the G. M. W. sent out this strictly personal interpretation to a knight in France:

> The church has not passed on our Order in the way of approval, it examined our law and found nothing to criticize except possibly minor details. The principal item to which they took exception was the wording of the preamble to the constitution of Local Assemblies. I never favored that section myself for the reason that under it any action whether of violence or otherwise would be considered lawful. These words are to be found as follows, 'In short, any action that will advance the cause of humanity, lighten the burden of toil, or elevate the moral and social condition of mankind, whether incorporated in the constitution or not, is the proper scope and field of operation of a Local Assembly.'

Powderly promised by way of eliminating this supposed point of friction between the Order and the Church to render an official decision restricting this broad statement only to acts within the bounds of the laws of the Knights of Labor and of the country.[83]

Even as Powderly by his silence was declining to assume again the position of ecclesiastical advocate within the Knights, he continued to suffer over the religious issue. Thomas Barry, who had flourished the religious firebrand until he was ousted from the Order, began his own Brotherhood of United Labor after the Indianapolis convention.[84] A few months later, in January, 1889, another schism, or founders' movement, took place occasioned by Powderly's dropping of Turner's office of treasurer and combining it with that of the secretary in the hands of John Hayes. It consisted of three members of the formerly powerful clique, the Home Club, and four of the original members.[85] Since this group who favored reform wanted to return to the original oath-bound secrecy, it was not without anti-Catholic sentiment. Its ritual, for example, asked that one bind himself to use his own judgment, "absolutely independent of the dictation of any church, prince, potentate, or authority whatso-

---

83 PP, Powderly to F. Veyssier, Scranton, December 29, 1888, copy.
84 Powderly, *Thirty Years*, pp. 574-576.
85 Ware, *op. cit.*, p. 115; *Thirty Years*, p. 577.

ever." [86]   At first Powderly took the revolt lightly, but in a short time he was writing letters against the charges they had made that the Order was under the control of the Church.[87]   He cited Uriah S. Stephens as precedent for all he had done, for he claimed that the founder had gone farther than his successor ever did, even to the extent of giving Bishop Wood of Philadelphia a copy of the ritual to study. Furthermore—and this remains otherwise unsupported— Powderly claimed that he had himself made explanations about parts of the constitution also to "several Bishops of the Episcopal church, Bishops of the Presbyterian, Methodist and Lutheran churches" [*sic*].[88] His public plea against "Ignorance Bigotry and Religious Intolerance," and "Religious War," was made along the same lines, plus a detailed refutation of the charge that he picked only Catholics as general officers. He showed that only six out of sixteen were his coreligionists and the statement, he pointed out, supposed further that he controlled the general assembly which elected them.[89]

Quite apart from the difficulty of maintaining docility to the Church in the face of such hostile dissenters, Powderly himself drifted away from any position compatible with his promise to Cardinal Gibbons. Not only he, but the Knights of Labor as an organization, explicitly adopted George's views at a time when they had come under the severest scrutiny of the Church. In his pastoral of January 20, 1889, Archbishop Corrigan had made attendance at the meetings of the Anti-Poverty Society in New York a reserved case, that is a penitent could not be absolved by an ordinary confessor in the diocese without special recourse to the bishop. This action he had based on the papal statement that McGlynn's opinions were "false and pernicious" and the judgment of the Congregation of the Inquisition that a Catholic's presence at such gatherings was "an open and a public sin." [90]   Even as Powderly

---

[86] *Ibid.,* p. 577.

[87] PP, Powderly to C. A. Shemke, Scranton, January 30, 1889.

[88] PP, Powderly to George B. Dechant, Scranton, January 14, 1889.

[89] *Journal of United Labor,* January 31, 1889.

[90] Zwierlein, *op. cit.,* III, 63. George, on the verge of a break with McGlynn who refused to go along in support of President Cleveland on his policy

grew in George's estimation for his budding espousal of the single
tax system an answer came from Rome condemning the latter's
books.[91]   A year had passed since Gibbons' successful efforts to
keep the works of the social philosopher off the Index. His reasons
had been based for the most part on the ill effects that would follow.
The Holy Office when it found them "deserving of condemnation" on
February 6, 1889, enjoined that the fact be kept *sub secreto* in its
enforcement and in the promulgation of the decree to the suffragan
bishops. On April 23 Corrigan received this document, dated April 9
from Simeoni by way of Baltimore. He noted, however, that Archbishop Ryan of Philadelphia had not yet obtained his copy.[92]   The
Archbishop of New York loosely translated a salient sentence for
the Bishop of Rochester [93] which more accurately amounted to the
following words of explanation of the decision. Gibbons had been
told that the cardinals of the Inquisition

> felt very sure that the Bishops of the country and yourself will
> exercise industry and zeal in order that the faithful and espe-
> cially clerics may retain without any admixture what the Church
> has always taught, has often defined and has most recently in-
> culcated through Pope Pius IX's Encyclical *Qui pluribus* and
> Leo XIII's *Quod apostolici muneris,* concerning the right of pri-
> vate property even respecting the land.[94]

Corrigan after his years of struggle over this question took this
Roman reply with the previous conditional toleration of the Knights
of Labor as justification of his original position. He said:

of tariff reduction, admitted there might have been "violent and abusive
language" at the meetings, but not false teaching. He advised the members quite
correctly that they could get absolution in Brooklyn or New Jersey. *Standard,*
January 26, 1888. George's own resignation from the society was accepted on
February 28, 1888, and the next month he said he was over the pain and was
"perfectly satisfied" since McGlynn had qualities which "would have made ultimate trouble." New York Public Library, Henry George Papers, George to
Thomas F. Walker, New York, March 17, 1888.

    [91] *Standard,* March 7, 1889.

    [92] RDA, Corrigan to McQuaid, Atlantic City, April 24, 1889. The only
copy found was addressed to Gibbons, BCA, 85-W-4.

    [93] Zwierlein, *Letters of Archbishop Corrigan to Bishop McQuaid and Allied
Documents* (Rochester, 1946), p. 126.

    [94] BCA, 85-W-4, Simeoni to Gibbons, Rome, April 9, 1889.

As my Pastoral was expressly based on these Encyclicals, and I was accused of stretching them too far—this new document is a complete vindication of my cause. The only trouble is that the decision is to be kept secret (on account of circumstances), and hence it will be hard to enforce it. . . . Both the pronouncements of the H. O. viz. in re Knights of Labor, and this, must have opened the eyes of some of our friends. They will be more careful, I trust, in future in closing their eyes to dangerous doctrines.[95]

In fact, however, one of Corrigan's "friends," Cardinal Gibbons, could have claimed almost equal vindication insofar as Rome had imposed secrecy in its condemnation. One of the results of this was that the Knights of Labor would prepare without possibly a greater perturbation of Catholic consciences to endorse the teachings of the banned George books. Powderly in the spring of 1889 was being coaxed into the fold by George himself, and his reactions showed promise.[96] His more favorable attitude toward the land reformers might have influenced the group of leading Catholic laymen who prepared the program of speakers for the Catholic Congress held November 11-12 at Baltimore in conjunction with the centennial of the American hierarchy. They were admittedly "a little afraid to have Powderly on the labor question."[97] They did finally tender him the offer and, perhaps to their relief, received his refusal to accept it, ostensibly because of the burden of his duties, although privately he looked on them with scorn.[98]

[95] RDA, Corrigan to McQuaid, New York, April 24, 1889.

[96] *Standard,* May 11, 1889.

[97] AUND, Henry Brownson Papers, Brownson to Joseph P. Roles, Detroit, August 29, 1889.

[98] *Ibid.,* Powderly to Brownson, n.p., September 18, 1889. He wrote about that time, "A change has taken place, we are being courted now by the good-goods who shunned us for fear of defilement and now attempt to take us under their wings in a patronizing sort of way. . . . The Order has forced a cowardly—miscalled conservative—church to recognize the doctrine of Christ. . . . Would you believe it, I am invited to nearly every synod, conclave, or congress of the clergy now. . . ." Interestingly enough, Powderly did not think highly of another group which also made overtures to him, "I have little respect for the Masons, they originally were Industrials, but followed the church when it started after Mammon and then lost sight of their principles." PP, Powderly to Miss A. A. Wright, October 27, 1889.

The convention, nevertheless, had two papers on the social question, although only one could be read for want of time. Peter L. Foy of St. Louis spoke on "The New Social Order." He was not at all easy on capital and predicted "the future belongs to organized labor" unless it should fall into radicalism.[99] Powderly's substitute, William Richards of Washington, had his paper published in the proceedings although it was not read at the convention. It was entitled "Labor and Capital" and Richards attacked the notion of free competition and pointed out that, more than unions and mutual benefit associations, what was needed in society was divine charity.[100] The American press gave this Catholic lay gathering, which was to be repeated only once more in 1893 at Chicago, wide publicity.[101]

Their inability to have Powderly on the program may have saved this group of laymen embarrassed explanations to episcopal authority. Not long after their congress the labor leader came out with his personal advocacy of the single tax idea.[102] Shortly afterwards it became part of the official program of the Knights of Labor, for the organization was becoming increasingly rural in mind as well as make-up, and it was ready to co-operate with the Farmers' Alliance and kindred reform groups.[103] At the Atlanta convention of the general assembly in 1889 the committee on law reported unfavorably on the proposed amendment since it held that the fourth section of the preamble "as worded at present sufficiently expressed the general stand of the Order upon the land question." It had in opposition to its views the recommendation of Powderly's presidential address.[104] On November 18, 1889,

[99] *Official Report of the Proceedings of the Catholic Congress held at Baltimore, Md., November 11th and 12th, 1889* (Detroit, 1889), p. 68.

[100] *Ibid.*, pp. 155-163.

[101] Cf. Vincent J. Donovan, "The First American Catholic Lay Congress Held at Baltimore, November 11-12, 1889." Unpublished master's thesis, Catholic University of America (1940), pp. 48-55. On the growth of this idea of congresses in Europe and the United States, cf. Martin Spahn and Thomas F. Meehan, "Catholic Congresses," *Catholic Encyclopedia*, IV, 242-251.

[102] *Standard,* October 19, 1889.

[103] *Proceedings* (Atlanta, 1889), pp. 33, 87-93, 94-95.

[104] *Ibid.,* pp. 4, 8.

the general assembly went into committee of the whole on this question, and "after prolonged discussion," came out with a substitute for the much mooted clause which was carried. It read:

> The land, including all the natural sources of wealth is the heritage of all the people, and should not be subject to speculative traffic. Occupancy and use should be the only title to the possession of land. The taxes upon land should be levied upon its full value for use, exclusive of improvements, and should be sufficient to take for the community all unearned increment.[105]

This "final plunge" was written up in the press and, of course, hailed by George, who proclaimed optimistically that it was the "most important event . . . the *Standard* has been able to record." [106]   If it caused even a slight reaction among the American hierarchy, their extant records have not revealed it.   This action was in effect the strongest proof that the loosely worded preamble of local assemblies which had particularly bothered the Holy Office would not be changed.   A copy of the constitution published in 1893 showed the key sentence still unaltered, and in the convention of that year Powderly offered the Knights' tenet on land as proof of their independence of Rome.[107]

From the point of view, therefore, of securing perfect conformity with the expressed will of Rome the outcome of all Gibbons' negotiations with Powderly ended in failure.   The activity of the cardinal, however, had already done its good work by producing a profound impression in the United States that the Catholic Church was friendly towards labor and even advocated its legitimate organization.   Beyond this it joined Gibbons for a time with the forces of the Catholic social thought in Europe, which were to close ranks

---

[105] *Ibid.,* p. 43.

[106] November 23, 1889.

[107] P. 32; also a copy from 1890, p. 47.   It read, ". . . Among the higher duties that should be taught in every Local Assembly are man's inalienable inheritance and right to a share, for use, of the soil; that the right to life carries with it the right to the means of living; and that all statutes that obstruct or deny these rights are wrong, unjust and must give away." *Proceedings* (Philadelphia, 1893), "Report of the General Master Workman," p. 12.

on the call of *Rerum novarum*. The Cardinal Archbishop of Rheims, for example, in sending him a copy of his address to the Holy Father on the occasion of another pilgrimage of French workers, prayed God, he told Gibbons, to grant himself, "a part of the great love which you have for the people and of the constant energy with which you support their interests." [108] Further events in Europe stimulated the memory of the aging Cardinal Manning. The proposal of the Swiss founder of the Catholic social movement, Gaspard Decurtins, for a conference regarding international labor legislation on hours and working conditions had been taken up both by Leo XIII and the young German Emperor William II.[109] This prompted Manning to write:

> We little thought when we were writing about the Knights of Labour in Rome, a few years ago that every word would be so soon published to the world by an Emperor and a Pope.
> This is surely the New World over-shadowing the old, and the Church walking like its Master among the people of Christendom.
> Were we Prophets? [110]

After seeing this extract, Archbishop Ireland answered Manning's question for Gibbons with no uncertain ring: "You were a prophet! The people are the power, and the Church must be with the people. I wish all our own bishops understood this truth." [111]

Gibbons, the prophet, continued to be honored outside of his own country for his interest in social problems while actually his time was becoming more absorbed at home by other national questions. In the early 1890's the Church in the United States had to face not only the continuation of Cahenslyism but especially the new difficulties and differences raised by Ireland's Faribault-Stillwater plan for partial state aid to parochial schools.[112] Although

---

[108] BCA, 86-S-2, Benoît Marie Langenieux to Gibbons, Rheims, October 25, 1889.

[109] Soderini, *op. cit.,* pp. 183-188.

[110] BCA, 87-G-8, Manning to Gibbons, n.p., March 31, 1890, also quoted in Leslie, *op. cit.,* pp. 365-366.

[111] BCA, 87-J-5, Ireland to Gibbons, St. Paul, April 21, 1890, also quoted in Leslie, *op. cit.,* p. 366.

[112] Cf. John J. Meng, "Cahenslyism: The Second Chapter, 1891-1910,"

these matters kept Gibbons occupied, the fame of his efforts for labor remained well established. Soderini mentioned his activities in two articles in *Osservatore Romano,* and he told Gibbons, too, of Leo XIII's great interest in the social question. The Italian nobleman likewise relayed the news of the expected coming to Rome of Bishop Gaspard Mermillod as a cardinal, whose presence would be considered "very useful" as he had "always taken the greatest interest in the social question." [113] This Swiss prelate was in fact influential in the formulation of *Rerum novarum,* not only by his presence at the Vatican but by his previous work of 1884 in convening the Fribourg Union, which had produced an important statement on Christian social principles that had been presented to the Pope in February, 1888.[114]

Further indication that some directive must soon come from Rome was seen in the fall of 1890. Not only was the Baltimore cardinal informed of the Pope's increasing attention to the problems of modern society, but he was asked to represent the United States at the Third International Social Congress of Liége in September.[115] His presence, he was assured, "would cast a brilliant effect on our work." [116] But Gibbons took no part in the congress which discussed such matters as the international aspects of labor and passed a double resolution favoring the temporal power of the Papacy and a place for the Pope in the arbitration of labor questions. He did, however, send a letter of good wishes.[117] The participation of Manning

Catholic Historical Review, XXXII (October, 1946), 302-340, and Daniel F. Reilly, O.P., *The School Controversy (1891-1893)* (Washington, 1943). The latter's neglect of the Corrigan Papers and the discovery of new materials detract, somewhat from the definitive character of this work.

[113] BCA, 87-N-4, Soderini to Gibbons, Rome, May 26, 1890.

[114] Kothen, *op. cit.,* pp. 244 ff. A most valuable study of the whole movement in France says this memorial of 1888 probably "more than anything else . . . proved to the pope that the time was ripe for an official pronouncement on the labor problem." Parker T. Moon, *The Labor Problem and the Social Catholic Movement in France* (New York, 1921), p. 139.

[115] BCA, 87-Y-4, Soderini to Gibbons, Rome, September 29, 1890.

[116] BCA, 87-S-4, Count Frederick L. Waldbott, St. Andreas, Belgium, August 3, 1890.

[117] *Tablet,* September 13, 1890.

in these deliberations also took the form of a letter which, he laughed to hear, "had the effect of bombshell among the continental bishops." [118]   His brash statement had been to favor a "just and suitable standard regulating profits and salary" as a guide for "free contracts between capital and labor." [119]   Unacquainted as he was with such intricacies of the problem, Cardinal Gibbons was, nevertheless, able to make one positive contribution to the cause by the encouragement he gave to Comte de Mun by reading and approving one of his articles as well as a pamphlet entitled, "Quelque mots d'explication," which de Mun wrote to vindicate his course of action.[120]   The cardinal advised this zealous layman:

> It is a sad reflection that one who has consecrated his time and talents to the best interests of society, should be obliged to defend his actions which eloquently speak for themselves. But you will derive consolation from the reflection that if he merits well who writes and speaks for the poor, he merits more who suffers for them.
>
> The efforts you are making to mitigate the hardship of the laboring classes are worthy of all praise. The restriction of female and child labor, and the judicious regulation of the hours of labor for men, is a humane mission. It may be difficult to determine by law how many hours should constitute a day's labor for men, but it is not difficult for the authorities to fix a maximum standard beyond which he should not be obliged to work. All fair-minded legislators will agree that labor should be so restricted as to allow a reasonable period for bodily rest and for healthful recreation.[121]

More than de Mun, it would seem, felt beholden to Cardinal Gibbons. It was O'Connell's opinion that, as European conditions deteriorated, Rome looked more and more to the United States where the Vatican considered the Archbishop of Baltimore to be the "guid-

---

[118] BCA, 88-D-4, J. E. C. Bodley to Gibbons, Paris, November 21, 1890.

[119] *Tablet,* September 13, 1890.

[120] BCA, 88-G-9, de Mun to Gibbons, Paris, January 15, 1891. On de Mun's important efforts with workingmen's clubs and his advocacy of social legislation in the Chamber of Deputies from 1883 to 1891, cf. Moon, *op. cit.,* pp. 80-112.

[121] BCA, 88-K-5, Gibbons to de Mun, Baltimore, February 21, 1891, copy.

ing star" of the Church. He explained, "I never had the slightest reason to suspect that the Holy See was not profoundly grateful to you for saving them from committing a great mistake in regard to the Knights of Labor and that I believe is the common opinion." [122] At least one Catholic layman—and he was from New York—expressed a higher motive for gratitude toward Gibbons. He praised him for being like the European prelates who identified themselves with the interests of the workingmen. Of all the episcopate he singled out Gibbons as "the only one in this country who has taken an open and decided stand in their behalf." [123]

Among the other bishops who were never represented before the American public as friends of labor may certainly be numbered Michael A. Corrigan. The threatened schism in his see had become aggravated when another Propaganda alumnus, Richard L. Burtsell, was disciplined by being removed to the town of Rondout from the pastorate of the Church of the Epiphany in New York City where he had been a neighbor as well as a friend and aide of Mc-Glynn. This move had to be defended in Rome by the archbishop in the early part of 1890.[124] While Corrigan was there, the rumors of the Pope's interest in the social question were rife and the American prelate evidenced an interest in learning what Leo XIII was thinking on socialism.[125] On May 16, 1890, moreover, the Archbishop of New York addressed a letter to Camillo Cardinal Mazzella of which the following is a "memorandum of points":

Need of some explicit declaration regarding the right of private property.
(a) to prevent the sophistry of McGlynn and his associates.
(b) because of the carelessness or inadvertence of certain Prelates
the promises required by the Holy See in tolerating the Knights of Labor have *not* been fulfilled
the letter of the Holy See *in re* has not been communicated to the Bishops, e.g. in the Provinces of St. Louis, Cincinnati and

[122] BCA, 88-D-9, O'Connell to Gibbons, Rome, November 29, 1890.

[123] BCA, Marc. F. Vallette to Gibbons, New York, February 20, 1891.

[124] Zwierlein, *op. cit.*, III, 65-68.

[125] ACUA, Keane Papers, John P. Farrelly to Keane, Rome, April 22, 1890.

Oregon City.   Proofs Bishops Burke and Brondel, now in Rome, Bishop Chatard of Vincennes.

This could be remedied by sending in future to the Metropolitan printed copies of Instructions intended for distribution to their suffragans.   The present moment is a critical one in the history of the Diocese of New York.[126]

Months after adding his voice to those who had been calling on the Holy See for clarification of its social teaching, Corrigan again had the Knights of Labor brought to his attention.   The question of such secret fraternal groups as the Knights of Pythias and Odd Fellows had continued to plague the bishops and, whereas men like Gibbons and Ireland were very slow to condemn because of the ill effects that might follow, others like Corrigan, McQuaid, and Healy were concerned with the strictly canonical approach to the problem.[127]   The Boston meeting of the archbishops in July, 1890, the only legal status of which was as a committee on secret societies, added further confusion to this issue.[128]   They decided that the only formally condemned society was the Masons, and, while Catholics were to be discouraged from joining the others, if they already were members the question of leaving them was to be "decided by the conscience of each individual."[129]   The bad results of the inaccurate divulging of such a discussion excited especially Bishop McQuaid, who said of the new attitude, "It is time for someone to call a halt!   The idea is spreading that no society is forbidden except Freemasonry."[130]   Thus aroused over secret societies in general, and possibly because of the publicity attendant on the New York Central strike, McQuaid caused one last flutter of interest in the Knights of Labor question among the hierarchy.   Powderly had addressed over 10,000 strikers in New York, and McGlynn along with

---

[126] NYAA, Private Record of the Case of Rev. Edward J. McGlynn (typescript of 510 pages, but pagination is irregular), p. 254.   Maurice F. Burke was Bishop of Cheyenne (1887-1893) and John B. Brondel of Helena (1884-1903).

[127] Macdonald, *op. cit.*, pp. 150-184.

[128] NYAA, Ryan to Corrigan, Philadelphia, October 3, 1890.

[129] Macdonald, *op. cit.*, p. 163.

[130] McQuaid to Gilmour, Rochester, December 24, 1890, quoted in Zwierlein, *op. cit.*, II, 436.

the Reverend Hugh O. Pentecost addressed another one of the Knights' rallies.[131] Both layman and priest continued in bitter public attacks on the railroad which linked the cities of New York and Rochester.[132] Whatever were his immediate motives, the Bishop of Rochester did quote the pertinent clause of Simeoni's letter of August 29, 1888, to Cardinal Gibbons, and he asked, "Will your Eminence be pleased to inform me if these conditions required for tolerance of the Knights of Labor have been complied with, and where I am to get a copy of the amended Constitution?"[133] McQuaid informed Corrigan of this inquiry, and he added, "His Eminence may wish me in heaven sooner than my appointed time."[134] The cardinal, however, merely replied tersely and without any patent betrayal of feelings.

In reply to your letter recently received, I beg to say that I have not at hand a copy of the Constitution of the Knights of Labor. I may be permitted to add that as the Archbishops of the country were constituted with approbation of H. See a standing committee on societies, that subject is now in their hands.[135]

Corrigan, of course, received a copy of this response with a notation of McQuaid's that Gibbons had dodged the question by not adverting to the fact that the Holy See had already condemned the Knights of Labor, "unless they expunge certain socialistic doctrines from their constitution." Apart from his strong feelings on the matter, the Bishop of Rochester was undoubtedly right in saying that unless that took place, "the condemnation of the K. of L. is by an authority higher than that of an American commission of

[131] Pentecost, a Congregationalist, had been forced out of his Newark pastorate for championing Henry George and the labor movement, and had become a publicist of "the gospel of social revolution." Abell, *Urban Impact on American Protestantism,* p. 100.

[132] *Journal of Knights of Labor,* September 4, 18; October 1, 1890.

[133] BCA, 88-G-7, McQuaid to Gibbons, Rochester, January 12, 1891.

[134] NYAA, McQuaid to Corrigan, Rochester, January 13, 1891.

[135] BCA, 88-H-6, Gibbons to McQuaid, Baltimore, January 23 [*sic*], 1891, copy.

Archbishops." [136]   Certainly Corrigan often was advised by his old associate of Seton Hall College days, but this time he did the calm counseling.   Although McQuaid had concluded, "My next letter to his Eminence will be an awkward one to answer," there is no evidence that such a one was ever written, for his metropolitan had cautioned him, "As the K. of L. are practically dead would it not be like galvanizing them into life to record the fact that their former condemnation has never been withdrawn?" That Corrigan remained however, the champion of private property could be seen in his saying further, "I hope the Encyclical on socialism will appear soon, and remove any doubts still remaining in the minds of good priests." [137]

In three months the long-awaited and eagerly sought document of the Holy See was published.   The evolution of the ideas of *Rerum novarum* and the various influences that shaped its teaching are of interest here only insofar as they pertain to the case of the Knights of Labor.   Many of the men and movements in Catholic social questions, already noted as having come under the observation of Gibbons especially, have been credited with providing the foundation for Leo XIII's work.[138]   Before it appeared on May 15, 1891, Denis O'Connell, who was by that time probably the shrewdest American observer in Rome, remarked not only that de Mun was being consulted on the encyclical and that Manning was "in direct correspondence with the Pope," but also that "the Pope

---

136 NYAA, McQuaid to Corrigan, Rochester, January 22 [*sic*], 1891.

137 RDA, Corrigan to McQuaid, New York, February 7, 1891.

138 The two standard works on Pope Leo XIII's social theory show no awareness of any American contribution, namely, *Die soziale Frage und de Katholizismus. Festschrift zum 40 jährigen Jubiläum der Enzyklika Rerum Novarum.* Herausgegeben von der Sektion fur Sozial-und Wirtschaftswissenschaft der Görres-Gesellschaft (Paderborn, 1931), and *Il XI anniversario della enciclica Rerum novarum.* Scritti commemorativi pubblicati a cura della Università Cattolica del Sacro Cruore con il contributo della Unione Cattolica per le Scienze Sociali (Milano, 1931).   In the former Wilhelm Schwer, "Zeitbedingte Elemente im Rundschreiben 'Rerum Novarum,'" p. 403, merely mentions the episode of the Knights as one of the many only apparently disparate events which preceded the issuance of the encyclical.   It was not overlooked by Clarence J. McCabe, "The Background of Rerum Novarum." Unpublished master's thesis, Catholic University of America (1941), pp. 38-44.

is trying to embody in it everybody's views." [139]   Apart from the two memorials of February, 1887, the only other elaborate statements of American views as yet revealed were the conversations of the Pope with members of the hierarchy.   In the case of Gibbons— as of Manning—this has been said to have been welcomed by the Pontiff as a support to his own ideas.[140]   The Church in the United States did not present a program of social thought, but its problem of Catholic participation in the Knights of Labor combined with the further obscurity of the land issue to act as one of the world events which stimulated Rome to action.[141]   Behind an advance guard of papal letters on the evils of society and on the state, Pope Leo XIII entrusted to the Dominican Cardinal, Tommaso Zigliara, the first drafting, according to Leo's outline, of the most famous of the social encyclicals.   The resulting profound, prolix, and "perhaps too theoretical" work of this leader in the revival of Thomistic philosophy was given over to the papal secretaries, Gabriele Boccali and Alessandro Volpini, for a complete remoulding.   They made more use of the practical experience of Christian reformers.[142]   Pope Leo then applied the finishing touches to the message, which began with a pithy historical background:

[139] ACUA, Keane Papers, O'Connell to Keane, Rome, March 20, 1891. Manning had won his fame in the settlement of the London dock strike of 1889; cf. Leslie, *op. cit.*, pp. 368-376, and Georgiana P. McEntee, *The Social Catholic Movement in Great Britain* (New York, 1927), pp. 71-76.

[140] Josef Schmidlin, *Papstgeschichte der neuesten Zeit* (München, 1934), II, 371. Pius XI in *Quadragesimo anno* seems to have left out the petitions of the hierarchy when he wrote of his predecessor Leo XIII, "To the feet of Christ's Vicar on earth were seen to flock, in unprecedented numbers, sociological students, employers, the very workmen themselves, begging with one voice that at last a safe road might be pointed out to them." Husslein, (Ed.), *Social Wellsprings*, II, 180.

[141] Mourret, *op. cit.*, IX, 405, ranks the Knights of Labor case with the Berlin Congress which Kaiser William II carried through and the French workers' pilgrimages on this score. Georges Goyau, *Le Pape, les catholiques et la question sociale* (Paris, 1893), p. 481, comparing Gibbons' trip to Rome to a pilgrimage rates it with the organized French visits to the Eternal City as calling forth the encyclical. Quoted in Lecanuet, *op. cit.*, p. 451.

[142] Soderini, *op. cit.*, pp. 192-193.

The spirit of revolutionary change, long predominant in the nations of the world, when once aroused gradually passed beyond the bounds of politics and made itself felt in the cognate field of practical economy. The elements of a conflict are unmistakable. We perceive them in the growth of industry and the marvellous discoveries of science; in the changed relation of employers and workingmen; in the enormous fortunes of individuals and the poverty of the masses; in the increased self-reliance and closer mutual combination of the labour population; and finally in a general moral deterioration.[143]

Although it is impossible to unravel all the strands which went into the texture of the encyclical, it may be of worth to trace as far as one can any possible relationship of its contents to the labor memorial of Cardinal Gibbons. That document of 1887 had mentioned the grinding greed of monopoly, and this was re-echoed by Leo. The Pope called for the state to take a part in the "relief and remedy" of the social problem, especially by protecting the workers, and this, Gibbons had pointed out, had already come to pass in the United States. Although the Holy Father was suggesting safeguards to prevent strikes more than was true in Gibbons' document, they both showed an awareness of how workers were often driven to this undesirable resort. Both agreed (and here Leo included also organization with employers) that the right of labor to organize was a natural one, but in the encyclical the notion of an American style, non-religious association of workmen for which the bishops had sought toleration in Rome, was not mentioned specifically. In germ, however, the endorsement was there, for the papal approval applied to organizations, "adapted to the requirements of the age in which we live." The American memorial had argued that there was no necessity or practicality in having distinctively Catholic workers' societies in the United States, whereas *Rerum novarum* imposed membership in such a union only where the only alternative was an organization incompatible with the Christian religion. Leo XIII allowed his description of the labor organization to remain in very general terms, which may be attributed in part to Gibbons and more especially to Manning both of whom had the institution

---

143 Husslein (Ed.), *Social Wellsprings,* I, 167.

of the non-religious trade unions in their own countries to defend. The danger of socialism to the welfare of the worker was especially attacked by Leo, but Gibbons' defense of the Knights of Labor had merely remarked that such views were a European importation into the United States.

In the light of this primary emphasis it was Archbishop Corrigan especially who rejoiced in the *Rerum novarum.* Fortified with its text, he used the gospel of the Good Shepherd to call back those "who have gone astray . . . on the question of property" in a sermon the text of which was later given two columns in the London *Tablet.*[144] More than that, with the bishops of his province he sent a superlative-studded letter of gratitude to the Pope.[145] Gibbons did not neglect to write a letter of appreciation himself on June 22 (the copy of which was not found) and, although Leo did not single him out in any way as a predecessor or even mention his contribution in answering, he did thank him for promulgating the encyclical and confirming in his prudence and experience the Pope's own conviction of its timeliness and value. His purpose in writing the encyclical, the Pope said, was "that equity might be brought about in the mutual relationship between employers and employees; that we may be of help to men of small means; that harmony be restored among the classes in society and that we contribute to public peace." [146]

Although not as a result of the new encyclical, by 1891 the troublesome contacts of the Church with the Knights had ceased, even though the condemnation of secret societies continued. For

---

[144] *Tablet,* July 4, 1891.

[145] NYAA, n.d., copy. Translation in London *Tablet,* October 10, 1891.

[146] BCA, 88-S-7, Leo XIII to Gibbons, Rome, July 9, 1891. The cardinal's published comments of that spring, evoked by Andrew Carnegie's essay on "Wealth," disagreed merely with the millionaire's notion that "so-called charity" was being unwisely spent. Besides offering the teaching and example of Christ as guides for all in the country's economic crisis, he said: "Above all, like the French workmen of the Val-de-Bois and that great Christian socialist le Comte de Mun, let employers and employed come together in amity, with a view to understanding. Let them state their mutual grievances and ascertain their mutual demands, and, temperate Christian counsels reigning, the result will be lasting peace." "Wealth and Its Obligations," *North American Review,"* CLII (April, 1891), 394.

some undiscovered reason, perhaps in considering the reopening of the case, Corrigan had the Vicar General of Quebec send him copies of the six important documents pertaining to the question in Canada.[147] Moreover, a general peace began to descend on New York when its most recalcitrant subject was reconciled to the Church on December 23, 1892, by Archbishop Francesco Satolli, the new apostolic delegate. With a committee of four professors of the Catholic University of America the delegate examined Edward McGlynn's written exposition of his teaching and accepted his adherence to *Rerum novarum*. The priest was appointed to St. Mary's Church in Newburgh, New York, as pastor in 1894 and died there in 1900.[148]

In Baltimore, on the other hand, Cardinal Gibbons continued to be known as a friend of the workers. He was called on not only to send a letter to a Catholic workingmen's demonstration in New York in honor of Leo XIII but also to send the Knights' statutes and the Roman "approbation" of the organization to a group in Spain.[149] The work of Gibbons in putting the Church and organized labor before the public in a friendly relationship was one of the keynotes of the congratulatory messages which poured in upon him

---

[147] NYAA, C. A. Marois to Corrigan, Quebec, November 23, 1891, with enclosures.

[148] Zwierlein, *op. cit.*, III, 75-81. The encyclical of 1891 did not condemn the single tax system as such, although it pointed out the error of denying the justice of full private ownership of land and of depriving a man of "improvements which he makes in the soil." It was against the former of these points that Henry George argued in his *Open Letter to Pope Leo XIII* (New York, 1891), rather than in favor of the peculiar system of land tenure connected with his name. Cf. John A. Ryan, *Distributive Justice* (New York, 1942), pp. 52-53. This same Catholic authority held that the right of private ownership was certainly valid against complete socialism and *"probably* valid even against these modified forms of common ownership." *Ibid.*, p. 49. Cf. also Vincent A. McQuade, O.S.A., "Rev. Dr. McGlynn's Statement on Private Land Ownership in the Light of the Teaching of Pope Leo XIII." Unpublished master's thesis, Catholic University of America (1935), which concludes, "Economically his proposals might be censured; theologically, they do not contain any false principles" p. 45.

[149] BCA, 89-S-2, Austin Ford to Gibbons, New York, March 19, 1892; unindexed, Fernando Nunes Robres, Valencia, June 7, 1892.

on the occassion of his silver episcopal jubilee.[150] John Ireland did not let the occasion pass without saying in his sermon that he was sure the incident of the Knights exercised "no small influence upon the preparation of the encyclical, 'The Condition of Labor.' "[151]

As late as 1894 the name of the Knights had not been forgotten in Rome, although they were not apparently specified by two American churchmen who were seeking to inform Leo XIII on American affairs. With Bishop Keane the Pope dwelt on the tendency toward socialism, but the university rector still protested strongly any condemnation of American labor organizations or even fraternal groups.[152] The Pontiff, according to one American priest, showed acquaintance with social disorders in the United States, and Thomas O'Gorman, professor of church history in the University, tried to pass them off "as the work of the foreign element." [153] The success of Keane and O'Gorman is shown in the encyclical to the American hierarchy of 1895 in which the right of workers to associate was reasserted, although they were warned to be careful of the men with whom they co-operated.[154] While the two university men were in the Eternal City the *Moniteur de Rome* was exonerating the Knights of Labor in the United States of any connection with recent strikes. It was merely a qualifying clause, "the Holy See never wished to condemn the Knights of Labor," which caused a reaction in Quebec and illustrated that although the case had come to an end it was not closed. A weekly in that city, *La Vérité*, undoubtedly with official help, since it used hitherto unpublished documents, printed six columns of a refutation of the "singulière légende" that existed in the United States and Europe that Cardinal Taschereau had been responsible for the condemnation of the

[150] E.g., BCA, 92-F-8, James McMahon to Gibbons, Brooklyn, October 17, 1893; 92-J-11, J. A. Rodier (D. A. 19 of K. of L.), Montreal, October 8, 1893.

[151] John Ireland, *The Church and Modern Society* (St. Paul, 1905), I, 128.

[152] ACUA, Bouquillon Papers, Keane to Thomas Bouquillon, Pegli, August 3, 1894.

[153] ADR, O'Gorman to O'Connell, n.p., August 25, 1894.

[154] John J. Wynne (Ed.), *The Great Encyclical Letters of Pope Leo XIII* (New York, 1903), pp. 331-332, *Longinqua oceani* of January 6, 1895.

Knights. It indicated the two Roman decisions of 1884 and 1886 which the Canadian cardinal had merely carried out, and which finally had only been conditionally suspended. *La Vérité* represented Taschereau's appeals for what actually, in the main, they had been, namely, requests for uniformity of discipline.[155] But the evidence of the cardinal's personal conviction that the Order was worthy of Rome's sanctions, as has been seen, was omitted. The Archbishop of New York somehow secured a copy of this exposition of the case, and he wrote to the cardinal's coadjutor archbishop:

> . . . I rejoice that His Eminence is so ably vindicated.
> Regarding the decree of the Holy Office 16 Aug. 1888, I would respectfully suggest that the latest edition of the constitution of the K. of L. will show if the Society has complied with the prescriptions of said decree, 'Societatem equitum laboris pro nunc *tolerari: dummodo emendentur* etc.
> For obvious reasons I do not enter into further details.[156]

Corrigan's judgment of the status of the question was a very correct one as the hindsight of history bears out, but nonetheless Taschereau's name was to be passed on as the first enemy and denouncer of the Knights of Labor.[157]

---

[155] *La Vérité*, August 25, 1894. It cited the note of Abbé Felix Klein in John Ireland's book of lectures, *L'église et le siècle* (Paris, 1894) and also the book which Klein used in his own footnote, Max Leclerc, *Choses d'Amérique* (Paris, 1891) as also offending in this regard. These writers in turn may have depended on such a work as the highly commended *Les Etats-Unis contemporains* of Claudio Jannet, the fourth edition of which was quoted by Bernard O'Reilly, in "Land and Labor in France and the United States," *American Catholic Quarterly Review*, XIV (January 1889), 21: "The Canadian bishops together with the Cardinal Archbishop of Quebec condemned the order." Apart from his unqualified praise of Powderly, Jannet erred further in attributing the Canadian hostility to the origin of the Order in Montreal under a Jewish Mason, named Heilbronner. (*Vide supra*, pp. 95-96) O'Reilly carried both these stories in his *Life of Leo XIII* (Philadelphia, 1903), p. 674.

[156] AAQ, E. U., IV, 95, Corrigan to Begin, New York, September 10, 1884.

[157] Cf. Mourret, *op. cit.*, IX, 405, and Schmidlin, *op. cit.*, II, 371. Less understandable are Gibbons, *Retrospect*, I, 188, "The Canadian bishops obtained from the Holy See a condemnation of the Knights," and Will, *op. cit.*, I, 324, who has the first condemnation coming from "the Catholic Hierarchy

What amounts almost to another legend has persisted since the days of the trouble between the Catholic Church and the Knights. It concerns Powderly's "being forced out of the Church by well-intentioned reactionaries."[158] It is not the province of the present study, but rather of the biography of that picturesque character, to trace Powderly's defection from his religious faith. As has been seen the religious issue made trouble within the Knights of Labor and weakened Powderly's position, but with the end of 1892 he came under fire from real Protestant bigotry outside the Order. Even his joke about the Pope's membership in the Knights came back at him as "Part of my Reward."[159] There seems to have been little directly pertaining to his religion in the move which ousted him from office in 1893. It resulted from an alliance of "the Western agrico-political faction and the New York socialist-fundamentalist crowd." His accuser was his erstwhile friend, Secretary John Hayes, and the new general master workman was James R. Sovereign of Iowa.[160] In answering the charges, however, he did once again have to deny that he had bought the Pope's favor, and he referred to the Minneapolis convention where he had defended himself. This attack Powderly labeled as framed only to appeal to minds friendly disposed to the anti-Catholic American Protective As-

of Canada." Naturally this version has gotten into works on labor history in the same way.

[158] Richard J. Purcell, "John A. Ryan, Prophet of Social Justice," *Studies,* XXXV (June, 1946), 162. In four pages of typescript, by his own hand, "omitted from chapter 27" of his memoirs, Powderly professed to have found many Catholic priests lacking in Christlike qualities—at least up to the time, "when the laboring men of America caused the world to acknowledge that the poor were as much the children of God as were other men." In truth, he could add, "I had something to do with that change in the attitude of society and the church."

[159] Powderly, *Path,* pp. 394-408. Herein he used documents unlike his usual procedure. His chief accuser was the Reverend J. G. White who even included him in an article, "Jesuitism in America," in the *Cumberland Presbyterian* (October 26, 1893), PP, unassorted.

[160] Ware, *op. cit.,* p. 369. In the convention some who voted for the acceptance of Powderly's resignation gave reasons, such as his blocking the will of the majority and using the Order for private gain. *Proceedings* (Philadelphia, 1893), pp. 59-61.

sociation.[161]. Likewise in his Philadelphia report to the convention of the general assembly in 1893 Powderly made public some of his correspondence on the religious issue, and herein he sought to protect himself against bigoted charges of subservience to Rome. He was especially weak when confronted with the text of both Simeoni's decree of conditional toleration, and Gibbons' letter of September 25, 1888, transmitting the decree to the other archbishops. The general master workman did not fear, however, to praise Pope Leo XIII, whose advice on labor and politics he considered, "in the direction of liberality and toleration." [162]

The activities of Catholics in the field of organized labor do not seem to have been a major target of the anti-Catholicism of the A. P. A. in the early 1890's, as were their progress into respectable positions in society and their disreputable representation in local politics.[163] Powderly suffered later on for the former of these reasons. After 1893 he returned to the study of law, and within a year he was admitted to the bar. In 1897, in return for his political services, he was appointed Commissioner General of Immigration by President William McKinley, but only after an American Protective Association attack on his Catholicism joined by an assault of the Democratic Knights on his APAism.[164] In his memoirs Powderly recalled difficulties with Catholic clerics, too, because of public positions he later took, but he remained friendly with others, especially with Archbishop Ireland, to whom he referred as a "warm friend." [165] Powderly was not beyond ap-

[161] Wisconsin State Historical Society, Manuscripts, Knights of Labor, "Statement of T. V. Powderly to the Order of the Knights of Labor," n.d., n.p.

[162] *Proceedings* (Philadelphia, 1893), "Report of the General Master Workman," p. 9; pp. 6-20.

[163] Cf. Humphrey Desmond, *The APA Movement* (Washington, 1912) and Gustavus Meyers, *History of Bigotry in the United States* (New York, 1943), pp. 219-247; On the influence of the labor situation, cf. Alvin P. Stauffer, "Anti-Catholicism in American Politics, 1865-1900." Unpublished doctoral thesis, Harvard University (1933), pp. 130-155.

[164] PP, Scrapbook, March-November, 1897, Scranton *Truth,* July 19; Chicago *Federationist,* September 11; Dayton *Journal,* September 15, 1897.

[165] PP, Powderly to "Col" Scranton, April 7, 1897; also to Emma Fichenscher, Washington, October 20, 1897.

pealing to Gibbons to aid in preventing a strike in the Pennsylvania anthracite fields as late as 1900. Although he used glowing terms in speaking of the cardinal's early help, he received a non-committal reply.[166] Corrigan, he insisted, used his influence against him in the controversy about affairs in the port of New York, which resulted in his dismissal from the office of Commissioner by President Theodore Roosevelt in 1902.[167] Whatever the influences were that held sway, it was only in 1901 that he openly gave up the Catholic Church by joining the Masons.[168] Yet he remained friendly with William J. Kerby, professor of sociology in the Catholic University of America, near the campus of which the former labor leader made his home in Washington, D. C.[169] In 1907 he was reinstated in the Information Division of the Bureau of Immigration after making a study in 1906 of the causes of European emigration for the Department of Commerce and Labor. Powderly continued with the bureau until 1921, but before his death on June 24, 1924, he also served as Commissioner of Conciliation in the Department of Labor.[170]

Powderly's recollections published after his death at the instance of his widow by a second marriage, Emma Fichenscher, his former secretary, are more bitter toward Catholic churchmen than the records would indicate he actually was at the time of his "ecclesiastical diplomacy." [171] Ironically enough, he was too close to the events to see what a paper in the birthplace of the Knights discerned at the time of his death, namely, "the thing for which Powderly will probably be most remembered was the long and

[166] PP, Powderly to Gibbons, Washington, August 29, 1900, copy; Gibbons to Powderly, Southhampton, L. I., August 31, 1900.

[167] Powderly, *Path,* p. 302.

[168] *Ibid.,* p. 380.

[169] ACUA, Kerby Papers, Powderly to Kerby, Washington, August 4, 1904. He sought to hear the "recital of the great struggle . . . at Rome" from Denis O'Connell, then rector of the University. ACUA, O'Connell Papers, June 10, 1903.

[170] Powderly, *Path,* pp. ix-x.

[171] Ware, *op. cit.,* p. 102, "In no other relationship did Powderly show so great dignity and ability as in his handling of the problem of the Order and the Church."

successful battle by which he prevented the Knights of Labor from coming under the ban of the Catholic Church." This editorial appreciated, too, the real connection between this action and the issuance of *Rerum novarum.*[172] Powderly chose to be remembered as a martyr to a cause, but he failed to appreciate the full effects of his efforts since the misunderstanding he bore was to save number-less Catholic workingmen after him. After 1891 American ec-clesiastical authority and Catholic labor leaders, too, had a guide, in Pope Leo's encyclical even though only a few hardy pioneers took it up. The existence of *Rerum novarum,* furthermore, brought some slow-dawning realization that in the training of the clergy attention must be given not only to the principles of social morality, but also to the serious problems of the society in which they must be made to work.[173]

All of which, however, does not mean that Pope Leo's encyclical marked the beginnings of a great Catholic social movement in the United States. Even Cardinal Gibbons was no longer found in the forefront for the workers' causes.[174] Among those Catholics who propagated the papal teaching—and they were far from a majority —the positive teaching and program of the Church were scarcely emphasized until the advent of John A. Ryan in 1906 with the publication of his volume, *A Living Wage.* Up to that time, and even after, the Catholic preoccupation in the labor movement was to oppose socialism.[175] Catholic laborers supported the current

[172] Philadelphia *Inquirer,* June 26, 1924, PP, unassorted.

[173] Cf. John Talbot Smith, *Our Seminaries* (New York, 1896), p. 303, "The new social conditions . . . call imperatively for the new moral theology." The discussion of seminary curricula at the Third Plenary Council of Baltimore in 1884 showed no awareness of this need. Cf. Francis P. Cassidy, "Catholic Education in the Third Plenary Council of Baltimore," *Catholic Historical Review,* XXXIV (October, 1948), 282-287.

[174] In an interview given in 1917 he maintained in favor of the railroads and as a warning to labor unions, "Class legislation is dangerous in this country. I sincerely hope that organizations working on such programmes will be restrained." *Outlook,* February 28, 1917.

[175] Cf. Aaron I. Abell, "The Reception of Leo XIII's Labor Encyclical in America, 1891-1919," *Review of Politics,* VII (October, 1945), 464-495; Sister M. Joan de Lourdes Leonard, "The Catholic Attitude toward American Labor, 1884-1919." Unpublished master's thesis, Columbia University (1941);

form of organization, the American Federation of Labor, and many of the leaders of that body were Catholics. The increasing interest and friendly attitude of ecclesiastics which made them even desirable as peacemakers in industrial disputes [176] was to be highlighted by the forward-looking "Bishops' Program of Social Reconstruction" in 1919.[177] The influence of the Catholic Church, it might be said, was exercised as a conserving force in American unionism, helping it to survive by at least the endorsement of silence, and aiding in the struggle which kept it an economic movement non-politicized by the socialists.[178]

In Europe after 1891 Catholic workingmen and their Church leaders were brought face to face with the problem of their membership in non-Catholic unions. Similar to Europe, sections of French-Catholic Canada also developed Catholic associations of workers which resulted in a debilitating dual unionism.[179] Only in 1912 and after much strife was Catholic membership in Christian but non-Catholic groups allowed in Germany.[180] In the United States the analogous trouble had long since been experienced in the case of

Purcell, *op. cit.*, pp. 153-174; Henry J. Browne, "Peter E. Dietz, Pioneer Planner of Catholic Social Action," *Catholic Historical Review*, XXXIII (January, 1948), 448-456; Abell, "The Catholic Church and Social Problems in the World War I Era," *Mid-America*, New Series, XIX (July, 1948), 139-151.

[176] Cf. Paul Stroh, C.SS.R., "The Catholic Clergy and American Labor Disputes, 1900-1937." Unpublished thesis, School of Social Science, Catholic University of America (1939); also, Sister Mary Evangela Henthorne, "Bishop Spalding's Work on the Anthracite Coal Strike Commission," *Catholic Historical Review*, XXVIII (July, 1942), 184-205.

[177] Cf. John A. Ryan, *Social Reconstruction* (New York, 1920), for text and commentary; also his autobiographical *Social Doctrine in Action* (New York, 1941), pp. 143-151.

[178] One view from the left by a labor historian, after judging Gibbons' Roman action and its outcome, "one of the most significant factors in making the American labor movement safe for Catholicism," goes on to say of the later period: "The Catholic domination has more than any other factor made the American Federation of Labor safe for capitalism and a violent opponent of socialism." David J. Saposs, "The Catholic Church and the Labor Movement," *Modern Monthly*, VII (May, 1933), 230; VII (June, 1933), 298.

[179] Cf. Allan B. Latham, *The Catholic and National Labor Union of Canada* (Toronto, 1930).

[180] By the letter *Singulari quadam* of Pope Pius X, September 24, 1912.

the Knights of Labor. The burden of it had been borne by the parish priests of Pennsylvania who first feared this secret and oath-bound society. Then the bishops scattered throughout the country had been puzzled as to how it could be anything but harmful. Powderly had striven mightily, especially after Rome's decision on the case in Canada had further confused the issue. Finally Gibbons, with far more episcopal support than opposition, in his Roman triumph had brought peace and friendly relations. This he did, not with canonical accuracy, but with a venturesome awareness of the threat of the present and the spirit of the future.

When Pius XI in 1931 in *Quadragesimo anno* explicitly recognized that in some countries peculiar conditions might not warrant Catholic unions it was no great innovation for American Catholics to be instructed, "Under some circumstances, they seem to have no choice but to enroll themselves in neutral trade unions." If that permission could be taken as a recognition of their early contribution to the Catholic social movement, what followed might well be considered as a future challenge to both clergy and laity:

> Side by side with these trade unions, there must always be associations which aim at giving their members a thorough religious and moral training, that these in turn may impart to the labor union to which they belong the upright spirit which should direct their entire conduct. Thus will these unions exert a beneficial influence far beyond the ranks of their own members.[181]

[181] Husslein (Ed.), *Social Wellsprings*, II, 189.

APPENDIX I

THE SECRET WORK[1]

WHEN admitted to the Assembly, immediately advance to the center and deliver the Sign of Obliteration to the Venerable Sage, who sits there to represent the dignity of the Order. It is made thus:

SIGN OF OBLITERATION

Place the palm of the right hand on the palm of the left hand—both hands in front of the body at the height of the elbow—elbows close to the body—right hand uppermost. Then separate the hands, right and left as if wiping something off the left hand with the right —elbows still touching the sides—right palm down—left palm up. Then drop both hands naturally to sides.

The language of that sign is: "to erase, obliterate, wipe out" everything on entering here, as the draughtsman erases useless lines. On retiring, you also come to the center and deliver the same sign, when it also signifies to obliterate, or to keep profoundly secret everything seen, heard, said or done by yourself or others, absolutely in accordance with your pledge. It is answered by the Venerable Sage by the Sign of Decoration thus:

SIGN OF DECORATION

Place the index finger of the right hand on the left breast, back of the hand to the front.

[1] Taken from Ezra A. Cook (Publisher), *Knights of Labor Illustrated. "Adelphon Kruptos." The Full Illustrated Ritual including the "Unwritten Work" and an Historical Sketch of the Order* (Chicago, 1886), pp. 32-37. Although this was a piece of exposé literature, it combined the items of the "Secret Work and Instructions" (received by Powderly, April 1, 1882) with the instructions of the Venerable Sage to new members as given in the A.K. after the beginning of 1882. The old ritual (Powderly's copy was pencil marked, 1880) includes an additional sign, "The A. of D. is made by * * * and * *, on all occasions when as *s we address the Universal Father. Its language is "I reverently adore." (p. 17). The term "Unwritten Work" was also used for "Secret Work." *Path*, Appendix II, pp. 431-443, contains an explanation sent out by circular to the Order of such things as the trappings of the "sanctuary" and the seal. Commons, *Documentary History*, X, 19-31, gives the text of the initiation and founding ceremonies.

The language of the answering sign is: "Labor is noble and holy." The grip is made thus:

GRIP

Extend the hand with the thumb parallel with the forefinger and close to it; clasp hands with the fingers, without locking the thumbs—with a side pressure of the thumbs on the outside—thumbs still extended parallel with each other. Then end by locking the thumbs and an ordinary shake of the hands.

The Grip signifies "Humanity." As the thumb distinguishes man from all other orders of creation, and by it alone man is able to achieve wonders of art and perform labor, we always, therefore, approach a member in this way, after which shake hands in the usual way.

SIGN OF INTELLIGENCE

The Sign of Intelligence is made by placing the index finger of the right hand in the center of the forehead—the last three fingers of the hand closed over the thumb—back of the hand to the front.

The language of that sign is: "I have determined," that being the seat of intelligence and wisdom. It is used in voting both in the affirmative and negative.

SIGN OF RECOGNITION

The sign is made with shield or left hand, thus: with the thumb and first two fingers of the left hand take hold of the end of the right sleeve, at the cuff on the right hand—thumb on the outside and the two fingers inserted on the inside. Make a motion as if to turn up the cuff.

The language of that sign is: "I am a worker," to be used in strange company or among or where craftsmen are employed, to ascertain if there are Knights present.

ANSWER

The answer is made in this manner: Draw the right hand open across the forehead from left to right, back of hand to the front.

The language of the answer is: "I, too, earn my bread by the sweat of my brow." To give assurance, if necessary, use it in reverse, the challenged giving the sign, and challenger giving the answer.

We also have a verbal challenge:

VERBAL CHALLENGE

The following words are used where a member might be seeking for work or information: "I have come," a member replying to the challenge with; "work your way." Any other words can be used after the words "come" and "way" so as not attract attention, such as "I have come to look for work," and "work your way and find it."

THE CRY OF DISTRESS

To be used in the dark, or when the Sign of Recognition cannot be used, is thus: "I am a stranger," giving emphasis to the word *stranger*. Any member of the Order hearing this will answer "a stranger should be assisted."

CAUTION

As the value of the cry of distress, for practical use, depends entirely on accuracy of wording, great care should be exercised in instructing candidates, especially as great irregularity now exists. The words given above are all of the official work, although members are allowed to suppliment [*sic*] the words given with others, so as not to attract attention from those not members, as for instance: "I am a stranger and need assistance." Answer; "a stranger should be assisted and I for one am willing to help you." Any other similar additional words may be used, but when instructing candidates use care not to confound the official part with the unofficial.

The Sign of Caution is made in this manner:

SIGN OF CAUTION

Close the last two fingers of the right hand, leaving the first fingers extended. Place the two extended fingers on the left side of the forehead—back of hand to the front. Then draw the fingers across the forehead toward the right and down over the right side of the face, then cross the mouth toward the left, the thumb under the line, in a careless manner.

It is used to warn any member whom you may see being imposed upon or cheated; or where a member is thoughtlessly revealing in the presence of those not members, something in regard to the Order that should only be known by members. In balloting, advance to the center, deliver the Sign of Obliteration to the Master Workman who will answer by the Sign of Decoration. You will then deposit your ballot and retire.

The special meeting sign is a perpendicular and horizontal line, meeting at right angles. The hour of meeting is placed over the *horizontal* line; the number of the Local under it. The month, designated by a figure, as 3 for March, is placed to the left of the *perpendicular* line; the day of the month to the right of it. The horizontal line may be placed either at the top or bottom of the perpendicular line, and may run either to the right or left of it. All that is required is two lines, one horizontal and the other perpendicular, meeting at right angles. When the hour of meeting is *before* noon, the sign X is placed *before* the hour of meeting. When it is *after* noon, then *after* the hour.

Wishing to announce a special meeting of Local Assembly No. 300 for September 5th, at 8 o'clock in the evening it is done as shown by figure.

$$9 \mid 5$$
$$8{:}00 \ X$$
$$300$$

This Assembly is known as .... Assembly No. ...., and is attached to (*the General Assembly, or District Assembly, No. ...., as the case may be.*) Your monthly dues are .... cents, and upon your prompt payment of the same to the Financial Secretary will depend, in a great measure, your good standing in the Order. Unknown Knight, you will please conduct the candidate to the Master Workman for the closing ceremony.

APPENDIX II

PROPOSED ADDRESS OF BISHOP JOHN J. KEANE BEFORE THE RICHMOND CONVENTION[1]

BOTH as an American citizen and as a Catholic Bishop I am glad to address this representative assembly of the workingmen of our country. The fundamental principle of our country's constitution is the declaration that every individual should freely possess and fully be protected in the inalienable rights bestowed on him by his Creator, the rights to life, liberty, and the pursuit of happiness. As an American citizen, I rejoice at every advance toward the perfect realization of that truest and noblest ideal of social organization and government; and therefore do I rejoice to behold you and the vast body of working men at your backs banded together, not for violence or injustice, but for the calm, orderly, dignified assertion and vindication of your God-given rights. The Catholic Church is the old Church of "the gospel preached to the poor." As a Catholic Bishop I welcome whatever really improves the poor man's condition, whatever lifts poverty out of squalor and degradation, places it beyond the power of oppression, and makes it worthy of the Divine Carpenter of Nazareth, who chose poverty for His Bride and deified labor in His sacred person; therefore do I hail this organization of the intelligence, the energy, and the conscientiousness of the sons of toil, which, if faithful to intelligence and conscience, cannot fail to win for them the respect as well as the justice that is their due.

In the utterances of your presiding officer you unfurl your banner to the world; and on its folds we read the motto: Justice to all; injustice to none. Under that banner, you cannot fail of victory; true to that motto, you will assuredly have with you the sympathy of every friend of justice, of every lover of his race. Seek justice for yourselves, but never at the cost of injustice to anyone. Let the rights of others be as sacred as your own. As true Americans love freedom always and everywhere, even in those who differ from you in conviction, or who are not within your aims and

---

[1] Powderly Papers, Attached to Keane to Powderly, October 21, 1886.

organization. Convince them all that it is to their interest to be with you, and you will soon have them all in your ranks; and as long as they either do not choose to be, or for any reason cannot be with you, respect their freedom, be true Americans, and act upon the good old rule: "Live and let live." Coercion will never do for conviction. You are powerful enough and noble enough to be able to be tolerant and magnanimous. Americans will always respect those, and only those, who respect the freedom and the rights of others, and who would rather suffer harm themselves than inflict wrong on anyone.

On your banner I read reverence for the majesty of the law. Cling to that principle, as the sheet-anchor that will keep you from being swept in to the whirlpool that has swallowed up many an organization before you. You must appeal to the law and the judiciary for protection of your own rights; assuredly then you will not forfeit your claim by slighting or evading any decisions of law and the judiciary in defense of others. How powerful soever may be any instrument of offense or defense, cast it from you as soon as the authority which we are all bound to respect, pronounces it an unlawful or dishonorable weapon.

Your every utterance proclaims you devoted patriotic citizens. As such, love your country's weal more than your private interests. Like brave soldiers, bear any hardship rather than escape from it to her disadvantage; spurn any gain that would cost her suffering or loss. She feared lately that the methods of some of your associates were oblivious of this patriotic unselfishness, that they sought their own advantage with great risk to her industrial interests and to that business-confidence which is the very life-energy of her prosperity. I am certain that you mean no such result, and that you will never countenance any methods that would lead to it.

Loud and clear then let your motto ring abroad: *Justice to all; injustice to none;* and to its music may you march on to a victory that will have on it the blessing of Church and of country, of God and of man.

APPENDIX III

THE QUESTION OF THE "KNIGHTS OF LABOR" [1]

To His Eminence Cardinal Simeoni, Prefect of the Sacred Congregation of the Propaganda:

YOUR EMINENCE:

In submitting to the Holy See the conclusions which after several months of attentive observation and reflection, seem to me to sum up the truth concerning the association of the Knights of Labor, I feel profoundly convinced of the vast importance of the consequences attaching to this question, which forms but a link in the great chain of the social problems of our day, and especially of our country.

In weighing [treating-jugeant] this question I have been very careful to follow as my constant guide the spirit of the Encyclicals, in which our Holy Father, Leo XIII, has so admirably set forth the dangers of our time and their remedies, as well as the principles by which we are to recognize associations condemned by the Holy See. Such was also the guide of the Third Plenary Council of Baltimore in its teaching concerning the principles to be followed and the dangers to be shunned by the faithful either in the choice or in the establishment of those associations toward which the spirit of our popular institutions so strongly impels them. And considering the dire [evil-funestes] consequences that might result from a mistake in the treatment of organizations which often count their members by the thousands and hundreds of thousands, the council wisely ordained (n. 255) [n. 225] that when an association is spread over several dioceses, not even the bishop of one of these dioceses shall condemn it, but shall refer the case to a standing com-

---

[1] Baltimore Cathedral Archives, 82-N-3. The "official" English version, first published in the *Moniteur de Rome*, March 28, 1887, has been reproduced in Will, *Life of Cardinal Gibbons*, I, 337-352; Gibbons, *Retrospect of Fifty Years*, I, 190-209; John T. Reily, *Passing Events in the Life of Cardinal Gibbons* (Martinsburg, 1890), I, 92-102; Zwierlein, *Life and Letters of Bishop McQuaid*, II, 445-455.

The lesser differences in the readings, which usually show the toning down of the original French for American readers, will be indicated in brackets within the text. The other variations will be cited in the notes.

mittee of all the archbishops of the United States; and even these are not authorized to condemn unless their sentence be unanimous; and in case they fail to agree unanimously, then only the supreme tribunal of the Holy See can impose a condemnation; all this in order to avoid error and confusion of discipline.

This committee of archbishops held a meeting, in fact, toward the end of last October, especially to consider the association of the Knights of Labor. [at which the Knights of Labor was specially considered—spécialement pour consider] We were not persuaded to hold this meeting because of any request on the part of our bishops, for none of them had asked for it; and it should also be said that, among all the bishops we know, only two or three desire the condemnation. But the importance of the question in itself, and in the estimation of the Holy See led us to examine it with greatest attention. After our discussion, the results of which have already been communicated to the Sacred Congregation of the Propaganda, only two out of the twelve archbishops voted for condemnation, and their reasons were powerless to convince the others of either the justice or the prudence of such a condemnation.

In the following considerations I wish to state in detail the reasons which determined the vote of the great majority of the committee—reasons whose truth and force seem to me all the more evident today; I shall try at the same time to do justice to the arguments advanced by the opposition.

1. In the first place, in the constitution, laws and official declarations of the Knights of Labor, there can clearly be found assertions and rules [though there may be found . . . things—peuvent bien se trouver des assertions ou des règles] which we would not approve; but we have not found in them those elements so clearly pointed out by the Holy See, which places them among condemned associations.

(a) In their form of initiation there is no oath.

(b) The obligation to secrecy by which they keep the knowledge of their business from strangers or enemies, in no wise prevents Catholics from manifesting everything to competent ecclesiastical authority, even outside of confession. This has been positively declared to us by their president. [their chief officers—leur président]

(c) They make no promise of blind obedience. The object and laws of the association are distinctly declared, and the obligation of obedience does not go beyond these limits.

(d) They not only profess no hostility against religion or the Church, but their declarations are quite to the contrary. The Third Plenary Council commands that we should not condemn an association without giving a hearing to its officers or representatives; "auditis ducibus, corypheis vel sociis praecipuis" (n. 254).[2] Now, their president in sending me a copy of their constitution, says that he is a Catholic from the bottom of his heart; [devoted Catholic— Catholique du fond de son coeur] that he practices his religion faithfully and receives the sacraments regularly; that he belongs to no Masonic or other society condemned by the Church; that he knows of nothing in the association of the Knights of Labor contrary to the laws of the Church; that, with filial submission he begs the Pastors of the Church to examine all the details of their organization, [their constitution and laws—tous les détails de leur organisation] and, if they find anything worthy of condemnation, they should indicate it, and he promises its correction. Assuredly one does not perceive in all this any hostility to the authority of the Church, but on the contrary a spirit in every way praiseworthy. After their convention last year at Richmond, he and several of the officers and members, devout Catholics, [principal members— officiers et membres] made similar declarations concerning their feelings [3] and the action of that convention, the documents of which we are expecting to receive.

(e) Nor do we find in this organization any hostility to the authority and laws of our country. Not only does nothing of the kind appear in their constitution and laws, but the heads of our civil government treat with the greatest respect [with respect— avec le plus grand respect] the cause which they represent. The President of the United States told me personally, a month ago [a few weeks ago—il y a un mois] that he was then examining a law for the amelioration of certain social grievances and that he had just had a long conference on the subject with Mr. Powderly, president of the Knights of Labor. The Congress of the United States, following the advice of President Cleveland [4] is busying itself at the present time with the amelioration of the working classes, in whose complaints they acknowledge openly [5] there is

---

[2] The Latin phrase was omitted in the English version.
[3] "leurs sentiments," was not translated.
[4] "in his annual message," was inserted in the English.
[5] "ouvertement," was not translated.

a great deal of truth. And our political parties, far from regarding them as enemies of the country, vie with each other in championing the evident rights of the poor workmen, [workmen—pauvres travailleurs] who seek not to resist [6] the laws, but only to obtain just legislation by constitutional and legitimate means.

These considerations, which show that in this association [these associations—cette association] those elements are not to be found which the Holy See condemns, lead us to study, in the second place, the evils which the associations contend against, and the nature of the conflict.

2. That there exists among us, as in the other countries of the world, grave and threatening social evils, public injustices, which call for strong resistance and legal remedy, is a fact which no one dares to deny, and the truth of which has been already acknowledged by the Congress and the President of the United States. Without entering into the sad details of these wrongs,—which does not seem necessary here,—it may suffice to mention only that monopolies on the part of both individuals and of corporations, have already called forth not only the complaints of our working classes but also the opposition of our public men and legislators; that the efforts of these monopolists, not always without success, to control legislation to their own profit, cause serious apprehension among the disinterested friends of liberty; that the heartless avarice which, through greed of gain, pitilessly grinds not only the men, but particularly the women and children in various employments, make it clear to all who love humanity and justice that it is not only the right of the laboring classes to protect themselves, but the duty of the whole people to aid them in finding a remedy against the dangers with which both civilization and the social order are menaced by avarice, oppression and corruption.

It would be vain to deny either the existence of the evils, the right of legitimate resistance, or the necessity of a remedy. At most doubt might be raised about the legitimacy of the form of resistance and the remedy employed by the Knights of Labor. This then ought to be the next point of our examination.

3. It can hardly be doubted that for the attainment of any public end, association—the organization of all interested persons—is the most efficacious means, a means altogether natural and just. This is so evident, and besides so conformable to the genius of our coun-

---

[6] "or overthrow," was inserted.

try, of our essentially popular social conditions, that it is unnecessary to insist upon it. It is almost the only means to invite public attention, to give force to the most legitimate resistance, to add weight to the most just demands.

Now there already exists an organization which presents a thousand attractions and advantages, but which our Catholic workingmen, with filial obedience to the Holy See, refuse to join; this is the *Masonic* organization, which exists everywhere in our country, and which, as Mr. Powderly has expressly pointed out to us, unites employer and worker in a brotherhood very advantageous for the latter, but which numbers in its ranks hardly a single Catholic. Freely [nobly—de grand coeur] renouncing the advantages which the Church and their consciences forbid, workingmen form associations, [join—se forment] having nothing in common with the deadly designs of the enemies of religion and seeking only mutual protection and help, and the legitimate assertion of their rights. But here they also find themselves threatened with condemnation, and so deprived of [hindered from—privés] their only means of defense. Is it surprising that they should be astonished at this and that they ask *Why?* [7]

4. Let us now consider the objections made against this sort of organization.

(a) It is objected that in these organizations Catholics are mixed with Protestants, to the peril of their faith. Naturally, yes, they are mixed with Protestants in the workers' associations,[8] precisely as they are at their work; for in a mixed people like ours, the separation of religions in social affairs is not possible. But to suppose that the faith of our Catholics suffers thereby is not to know the Catholic workers of America who are not like the workingmen of so many European countries—misguided and perverted children, looking on their Mother the Church as a hostile stepmother—but they are intelligent, well instructed and devoted children ready to give their blood, as they continually give their means (although small and hard-earned) [hard-earned—chétifs et péniblement gagnés] for her support and protection. And in fact it is not in the present

---

[7] The last sentence of the paragraph was entirely omitted in the English version.

[8] The first part of the parallel was omitted in the English "avec les Protestants dans les associations des travailleurs, précisément comme ils sont dans les travaux mêmes."

case that Catholics are mixed with Protestants, but rather that Protestants are admitted to the advantages of an association, two-thirds of whose members and the principal officers [many of whose members and officers—des deux tiers des membres et les officiers principaux] are Catholics; and in a country like ours their exclusion would be simply impossible.

(b) But it is said, could there not be substituted for such an organization confraternities which would unite the workingmen under the direction of the priests and the direct influence of religion? I answer frankly that I do not believe that either possible or necessary in our country. I sincerely admire the efforts of this sort which are made in countries where the workers are led astray by the enemies of religion; but thanks be to God, that is not our condition. We find that in our country the presence and explicit influence of the clergy would not be advisable where our citizens, without distinction of religious belief, come together in regard to their industrial interests alone. Without going so far, we have abundant means for making our working people faithful Catholics, and simple good sense advises us not to go to extremes.

(c) Again, it is objected that the liberty of such an organization exposes Catholics to the evil influences of the most dangerous associates, even of atheists, communists and anarchists. That is true; but it is one of the trials of faith which our brave American Catholics are accustomed to meet almost daily, and which they know how to disregard with good sense and firmness. The press of our country tells us and the president of the Knights of Labor has related to us, how these violent and aggressive elements have endeavored to seize authority in their councils, or to inject their poison into the principles of the association; but they also verify with what determination these evil spirits [machinators—mauvais esprits] have been repulsed and defeated. The presence among our citizens of this destructive element, which has come for the most part from certain nations of Europe, is assuredly for us an occasion of lively regrets and careful precautions; it is an inevitable fact, however, but one which the union between the Church and her children in our country renders comparatively free from danger. In truth, the only grave danger would come from an alienation between the Church and her children, which nothing would more certainly occasion than imprudent condemnations.

(d) An especially weighty charge is drawn from the outbursts of violence, even to bloodshed, which have characterized [accompanied—charactérize] several of the strikes inaugurated by labor organizations. Concerning this, three things are to be remarked: first, strikes are not an invention of the Knights of Labor, but a means almost everywhere and always resorted to by employees in our land and elsewhere to protest against what they consider unjust and to demand their rights; secondly in such a struggle of the poor and indignant multitudes against hard and obstinate monopoly, anger and violence [outbursts of anger—colère et le violence] are often as inevitable as they are regrettable; thirdly, the laws and chief authorities of the Knights of Labor, far from encouraging violence or the occasions of it, exercise a powerful influence to hinder it, and to keep strikes within the limits of good order and legitimate action. A careful examination of the acts of violence which have marked the struggle between capital and labor during the past year, leaves us convinced that it would be unjust to attribute them to the association of the Knights of Labor. This was but one of several associations of workers that took part in the strikes, and their chief officers, according to disinterested witnesses, used every possible effort to appease the anger of the crowds and to prevent the excesses which, in my judgment, could not justly be attributed to them. Doubtless among the Knights of Labor as among thousands of other workingmen, there are violent, or even wicked and criminal men, who have committed inexcusable deeds of violence, and have urged their associates to do the same; but to attribute this to the organization, it seems to me, would be as unreasonable as to attribute to the Church the follies and crimes of her children against which she protests.[9] I repeat that in such a struggle of the great masses of the people against the mail-clad power, which, as it is acknowledged, often refuses them the simple rights of humanity and justice, it is vain to expect that every error and every act of violence can be avoided; and to dream that this struggle can be prevented, or that we can deter the multitudes from organizing, which is their only practical means [hope—moyen pratique] of success, would be to ignore the nature and forces of human society in times like ours. The part of Christian prudence evidently is to try to hold the hearts of the multitude by the bonds of love, in order to control their actions by the principles of faith, justice and charity, to acknowledge frankly the truth and justice in their cause,

[9] "proteste," was translated, "strives and protests."

in order to deter them from what would be false and criminal, and thus to turn into a legitimate, peaceable and beneficent contest what could easily become for the masses of our people a volcanic abyss, like that which society fears and the Church deplores in Europe.

Upon this point I insist strongly, because, from an intimate acquaintance with the social conditions of our country I am profoundly convinced that here we are touching upon a subject which not only concerns the rights of the working classes, who ought to be especially dear to the Church which our Divine Lord sent to evangelize the poor, but with which are bound up the fundamental interests of the Church and of human society for the future. This is a point which I desire, in a few additional words to develop more clearly.

5. Whoever meditates upon the ways in which divine Providence is guiding contemporary history cannot fail to remark how important is the part which the power of the people takes therein at present and must take in the future. We behold, with profound sadness, the efforts of the prince of darkness to make this power dangerous to the social weal by withdrawing the masses of the people from the influence of religion, and impelling them towards the ruinous paths of license and anarchy. Until now our country presents a picture of altogether different [most consolingly different—tout différent] character—that of a popular power regulated by love of good order, by respect for religion, by obedience to the authority of the laws, not a democracy of license and violence, but that true democracy which aims at the general prosperity through the means of sound principles and good social order.

In order to preserve so desirable a state of things it is absolutely necessary that religion should continue to hold the affections, and thus rule the conduct of the multitudes. As Cardinal Manning has so well written,[10] "In the future era the Church has no longer to deal with princes and parliaments, but with the masses, with the people. Whether we will or no this is our work; we need a new spirit, a new direction of our life and activity." To lose influence over the people would be to lose the future altogether; and it is by the heart, far more than by the understanding, that we must hold and guide this immense power, so mighty either for good or for evil. Among all the glorious titles of the Church which her

---

[10] In the English version this quotation is introduced with the words, "A new task is before us."

history has merited for her, there is not one which at present gives her so great influence as that of *Friend of the People*. Assuredly, in our democratic country, it is this title which wins for the Catholic Church not only the enthusiastic devotedness of the millions of her children, but also the respect and admiration of all our citizens, whatever be their religious belief. It is the power of precisely this title which renders persecution almost an impossibility, and which draws toward our holy Church the great heart of the American people.

And since it is acknowledged by all that the great questions of the future are not those of war, of commerce or finance, but the social questions, the questions which concern the improvement of the condition of the great masses of the people, and especially of the working people, it is evidently of supreme importance that the Church should always be found on the side of humanity, of justice toward the multitudes who compose the body of the human family. As the same Cardinal Manning very wisely wrote, "We must admit and accept calmly and with good will that industries and profits must be considered in second place; the moral state and domestic condition of the whole working population must be considered first. I will not venture to formulate the acts of parliament, but here is precisely their fundamental principle for the future. The conditions of the lower classes as are found at present among our people, can not and must not continue. On such a basis no social edifice can stand." [11] In our country, especially, this is the inevitable program of the future, and the position which the Church must hold toward the solution is sufficiently obvious. She must certainly not favor the extremes to which the poor multitudes are naturally inclined, but, I repeat, she must withhold them from these extremes by the bonds of affection, by the maternal desire which

[11] The *Moniteur* version of Manning's text was cited as from, "Miscellanies, Vol. 2, p. 81," and read as follows: "I know I am treading on a very difficult subject, but I feel confident of this, that we must face it, and that we must face it calmly, justly, and with a willingness to put labor and the profits of labor second—the moral state and domestic life of the whole working population first. I will not venture to draw up such an act of Parliament further than to lay down this principle. These things (the present condition of the poor in England) cannot go on; these things ought not to go on. The accumulation of wealth in the land, the piling up of wealth like mountains, in the possession of classes or individuals, cannot go on. No commonwealth can rest on such foundations."

she will manifest for the concession of all that is just and reasonable in their demands, and by the maternal blessing which she will bestow upon every legitimate means for improving the condition of the people.

6. Now let us consider for a moment the consequences which would inevitably follow from a contrary course, from a lack of sympathy for the working class, from a suspicion of their aims, from a hasty condemnation of their methods.

(a) First, there is the evident danger of the Church's losing in popular estimation her right to be considered the friend of the people. The logic of men's hearts goes swiftly to its conclusions, and this conclusion would be a pernicious one for the people and for the Church. To lose the heart of the people would be a misfortune for which the friendship of the few rich and powerful would be no compensation.

(b) There is a great danger of rendering hostile to the Church the political power of our country, which openly takes sides with the millions who are demanding justice and the improvement of their condition. The accusation of being, *"un-American,"* that is to say, alien to our national spirit, is the most powerful weapon which the enemies of the Church know how to employ against her. It was this cry which aroused the Know-Nothing persecution thirty years ago, and the same would be quickly used again if the opportunity offered itself. To appreciate the gravity of this danger it is well to remark that not only are the rights of the working classes loudly proclaimed by each of our two great political parties, but it is very probable [not improbable—très probable] that, in our approaching national elections there will be a candidate for the office of President of the United States as the special representative of these complaints and demands of the masses. Now, to seek to crush by an ecclesiastical condemnation an organization which represents nearly [more than—presque] 500,000 votes, and which has already so respectable and so universally recognized a place in the political arena, would to speak frankly, be considered by the American people as not less ridiculous as it is rash. To alienate from ourselves the friendship of the people would be to run great risk of losing the respect which the Church has won in the estimation of the American nation, and of destroying the state of peace and prosperity which form so admirable a contrast with her condition in some so-called Catholic countries. Already in these months past, a murmur of popular anger and of threats against the Church has made itself heard, and it is necessary that we should move with much precaution.[12]

(c) A third danger, and the one which touches our hearts the most, is the risk of losing the love of the children of the Church, and of pushing them into an attitude of resistance against their Mother. The whole world presents no more beautiful spectacle than that of their filial devotion and obedience. But it is necessary to recognize that, in our age and in our country, obedience cannot be blind. We would greatly deceive ourselves if we expected it. Our Catholic working men sincerely believe that they are only seeking justice, and seeking it by legitimate means. A condemnation would be considered both false and unjust, and would not be accepted [and therefore, not binding—et ne serait pas acceptée]. We might indeed preach to them submission and confidence in the Church, but these good dispositions could hardly go so far. They love the Church, and they wish to save their souls, but they must also earn their living, and labor is now so organized that without belonging to the organization there is little chance to earn one's living.

Behold, then, the consequences to be feared. Thousands of the most devoted children of the Church would believe themselves repulsed by their Mother and would live without practicing their religion. The revenues of the Church, which with us come entirely from the free offerings of the people, would suffer immensely, and it would be the same with Peter's pence. The ranks of the secret societies would be filled with Catholics, who had been up to now faithful.[13] The Holy See, which has constantly received from the Catholics of America proofs of almost unparalleled devotedness, would be considered not as a paternal authority, but as a harsh and unjust power. Here are assuredly effects, the occasion of which wisdom and prudence must avoid.

In a word, we have seen quite recently the sad and threatening confusion caused by the condemnation inflicted by an Archbishop

[12] The English read, "Angry utterances have not been wanting of late, and it is well that we should act prudently."

[13] The variant reading in English was, "Thousands of the Church's most devoted children, whose affection is her greatest comfort, and whose free offerings are her chief support, would consider themselves repulsed by their Mother, and would live without practising their religion. Catholics who have hitherto shunned the secret societies, would be sorely tempted to join their ranks."

upon a single priest in vindication of discipline—a condemnation which the Archbishop believed to be just and necessary, but which fell upon a priest who was regarded as the friend of the people. Now, if the consequences have been so deplorable for the peace of the Church from the condemnation of only one priest, because he was considered to be the friend of the people, what will not be the consequences to be feared from a condemnation which would fall directly upon the people themselves in the exercise of what they consider their legitimate right? [14]

7. But besides the danger which would result from such a condemnation and the impossibility of having it respected and observed [putting it into effect—de la faire respecter et observer] one should note that the form of this organization is so little permanent, as the press indicates nearly every day, that in the estimation of practical men in our country, it cannot last very many years.[15] Whence it follows that it is not necessary, even if it were just and prudent, to level the solemn condemnations of the Church against something which will vanish of itself. The social agitation will, indeed, last as long as there are social evils to be remedied; but the forms of organization and procedure meant for the attainment of this end are necessarily provisional and transient. They are also very numerous, for I have already remarked that the Knights of Labor is only one among several forms of labor organizations. To strike, then, at one of these forms would be to commence a war without system and without end; it would be to exhaust the forces of the Church in chasing a crowd of changing and uncertain phantasms. The American people behold with perfect composure and confidence the progress of our social contest, and have not the least fear of not being able to protect themselves against any excesses or dangers that may occasionally arise. And, to speak with the most profound respect, but also with the frankness which duty requires of me, it seems to me that prudence suggests, and that even the dignity of the Church demands that we should not offer

----

[14] This whole paragraph referring to the case of Dr. Edward McGlynn was elided in the official English version.

[15] The English read: "It is also very important that we should carefully consider another reason against condemnation, arising from the unstable and transient character of the organization in question. It is frequently remarked by the press and by attentive observers that this special form of association has in it so little permanence that, in its present shape, it is not likely to last many years."

to America an ecclesiastical protection for which she does not ask, and of which she believes she has no need.

8. In all this discussion I have not at all spoken of Canada, nor of the condemnation concerning the Knights of Labor in Canada. For we would consider it an impertinence to involve ourselves in the ecclesiastical affairs of another country which has a hierarchy of its own, and with whose needs and social conditions we do not pretend to be acquainted.[16] We believe, however, that the circumstances of a people almost entirely Catholic, as in lower Canada, must be very different from those of a mixed population like ours; moreover, that the documents submitted to the Holy Office are not the present constitution of the organization in our country, and that we, therefore, ask nothing involving an inconsistency on the part of the Holy See, which passed sentence *juxta exposita*.[17] It is of the condition of things in the United States that we speak, and we trust that in these matters we are not presumptuous in believing that we are competent to judge. Now, as I have already indicated, out of the seventy-five archbishops and bishops of the United States, there are about five who would desire a condemnation of the Knights of Labor, such as we know them in our country; so that our hierarchy are almost unanimous in protesting against such a condemnation. Surely, such a fact ought to have great weight in deciding the question. If there are difficulties in the case, it seems to me that the prudence and experience of our bishops and the wise rules of the Third Plenary Council ought to suffice for their solution.

9. Finally, to sum it all up, it seems clear to me that the Holy See should not entertain the idea of condemning an association:

1. When the condemnation does not seem to be *justified* either by the letter or the spirit of its constitution, its law and the declaration of its leaders.

2. When the condemnation does not seem *necessary*, in view of the transient form of the organization and the social condition of the United States.

3. When it does not seem to be *prudent*, because of the reality of the grievances of the workers, and the admission of them made by the American people.

4. When it would be *dangerous* for the reputation of the Church in our democratic country, and possibly even arouse persecution.

---

[16] "les besoins" was not translated.
[17] In the *Moniteur*, it read, *"localiter et juxta exposita."*

5. When it would be *ineffectual* in compelling the obedience of our Catholic workers, who would regard it as false and unjust.[18]

6. When it would be *destructive* instead of beneficial in its effects, impelling the children of the Church to disobey their Mother, and even to join condemned societies, which they have thus far shunned.

7. When it would be almost *ruinous* for the financial maintenance of the Church in our country, and for the Peter's pence.[19]

8. When it would turn into suspicion and hostility the outstanding devotedness of our Catholic people toward the Holy See.

9. When it would be regarded as a cruel blow to the authority of the bishops of the United States, who, it is well known, protest against such a condemnation.

Now, I hope the considerations here presented have shown with sufficient clearness that such would be the condemnation [20] of the Knights of Labor in the United States.

Therefore, with complete confidence, I leave the case [21] to the wisdom and prudence of your Eminence and the Holy See.

Rome, February 20, 1887.

J. CARDINAL GIBBONS,
Archbishop of Baltimore.

[18] The fifth reason in the official English version was: "When it would probably be inefficacious, owing to the general conviction that it would be unjust."

[19] This point was completely omitted in the *Moniteur* translation.

[20] The official English read, "the effect of condemnation."

[21] The English inserted, "the decision of the case."

ESSAY ON SOURCES

THIS study has been based almost entirely on previously un-exploited manuscript sources.[1] Some of the depositories proved to be highly rewarding, while in the case of others the expectation exceeded the finding. Still a third group of archival material might be classified as not available, either because of its non-existence or present inaccessibility.

Although the subject of this investigation lay in the field of ecclesiastical history one of the most important collections was the papers of Terence Vincent Powderly, which are in the possession of the Mullen Library of the Catholic University of America. This is made up of a vast amount of material—estimated at about 75,000 letters—which had to be used while still only roughly arranged and lacking completely in any finding-aid except its own general indices. Letter-books, files of incoming mail, diaries, scrapbooks of press clippings, and unattached jottings were utilized.[2] Of much less importance and extent, but in a more chaotic condition, were the papers of John Hayes, Powderly's last successor, which are in the custody of the same institution. But since these latter records of the Knights of Labor begin with the 1890's only one unit of the Powderly-Hayes correspondence, from 1886 to 1890, proved of value.[3] A few items

---

[1] The symbols, BCA, NYAA and RDA, which do not conform with the normal way of citing an archival depository, have been retained since they have been somewhat canonized by usage.

[2] Cf. Terence V. Powderly, *The Path I Trod* (New York, 1940), p. xi. The Columbia University editors of this posthumously published autobiography, Harry J. Carman, Henry David, and Paul N. Guthrie, had access to the collection, but they made little use of it in editing the manuscript which Powderly had left in a rather complete state. Hence Carman's remark in good faith, "Powderly's chapter entitled 'Ecclesiastical Opposition' . . . is one of the most illuminating in the book." "Terence Vincent Powderly—An Appraisal," *Journal of Economic History,* I (May, 1941), 85.

[3] These records were deposited in "a leaky shed" in Washington D. C. when Hayes closed down the national office in 1917, and their present condition shows the results of it. Norman J. Ware, *The Labor Movement in the United States, 1860-1895* (New York, 1929), p. xi. A district office existed in Boston in 1937, but by 1943 it had fallen out of the city directory. Cf. Fred Landon, "The Knights of Labor: Predecessors of the C. I. O.," *Quarterly Review of Commerce* (University of Western Ontario, Summer-Autumn, 1937), pp. 1-7.

of interest were found on the Knights in the manuscript room of the Wisconsin Historical Society at Madison, and the labor collection in the society's library provided for examination an almost complete series of constitutions of the Knights of Labor.[4]

In tracing the development of the problem under study one of the chief obstacles, especially for the early years of the Knights of Labor, was the condition of ecclesiastical archives in Pennsylvania. In the Archives of the Archdiocese of Philadelphia there were found only a few unimportant scraps of paper pertaining to the adminstration of Archbishops Wood (1860-1883) and Ryan (1884-1911).[5] It would have been more important in some ways to have church records in the suffragan Diocese of Scranton, but the adminstration of Bishop William O'Hara (1868-1899) left very few papers and nothing of any use to the historian of this question.[6] In this instance the secular press was put to good use at the Scranton Public Library and the Lackawanna Historical Society in that city. Of the three other Pennsylvania dioceses of those days the archives of Harrisburg, fortunately, were not important since they are barren for this period, and those of Pittsburgh and Erie were searched for the writer and found to contain nothing relating to the Knights of Labor.[7]

As the Church and the Knights' story had to be followed outside of the state of its origin other ecclesiastical archives happily proved more fruitful.[8] This was especially true of those of the Archdiocese of Baltimore, the chief source utilized for this work. They are housed

The Knights of Labor enjoyed a brief revival in Canada as late as 1899-1902. Norman J. Ware, "The History of Labor Interaction," *Labor in Canadian-American Relations* (New Haven, 1937), p. 16.

[4] Cf. Alice E. Smith (Ed.), *Guide to the Manuscripts of the Wisconsin Historical Society* (Madison, 1944), pp. 117, 120.

[5] John Tracy Ellis, "Can We have a History of the Church in the United States," *The Catholic University Bulletin,* XII (March, 1945), 3. Ryan destroyed a large part of his correspondence before his death.

[6] Letter of William Dolan, chancellor, to the author, Scranton, December 14, 1945, and personal visit to Scranton.

[7] Ellis, *Catholic University Bulletin,* XIII, 3; Letters of John Canova, Monaca, May 18, 1948, and Robert D. Goodill, Erie, April 26, 1948, to the author.

[8] Cf. Thomas F. O'Connor, "Catholic Archives of the United States," *Catholic Historical Review,* XXXI (January, 1946), 414-430. Since this was written important finds have been made in hitherto buried manuscripts, especially in the Diocese of Richmond, the National Catholic Welfare Conference, and the Catholic University of America.

at the Chancery Office, 408 N. Charles Street, and because of the systematic arrangement and the calendar index of the Gibbons Papers they readily surrendered all their rich contents.[9] Next in importance were the records remaining from the Corrigan adminstration in the New York Archdiocesan Archives at St. Joseph's Seminary, Yonkers, New York. There are notable gaps in individual containers of this material and the traditions of lost material pertaining to the McGlynn trouble are discouraging. The search there was satisfying only after a complete survey, and some further material in the archiepiscopal residence in New York City was found to include nothing pertinent. Related to New York by ties of friendship in this period was Bishop McQuaid; for that reason it was necessary to examine the contents of the Rochester Diocesan Archives at St. Bernard's Seminary, Rochester, New York. The Rochester archives, of course, had already been rather thoroughly used by Zwierlein in his published works. A search in the Archives of the Archdiocese of Cincinnati, at Mount Saint Mary's Seminary of the West, Norwood, Ohio, was also rewarding since the papers of Archbishop Elder are well preserved and easily used. In Cleveland the Gilmour Papers were examined in the archives at the diocesan chancery, and it may be said that while they are of genuine historical value, they are not in quite the state described by one writer twenty-five years ago.[10] The University of Notre Dame with its rich holdings of Catholic manuscripts, some of which were well preserved and processed there when the dioceses that had produced them did not appreciate their value, provided items from the records of Fort Wayne (Bishop Dwenger) and Vincennes (Bishop Chatard) and one letter of interest from the earlier Cincinnati material of Archbishop John B. Purcell. In addition, several letters in the personal papers of Henry F. Brownson and James A. McMaster provided minor sidelights on the general story. In New England, the ordinarily out-of-the-way Diocese of Portland, Maine, fortunately was able to supply from its archives in the basement of the old episcopal residence the letterbooks of Bishop Healy, but the writer was informed that no incoming correspondence of those years was

---

[9] Cf. John Tracy Ellis, "A Guide to the Baltimore Cathedral Archives," *Catholic Historical Review*, XXXII (October, 1946), 341-360.

[10] Paul J. Foik, C.S.C., in "Proceedings of the Third Annual Meeting of the American Catholic Historical Association," *Catholic Historical Review*, IX (April, 1923), 17-20.

extant. The diocesan announcements and pastorals were found in the attic of the same building. Boston's ecclesiastical archives, housed in the chancery office, were practically speaking bare on the period of this study, due in part, of course, to the writing habits, or lack of them, of Archbishop Williams.

Because of the Canadian character of the story of the relations of the Church and the Knights of Labor, the principal ecclesiastical depositories in the Dominion were visited. In Quebec, where a fine sense of tradition was evident, the most complete files of correspondence were found, although unlike their American counterparts —lacking in personal and gossipy letters. With the excellent tools available the Taschereau Papers were readily examined and an exception was graciously made to the rule restricting the copying of items that are not yet one hundred years old. Two personal letters of the cardinal were found among the papers of Cyrille Legaré in the Archives of the Seminary of Quebec. In the Archdiocese of Montreal the archives when visited were going through a period of transition in an attempt to restore them to a former and better condition. Here there were no guides for the searcher, and only by enjoying full freedom did the present writer find as much as he did of the administrative records of Archbishop Fabre. The Archives of the Archdiocese of Toronto, with regard to the period of Archbishop Lynch, were less well preserved than Montreal. Only scattered letters of the prelate could be located and some few of his letterbooks. Since that time a complete renovation has been effected but no new material pertinent to this study has been uncovered. In all three of the Canadian cases the archives are connected with the respective chancery offices.

As seems to be inevitable in seeking the raw stuff of history, the author suffered several disappointments in his research. The major one, of course, although mitigated by the foreknowledge of the hundred year regulation, was the inaccessibility of the Archives of the Congregation of the Propaganda Fide. They remained unavailable for that reason, "apart from the delicate character of certain documents such as those relative to the Knights of Labor in America." [11] Other Roman aspects of the question suffered also by the unexplained gap of the earliest years in the Roman cor-

[11] Note of Guiseppe Monticone, archivist of the Congregation of the Propaganda Fide, February 13, 1947, to the author through the Reverend Charles Kenny, M.M.

respondence of Denis O'Connell which was discovered in a trunk in the old chancery building in Richmond, Virginia, where O'Connell died in 1927. This precious collection has been systematically arranged since the writer's visit to Richmond. O'Connell was active in Rome as middleman for the American hierarchy from 1885, but his extant papers begin with regularity only in 1888, and so only a few, although very important, documents relevant to this study were unearthed. Because O'Connell's effects were said to have been at one time at Mount Saint Mary's College, Emmitsburg, Maryland, a search was made of the archives of that institution, but to no avail. Likewise in Richmond, the scanty Keane Papers (1878-1888) proved of no help. A few things, however, among the records of the respective administrations of Bishops Keane and O'Connell as Rectors of the Catholic University of America, and preserved in the recently reorganized archives of that institution, proved of interest. Another private archives that provided one important item was that of Woodstock College at Woodstock, Maryland. Here the writer found a manuscript of Aloysius Sabetti, S.J., dealing with the Knights of Labor. The archives of the New York Province of the Jesuits at Fordham University revealed nothing on the other members of the Society of Jesus who were involved in the case of the Knights as advisers of the hierarchy. In a similar way the Sulpician Archives of St. Mary's Seminary at Roland Park, Maryland, proved to have nothing among the papers of Abbé Magnien when Cardinal Gibbons would have been expected to have been corresponding with him, i.e., during his stay in Rome in 1887. The Roland Park archives, as also those of Georgetown University contained, in general, nothing of value for this work. This was true also of the library and archives of the Catholic Central Verein of America in St. Louis.[12] The Isaac Hecker Papers in the Paulist Archives in New York City had a single letter that was pertinent and the diary of Archbishop Robert Seton in the possession of the New York Historical Society of the same city had one illuminating entry. The snatches of Wood-Gowen correspondence in the hands of the American Catholic Historical Society of Philadelphia were other stray items which were much more eagerly seized upon.

Clarification of some elements of the problem was naturally sought in non-ecclesiastical archives. The recently released material

[12] Letter of F. P. Kenkel to the author, St. Louis, April 27, 1948.

of the Philadelphia and Reading Railroad pertaining to the Molly Maguires remained inaccessible to this investigator, although he was assured it contained nothing relevant to his interest.[13] The files of Pinkerton's National Detective Agency, in New York City, contained nothing to alter the story of the Church's contacts with the Knights of Labor, while the Missouri Pacific Railroad held out no hope of finding anything in its records pertaining to this study.[14] Among non-institutional manuscript holdings the Henry George Papers at the New York Public Library were woefully lacking in anything on George's relations with churchmen. Likewise the Grover Cleveland Papers in the Library of Congress had nothing on his relations with Gibbons or Powderly concerning the Knights of Labor.

The present writer depended on fellow workers and friends to inform him that there was nothing of interest in the archives of various American dioceses other than those of the bishops who were most active in the question under study. By correspondence he learned from the archivist of the lamentable lack of material on the Knights in the Archives of the Archdiocese of St. Louis,[15] and from a kind friend who made a search in his behalf he was told of the not so important deficiency of San Francisco.[16] By personal contacts and mail it was established that New Orleans, Milwaukee, Santa Fe, Omaha, Chicago,[17] Albany, and Hamilton, Ontario, had nothing to offer, while Detroit produced one valuable letter. Personal visits determined there was nothing of value in the diocesan archives of Columbus and Covington. The lack of personal manuscripts pertaining to John Ireland of St. Paul and John L. Spalding of Peoria is regretted by every student of the history of the American Church of the late nineteenth century. The former, remembering Purcell's life of Manning destroyed most of his while the fate of the Spalding Papers remains a mystery.[18] Furthermore, Cardinal

[13] Letter of Roy F. Nichols to the author, Philadelphia, May 4, 1948; letter of I. L. Gordan to the author, Philadelphia, August 23, 1948.

[14] Letter of R. C. White to the author, St. Louis, July 28, 1948.

[15] Letter of Jasper J. Chiodini, archivist, to the author, St. Louis, November 4, 1946.

[16] Letter of Timothy J. Casey to the author, San Francisco, July 10, 1946.

[17] Ellis, *Catholic University Bulletin*, XII, 3, reports the papers of Patrick A. Feehan (1880-1902) as missing.

[18] *Ibid*,

Manning's activities for the Knights remain still pretty much as related by Leslie since no further documentation was available.[19]

Besides the unpublished manuscripts important sources for this study were pastoral letters and the press. The former were obtained in the Treasure Room of the Library of the University of Notre Dame, as well as in bound volumes in the Mullen Library of the Catholic University of America. The wealth of Catholic newspaper material covering the late nineteenth and early twentieth centuries in the holdings of the American Catholic Historical Society of Philadelphia, housed at St. Charles Borromeo Seminary, Overbrook, Pennsylvania, was extensively used for the first time. Some of the papers, however, were more conveniently accessible at the libraries of the Catholic University of America and Georgetown University.[20] A sampling of the Canadian press was made at the Library of Laval University, Quebec, and some few items were found in the Provincial Library at Toronto. The investigation of labor papers was made at the Wisconsin Historical Society Library, except for the *Standard* which was available in the New York Public Library, although in poor condition. The library of the Henry George School in New York City had only one rare booklet of minor interest for this subject. The ordinary secular press was readily worked over at the Library of Congress when not enough was found in scrapbooks of some of the principals in the story of the Church and the Knights of Labor.

The following printed sources, newspapers, books, unpublished material, and articles were consulted:

PRINTED SOURCES

Acta et decreta concilii plenarii Baltimorensis II. Baltimore, 1868.
Acta et decreta concilii plenarii Baltimorensis II. Baltimore, 1877.
Acta et decreta concilii plenarii Baltimorensis tertii. Baltimore, 1884.
Acta et decreta concilii plenarii Baltimorensis tertii. Baltimore, 1886.
Acta et decreta concilii provincialis Milwaukiensis primi. Milwaukee, 1888.

[19] Letter of Bernard C. Fisher to John Tracy Ellis, Westminster, July 1, 1948.

[20] Cf. "Old Catholic Newspapers in Some Eastern Catholic Libraries," *Catholic Historical Review*, XXXIII (October, 1947), 303, for Catholic University of America's holdings and Thomas F. Meehan, "Early Catholic Weeklies," *Historical Records and Studies*, XXVIII (1937), 237-241, for Georgetown. A check-list of the Philadelphia collection is in the process of preparation.

Acta et decreta concilii provincialis Neo-Eboracensis IV. New York, 1886.
Acta et decreta quatuor conciliorum provincialium Cincinnatensium, 1855-1882. Cincinnati, 1886.
Adelphon Kruptos [1880], [1886] Toledo, 1891. French version, [after 1882].
Archeon Work for District Assemblies of the Order of the Knights of Labor, n. p., 1883.
Brownson, Henry (Ed.), *Brownson's Works,* V. Detroit, 1884.
Buchanan, Joseph R., *The Story of a Labor Agitator.* New York, 1903.
Collectanea sacrae congregationis de propaganda fide, II. Rome, 1907.
Commons, John R., et al (Eds.), *A Documentary History of American Industrial Society,* X. Cleveland, 1911.
Concilia provincialia Baltimorensia. Baltimore, 1851.
Constitution of the General Assembly, District Assemblies and Local Assemblies of the Order of the Knights of Labor in America [1881] [1885] [1887]. Philadelphia, 1888, 1890.
Constitution de l'assemblée générale des assemblées districts et des assemblées locales de l'ordre des Chevaliers du Travail de l'Amérique [n. p., 1884].
Cook, Ezra (Ed.), *Knights of Labor Illustrated.* Chicago, 1886.
Decreta concilii provincialis Philadelphiensis I. Philadelphia, n. d.
Founding Ceremony and Adelphon Kruptos. [n. p., 1882].
Gibbons, James, *A Retrospect of Fifty Years,* I. Baltimore, 1916.
Guilday, Peter (Ed.), *The National Pastorals of the American Hierarchy (1792-1919).* Washington, 1923.
Husselein, Joseph, S.J. (Ed.), *Social Wellsprings,* I, II. Milwaukee, 1940, 1943.
Ireland, John, *The Church and Modern Society,* I. St. Paul, 1905.
Mandements, lettres pastorales, circulaires et autres documents publiés dans diocèse de Montréal depuis son érection, X, XI. Montreal, 1893, 1894.
Memorial Volume. A History of the Third Plenary Council of Baltimore. Baltimore, 1885.
Official Report of the Proceedings of the Catholic Congress held at Baltimore, Md., November 11th and 12th, 1889. Detroit, 1889.
Pastorals.
Mullen Library, Catholic University of America:
   Pastoral Letter of the Archbishop and Bishops of New Orleans assembled in Council. 1873.
   Pastoral Letter of the Right Reverend, the Bishop of Rochester. 1878.
   Lenten Pastoral of Right Rev. Richard Gilmour, D.D., Bishop of Cleveland. 1879.
   Pastoral Letter addressed by the Archbishop of New York to the Faithful of his Charge on occasion of the Celebration of the Fifth Diocesan Synod, November 17th and 18th, 1886.
Treasure Room, University of Notre Dame:
   Pastoral Instruction of the Bishop of Alton to the Clergy, Secular and Regular, and to the Religious Communities, etc. of his Diocese, April 12, 1872.

Pastoral Instruction of Peter J. Baltes, Bishop of Alton, January 23, 1879.

Pastoral Letter of the Bishop of Vincennes on the Occasion of the Diocesan Synod. Indianapolis, 1879.

Pastoral of Right Rev. Joseph Dwenger, Septuagesima Sunday. Fort Wayne, 1885.

Pastoral Letter of Right Rev. Francis Silas Chatard, D.D., Bishop of Vincennes, December 18. Indianapolis, 1886.

Pope, Joseph (Ed.), *Memoirs of Right Honourable Sir John Alexander Macdonald,* II. London, 1894.

Powderly, Terence V., *Thirty Years of Labor.* Columbus, 1890.

———, *The Path I Trod.* New York, 1940. Edited by Harry J. Carman, Henry David, and Paul Guthrie.

Record of the Proceedings of the General Assembly.

    Reading, January, 1878.

    Philadelphia, June, 1878.

    St. Louis, January, 1879.

    Chicago, September, 1879.

    Pittsburgh, 1880.

    Detroit, 1881.

    New York, 1882.

    Cincinnati, 1883.

    Philadelphia, 1884.

    Hamilton, 1885.

    Cleveland, May, 1886.

    Richmond, October, 1886.

    Minneapolis, 1887.

    Indianapolis, 1888.

    Atlanta, 1889.

    Denver, 1890.

    Philadelphia, 1893.

Relatio collationum quae Romae coram S. C. de P. F. praefecto habuerunt archiepiscopi pluresque episcopi Statuum Foederatorum Americae. Baltimore, n. d.

Relationes eorumque disceptata fuerunt ab illmis ac revmis metroplitis cum suis suffraganeis in suis singulis provinciis super schema futurii concilii praesertim vero super capita cuique commissa. Baltimore, 1884.

Richardson, James D. (Ed.), *A Compilation of the Messages and Papers of the Presidents,* XI. New York, 1897.

Schema decretorum concilii plenarii Baltimorensis tertii. Baltimore, 1884.

Taschereau, E. A., *Discipline du diocèse de Québec.* Quebec, 1879.

Têtu, H. and Gagnon, C.-O., *Mandements, lettres pastorales et circulaires des évêques de Québec,* II (Nouvelle série). Quebec, 1890.

Thébaud, Augustus J., S.J., *Forty Years in the United States of America, 1839-1885.* New York, 1904.

United States House of Representatives, 49th Congress, 2d Session, Report
    No. 4174. *Investigation of Labor Troubles in Missouri, Arkansas, Kansas,
    Texas, and Illinois,* Part I, 1887.
Wynne, John J., S.J. (Ed.), *The Great Encyclical Letters of Pope Leo XIII.*
    New York, 1903.

NEWSPAPERS

Catholic:
    Baltimore *Catholic Mirror*
    Baltimore *Katholische Volkszeitung*
    Boston *Pilot*
    Boston *Republic*
    Brooklyn *Examiner*
    Chicago *Western Catholic*
    Chicago *Catholic Home*
    Cincinnati *Catholic Telegraph*
    Cincinnati *Wahrheits-Freund*
    Cleveland *Catholic Knight*
    Cleveland *Catholic Universe*
    Columbus *Catholic Columbian*
    Denver *Colorado Catholic*
    Detroit *Michigan Catholic*
    Hartford *Connecticut Catholic*
    Kingston, Ontario, *Canadian Freeman*
    Leavenworth, *Kansas Catholic*
    London, England, *Tablet*
    Louisville *Central Catholic Advocate*
    Memphis *Adam*
    New Orleans *Le Propagateur Catholique*
    New Orleans *Morning Star*
    New York *Catholic Herald*
    New York *Catholic News*
    New York *Catholic Review*
    New York *Freeman's Journal and Catholic Register*
    New York *Illustrated Catholic American*
    Philadelphia *Catholic Herald*
    Philadelphia *Catholic Standard*
    Philadelphia *I. C. B. U. Journal*
    Pittsburgh *Catholic*
    Quebec *La Vérité*
    St. Louis *Catholic World*
    St. Louis *Western Watchman*
    St. Paul *Northwestern Chronicle.*
    San Francisco *Monitor*

Scranton *Catholic Record*
Toronto *Irish Canadian*
Troy *Catholic Weekly*
Washington, D. C. *Church News*
Labor:
Chicago *Knights of Labor*
Denver *Labor Enquirer*
New York *Irish World and Industrial Liberator*
New York *John Swinton's Paper*
New York *Standard*
Philadelphia *The Journal of United Labor*
General:
Baltimore *Sun*
New York *Herald*
New York *Sun*
New York *Times*
New York *World*
Quebec *Le Canadien*
Quebec *L'Evénement*
Quebec *Morning Chronicle*
Richmond *Dispatch*
Richmond *State*
Scranton *Daily Times*
Scranton *Republican*

GENERAL WORKS

Abell, Aaron I., *The Urban Impact on American Protestantism, 1866-1900*. Cambridge, 1943.

Alexis, P., *Histoire de le province ecclésiastique d'Ottawa et de la colonisation dans la vallée de l'Ottawa*. Ottawa, 1897.

Allen, Ruth A., *The Great Southwest Strike*. Austin, 1942.

Beard, Charles and Mary, *The Rise of American Civilization*, II. New York, 1942.

Beard, Mary R., "Knights of Labor," *Encyclopedia of the Social Sciences*, VIII. New York, 1932.

Bell, Stephen, *Rebel, Priest and Prophet*. New York, 1937.

Billington, Ray Allan, *The Protestant Crusade, 1800-1860*. New York, 1938.

Brophy, Sister M. Liguori, *The Social Thought of the German Roman Catholic Central Verein*. Washington, 1941.

Byrne, John F., C.SS.R., *The Redemptorist Centenaries, 1732-1932*. Philadelphia, 1932.

Canova, John, "Bishop Michael Domenec and Bishop John Tuigg," *Catholic Pittsburgh's One Hundred Years*. Chicago, 1943.

Coats, R. H., "The Labor Movement in Canada," *Canada and Its Provinces,* IX. Toronto, 1914.

Coleman, J. Walter, *Labor Disturbances in Pennsylvania, 1850-1880.* Washington, 1936.

Commons, John R. and Associates, *History of Labor in the United States,* I, II. New York, 1918.

Connaughton, Sister M. Stanislaus, *The Editorial Opinion of the Catholic Telegraph of Cincinnati on Contemporary Affairs and Politics, 1871-1921.* Washington, 1943.

Cross, Ira B., *A History of the Labor Movement in California.* Berkeley, 1935.

David, Henry, *The History of the Haymarket Affair.* New York, 1936.

Davitt, Michael, *The Fall of Feudalism in Ireland.* London, 1904.

Desmond, Humphrey J., *The APA Movement.* Washington, 1912.

Ellis, John Tracy, *The Formative Years of the Catholic University of America.* Washington, 1946.

Ely, Richard T., *The Labor Movement in America.* New York, 1886.

Farley, John [P. Guilday], *The Life of Cardinal McCloskey.* New York, 1918.

George, Henry, Jr., *The Life of Henry George.* New York, 1900.

Gompers, Samuel, *Seventy Years of Life and Labor.* New York, 1925.

Grossman, Jonathan, *William Sylvis, Pioneer of American Labor.* New York, 1945.

Guilday, Peter, *A History of the Councils of Baltimore, 1791-1884.* New York, 1932.

Hansen, Marcus L. and John B. Brebner, *The Mingling of the Canadian and American Peoples.* New Haven, 1940.

Hassard, John R. G., *The Life of the Most Reverend John Hughes.* New York, 1866.

Healy, Patrick J., "Catholic Economic Thought," *Catholic Builders of the Nation,* III. Boston, 1923.

Hillquit, Morris, *History of Socialism in the United States.* New York, 1910.

Hogan, William E., *The Development of Bishop Wilhelm Emmanuel von Ketteler's Interpretation of the Social Problem.* Washington, 1946.

Hopkins, Charles H., *The Rise of the Social Gospel in American Protestantism, 1865-1915.* New Haven, 1940.

Hughes, H. L., *The Catholic Revival in Italy, 1815-1915.* London, 1935.

Josephson, Matthew, *The Robber Barons.* New York, 1934.

Kelly, Sister M. Gilbert, *Catholic Immigrant Colonization Projects in the United States, 1815-1860.* New York, 1939.

Kirlin, Joseph L., *Catholicity in Philadelphia.* Philadelphia, 1909.

Kothen, Robert, *La pensée et l'action sociales des catholiques (1789-1944).* Louvain, 1945.

Lamott, John L., *History of the Archdiocese of Cincinnati, 1821-1921.* Cincinnati, 1921.

Latham, Allan B., *The Catholic and National Labour Union of Canada.* Toronto, 1930.

Lecanuet, Edouard, *Les premières années du pontificat de Léon XIII, 1878-1894.* Paris, 1931.

Lescohier, Don D., *The Knights of St. Crispin, 1867-1874.* Madison, 1910.

Leslie, Shane, *Henry Edward Manning, His Life and Labours.* London, 1921.

Levasseur, E., *The American Workman.* Translated and edited by Thomas S. Adams and Theodore Marburg. Baltimore, 1900.

Logan, Harold, *The History of Trade-Union Organization in Canada.* Chicago, 1928.

Lyons, Sister M. Laetitia, *Francis Norbert Blanchet and the Founding of the Oregon Missions, 1838-1848.* Washington, 1940.

Macdonald, Fergus, C.P., *The Catholic Church and the Secret Societies in the United States.* New York, 1946.

McEntee, Georgiana P., *The Social Catholic Movement in Great Britain.* New York, 1927.

McNeil, George (Ed.), *The Labor Movement, the Problem of Today.* New York, 1891.

Malone, Sylvester L. (Ed.), *Dr. Edward McGlynn.* New York, 1918.

Meehan, Thomas F., "Emigrant Aid Societies," *Catholic Encyclopedia,* V. New York, 1909.

Metlake, George (John J. Laux), *Christian Social Reform.* Philadelphia, 1912.

Meyers, Gustavus, *History of Bigotry in the United States.* New York, 1943.

Millis, Harry A. and Royal E. Montgomery, *Organized Labor.* New York, 1945.

Moon, Parker T., *The Labor Problem and the Social Catholic Movement in France.* New York, 1921.

Mourret, Fernand, S.S., *Histoire générale de l'église,* IX. Paris, 1923.

Nevins, Allan, *Grover Cleveland. A Study in Courage.* New York, 1934.

O'Dea, John, *History of the Ancient Order of Hibernians,* III. Philadelphia, 1923.

O'Donoghue, Daniel J. "Labor Organization in Ontario," *Annual Report of the Bureau of Industries for the Province of Ontario, 1886.* Toronto, 1887.

O'Reilly, Bernard, *Life of Leo XIII.* Philadelphia, 1903.

Parsons, Lucy E., *Life of Albert K. Parsons.* Chicago, 1889.

Pinkerton, Allan, *Strikes, Communists, Tramps and Detectives.* New York, 1900.

Post, Louis F. and Fred C. Leubuscher (Eds.), *An Account of the George-Hewitt Campaign in the New York Municipal Election of 1886.* New York, 1887.

Il XL anniversario della enciclica Rerum Novarum. Milano, 1931.

Quigley, Joseph A., *Condemned Societies.* Washington, 1927.

Reilly, Daniel F., O.P., *The School Controversy (1891-1893).* Washington, 1943.

Ring, Sister M. Ignatius, *Villeneuve-Bargement, Precursor of Modern Social Catholicism, 1784-1850.* Milwaukee, 1935.

Rosebloom, Eugene H., and Francis P. Weisenburger, *A History of Ohio.* New York, 1934.

Rothensteiner, John, *History of the Archdiocese of St. Louis,* II. St. Louis, 1928.

Rumilly, Robert, *Histoire de la province de Québec,* V. Montreal, 1943.

Ryan, John A., *Distributive Justice.* New York, 1942.

——, "Edward McGlynn," *Dictionary of American Biography,* XII. New York, 1943.

——, "Moral Aspects of Labour Unions," *Catholic Encyclopedia,* VIII. New York, 1910.

——, *Social Doctrine in Action.* New York, 1941.

——, *Social Reconstruction.* New York, 1920.

Schlegel, Marvin W., *Ruler of the Reading: the Life of Franklin B. Gowen.* Harrisburg, 1947.

Schmidlin, Josef, *Papstgeschichte der neuesten Zeit,* II. Munchen, 1934.

Shaughnessy, Gerald, S.M., *Has the Immigrant Kept the Faith?* New York, 1925.

Shea, John Gilmary, *History of the Catholic Church in the United States,* III, IV. New York, 1890, 1892.

Skelton, Elizabeth, *Life of Thomas D'Arcy McGee.* Gardenvale, 1925.

Skelton, O. D., "General Economic History, 1867-1912," *Canada and Its Provinces,* IX. Toronto, 1914.

Smith, John Talbot, *Our Seminaries.* New York, 1896.

Soderini, Eduardo, *The Pontificate of Leo XIII,* I. London, 1934.

Solow, Herbert, "Uriah Smith Stephens," *Dictionary of American Biography,* XVII. New York, 1943.

Die soziale Frage und de Katholizismus. Festschrift zum 40 jährigen Jubiläum der Enzyklika Rerum Novarum. Paderborn, 1931.

Spahn, Martin and Thomas F. Meehan, "Catholic Congresses," *Catholic Encyclopedia,* IV. New York, 1908.

Spalding, John L., *Life of the Most Rev. M. J. Spalding, D.D.* New York, 1873.

Speek, Peter A., *The Single Tax and the Labor Movement.* Madison, 1915.

Tansill, Charles C., *Canadian American Relations, 1875-1911.* New Haven, 1943.

Walsh, Patrick J., *William J. Walsh, Archbishop of Dublin.* Dublin, 1928.

Ware, Norman J., *The Labor Movement in the United States, 1860-1895.* New York, 1929.

Ware, Norman J. and H. A. Logan, *Labor in Canadian-American Relations.* New Haven, 1937.

Will, Allen S., *Life of Cardinal Gibbons,* I, II. New York, 1922.

Yeager, Sister M. Hildegarde, *The Life of James Roosevelt Bayley, First Bishop of Newark and Eighth Archbishop of Baltimore, 1814-1877.* Washington, 1947.

Zwierlein, Frederick J., *The Life and Letters of Bishop McQuaid,* II, III. Rochester, 1926, 1927.

————, *Letters of Archbishop Corrigan to Bishop McQuaid and Allied Documents.* Rochester, 1946.

UNPUBLISHED MATERIAL

Donovan, Vincent J., "The First American Catholic Lay Congress held at Baltimore, November 11-12, 1889." Unpublished master's thesis, Catholic University of America, 1940.

Kennedy, Douglas R., "The Knights of Labor in Canada." Unpublished master's thesis, University of Western Ontario, 1945.

Killeen, Charles Edward, O. Praem., "John Siney: The Pioneer of American Industrial Unionism and Industrial Government." Unpublished doctoral thesis, University of Wisconsin, 1942.

Leonard, Sister Joan de Lourdes, "Catholic Attitude Toward American Labor, 1884-1919." Unpublished master's thesis, Columbia University, 1941.

McCabe, Clarence J., "The Background of Rerum Novarum." Unpublished master's thesis, Catholic University of America, 1941.

McGray, Sister M. Gertrude, "Evidences of Catholic Interest in Social Welfare in the United States, 1830-1850." Unpublished master's thesis, University of Notre Dame, 1937.

McHale, Sister M. Loretta, "The Social Thought of the Knights of Labor." As yet unpublished doctoral thesis, Catholic University of America, 1948.

McQuade, Vincent A., O.S.A., "Rev. Dr. McGlynn's Statement on Private Land-Ownership in the Light of the Teaching of Pope Leo XIII." Unpublished master's thesis, Catholic University of America, 1935.

Powers, Joseph L., C.S.C., "The Knights of Labor and the Church's Attitude on Secret Societies." Unpublished master's thesis, University of Notre Dame, 1943.

Stauffer, Alvin P., "Anti-Catholicism in American Politics, 1865-1900." Unpublished doctoral thesis, Harvard University, 1933.

Stroh, Paul, C.SS.R., "The Catholic Clergy and American Labor Disputes, 1900-1932." Unpublished doctoral thesis, Catholic University of America, 1939.

PERIODICALS

Abell, Aaron I., "The Catholic Church and Social Problems in the World War I Era," *Mid-America,* XXX (July, 1948), 139-151.

————, "The Reception of Leo XIII's Labor Encyclical in America, 1891-1919," *Review of Politics,* VII (October, 1945), 464-495.

Becker, Thomas A., "Secret Societies in the United States," *American Catholic Quarterly Review,* III (April, 1878), 193-219.

Brann, Henry A., "Henry George and his Land Theories," *Catholic World,* XLIV (March, 1887), 810-828.

Browne, Henry J., "The 'Italian Problem' in the Catholic Church of the United States, 1880-1900," *Historical Records and Studies,* XXXV (New York, 1946), 46-72.

———, "Peter E. Dietz, Pioneer Planner of Catholic Social Action," *Catholic Historical Review,* XXXIII (January, 1948), 448-456.

———, "Terence V. Powderly and Church-Labor Difficulties of the Early 1880's," *Ibid.,* XXXII (April, 1946), 1-27.

Cassidy, Francis P., "Catholic Education in the Third Plenary Council of Baltimore," *Catholic Historical Review,* XXXIV (October, 1948), 257-305.

Chatard, Francis S., "Catholic Societies," *American Catholic Quarterly Review,* IV (April, 1879), 212-221.

The Churchman, LV (March-April, 1887), Editorials.

Clancy, Raymond J., C.S.C., American Prelates in the Vatican Council," *Historical Records and Studies,* XXVIII (New York, 1937), 7-135.

Gibbons, James Cardinal, "My Memories," *Dublin Review,* CLX (April, 1917), 163-172.

———, "Wealth and Its Obligations," *North American Review,* CLII (April, 1891), 385-394.

Griffiths, Carl Warren, "Some Protestant Attitudes on the Labor Question in 1886," *Church History,* XI (June, 1942), 138-148.

Haas, Francis J., "Three Economic Needs of the 1880's and of the 1940's," *American Ecclesiastical Review,* CXVII (December, 1947), 40-425.

Henthorne, Sister M. Evangela, "Bishop Spalding's Work on the Anthracite Coal Strike Commission," *Catholic Historical Review,* XXVIII (July, 1942), 184-205.

The *Independent,* XXXIX (March-April, 1887), Editorials.

M. F. S., "The Labor Question," *American Catholic Quarterly Review,* III (October, 1878), 721-746.

McGlynn, Edward, "The Bugbear of Vaticanism," *American Catholic Quarterly Review,* I (January, 1876), 73-99.

McSweeney, Edward, "Social Problems," *Catholic World* XLIV (February, 1887), 577-588.

Massicote, E.-Z., "Les Chevaliers du Travail," *Le bulletin des recherches historiques,* XL (August, 1934), 452-453.

Matt, Joseph, "The German Roman Catholic Central-Verein," *Offizielles Souvenir Goldenes Jubilaeum* (Cincinnati, 1905), pp. 129-159.

Meng, John J., "Cahenslyism: the First Stage, 1883-1891," *Catholic Historical Review,* XXXI (January, 1946), 389-413.

———, "Cahenslyism: the Second Chapter, 1891-1910," *Ibid.,* XXXII (October, 1946), 302-340.

The *Nation,* XLIV (March 17, 1887), Editorial.

O'Donoghue, John G., "Daniel John O'Donoghue, Father of the Canadian Labor Movement," *Report, 1942-1943,* of the Canadian Catholic Historical Association (Ottawa, 1943), pp. 87-96.

O'Reilly, Bernard, "Land and Labor in France and the United States," *American Catholic Quarterly Review,* XIV (January, 1889), 1-22.

Puck, XXI (March 23, April 13, 1887), 60-61; 114-115, Cartoons by J. Keppler.

Purcell, Richard J., "John A. Ryan, Prophet of Social Justice," *Studies,* XXXV (June, 1946), 153-174.

Ronayne, M., S.J., "Land and Labor," *American Catholic Quarterly Review,* XII (August, 1887), 233-252.

Saposs, David J., "The Catholic Church and the Labor Movement," *Modern Monthly,* VII (May, June, 1933), 225-230; 294-298.

Shea, John Gilmary, "The Coming Council of Baltimore," *American Catholic Quarterly Review,* IX (April, 1884), 340-357.

———, "The Rapid Increase of the Dangerous Classes in the United States," *Ibid.,* IV (April, 1879), 240-268.

Smith, John Talbot, "The Eight Hour Law," *Catholic World,* XLIV (December, 1886), 397-406.

———, "Kitchens and Wages," *Ibid.,* XLIV (March, 1887), 779-786.

Steckel, Alfred, "German Roman Catholic Society of the United States," *Records* of the American Catholic Historical Society of Philadelphia, VI (1895), 252-265.

Wolff, George D., "Socialistic Communism in the United States," *American Catholic Quarterly Review,* III (July, 1878), 522-562.

Wright, Carroll D., "An Historical Sketch of the Knights of Labor," *Quarterly Journal of Economics,* I (January, 1887), 137-168.

Chicago: S. J. Clarke Publishing Co., 1920.

ALPHABETICAL INDEX

Abbelen, Rev. P. M., 213n
Adam (Memphis), 247
Adelphon Kruptos (or A. K.), 36, 41, 50, 63, 67, 68, 70, 71, 106, 107n, 128, 215, 278, 302
Age of Steel, 262-263
Albany, N. Y., 135
Alemany, Abp. Joseph S., 115-116
American Catholic Quarterly Review, article of Bp. Becker on secret societies, 48; articles on land question, 250
American College, Rome, 54, 234, 243
American Federation of Labor, 357
American Protective Association, 353-354
Amerika (St. Louis), 248
Anarchism, 88-89, 299. See socialism, communism.
Ancient Order of Hibernians, 22, 23, 48, 73, 100, 115, 116, 131n, 160, 174, 175, 187, 198, 202, 207, 219-220, 304
Ancient Order of United Workmen, 27, 27n, 131n
Anti-Catholicism, in K. of L., 334. See A.P.A.
Anti-Poverty Society, 304, 335
Arbitration, Gibbons on, 287
Archibald, James, 295
Arthur, Pres. Chester A., 138

Bailey, William H., 299
Baird, William, 57
Baltes, Bp. Peter J., 25
Baltimore, 112; Second Plenary Council of, 96, 101; Third Plenary Council of, 98, 106, 110-119; Catholic Congress in, 337; meeting of archbishops' committee in, 195-198; visit of Powderly to, 326. See Catholic Mirror.

Baltimore Morning Herald, 251; Sun, 180, 210, 214
Barnabò, Alessandro Cardinal, 15, 17n, 31, 197n
Barry, Mrs. L. M., 312
Barry, Rev. Thomas, 149n
Barry, Thomas B., 206, 232, 295, 299, 329, 334
Bayley, Abp. James Roosevelt, 16
Becker, Bp. Thomas A., 29-30, 48
Beecher, Rev. Henry Ward, 305
Bilio, Luigi Cardinal, 101
Bishops. See Hierarchy; also names of individual bishops.
"Bishops' Program of Social Reconstruction," 357
Black International, 89
Blanchet, Abp. Francis Norbert, 4
Boccali, Rev. Gabriele, 347
Borgess, Bp. Caspar H., 77, 166-167, 320
Boston, Powderly in, 106, 279; meeting of archbishops in, 344. See Pilot, Republic, Williams.
Boycotting, Gibbons on, 294
Brondel, Bp. John B., 344
Brooklyn. See Examiner, K. of L.
Brotherhood of United Labor, 334
Brownson, Orestes, 6
Buchanan, Joseph R., 89, 276, 278, 296
Burke, Bp. Maurice F., 344
Burns, Rev. C. J., 141
Burtsell, Rev. Richard L., 217, 258, 343

Cahenslyism, 228, 340
Calvary Cemetery, 265, 270-271
Canada, Church and unions in, 31-32; K. of L. in, 141-142, 171; O'Reilly trip to, 290; Catholic unionism in, 357

Canadian Labor Union, 31, 142
Canal Fulton, Ohio, K. of L. in, 83-84
Canon Law, Code of, on secret societies, 7
Capital and labor, Gibbons on, 293; Leo XIII on, 325; Place on, 331
Capitalism, Chatard on, 28; Dwenger on, 119-120; Milwaukee council on, 136-137; Catholic press on, 155-156; and Church in U. S., 319
Capitalists, concern over Gibbons' action in Rome on K. of L., 262; complaints to Taschereau, 307; Bp. O'Connor on, 321-322
Careau, Rev. M., 31
Carey, Matthew, 4
Carew, Rev. Francis, 189, 231, 259
The Catholic (Pittsburgh), 156, 251, 302
Catholic Beneficial Society, Richmond, 205n
Catholic Benevolent Legion, 118
Catholic Church, and pre-Civil War labor movement, 3-7; and secret societies, 7-11; and post-Civil War labor movement, 11-30; attempt of K. of L. to placate, 44; clerics against K. of L. secrecy, 47; in Pa. coal fields, 52-54; pastoral influence on workers, 55; "missions" and K. of L., 59-60; and K. of L. in Phila., 84-86; and K. of L. in Chicago, 85-86; attitude of K. of L. toward, 87-88, 298; archbishops' Roman conference, on secret societies, 98-101; Third Plenary Council, on societies for Catholics, 110-119; and K. of L. in Montreal, 121-122; in Quebec, 122-126; in Maine, 130-133; in Ottawa, 142-144; loss of workers to, 241; relations with K. of L. publicized, 289; labor's relationship with, 311-312; social awareness of, 313, 339-340; problems of in U. S., 1890's, 340. See

clergy, congregations, hierarchy, Leo XIII, names of individual bishops.
Catholic Columbian (Columbus), 157
Catholic Congress, Baltimore, 337-338
Catholic Herald (New York), 246-247, 268-269, 286
Catholic Home (Chicago), 247
Catholic Knight (Cleveland), 246
Catholic Knights of America, 118
Catholic Mirror (Baltimore), 170, 246, 248, 251, 268, 301
Catholic Mutual Benevolence Association, 118
Catholic News (New York), 225, 247, 267, 285, 326
Catholic Record (Scranton), 248
Catholic Review (New York), 157, 159, 160, 245, 251, 301
Catholic Standard (Philadelphia), 140, 156-157, 183, 250, 252, 269, 301, 331
Catholic Telegraph (Cincinnati), 155, 232, 251
Catholic Universe (Cleveland), 249, 332
Catholic University of America, 206, 229, 350
Catholic workingmen, societies of, 100, 102-103
Catholic Workingmen's Society, Girardville, Pa., 53-54
Catholic Workmen's Benevolent Union, 118
Catholic World (St. Louis), 220, 227, 245, 301
Catholic World, periodical, on land question, 250
Catholic Young Men's National Union, 118
Central Labor Union, 285
Cercles catholiques d'ouvriers, 315
Chapelle, Rev. Placide L., 166n, 183, 186
Chatard, Bp. Francis S., on secret so-

cieties, 27-28; on K. of L., 54, 75-76, 173, 202-203, 242; at Roman conference, 1883, 99-100; at Third Plenary Council, 115; on labor problems, 160; on Corrigan's pastoral, 224-225; on K. of L. decree of Holy Office, 331

Chicago, Church and K. of L. in, 85

Chicago *Knights of Labor*, 252

Chicago *Times*, 157; *Tribune*, 160, 251

Churchman (New York), 252, 267

Cigar Makers International Union, 204

Cincinnati, Fourth Provincial Council of, 81-82; bishops of Province of on social movements, 318-319; Powderly invited to, 325

Cleary, Rev. M. J., 96

Clergy, on Powderly's temperance views, 279

Clergy, Catholic, and K. of L., 76-79, 86-87, 126, 230-231; concern with labor radicalism, 92-94; defense of labor, 97; and decrees on secret societies, 119; on Md. K. of L., 127; applying decree on K. of L., 133; on Pa. K. of L., 133-134; on Milwaukee K. of L., 135-136; reaction in U. S. to Taschereau mandement, 163-168; social thought among, 312; training of, 356. See also Catholic Church, hierarchy, names of individual bishops and priests.

Clergy, Protestant, and Powderly's conservatism, 154-155; on labor problems, 174n; membership in K. of L., 303

Cleveland, K. of L. in, 83

Cleveland, Pres. Grover, confers with Powderly and Gibbons, 239; sympathy with Gibbons, 282-283

Cluever, Msgr. John H., 135

Coffey, Rev. Thomas F., 47n

Colorado Catholic (Denver), 248, 250

Columbus, K. of L. in, 82

Committee (Commission) of archbishops on secret societies, formed, 115-117; functioning, 138, 187-188, 195; preparations for meeting of, 195-198; meeting in Baltimore, 211-221; Gibbons-McQuaid on, 345-346

Communism, 27, 28, 89. See socialism, anarchism.

Congregation of the Index, 317, 322

Congregation of the Inquisition, see Holy Office.

Congregation of the Propaganda, see Propaganda.

Congregationalists, Chicago group of, 303

Congresses, Catholic, 314; in Germany, 6, 314; at Liége, 316, 341, at Baltimore, 337-338

Connecticut Catholic (Hartford), 184, 291-292

Consolidated Coal Company, 80

Constitution and By-Laws and Rules of Order of the Trade and Labor Assembly of Cincinnati and Vicinity, 75

Conway, Rev. P. J., 147-148, 163

Coopers' Union, 75

Corrigan, Abp. Michael A., friend of McQuaid, 25; rumor of red hat for, 101; prepares for Third Plenary Council, 113; defends Gibbons, 115; on conciliar decrees, 117; on K. of L., 160, 163-164, 173-174, 179-180, 183, 203, 211, 324; on fraternal societies, 188, 344; on convening committee of archbishops, 195-196, 198; at meeting of archbishops, 217-219; pastorals of, 222-226, 335; relations with Gibbons, 233; visit to Bahamas, 234; Gibbons' explanation of K. of L. memorial to, 264; troubles described by, 264-265; Taschereau copy of H. Of. decree sent to, 268; Gibbons' explanation to, 270;

Examiner's opinion of, 271; summary of position vis-à-vis Gibbons, 273; editor Preston's opinion of, 305; congratulated by Farren, 306; agrees with Taschereau, 307; denies *World* interview, 310; explains press report to Healy, 310; supposed interview of Powderly with, 311n; forces of against George, 317; congratulates Gibbons, 328-329; self-justification of, 336-337; request for papal statement, 343-344; advises McQuaid, on K. of L., 345-346; on *Rerum novarum,* 349; seeks Quebec documents, 350; agrees with Taschereau, 352

Cuno, Theodore, 90

Curtin Committee, Fr. O'Leary before, 280

Czack, Vladimir Cardinal, 272

Davis, John N., 38

Davitt, Michael, 235, 302

"De secta massonum," 102, 115, 123, 162

De socialistarum secta, 89

De Soto, Mo., Fr. O'Leary in, 158

"Declaration of Seven Pastors," 22

Decurtins, Gaspard, 340

Denver *Labor Enquirer,* 90, 157, 212n

Depression of 1883-1885, 105

Detroit, K. of L. in, 77. See also *Michigan Catholic.*

Dever, Hannah, 39

Dillon, Rev. John R., 106, 126

Discipline du diocèse de Québec, 31-32

Dissez, Paulinus F., S.S., 189n, 324

Donahoe, Patrick, 106

Doutreloux, Bp. Victor, 316

Drury, Victor, 140

DuBois, Pa., K. of L. in, 55

Ducey, Rev. Thomas J., 248

Dufresne, James, 143

Duhamel, Bp. Joseph T., 142-145

Dunn, Rev. William J., 20n

Dunne, Rev. John W., 41, 47n

Dwenger, Bp. Joseph, 28, 119-120, 127n, 140, 187, 202

Easton, Pa., K. of L. in, 106

Eccleston, Abp. Samuel, 19n

Eckhart, Md., K. of L. in, 80

Edes, Ella, 197, 243, 329

Egan, Maurice Francis, 245, 286, 301

Elder, Abp. William H., convenes Fourth Provincial Council of Cincinnati, 81; on Canadian action on K. of L., 164-165, 188; on meeting of archbishops on secret societies, 174-175, 193-194, 220; on K. of L., 216, 218; shows K. of L. memorial to bishops, 259; to Rome on American social questions, 319-321; final letter on K. of L. publicized, 332

Emeralds, 73, 96

Employers, opposition of to K. of L., 288-289

Encyclicals. See titles.

Erie, Pa., K. of L. in, 55, 75, 79-80

Examiner (Brooklyn), *Catholic . . .,* 140; 147, 172, 183, 185, 220, 226, 244, 268, 284, 286. See also, Preston, Thomas, editor.

Fabre, Abp. Edouard, and K. of L. into Canada, 95; on K. of L. condemnation, 108; contacts with K. of L., 121-123, 144-145, 168; advised by Taschereau on K. of L., 141, 202; independent action on K. of L., 177-179, 198; and revision of K. of L. constitution, 201, 221

Farren, Bernard N., 224, 306

Farmers' Alliance, 338

Federation of Organized Trades and Labor Unions, 204n

Feehan, Abp. Patrick A., 99, 115, 163, 194, 218

Fehrenbatch, John, 20

Fenianism, 31

Fennimore, William, 37
Fenwick, James, 224n
Fickenscher, Emma, 205n
Fink, Bp. Louis, 126
First Diocesan Synod of New York, 9n
First International, 90
First Plenary Council of Baltimore, 11
First Provincial Council of Milwaukee, 136, 174
First Provincial Council of Philadelphia, 73
First Provincial Council of Quebec, 30, 110
First Provincial Council of San Francisco, 73
Fitzgerald, David, 54
Fitzgerald, Bp. Edward, 100n, 114n, 258
"Five Stars" (for K. of L.), 49
Flannigan, Rev. P. M., 206, 232, 295
Flickeissen, Frederick E., 136n
Foley, Rev. M. F., 213, 215, 218, 221
Foley, Bp. Thomas, 19, 30n
Ford, Patrick, introduces Powderly, 235; opinion on K. of L. gesture to Gibbons, 301-302; break with George, 305; reaction to K. of L. toleration, 322; praises Gibbons, 332. See also *Irish World.*
Founders' movement, 334
Founding and Installation Ceremonies, 63, 70
Fourth Provincial Council of Baltimore, 8-9
Fourth Provincial Council of Cincinnati, 81-82
Fourth Provincial Council of New York, 93
Fourth Provincial Council of Quebec, 162
Foy, Peter L., 338
Fulton, Robert, S.J., 174, 324
Free Religious Society, 141

Fribourg Union, 341
Franzelin, Giovanni Cardinal, 98
Freeman's Journal (New York), 148n, 157, 220, 245, 248, 268, 286, 301, 307. See also McMaster, James.
Freemasons, 73, 123
Freemasonry, 7-8; influence on K. of L., 35; in Canada, 96, 101; encyclical and instruction on, 102-104; American archbishops on, 344
Frostburg, Md., 80

Garment Cutters' Union, 34
George, Henry, N. Y. mayorality campaign, 1886, 223; Catholic press on, 225; issue before hierarchy, 228; Gibbons on condemning works of, 229; Rome's concern with, 230; on Gibbons K. of L. action in Rome, 252; Gibbons' memorial on writings of, 256; influence on K. of L., 285, 333; 1887 defeat of, 306; on Powderly's church contacts, 308; writings of, problem in Rome, 317; noticed in toleration of K. of L., 330; Church and the views of, 335-337; and McGlynn, 335-336n; and Powderly, 337; Catholic teaching on system of, 350n.
German Roman Catholic Central-Verein, 6-7, 291
Gibbons, James Cardinal, early attitude toward labor, 18; and Order of American Union, 26; in Spalding household, 30n; Powderly's statement of case of K. of L. to, 38, 189-192; attention to K. of L. in Md., 57; on labor unions, Roman conference, 1883, 99; rumor of red hat for, 101; at Third Plenary Council, 114-115; position on K. of L., 127; on Church-labor policy, 138; supposed comment for labor meeting, 159-160; reaction to Taschereau's action on K. of L., 165-166;

made cardinal, 171; on meeting of archbishops, 175; interview on K. of L., 180, 183, 184; on convening committee of archbishops, 188, 193, 196, 198; action on adjudication of K. of L., 188-193; own report to Rome on K. of L., 192-193; delay in presenting defense of K. of L., 197; conference with Powderly, 208-211, 213-215; at conference of archbishops, 216; on rights of labor, 219; report of meeting to Propaganda, 221; on Corrigan's pastoral of 1886, 224; opposes condemnation of George's works, 229; reputation failing in Rome, 230; relations with Corrigan, 233; called for cardinal's hat, 233; in N. Y. before sailing for Rome, 234; praised by Ryan, 235; arrival in Rome, 235; request to McGlynn, 236; work in Rome, 237; presents memorial on K. of L., 238; interview with Cleveland, 239; reaction to own work in Rome, 242; on release of *Herald* story, 243; approval of action in Rome, 247; disclaiming *Herald* story, 249; Protestant press on action in Rome, 252; opinion of George on, 252; apprehension on memorial publication, 255; Roman action endorsed by Manning, 255; acknowledges Manning's help, 256; Roman action approved by Lynch, 257; receives *Nation*, 257-258; reported interview in Rome, 257; co-operation with Taschereau, 260-261; petition to Holy Office in favor of K. of L., 261-262; receives reports of reactions in U. S., 262-264; explanation to Corrigan on publication of memorial, 264; on revelation of secret document, 269; visits Manning, 270; work in Rome acknowledged by Corrigan, 271; homecoming of,

271; views vis-à-vis Corrigan, 273; reactions of K. of L. leaders to Roman efforts of, 276; revelation of K. of L. secrets to, 278; Powderly's thanks to, 281-282; sympathy of Cleveland with, 282-283; speech in titular church, 282; thanks to Powderly, 286-287; K. of L. committee to call on, 289; letter to K. of L. convention sought, 292-293; visit of O'Reilly to, 293; reply to petition of Powderly, 292-295; appreciation of Powderly by, 295; McQuaid's opinion of, 307; contacts with European social Catholicism, 314; arrangements for meeting with Powderly, 325; trip to Val de Bois, 315; applauded at Liége congress, 316; praised by Langenieux, 316-317; contacts with Manning, 317-318; social encyclical sought by, 318; organizes opposition to George's condemnation, 318-322; Protestant opinion on success in Rome, 322-323; Satolli's opinion on Roman action of, 323; forwarded final decision of Holy Office on K. of L., 324; handling of decree of toleration by, 327-328; displeasure at Barry publicity, 329; Place's congratulations to, 331; Rampolla's praise of, 332; receipt of decree on George, 336-337; result of K. of L. activity of, 339; Manning's praise of, 340; continued labor fame of, 340-341, 350; invitation to Liége congress, 341; encouragement to de Mun, 342; gratitude of Rome toward, 342-343; answer to McQuaid's inquiry, 345; and *Rerum novarum,* 347; reception of *Rerum novarum* by, 349; on Canadian action, 352n; 1900 appeal of Powderly to, 355

Gilmour, Bp. Richard, and Order of American Union, 26; pastoral on labor, 29; prepares Cincinnati pastoral, 82; on K. of L., 83, 194; in Rome, 187; on K. of L. condemnation, 202; on A.O.H., 207; learns action on K. of L., 220; receives copy of memorial on K. of L., 242; agreement with Gibbons, 258; thanks Gibbons for stand in Rome, 283-284; statement of labor problem, 284; ideas on Church and social problem, 319

Gompers, Samuel, 13n

Gould, Jay, 120, 157

Gowen, Franklin B., 22, 23, 46, 52, 85

Graham, Rev. T. W., 148n

Grand Army of the Republic, 131n, 132, 187, 195-198, 219-220

Grand Trunk Railroad, 141

Grannan, Rev. Charles P., 114n

Griffin, Martin I. J., 250

Griffiths, Richard, 64, 85

Gross, Abp. William H., 212

Haid, Leo, O.S.B., 321

Harmel, Léon, 315

Haskell, Burnette G., 90, 212n, 277

Hamilton, Ont., 96, 107

Harel, Rev. F., 178

Harrington, Rev. John M., 129, 131

Hayes, John W., 117n, 209, 326, 334, 353

Haymarket affair, 168-169, 230, 275, 306

Healy, Bp. James A., on secret societies, 25, 103, 344; on K. of L., 84, 128-133, 242, 257; on labor unions, 103-104; on Powderly, 310

Heiss, Abp. Michael, 135-136, 212-213, 321

Hennessey, Rev. J. J., 216

Hennessy, Rev. Richard, 40

Hewitt, Abram S., 223

Hickey, Patrick, 160

Hierarchy, American, position on K. of L., 72-73, 81-82, 104, 173-176; on labor problems, 159-161; problems of in Rome, 228; advice to H. Office on K. of L., 242; opinions on Gibbons' action for K. of L. in Rome, 257-258; for papal clarification on Church's social teaching, 318; opinions on George issue, 320; compared with Irish, 323; final interest on K. of L. among, 344. See also committee of archbishops on secret societies, councils, names of individual bishops.

Hierarchy, Canadian, on K. of L., 200-202. See also names of individual bishops, councils.

Hinckley, Rev. F. A., 141

Hitze, Rev. Franz, 314

Holy Office (Congregation of the Inquisition), on secret societies, 15, 31; "De secta massonum," 102; first decision on K. of L., 108, 130, 133; second decree on K. of L., 176-177; recourse to by American archbishops, 217-218; decree changing K. of L. status in Canada, 261; K. of L. material given to, 272; apparent approval of K. of L., 275-276; final decree on K. of L., 322-324, 339; on George's works, 336

Holy See, gratitude to Gibbons for K. of L. case, 343. See also Leo XIII, Simeoni, congregations.

Home Club, 91n, 170, 295, 334

Horstmann, Rev. Ignatius, 259n

Howes, John, 209

Hoxie, H. M., 152, 215

Hughes, Abp. John, 5

Hughes, William H., 167n

Humanum genus, 102

Hyde, John, 167n

Illustrated Catholic American (New York), 248

Immigrants, German, 6; Irish, 6

Immigration, problems arising out of, 228

Index of Prohibited Books, 317

Industrial Brotherhood, 13, 34, 39, 46

Inquisition, Congregation of the, see Holy Office.

Inscrutabili, 26

International Union of Machinists and Blacksmiths of North America, 20

International Working Peoples' Association, 89

International Workingmen's Association, 90

Ireland, Abp. John, 185, 301; to take K. of L. case to Rome, 188, 193, 206; activity in Rome, 229; work in preparing K. of L. memorial, 238; suggests bribery by *Herald,* 243; interview in Rome of, 262n; advice to K. of L., 274; on George's failure, 306-307; report on Gibbons in France, 315; work in George case, 318, 322; reaction to K. of L. toleration, 329; opinion on Gibbons' K. of L. stand, 340; claim for Gibbons, 351

Irish Canadian (Toronto), 163

Irish Catholic Benevolent Societies, 16n

Irish Catholic Benevolent Union, 118

Irish Emigrant Aid Society, 6

Irish World and Industrial Liberator, 134, 157, 183, 204, 252, 301, 306, 322, 326, 332. See also Ford, Patrick.

Iron Moulders' Union, 11

Irons, Martin, 153, 157

Jacobini, Abp. Domenico, 98, 197, 269, 272

Jacobini, Lodovico Cardinal, 98

Janssens, Abp. Francis, 321

Jesuits, 59

John Swinton's Paper, 154, 169, 184, 199, 253

Journal of United Labor, 60-61, 92, 139, 226, 253, 280, 326-327

Kain, Bp. John J., 211, 262-263, 312, 321

Kansas Catholic (Leavenworth), 248, 267

Katholische Volkszeitung (Baltimore), 182

Keane, Bp. John J., 114n, 188, 193; sermon on societies, 117n; first rector of Catholic University of America, 165n; on K. of L., 182, 183, 207-208; contacts with Powderly, 203, 205-206; activities in Rome, 229-230, 272; advice to Gibbons, 230; enlists Manning's aid, 236; work in preparing memorial on K. of L., 238; thanks Manning, 242; on Gibbons action in Rome, 255; letter to *Catholic Standard,* 269; contact with Maes, 318; and Leo XIII, 351

Keily, John, 234, 283

Kenrick, Abp. Francis Patrick, 10, 19n

Kenrick, Abp. Peter Richard, and local labor trouble, 158-159, 280; policy on fraternal societies, 161; on K. of L., 211, 215-216, 218; opinion on K. of L. disclosed, 244, 258

Kerby, Rev. William J., 355

Ketteler, Bp. Wilhelm Emmanuel von, 6-7, 314

Keys, William, 95, 121-122, 145, 232

King, Thomas, 41, 44

Knights of Labor, and Molly Maguires, 21, 45, 78-79; in Quebec, 30; origin of, 34-39; ritual and secrecy of, 35-36, 54; early growth of, 36-38; Reading priests on, 41; Fr. O'Reilly on, 48; Bp. O'Hara on, 42-43, 48-49; publicizing name of, 44, 46, 50, 51, 54, 57, 62-63; attempt to placate Church, 44, 58-59;

Bp. Tuigg on, 45, 74; changes in ritual, 46-47, 63, 70-71; membership, 50, 61, 62n, 66, 88, 105, 203, in Boston, 215n, in Maine, 128n, Catholic, 113n, 215; in Pa. coal fields, 52; Catholic members and the oath, 55-56; and Catholic opposition, 56-57; and Catholic "missions," 59-60; early problems of, 61-62; women admitted to, 63n; opposition to ritual changes, 63-67; secrecy after oath out, 68; early stand of hierarchy on, 72-73; Abp. Wood on, 74; Bp. Mullen on, 75; Bp. Chatard on, 75-76; Catholic clergy on, 76-79, 86-87, 126-127, 130-134; and use of violence, 78-79; Bp. Watterson on, 82; Bp. Gilmour on, 83; Bp. Healy on, 84; and Church in Philadelphia, 84-86; attitude toward Catholic clergy, 87-88; and clergy in Schuylkill County, 85; and Church in Chicago, 85-86; growth of, early 1880's, 88; socialism in, 88, 90; anarchists in, 89; radical influence on, 90-92; move for conservatism in, 92; in Canada, 94-96, 101, 107, 141-142, 144, 171; on strikes, 105; committees visiting pastors, 106; Catholic suspicion toward, 106; change in constitution, 107; translation of ritual, 107; condemned by H. Office, 108; Abp. Lynch on, 110, 200-201; Abp. Ryan on, 111; Fr. Wm. Walsh on, 111; arbitration with Gould, 120; and Church in Montreal, 121-122; and Church in Quebec, 122-126; Taschereau on, 123-124; new form of pledge, 126-127; Bp. Healy on, 128-133; condemned by Holy See, 130; Irish Catholics on, 134; growth of German Catholics in, 135; *Pilot* on, 135; in Milwaukee, 135-136; position in 1886,

138; in Ottawa, 142-144; Bp. Duhamel on, 145; position of Taschereau on, 147, 161-163; Quebec report to Propaganda on, 148; Protestant clergy on, 154-155; and Southwest railroad strike, 158; American hierarchy on, 104, 163-168, 173-176, 202-203, 211-213, 215-220, 344; Gibbons on, 165-166, 192-193; circular on labor disturbances, 1886, 169; reaction to Canadian action on, 172-173; letter of Simeoni on, 176-177; Fabre on, 95, 177-179; Corrigan on, 179-180, 222; Roman condemnation of, 182; Catholic press reactions to condemnation of, 182-187; American hierarchy's reactions, 187-191; concern of Propaganda with, 194-195; leaders of concerned with Catholic Church, 199; Canadian prelates on, 200-202; appearance of in Quebec, 201-202; Catholic press on, 204; revision of constitution, 205-206; report of J. J. Murphy, S.J., on, 218-219; Straniero on, 222, 248; case of transferred to Rome by archbishops, 222; on N. Y. election, 226; threatened condemnation of, 236; Gibbons' memorial on, 239-242; and Catholic workmen, 240; impermanence of, 241-242; advice of hierarchy on, 242; Taschereau's charges against, 254; same in U. S. and Canada, 254; constitution of, 259; Gibbons' plea for, 262; trouble of Corrigan with, 265, 271; on final Canadian circular, 266; report of approval of, 267; temporary toleration of, 268; Manning's defense of, 270; Gibbons and Corrigan on, 273; advice of Ireland to, 274; decline of, 275; leaders' reactions to Gibbons' defense of, 276; and McGlynn, 284-285, 304, 309-

310; temperance praised by religious press, 286; influence of religious issue in decline of, 288; Powderly spends funds of, 290; identified with revolutionists, 291; and George, 292; trade unions in, 296; official report on Church relations, 296-298; resignation of general officers of, 299; reactions of Protestants to, 302-303; Leo XIII's attitude toward, 307; result of agitation on, 313; Roman toleration of, 322, 324; advocacy of single tax by, 338-339; case of and *Rerum novarum*, 347n; *Moniteur de Rome* on, 351

Knights of Labor, district assemblies, Camden, 38; Philadelphia, 38; Reading, 41; Scranton, 44; New Bethlehem, 58; New York (D.A. 49), 140, 204, 285; Denver, 277-278

Knights of Labor, general assembly, conventions of, Philadelphia, 1876, 41; Pittsburgh, 1877, 43-44; Reading, 1878, 37, 46; Philadelphia, 1878, 49-50; Chicago, 1879, 54; Pittsburgh, 1880, 57; Detroit, 1881, 62; New York, 1882, 66, 71; Cincinnati, 1883, 72; Philadelphia, 1884, 107, 259n; Hamilton, Ont., 1885, 134-135; Cleveland, 1886, 169; Richmond, 1886, 199-200, 203-206; Minneapolis, 1887, 209, 295; Indianapolis, 1888, 333; Atlanta, 1889, 338; Philadelphia, 1893, 354

Knights of Labor, general executive board of, 299

Knights of Labor, general (grand) master workman, see Stephens, Powderly, Sovereign.

Knights of Labor, local assemblies, Philadelphia, 36-39, 63-64; Scranton, 39, 41; Brooklyn, 41, 65; New York, 65; Hamilton, 94

Knights of Pythias, 36, 344

Knights of St. Crispin, 12, 31, 61

Kolping, Rev. Adolphe, 314

La Vérité (Quebec), 170, 351-352

Labadie, Joseph, 91-92, 139n, 306

Labor, Catholic churchmen on, 18-19, 24, 29, 119-120; religious strife in, 231; opinions of on Gibbons' action for K. of L., 252; Bp. Phelan on, 263; Gibbons on state of in U. S., 273-274; political activity of, 304; M. F. Egan on, 286; crisis diagnosed by Phineas, 287; Church's relationship with, 311-312; papal statement desired on, 320-321; Leo XIII and claims of, 325; Cardinal Place on, 331-332; international conference on, 340

Labor and capital, Gibbons on, 293; Place on, 331

Labor disturbances, 1870, 21-24; 1877, 45; early 1880's, 88; 1884, 105; 1885, 120; 1886, 168-169; in Canada, 110. See also Haymarket affair, Molly Maguires, strikes.

Labor Enquirer (Denver), 250, 252, 277, 279, 284

Labor movement, pre-Civil War and Church, 3-7; post-Civil War, 11-30; radical elements in, 92-93; in 1886, 138; effect of bigotry in, 288; Catholic influence on, 357

Labor organizations, in conciliar legislation, 14; Abp. Bayley on, 16; Abp. Lynch on, 17; Bp. Wm. McCloskey on, 18-19; Catholic churchmen on, 20, 24, 73; Leo XIII on, 27; Bp. Chatard on, 27-28; Bp. Dwenger on, 28; Bp. Gilmour on, 29; Bp. Becker on, 30; Fr. McGrath on, 42; Bp. Borgess on, 77; archbishops' Roman conference on, 99-101; under Catholic auspices, 102, 114, 117-118, 315; Abp. Lynch on, 109-110; discussed at Third Plenary Council, 113-119;

Abp. Heiss on, 136; Fr. P. J. Conway on, 147-148; Catholic press on, 155-156; committee of archbishops on, 219; Roman mind on, 324; Bp. Keane on, 351; Catholic ideas on, 348-349, 358

Labor problems, individual Catholics' concern with, 4-6; Catholic collective concern with, 6-7; Catholic press on, 140; hierarchy on, 159-161; M. F. Egan on, 301; Baltimore congress on, 338; Liége congress on, 341; Gibbons on legislation for, 342

Land League, 91, 151n

Land question, K. of L. on, 304; Powderly's recommendation on, 338

Langenieux, Abp. Benoît, 315, 316-317, 340

Layton, Robert D., 63, 72, 76, 302

Le Propagateur Catholique (New Orleans), 182

The *Leader* (New York), 225

Leary, M. A., 52

Leclerc, Rev. J. V., 146

Lee, John, 43

Lee, Msgr. Thomas S., 183

Legaré, Rev. Cyrille E., 108, 236

Leo XIII, Pope, and *Rerum novarum,* 7, 347, 349; initial encyclicals of, 26, 224; on workers' societies, 82; on socialism, 89, 313; on Freemasonry, 102; summons to McGlynn, 234; favor to Taschereau, 261; contrasted with Taschereau, 297; Gibbons on, 317; and toleration of K. of L., 325; and international conference on labor, 340; interest in social question, 341; encyclical to U. S., 351; Powderly on, 354

Leray, Abp. Francis X., 114n, 215, 217, 219

Litchman, Charles, 51, 55, 57, 59, 65, 73, 247, 298, 299

A Living Wage, 356

Locomotive Brotherhood of Engineers, 76, 131n

Locust Gap, Pa., K. of L. in, 134

Lonaconing, Md., K. of L. in, 127

Lonergan, James, 325

Longinqua oceani, 351

Loughlin, Bp. John, 113

Lutherans, Missouri Synod of, 303

Lynch, Rev. B., 80

Lynch, Abp. John J., on labor unions, 17, 109-110; on Quebec strike, 1851, 30; on Freemasonry, 103; on K. of L., 125, 163, 200-201, 203; on Gibbons' K. of L. action, 257

McCartney, J. J., 211n

McCauley, Robert, 36

McCloskey, John Cardinal, 27, 121

McCloskey, Bp. William G., 18-19, 81, 259

McColgan, Msgr. Edward, 183, 211n

Macdonald, Sir John, 142, 171n

McDonnell, Rev. Charles E., 203, 234

McDonnell, J. P., 13n

McElrone, Hugh P., 310

McEnroe, Rev. Peter C., 312

McEvela, William, 143

McGee, Thomas D'Arcy, 5

McGlynn, Rev. Edward, and George campaign, 222-223; Abp. Riordan on, 225; called to Rome, 226, 229, 234; hierarchy on case of, 228; Gibbons' letter to, 236-237; paragraph in K. of L. memorial on, 241; Abp. Ryan on, 258; Gibbons explains memorial comment on, 270; Corrigan on, 271, 343; Powderly on, 278; Gilmour on, 283; case linked with K. of L., 284, 292; N. Y. demonstration for, 284-285; Phineas' comment on, 288; relations with K. of L., 304; continues support of George, 304; attack on Powderly, 307-309; papal statement on, 235;

split with George, 335-336n; addressing K. of L. rally, 344-345; reconciliation of, 350

McGrath, Rev. John, 42, 57n

McGregor, George N., 128, 133

McGuire, Peter J., 13n, 90, 922

Macheboeuf, Bp. Joseph P., 217n, 277

Machinists' and Blacksmiths' Union, 39, 40

McKinley, Pres. William, 354

McManus, Rev. P. J., 127

McMaster, James, 157, 170, 186, 197, 199, 245. See also *Freeman's Journal*.

McNeirny, Bp. Francis, 114, 135

McNulty gang, 52

McParlan, James, 22

McQuaid, Bp. Bernard J., on secret societies, 25, 160, 198, 344; queried on K. of L., 96; at Third Plenary Council, 116; on Catholic Mutual Benevolence Association, 118; on K. of L., 166, 307; on McGlynn, 226, 305; on publication of K. of L. memorial, 264; on George's defeat at polls, 307; on social encyclical, 318; asks Gibbons' status of K. of L., 345

Maes, Bp. Camillus P., 220-221, 259, 318

Magnien, Abbé Alphonse, 262

Mahanoy, Pa., K. of L. in, 48

Mahanoy Plane, Pa., Molly Maguire trouble in, 22

"Mandement sur certaines sociétés défendues," 161-163; reaction to in U. S., 163-168

Manning, Henry Edward Cardinal, 160n, 171n; aid sought in K. of L. case, 236; name used in Rome, 242; endorses Gibbons on K. of L., 255-256; on Gibbons' cause in Rome, 269-270; Gibbons' visit to, 270; letter used in K. of L. report, 296; aid to Gibbons in George case, 317-

318; recalls K. of L. episode, 340; and Liége congress, 341-342; and *Rerum novarum,* 346-347

Manning, Rev. Peter C., 127

Manucy, Bp. Dominic, 114n

March, Charles, 143, 200

Marois, Rev. A., 350

Marty, Bp. Martin, 114n

Matengier, Rev. A., 146

Mattingly, Rev. Charles A., 43

Mazzella, Camillo Cardinal, 194, 195, 257, 343-344

Meagher, Rev. Martin, 75, 80

Mechanics' Union of Trade Associations, 2

Memorial on the Knights of Labor, presented in Rome by Gibbons, 238; contents of, 239-242; dispute on versions of, 268; effects of publication of, 269; used in K. of L. report, 296; leakage of from Rome, 332; relation to *Rerum novarum,* 348-349

Mermillod, Bp. Gaspard, 341

Michigan Catholic (Detroit), 167, 173, 183, 246, 301

Milwaukee, K. of L. in, 135; First Provincial Council of, 136, 174

Minneapolis, G. A. convention at, 209, 299, 332, 353

Miners' National Association, 20

Missouri Pacific Railroad, 153, 158-159.

Mitsch, George, 291

Molly Maguires, 21-24, 45, 48, 78-79, 89

Monaco, Raffaele Cardinal, 194, 237, 260-261, 272

Moniteur de Rome, article on K. of L., 172; article on social question in U. S., 229; version of memorial on K. of L., 264, 267; editor Preston on memorial version of, 268; Manning's letter in, 269; Ireland on

George in, 322; on K. of L. and strikes, 351

Monitor (San Francisco), 249

Montreal, 95, 108, 121, 141, 163, 172, 232. See also Fabre, Keys.

Montreal *Daily Witness*, 147n, 181n.

Montreal *True Witness and Catholic Chronicle*, 172

Moore, Bp. John, 187

Morning Star (New Orleans), 185, 220

Most, Johann, 89, 92

Moulders' Association, 17

Mount Carmel, Pa., K. of L. in, 134

Mourret, Rev. Fernand, S.S., 325

Mullen, Bp. Tobias, 55, 75, 79-80

Mun, Albert de, 315, 342

Murphy, Rev. John J., S.J., 218-219

The *Nation*, 257-258

National Labor League of North America, 43

National Labor Union, 12, 34

Nativism, 3

Neasham, Thomas, 278

New Orleans, coadjutor for, 233

New York, K. of L. in, 65-66, 91; Fourth Provincial Council of, 93.

New York *Herald*, 211, 243, 255, 264; *Independent*, 155; *Mail and Express*, 251; *Post*, 253; *Times*, 250. See also *Freeman's Journal, Catholic News, Catholic Review, Catholic Herald, Tablet.*

Northcumberland Co., Pa., K. of L. in, **133**

Northrup, Bp. Henry P., 321

Northwestern Chronicle (St. Paul), 186, 251, 301, 330-331

Nunciature, papal in U. S., opposition to, 233

O'Brien, Abp. Cornelius, 181

O'Brien, Rev. James, 57

O'Brien, Jerry, 43

O'Bryen, Msgr. Richard, 173, 200

Observateur Français, 330

O'Connell, Msgr. Denis J., work on Baltimore legislation, 117n; reports to Gibbons on K. of L. case in Rome, 175-176, 194-195, 196-197, 229, 272, 283; to Corrigan on affairs in Rome, 195, 230; on Straniero's trip to U. S., 222; on Roman reaction to Gibbons' work for K. of L., 272-273; aids Gibbons on George question, 318, 320; on final Roman decision in K. of L. case, 322-323, 330; on Rome's feelings toward Gibbons, 342-343; on preparation of *Rerum novarum*, 346-347

O'Connor, Bp. James, 126n, 263, 321-322

O'Connor, Rev. Daniel, 22, 23n, 53-54, 170

Odd Fellows, 8, 10, 73, 174, 344

O'Donoghue, Daniel, interview with Abp. Lynch, 109-110; on Taschereau, 125; on socialism, 139; and Bp. Duhamel, 142-144; urges Powderly to go to Rome, 149, 151-153; and churchmen in Toronto, 200; on Montreal K. of L., 221; answers Thomas Barry, 232; to Powderly on Gibbons' K. of L. stand in Rome, 276

O'Hara, Bp. William, visited by Powderly, 42; on secret societies, 48; supposed approval of K. of L., 48-49; opposition to K. of L. in jurisdiction of, 84; Powderly's attempt to see, 132; invitation to Powderly, 312

O'Flanaghan, John, 186

O'Gorman, Rev. Thomas, 351

Der Ohio Waisenfreund, 135

O'Leary, Rev. Cornelius, and St. Louis labor troubles, 158-159; on Abp. P. R. Kenrick and Hoxie, 215-216; and Straniero, 222; suspension of, 279-280; conveys Powderly's message to Gibbons, 280-281

O'Leary, Daniel, 54
Ontario, K. of L. in, 107
Order of the American Union, 26
Order of United Americans, 3
O'Reilly, Rev. Bernard, 248
O'Reilly, Rev. Henry F., 47-48, 52-53
O'Reilly, Rev. John J., 134
O'Reilly, Thomas, in Richmond, 206; arranges with Powderly matter of ecclesiastical negotiations, 207-210, 289-291; account of call on Gibbons, 213; congratulates Powderly on Gibbons' K. of L. action, 276; prepares for Minn. G.A., 289; on affiliating with George, 292; report to G. A. on Church and Order, 293, 296-298; secret services for Powderly, 300; confidant of Powderly, 326
Osservatore Romano, 341
Ottawa, K. of L. in, 142-144, 145; a metropolitan see, 172

Panic of 1837, 2, 8
Parsons, Albert R., 89, 169, 186
Parysso, Anton, 231
Pastorals, see names of bishops and councils.
Pennsylvania coal fields, 21-24, 52
Pentecost, Rev. Hugh O., 345
Peter Cooper Club, 39
Peter's Pence, 241
Peterson, Rev. James, 128
Phelan, Rev. David S., 186
Phelan, Bp. Richard, 164, 166, 263
Philadelphia, 84, 107; First Provincial Council of, 73. See also *Catholic Standard,* K. of L., Ryan, Abp. Wood.
Philadelphia and Reading Railroad, 22, 307
Philadelphia *Times,* 53
Phineas, 185, 287, 288
Pilot (Boston), 135, 140, 157, 185,

204, 244, 248, 282. See also Donahoe, Phineas.
Pinkerton, Allan, 89
Pinkerton Detective Agency, 52
Pittsburgh, K. of L. in, 74, 76. See also the *Catholic.*
Pittsburgh *Dispatch,* 164, 251
Pittsburgh labor convention of 1876, 12
Pius IX, Pope, 15
Pius XI, Pope, 358
Place, Charles P. Cardinal, 331-332
Portland, Me., Bp. on K. of L. in, 84, 128, 130
Pottsville, Pa., K. of L. in, 52
Powderly, Terence Vincent, 21, 33, 34; and Abp. Wood, 38, 74; religious practices, 39; initiated into K. of L., 39; background, 39; and Fr. Hennessy, 40; aware of Church's teaching, 40; and Abp. Ryan, 40-41, 112; and Catholics in K. of L., 41; and Bp. O'Hara, 41-42, 49; vs. religious bigotry in K. of L., 43-44; resigns delegateship, 44; on publicizing name of K. of L., 44-45, 46, 50, 51, 55, 58, 60, 62-63; elected Mayor of Scranton, 45; to change ritual, 47; and Church in Pa., 52-53; and Shenandoah picnic, 53-54; and Catholic workers' societies, 54; elected grand master workman, 54; for word of honor, 55; on critical clerics, 62-63; on changes in ritual, 64-68; on ecclesiastical troubles, 68-69, 125; on Bp. Tuigg, 74-75; on Bp. Watterson, 82-83; and clerical connections, 84, 87, 170-171, 230, 289n, 325-326; on communism and socialism, 90-91, 109, 112, 138-139, 140-141; plea of conservatism, 92, 139-140; tour of Ontario, 108-109; called a Mason, 111; defense to Abp. Ryan, 112-113; and K. of L. in Montreal, 121-122, 144-145; on

sympathetic clergy, 127; and Bp. Healy, 128; on Church and K. of L., 128, 153-154, 190-192, 199-200, 279, 298, 327; reaction to clerical opposition in Me., 130-133; in Pa., 134; endorsed by Irish Catholics, 134; as politician, 138; on Ottawa difficulties, 146; and Taschereau, 147, 164, 177; on going to Rome, 149-151; on labor disorders, 153-154; Catholic press on, 155, 156-157, 169-170, 246, 300-302; and Fr. O'Leary, 158, 280; on Haymarket affair, 169, 306; on condemnation in Canada, 173; on strikes, 183; *Freeman's Journal* on, 186-187; and Gibbons, 192n, 208-211, 213-215, 276, 280-281, 286-287, 293, 295, 325, 327-328; Chatard on, 203; and Bp. Keane, 205, 206-207; and committee of archbishops in Baltimore, 207-211, 213-215; and George, 222-223, 335-336; and McGlynn, 223, 284-285, 292n, 307-309; defense of in *Moniteur,* 229; opposed for his religion, 232; public appearance in N. Y., 235; confers with Cleveland, 239; on Fr. Horstmann, 259n; accusations vs. in Denver, 276-277; reception in Boston, 279; M. F. Egan on, 286; and Thomas O'Reilly, 289-290; and German R. C. Central-Verein, 291; and Home Club, 295; G. A. on relations of with Church, 298-299; answers opposition in K. of L., 300; humor on Roman negotiations, 308-309; reactions to reported approval in *World,* 310-311; and Abp. Corrigan, 311n; gift of to prelates, 329; Ford's praise of, 332; on changing K. of L. constitution, 333; on Rome's decree of toleration, 334; on anti-Catholic charges, 335; invited to Catholic congress, 337; on land

question, 338; and N. Y. Central strike, 344; later career of, 353-355; publication of recollections of, 355; contribution of, 356

Press, on N. Y. mayoralty election of 1886, 226-227; evidences in of division in labor, 232; reactions of to K. of L. memorial, 244, 250-251; reactions to Taschereau, 253; reports of Roman approval of K. of L., 267, 322-323, 326-327; carrying documents on K. of L., 266-267. See also names of individual papers.

Press, Catholic, on labor problems, 140, 155; on Powderly, 156-157, 169-170, 300-302; on condemnation of K. of L., 182-187; on K. of L., 204; on archbishops' conference on secret societies, 200; on Corrigan's pastoral, 1886, 223-226; on K. of L. memorial, 244-250, 268-269; on Haymarket affair, 306; rumor of encyclical in, 313-314; and European social Catholicism, 313-316; and decree of toleration of K. of L., 330

Press, European, notice of Roman action on K. of L., 269, 330

Press, Protestant religious, 155, 251

Preston, Msgr. Thomas, 118, 174n, 223, 243, 306, 309-310

Preston, Thomas, 184, 220, 226, 231, 249, 268, 305

Primrose League, 160, 163

Progress and Poverty, 317

Propaganda, Congregation of, 26; on secret societies, 15, 96; and Baltimore legislation on unions, 17; and Taschereau, 97, 108, 148; and archbishops' Roman conference, 1883, 100; and Third Plenary Council, 115; interest in G.A.R., 188; convening archbishops' committee on secret societies, 195; supplied with material on K. of L., 229, 233, 272; leakage of secret documents from,

258; K. of L. decree of toleration from prefect of, 323

Property, private, teaching on sought from Rome, 318, 320-321, 343; defense of by Corrigan, 223-227, 328-329, 337, 346; principles of K. of L. on, 332-333

Protestants, Catholic contact with in K. of L., 240; concern with K. of L. case in Rome, 251; in K. of L., 298; reactions to K. of L., 302-303. See also clergy, Protestant.

Providence, R. I., Powderly in, 140-141

Puck (New York), 263

Purcell, Abp. John B., 11, 24

Quadragesimo anno, 358

Quebec, 107, 108, 123, 161, 172, 177, 200, 201, 350; Provincial Councils of, First, 110; Fourth, 162; Seventh, 171. See also *La Vérité*, Taschereau.

Quebec *Le Canadien*, 265; *L'Électeur*, 247; *L'Événement*, 253; *Morning Chronicle*, 141, 266

Qui pluribus, 336

Quinliven, Rev. J., 146

Quinn, Msgr. William, 163

Quod apostolici muneris, 26, 89, 224, 336

Radicals, attempt to discredit Church, 231; Catholic contacts with, 240; in Minn. G.A., 295-296. See also socialism, anarchism, communism.

Rampolla, Mariano Cardinal, 332

Rawley, William, 124

Red International, 90

Rende, Camillo Cardinal de, 328

"Report of J. J. Murphy, S.J., upon the Constitution, By-Laws, etc., of the Ancient Order of Hibernians and the Knights of Labor," 218

Republic (Boston), 184, 220

Rerum novarum, American contribu-

tion to issuing of, 313; petitions for, 318; influence on, 340-341, 346; relation of to memorial on K. of L., 348-349; American prelates' reception of, 349; McGlynn acceptance of, 350; and Powderly, 356; and American Catholic social movement, 356-357

Richards, William, 338

Richmond, G.A. convention at, 199-200

Richter, Bp. Henry J., 167, 259, 320

Riel, Louis, 123

Riordan, John J., 248

Riordan, Abp. Patrick W., 207, 211-212, 225

Der Ritter der Arbeit, 136n

Robot, Isidore, O.S.B., 114n

Roche, Rev. Patrick, 54

Rochester, N. Y., clergy on labor in, 86

Rome, opposition to K. of L. toleration in, 329

Ryan, Rev. John A., 350n, 356

Ryan, Abp. Patrick J., Powderly's defense to, 38, 40-41, 109; on K. of L., 111; on Catholics in societies, 160-161; on Canadian action on K. of L., 183; at meeting of archbishops' committee on secret societies, 196, 217-219; on Gibbons' going to Rome, 234, 235; message to Powderly, 259; to Gibbons after action on K. of L. in Rome, 263-264; and George issue, 318, 336

Ryan, Bp. Stephen V., 94, 226

Sabetti, Rev. Aloysius, S.J., 189n, 192

St. Louis, 153, 158-159. See also Kenrick, Abp. P. R., O'Leary, Rev. C., *Catholic World, Western Watchman.*

Sallua, Rev. Vincenzo, O.P., 237, 260

Salpointe, Abp. John Baptist, 217, 218, 245, 258

San Francisco, First Provincial Council of, 73

Satolli, Abp. Francesco, 323, 350

Sbarretti, Canon Donato, 175, 195, 229

Schiaffino, Placide Cardinal, 322

Schilling, Robert, 136

Schmitt, Rev. Valentine F., 57, 80-81

School controversy of the 1890's, 340

Schuylkill Co., Pa., labor in, 46, 47, 52, 53, 57, 85, 106, 111, 112, 133, 312

Scranton *Daily Times,* 48, 52; *Republican,* 48, 52. See also *Catholic Record,* O'Hara.

Second Plenary Council of Baltimore, 13-14, 20, 96, 101

Secrecy in labor movement, 12-13

"Secret Brotherhood," 42

Secret societies, and labor unions in conciliar legislation, 14-15; Church's attitude on, 7-11, 15-16; conciliar legislation on, 13-14, 17; in Canada, 17; in Boston, 20n; in other American dioceses, 25, 28; archbishops' Roman conference on, 98-100; discussed in Third Plenary Council, 113-119; Taschereau on, 123; meeting of archbishops' committee on, 344

"Secret Work," 36, 107n, 302-303

Seghers, Abp. Charles J., 99

Sepiacci, Bp. Luigi, 98, 101, 187

Seton, Abp. Robert, 197n

Seventh Provincial Council of Quebec, 171

Shamokin, Pa., K. of L. in, 134

Shea, John Gilmary, 27n, 116n

Simeoni, Giovanni Cardinal, 26; at archbishops' conference, 1883, 98; work on K. of L. in Rome, 176-177, 194-195, 229; on convening committee of archbishops, 188, 198; Gibbons' private report to on K. of L., 192; Gibbons to on archbishops' conference, 221; attacked by Davitt,

235; petitioned by Taschereau on K. of L., 254; informed on American reaction to Gibbons' K. of L. stand, 283; toleration of K. of L. sent by, 324; Gibbons' reassurance to on K. of L. co-operation, 328; sends decree on George, 336

Siney, John, 20-21

Single tax, 332-333, 336, 338-339, 350n

Singulari quadam, 357

Slattery, Rev. E. F., 248

Smith, Senator Frank, 200

Social Catholicism, 313-316, 346

Social reform, Church's concern with, 2

Socialism, in labor movement, 12-13, 93; Leo XIII on, 26, 313, 343, 346, 349, 351; and K. of L., 88, 138-141, 189n, 254, 324, 333; Catholic attitude toward, 214, 356; Bp. O'Connor on danger of, 321; Gibbons and, 330. See also anarchism, communism.

Socialist Labor Party, 90; Powderly and, 57, 277, 298

Socialists, on secrecy of K. of L., 57; on ritual, 67; and George, 304

Société des Cordonniers, 17

Soderini, Eduardo, 314, 325, 341

Sons of St. Joseph, 73

Sons of Temperance, 9, 10

Sources, lack of, in Pennsylvania archives, 86; on Roman negotiations over K. of L., 236

Sovereign, James R., 353

Sovereigns of Industry, 13

Spalding, Bp. John L., 115, 116, 220

Spalding, Abp. Martin J., 18, 19n, 30n

Standard (New York), 231, 252, 285, 305, 339

Starkey, George, 43

Stephens, Uriah S., 35; praise of Catholic members, 50-51; on socialism, 90; on ritual change, 63-64, 65n; precedent of for Powderly, 279, 335

Stevens, E. A., 56

Stewart, John T., 125-126

Straniero, Msgr. Germano, 221-222, 248

Strikes, telegraph operators, 94; in Southwest, 153, 157-159, 164; Chicago meatpackers, 206, 275, 295; in St. Louis, 215; N. Y. waterfront, 275; Gibbons on, 294; Bp. Gilmour on, 311-312; on N. Y. Central, 344; Leo XIII and Gibbons on, 348

Sylvis, William, 11

Tablet (London), 256, 270, 349

Tablet (New York), 247

Taschereau, Elzear-Alexandre Cardinal, 94; on secret societies, 31, 123; on labor associations, 32, 103; seeks decision on K. of L. in Rome, 96-97; made cardinal, 101, 171; receives answer from Rome, 108; American reaction to pronouncement of, 120; circular on K. of L., 123-124; interview with K. of L., 122-125; opinion of decree on K. of L., 124-125; concern with K. of L. in Canada, 141-142; mandement on K. of L., 147; report to Propaganda on K. of L., 148; mandement on prohibited societies, 161-163; report on American reactions, 167-168; pastoral mention of K. of L., 171; second Roman answer on K. of L., 176-177; for extension of decision on K. of L., 180-181; action on K. of L. publicized, 182-187; on convening of American archbishops' committee, 198; effect of action of on K. of L., 200; on K. of L. in Quebec, 201-202; continued opposition to K. of L., 234; in Rome, 235-237; corresponds with Legaré, 236; and press, 253; renewing K. of L. case in Rome, 253-254; seeks favor from H. Office, 259-261; final cir-

cular on K. of L., 265-266; informs Corrigan on K. of L. status, 268; contrasted with Leo XIII, 297; anxiety about K. of L., 307; views unchanged, 310; case for in *La Vérité,* 351-352

Tello, Manly, 249

Temperance, Powderly on, 279, 298; religious press on in K. of L., 286

Terry, Fr. Edward A., 135

Texas and Pacific Railroad, 153

Thébaud, Rev. Augustus J., S.J., 5

Third Plenary Council of Baltimore, 106, 110-119

Thirty Years of Labor, 38

Toner, Fr. Patrick, 43

Toniolo, Guiseppe, 314

Toronto, 31, 94, 107, 200. See also Lynch, Abp., O'Donoghue.

Toronto Trades' Assembly, 31

Toronto Trades and Labour Council, 94, 142

Toronto *Tribune,* 109

Tour du Pin, René de la, 315

Trades and Labour Congress of Canada, 142

Trade Union Act of 1872, 31

T'Serclaes, Charles de, 325

Tuigg, Bp. John, 45, 74

Turner, Frederick, 111, 121, 334

Unionism, a Catholic contribution to, 302

United Labor Party, 304

Universalist church, Dubuque, 303

Van Patten, Philip, 90, 277

Vatican Council, 17n

Vettman, Rev. E. J., 83-84

Villeneuve-Bargemont, Alban de, 315

Vinal Haven, Me., K. of L. in, 130

Vincennes, Ind., labor in diocese of, 75-76

Vogelzang, Charles von, 315

Volpini, Rev. Alessandro, 347

Wahrheits-Freund (Cincinnati), 182, 248
Walsh, Rev. William, 111, 120
Walsh, Abp. William J., 150n, 226n
Walsh, Rev. Maurice A., 74, 111n
Warren, George S., 144
Washington *Republic*, 180
Watterson, Bp. John A., 82, 320
"Wealth," Carnegie essay, 349n
Wesleyan Methodist, 303
Western Watchman (St. Louis), 155, 186, 220, 249, 267
Wigger, Bp. Winand M., 114
Williams, Abp. John J., 196, 215-218, 234, 272, 279
Wood, Abp. James F., and Molly Maguires, 22-23; and tradition of friendly relations with K. of L., 37-38, 72, 74, 335; on secret societies, 40; and Catholic workers' societies, 54n; reported action of K. of L., 84-85; death, 111
Workingmen's Benevolent Association, 21
Workingmen's Party, 2, 6
Wright, Duncan, 43
Wright, James A., 38, 74, 111
Wright, James L., 35, 44

Zigliara, Tommaso Cardinal, 347

THE IRISH-AMERICANS

An Arno Press Collection

Athearn, Robert G. **THOMAS FRANCIS MEAGHER:** An Irish Revolutionary in America. 1949

Biever, Bruce Francis. **RELIGION, CULTURE AND VALUES:** A Cross-Cultural Analysis of Motivational Factors in Native Irish and American Irish Catholicism. 1976

Bolger, Stephen Garrett. **THE IRISH CHARACTER IN AMERICAN FICTION, 1830-1860.** 1976

Browne, Henry J. **THE CATHOLIC CHURCH AND THE KNIGHTS OF LABOR.** 1949

Buckley, John Patrick. **THE NEW YORK IRISH:** Their View of American Foreign Policy, 1914-1921. 1976

Cochran, Alice Lida. **THE SAGA OF AN IRISH IMMIGRANT FAMILY:** The Descendants of John Mullanphy. 1976

Corbett, James J. **THE ROAR OF THE CROWD.** 1925

Cronin, Harry C. **EUGENE O'NEILL:** Irish and American; A Study in Cultural Context. 1976

Cuddy, Joseph Edward. **IRISH-AMERICAN AND NATIONAL ISOLATIONISM, 1914-1920.** 1976

Curley, James Michael. **I'D DO IT AGAIN:** A Record of All My Uproarious Years. 1957

Deasy, Mary. **THE HOUR OF SPRING.** 1948

Dinneen, Joseph. **WARD EIGHT.** 1936

Doyle, David Noel. **IRISH-AMERICANS, NATIVE RIGHTS AND NATIONAL EMPIRES:** The Structure, Divisions and Attitudes of the Catholic Minority in the Decade of Expansion, 1890-1901. 1976

Dunphy, Jack. **JOHN FURY.** 1946

Fanning, Charles, ed. **MR. DOOLEY AND THE CHICAGO IRISH:** An Anthology. 1976

Farrell, James T. **FATHER AND SON.** 1940

Fleming, Thomas J. **ALL GOOD MEN.** 1961

Funchion, Michael F. **CHICAGO'S IRISH NATIONALISTS, 1881-1890.** 1976

Gudelunas, William A., Jr. and William G. Shade. **BEFORE THE MOLLY MAGUIRES:** The Emergence of the Ethno-Religious Factor in the Politics of the Lower Anthracite Region, 1844-1872. 1976

Henderson, Thomas McLean. **TAMMANY HALL AND THE NEW IMMIGRANTS:** The Progressive Years. 1976

Hueston, Robert Francis. **THE CATHOLIC PRESS AND NATIVISM, 1840-1860.** 1976

Joyce, William Leonard. **EDITORS AND ETHNICITY:** A History of the Irish-American Press, 1848-1883. 1976

Larkin, Emmet. **THE HISTORICAL DIMENSIONS OF IRISH CATHOLICISM.** 1976

Lockhart, Audrey. **SOME ASPECTS OF EMIGRATION FROM IRELAND TO THE NORTH AMERICAN COLONIES BETWEEN 1660-1775.** 1976

Maguire, Edward J., ed. **REVEREND JOHN O'HANLON'S** *THE IRISH EMIGRANT'S GUIDE FOR THE UNITED STATES:* A Critical Edition with Introduction and Commentary. 1976

McCaffrey, Lawrence J., ed. **IRISH NATIONALISM AND THE AMERICAN CONTRIBUTION.** 1976

McDonald, Grace. **HISTORY OF THE IRISH IN WISCONSIN IN THE NINETEENTH CENTURY.** 1954

McManamin, Francis G. **THE AMERICAN YEARS OF JOHN BOYLE O'REILLY, 1870-1890.** 1976

McSorley, Edward. **OUR OWN KIND.** 1946

Moynihan, James H. **THE LIFE OF ARCHBISHOP JOHN IRELAND.** 1953

Niehaus, Earl F. **THE IRISH IN NEW ORLEANS, 1800-1860.** 1965

O'Grady, Joseph Patrick. **IRISH-AMERICANS AND ANGLO-AMERICAN RELATIONS, 1880-1888.** 1976

Rodechko, James Paul. **PATRICK FORD AND HIS SEARCH FOR AMERICA:** A Case Study of Irish-American Journalism, 1870-1913. 1976

Roney, Frank. **IRISH REBEL AND CALIFORNIA LABOR LEADER:** An Autobiography. Edited by Ira B. Cross. 1931

Roohan, James Edmund. **AMERICAN CATHOLICS AND THE SOCIAL QUESTION, 1865-1900.** 1976

Shannon, James. **CATHOLIC COLONIZATION ON THE WESTERN FRONTIER.** 1957

Shaw, Douglas V. **THE MAKING OF AN IMMIGRANT CITY:** Ethnic and Cultural Conflict in Jersey City, New Jersey, 1850-1877. 1976

Sylvester, Harry. **MOON GAFFNEY.** 1947

Tarpey, Marie Veronica. **THE ROLE OF JOSEPH McGARRITY IN THE STRUGGLE FOR IRISH INDEPENDENCE.** 1976

Vinyard, JoEllen McNergney. **THE IRISH ON THE URBAN FRONTIER:** Nineteenth Century Detroit. 1976

Walsh, James P., ed. **THE IRISH: AMERICA'S POLITICAL CLASS.** 1976

Weisz, Howard Ralph. **IRISH-AMERICAN AND ITALIAN-AMERICAN EDUCATIONAL VIEWS AND ACTIVITIES, 1870-1900:** A Comparison. 1976